The story of Australia's great race drivers

LEGENDS OF SPEED

Brabham to Webber, Beechey to Brock

Bill Woods

HarperSports
An imprint of HarperCollins*Publishers*

Harper*Sports*

An imprint of HarperCollins*Publishers*, Australia

First published in 2004
by HarperCollins*Publishers* Pty Limited
ABN 36 009 913 517
A member of the HarperCollins*Publishers* (Australia) Pty Limited Group
www.harpercollins.com.au

HarperCollins*Publishers*

25 Ryde Road, Pymble, Sydney, NSW 2073, Australia
31 View Road, Glenfield, Auckland 10, New Zealand
77-85 Fulham Palace Road, London W6 8JB, United Kingdom
2 Bloor Street East, 20th floor, Toronto, Ontario M4W 1A8, Canada
10 East 53rd Street, New York, NY 10022, USA

National Library of Australia Cataloguing-in-Publication data:

Woods, Bill.
    Legends of speed.
    ISBN 0 7322 7766 3.
    1. Automobile racing drivers - Australia - Biography.
    2. Motorcyclists - Australia - Biography. 3. Motorsports -
    Australia - History. I. Title
796.7092294

Cover images by Getty Images and Newspix
Cover design by Stuart Horton-Stephens
Author photo: Katie Wilson
Typeset in 9.5/15.5 Palatino by HarperCollins Design Studio
Printed and bound in Australia by Griffin Press on 79gsm Bulky Paperback White

7 6 5 4 3 2 1   04 05 06 07

LEGENDS OF SPEED

To the loves of my life:
Leeanne, Robert, Michael
and Lauren.
It is their precious time
that this book has stolen.

CONTENTS

FOREWORD

BY MARK WEBBER

Australians are very spoilt when it comes to success on the international sporting stage and the achievements of many of our sportsmen and sportswomen have been well documented. However, for some odd reason our success in international motor sport has never achieved national prominence. It always strikes me as rather strange that many of the Australian names etched into the history of international motor sport are probably better known and respected overseas than here in their own backyard.

So, when Bill told me he was writing a book in recognition of the achievements of Australian racing drivers through the ages, I was delighted their stories would finally be told and appreciated.

I think it's incredibly difficult for people to understand what has to happen to achieve success internationally as a racing driver. It's not that it's unbelievably complicated but the path can be littered with so many potholes and variables that even the most talented driver in the world may never reach the pinnacle of the sport.

When I left Australia for Europe in 1996, I never considered it to be a sacrifice. I had absolutely nothing to lose and everything to gain. Planted deeply in the back of my mind, too, were the success stories that had gone before me, and there's no doubt that these helped to give me the confidence that they could be repeated and that you can be noticed if you have enough belief in yourself and perform on the big days.

With a burning ambition to race in Formula 1 myself one day, there were always two names which meant more to me than any others — Sir Jack

Brabham and Alan Jones. My father was a big fan of Black Jack and it was Jack who was to become the catalyst for my own motor racing career. Yet, I never saw either he or Alan race in a grand prix on TV and even to this day, I've only seen very limited footage of them in action.

Instead, it was the reputation they carved for themselves that provided me with the inspiration to try and follow in their footsteps. Their dogged determination and strong work ethics ... the good old Aussie battler prepared to have a go — often against all odds. Maybe it was because there were so few Aussies competing internationally, that their attitude and strength of character made them stand out from the crowd. Even today, there are people in Europe for whom I have the utmost respect, who remember and continue to praise the way Brabham, Jones and Frank Gardner went about their business. And that means more to me than anything else.

Of course, not everyone was focused on Formula 1. For home-grown legends such as Peter Brock, Allan Moffat, Norm Beechey and Bob Jane, it must have been a great thrill when they had the opportunity to mix it with — and often beat — Europe's best on our home turf, and sometimes on theirs.

And finally, although this book is dedicated to those who enjoyed on-track successes, we shouldn't forget the unsung heroes who have succeeded in less glamorous but equally demanding areas of the sport. Across the board, there has always been a liberal smattering of Australian team owners, designers, engineers and mechanics, who have helped Australia to achieve respect in international motor sport. Long may it continue!

Mark Webber
2004

INTRODUCTION

Race driving is one of the least understood of sporting pursuits. For a start, it is inherently unfair, because in many races there is inequality of machinery and budget. That only serves to make it more interesting.

Motor racing is maligned by its critics for its lack of human endeavour and yet it is more about human endeavour than most sports because the path from pencil drawing to podium is a painstaking development cycle exhibiting our finest attributes: intellect, fitness, determination, concentration, courage, teamwork.

The drivers chosen for this book have been outstanding for a variety of reasons. They are not all popular or well known. Not all are world champions. Some have rarely competed internationally. There are those for whom success has been measured not so much by trophies and wealth but by the enormous respect of their peers and fans. They are all there because they have made important contributions to the heritage that Mark Webber speaks so proudly of. Many are cult heroes already. I hope the others soon will be, now that their stories have been told.

Jack Brabham, Frank Gardner and Frank Matich are among few with a distinction that will remain forever because it is almost impossible to emulate now. They are rare because they *were* the production line. They and the handful of people whom they employed, achieved what is today the work of hundreds, in an era when the process from design to drive is mind-numbing in its complexity and cost.

This process is what many of us cannot understand. Some believe it is simply a case of 'build a better machine, go faster and win'. However, finding the best technology, developing it, and finding the right driver to exploit it is no less fascinating than a football coach or manager putting together the best team and training it to win a title. The chassis, engine, suspension, tyres and drivers are components of motor racing, just as players are components of a football team. Nor should you assume that weight of money always wins, any more than weight of money guarantees Real Madrid or the LA Lakers every championship they contest.

It is the drivers who fascinate us most, for they are the end of the line, the men whose job it is to take the machine and find its extremities. For all the accuracy of design drawings and construction, the limits of a race car's performance are never clearly defined. They vary with track layout and surface, even air temperature, and they are found like one finds the edge of a precipice in thick fog. The drivers' level of involvement is the first thing that intrigues us, the component valued most by the fans, and yet are the most expendable. They are a special breed. There are the pure drivers, like jockeys on thoroughbreds, mercenaries who can be strapped in and trusted to maximise the machine, always with astonishing courage and sometimes fatal results. There are the technical drivers, capable of understanding the machine without punishing it, working towards a pace that may not have the breathtaking peaks of the pure drivers but are far more reliable because they sympathise with the components. There are the engineer drivers, who design and build their own cars, welding themselves to the entire process in an exhausting but ultimately more satisfying achievement.

One of those is Frank Matich, who says, 'A driver's performance is limited by two things: 1) Their ability to get the car in and out of corners etc., but that is always limited by the car's behaviour; 2) If you can find synergy between car and driver, so the driver knows what the car will do, it's not so important whether the car oversteers or understeers, so long as you know it will do the same thing every time. That's what you strive for with testing.'

Five times Australian Touring Car Champion Mark Skaife once tried to explain to me the process by which a driver pursues perfection. It is a process that is so often mistaken for technology, when in fact it is entirely human. Like a pole vaulter searches a length of carbon fibre to find height, Skaife searches his car to find speed. 'It's maximising the performance envelope, constantly trying to extract 100 per cent from the car at every corner, every lap. Searching for the perfect lap in motor sport is what drives us to find the edge of adhesion, this absolute limit. The rewards? Sheer exhilaration, especially at the fastest, least forgiving tracks like Bathurst.'

Bathurst is a focal point of this book, because it is a focal point for the Australian driver. Skaife again, this time telling Network Ten in 2003 what it feels like to challenge the malevolent mountain: 'Right across from McPhillamy to Skyline you're doing 220 kilometres an hour and you can't see where the road goes. You put your foot on the brake at a ridiculous point and you slide the car all the way down the esses just trying to slow it down enough so you can get through the dipper. I mean, an average, sensible human being would say, "This just can't be done." And when you put your foot on the brake, you go "Whooaaa ... " It's a big, deep breath as you slide off the first part, then slide around the next bit, back to second gear and you're over the next bit. You go, "Whooaaa ... geez ... I did it again!" You do that 161 times. It's bloody tough.'

John Bowe, long-time team-mate of Dick Johnson, was the 1995 Australian Touring Car Champion and winner of two Bathurst 1000s. When he recently turned 50, he was still among the top-10 drivers in the championship. 'I charge any athlete,' he says, 'to sit for 3 hours in temperatures in excess of 55 degrees with three layers of clothes on, a heart beat averaging at around 160 beats per minute and having to maintain the highest levels of concentration every second of the way.'

In an article about racing psyche in the *International Herald Tribune* on 11 June 2004, Vancouver sports psychologist Saul Miller was quoted as saying, 'It is about an ability to read a situation, to deal with multiple stimuli, to be able to have a big-picture sense of the race, to be able to have a remarkable reaction time, a rapport with the car. It's like playing chess at 150 miles per hour.'

This, of course, is all reliant on the assumption that the driver, on any given day, will be physically and mentally at his or her peak, which is often not the case. Nor is the car always in peak working order. A driver's performance relies heavily on so many other people in the process. Many of us forget that motor racing is more of a team sport than most.

How does a driver prove his talents when trapped in a mediocre team? Ask Mark Webber, who forged an impressive reputation for three seasons without ever reaching the podium. 'The main thing in a works team is beating your team-mate. That's your first priority, whatever happens off the circuit.'

In that period, Webber saw the dismissal of four team-mates. 'Your other goals are to get the most out of the car, the people around you, and accumulate as many points as you can. You can't beat yourself up too much when Michael Schumacher goes past, lapping you. You must do the job with what you have.'

It is also about psychology, not just the individual's struggle to go beyond the boundaries of fear and rationality, to abandon their instincts and trust a machine, or vice versa, but about outmanoeuvring their rivals. Frank Matich recalls a time when he and Bib Stillwell were locked in a sports car war that was lighting up Australia's circuits. To stay a step ahead, both drivers were constantly upgrading their cars, finding new ways to make them lighter or faster or stiffer. Matich claims that at one meeting he had made cuts in his chassis to break up some air flow behind the front wheel arches and noticed that at the next meeting Stillwell had copied him. To test his theory that his rivals were shadowing his development, Matich decided to play a trick. There was a tubular cross member which spanned the open engine bay in the front of his car. The bay was left open to keep a steady air flow from under the car through the radiator and out through the bonnet. The tube was there simply to stiffen the chassis, but it was hollow, so Matich fixed a truck's tyre valve to the tube, and during the next race meeting, took a compressed air hose and pretended to fill the tube with air. Stillwell's team apparently believed that Matich was actually pumping air through his car's space frame to make the chassis more stiff.

The world's paddocks are filled with similar stories about mind games played among team members and drivers. Jack Brabham was also famous for pretending to notice problems with his rivals' cars while on the grid, sending the more susceptible of them into panic.

While the entire process is about sheer competition, which is what ultimately drives the drivers, it is also inevitably tied to its lifeblood: money. Motor racing, since its birth, has been at the whim of commercialism. It has always cost money to race. At first, rich men bought their own cars and competed in them. Poor men had to find sponsors, and sponsors do not suffer defeat. The golden rule has always been that if you had no money and were successful, you must be good. That is another reason why Webber is so greatly admired. He has paid for his career with toil and tenacity. Sustaining sponsorship, however, is not always so simple. In fickle economic climates, where on-track success is not always a guarantee of support, it becomes an art form. That is why so many people in motor racing are good communicators. They've been hustling for cash since they were teenagers.

Frank Gardner, in his typically laconic style, summarises the relationship: 'Too many people are quite happy to take their sponsor's money and go out backwards. If you are going to be there year after year, doing the job for your sponsor you must maintain credibility and ethics. Otherwise you are an overnight wonder, verging on misappropriation of funds. The funds are there to maintain a team ... not a lifestyle.'

It is these levels of interest and participation that make motor racing, like horse racing, a microcosm of society. Walk onto any track and you will see the rich, the middle class, the intelligentsia and the proletariat, all circulating in their own affordable environments from muddy hillsides to concrete stands to corporate boxes. Similarly, walk from a plush motor home to the front of the pit garage and you will walk past multi-millionaire owners, millionaire team managers, wealthy technical staff, reasonably paid mechanics and poorly paid or volunteer 'gophers', each with an eye on some place higher up the ladder.

The drivers in this book have lived among all this, and for various reasons, risen above it. They are vastly different personalities with vastly differing methods and have dispersed, in retirement, in vastly different directions.

It's important to note that this book is about recollections of the drivers. It is not a definitive history or a statistical record. No driver is rated higher than any other. This is a story, and the perspectives are personal. Occasionally they even conflict. Some of the more dramatic contradictions, for legal reasons, have been kept out of the book. Sometimes you just have to agree to disagree. The more recent the events depicted, the more people there are still alive today who have seen them and they may have different perspectives too. They are welcome to write their own accounts.

Another important aspect of this book is that it is chronological. It begins with two pioneers who shaped their sport from either side of the world, and from the roots of their success a wondrous sequence of stories grew, the branches reaching every level of motor racing and weaving through all of its major evolutions. This is not just a story of individual achievements but remarkable associations and, in some cases, coincidence. One example is a period in the mid-1970s when it seemed likely that Tim Schenken, Vern Schuppan, Alan Jones and Larry Perkins would be driving in Formula 1 at the same time, a coincidence which never came to pass because of the political intrigue of the day. The four orbited for months without ever colliding, although on one occasion three of them managed to compete in the same event.

Another example of career intersection was the 1977 Bathurst 1000 which, curiously, brought together 15 of the 20 men featured in this book. Of course, they were at various stages of their careers, which collectively spanned from 1950 to the present day. Some were already legends, others legends in the making. It was one of the richest collections of Australian motor racing achievers ever to compete in the same event. There is probably no better circuit than Mt Panorama on which to hinge half a century of heritage. Allan Moffat won that race in the famous (or infamous, depending on your point of view) form finish with Ford team-mate Colin Bond. The result, however, was secondary to the curious fact that the race was run at almost exactly the mid-point of the 54 competitive years this book covers.

The origins and methods of these drivers will vary as widely as their opinions, but they all shared an almost disturbing modesty when I spoke with them, even if it was occasionally painted over a healthy ego. On that subject, the final word, before we launch into this rich story of remarkable achievement, belongs to Australia's most recent Formula 1 World Champion, Alan Jones. He typically plays down, with eloquent cynicism and a mischievous wink of the eye, the glorious attributes we like to associate with our favourite drivers and by doing so reveals the strength of character that has forged these legends of speed.

'What's it all about?' he smiles, 'It's all about politics, psychology, lying ... to a degree ... well, at the very least, bluffing. That's motor racing.'

TIME LINE

1940–45:   Tony Gaze flies Spitfires for RAF, awarded DFC with two bars
Harry Firth serves with Australian Signals Corp

1948:   Tony Gaze enters his first Australian Grand Prix, DNF (Alta), while
Harry Firth prepares winning BMW 328 for Frank Pratt
Jack Brabham wins Australian Speedway Championship
(Brabham/Ward Midget JAP 880)

1949:   Goodwood Racing Circuit opens, on the instigation of Tony Gaze
Jack Brabham wins Australian Speedway Championship
(Brabham/Ward Midget JAP 880)

1951:   Jack Brabham wins Australian Hill Climb Championship
(Brabham Midget)

1952:   Tony Gaze makes Formula 1 debut in Belgian Grand Prix
(HWM Alta)

1954:   Tony Gaze finishes 3rd to Stan Jones in first New Zealand Grand Prix
(HWM Alta)

1955:   Jack Brabham wins Australian Grand Prix (Cooper Bristol)
Jack Brabham makes Formula 1 debut at British Grand Prix
(Cooper Bristol T40)
Tony Gaze finishes 3rd to Prince Bira in New Zealand Grand Prix
(Ferrari 500/625)

1956:   Tony Gaze finishes 2nd to Stirling Moss in New Zealand Grand Prix
(Ferrari 500/750S)

1957:   John Harvey wins Australian Speedway Championship
(Kurtis Offenhauser)

1958: Jack Brabham wins New Zealand Grand Prix (Cooper T43 Climax)

John Harvey wins Australian Speedway Championship
(Kurtis Offenhauser)

1959: Jack Brabham wins Formula 1 Drivers Championship
(Cooper T51 Climax)

John Harvey wins Australian Speedway Championship
(Kurtis Offenhauser)

1960: Jack Brabham wins Formula 1 Drivers Championship
(Cooper T51–T53 Climax)

Jack Brabham wins New Zealand Grand Prix (Cooper T51 Climax)

Leo Geoghegan wins Australian GT Championship (Lotus Elite)

1961: Jack Brabham wins New Zealand Grand Prix (Cooper T53 Climax)

Bob Jane and Harry Firth win Armstrong 500 at Phillip Island
(Mercedes Benz 220SE)

Frank Matich wins Australian GT Championship (Jaguar D-Type)

1962: Bob Jane and Harry Firth win Armstrong 500 at Phillip Island
(Ford Falcon)

Bob Jane wins ATCC (Jaguar)

Frank Matich wins Australian Formula Junior Championship
(Elfin 1100)

1963: Jack Brabham wins Australian Grand Prix (Brabham BT4 Climax)

Bob Jane and Harry Firth win first Armstrong 500 at Bathurst
(Ford Cortina)

Bob Jane wins ATCC (Jaguar)

Bob Jane wins Australian GT Championship (Jaguar E-Type)

Leo Geoghegan wins Australian Formula Junior Championship
(Lotus 20)

1964: Jack Brabham wins Australian Grand Prix and finishes 2nd in
Tasman series (Brabham BT7A Climax)

Bob Jane and George Reynolds win Bathurst 500 (Ford Cortina)

Harry Firth wins Ampol Round Australia Trial (Ford Cortina GT)

Frank Matich wins Australian Sports Car Championship (Lotus 19B)

1965: Norm Beechey wins Australian Touring Car Championship
(Ford Mustang)

Jack Brabham becomes constructor, forming Motor Racing
Developments with Ron Tauranac

Tim Schenken wins Australian Hill Climb Championship
(White-JAP)

1966:   Jack Brabham wins Formula 1 Drivers and Constructors
championships (Brabham Repco BT19–BT20)

Spencer Martin, with Bob Jane owning the team, wins Australian
Drivers Championship 'Gold Star' (Brabham BT11A Climax)

Harry Firth wins Southern Cross Rally (Ford Cortina GT)

Frank Gardner finishes 2nd in Australian Grand Prix
(Brabham BT11A Climax)

John Harvey wins Australian Formula 2 Championship
(Brabham BT14)

Frank Matich wins Australian Sports Car Championship (Traco 400)

1967:   Jack Brabham wins Formula 1 Constructors Championship, finishes
2nd in Drivers Championship (Brabham Repco BT20–24)

Harry Firth and Fred Gibson win Armstrong 500 at Bathurst (Ford
Falcon XRGT)

Frank Gardner wins British Touring Car Championship (Ford Falcon)

Frank Gardner finishes 2nd in Tasman series
(Brabham BT16 Climax 2.5)

Leo and Ian Geoghegan finish 2nd in Bathurst 500 (Ford Falcon)

Spencer Martin, with Bob Jane owning the team, wins Australian
Drivers Championship 'Gold Star' (Brabham BT11A Climax)

Frank Matich wins Australian Sports Car Championship
(Matich SR3)

1968:   Tim Schenken wins British Formula Ford Championship (Merlyn)
and British Formula 3 Championship (Chevron Ford)

Kevin Bartlett wins Australian Drivers Championship 'Gold Star'
(Brabham BT23D)

Harry Firth wins Australian Rally Championship (Ford Cortina)

Frank Gardner wins British Touring Car Championship
(Ford Cortina, Ford Escort)

Frank Matich wins Australian Sports Car Championship
(Matich SR3)

1969:   Kevin Bartlett wins Australian Drivers Championship 'Gold Star'
and Macau Grand Prix (Mildren Waggott)

Leo Geoghegan wins Japanese Grand Prix (Lotus 39T)

Colin Bond and Tony Roberts, with Harry Firth as Team Manager
win Hardie Ferodo 500 at Bathurst (Monaro GTS350)

Frank Matich wins Australian Sports Car Championship
(Matich SR4)

1970: Frank Matich wins Australian Grand Prix (McLaren M10)

Leo Geoghegan wins Japanese Grand Prix (Lotus 39T)

Kevin Bartlett finishes 3rd in Tasman series (Mildren Waggott)

Allan Moffat wins Bathurst 500 (Falcon GTHO)

Norm Beechey wins Australian Touring Car Championship
(Monaro 350GTS)

1971: Frank Matich finishes 2nd in Tasman series, wins Riverside USA
(McLaren M10), wins Australian Grand Prix (Matich A50)

Frank Gardner wins British F5000 Championship (Lola T192 Chevrolet)

Frank Gardner wins Rothmans 100 at Warwick Farm
(Lola T192 Chevrolet)

Kevin Bartlett finishes 2nd in Australian Grand Prix (McLaren M10B)

Larry Perkins wins Driver-to-Europe Formula Ford Championship
(Elfin 600)

Tim Schenken finishes 3rd in Austrian Formula 1 Grand Prix
(Brabham BT33)

Vern Schuppan wins British Formula Atlantic Championship
(Palliser/BRM)

Colin Bond, with Harry Firth as Team Manager, wins Australian
Rally Championship (Holden Torana XU1), Southern Cross Rally
(Holden Torana XU1), Sandown Enduro (Holden Torana XU1)

John Harvey, with Bob Jane owning the team, wins Australian Sports
Car Championship (McLaren M6A)

Allan Moffat wins Bathurst 500 (Ford Falcon GTHO)

Bob Jane wins ATCC (Chevrolet Camaro)

1972: Frank Gardner wins New Zealand Grand Prix (Lola T300 Chevrolet)

Frank Gardner finishes 2nd Australian Grand Prix
(Lola T300 Chevrolet)

Frank Gardner wins British Driver's Championship for the 3rd time
(Touring cars, Sports cars, F5000)

Peter Brock wins Bathurst 500, with Harry Firth as Team Manager
(Holden Torana XU1)

Bob Jane wins ATCC (Chevrolet Camaro)

Frank Matich wins Australian Drivers Championship 'Gold Star'
(Matich A50)

Larry Perkins wins Australian Formula 2 Championship (Elfin 600B)

Colin Bond, with Harry Firth as Team Manager, wins Australian
Rally Championship (Holden Torana XU1)

John Harvey, with Bob Jane owning the team, wins Australian Sports
Car Championship (McLaren M6A)

Tim Schenken, with Ronnie Peterson, wins Buenos Aires 1000km and
Nurburgring 1000km sports car races (Ferrari 312P)

1973:   Allan Moffat wins ATCC and Bathurst 1000 (Ford Falcon)

Frank Gardner wins British Touring Car Championship
(Chevrolet Camaro)

Leo Geoghegan wins Australian Formula 2 Championship
(Birrana 173)

1974:   Kevin Bartlett and John Goss win Bathurst 1000 (Ford Falcon XA GT)

Peter Brock wins ATCC, with Harry Firth as Team Manager
(Holden Torana XU1/SLR5000)

Colin Bond, with Harry Firth as Team Manager, wins Australian
Rally Championship (Holden Torana XU1)

Leo Geoghegan wins Australian Formula 2 Championship
(Birrana 273)

Vern Schuppan wins Macau Grand Prix, Formula Pacific
(March 72B)

1975:   Peter Brock, with Harry Firth as Team Manager, wins Bathurst 1000
(Holden Torana L34)

Colin Bond, with Harry Firth as Team Manager, wins Australian
Touring Car Championship (Holden Torana L34)

Larry Perkins wins European Formula 3 Championship (Ralt RT1)

Geoff Brabham wins Australian Formula 2 Championship
(Birrana Ford)

1976:   John Goss wins Australian Grand Prix in a Matich A53

Allan Moffat wins ATCC (Ford Falcon) and Australian GT/Sports
Sedan Championship (Ford Capri/Chevrolet Monza)

Vern Schuppan wins Macau Grand Prix (Ralt) and Rothmans
International F5000 series (Lola T332)

1977: Allan Moffat wins ATCC and with Colin Bond the Bathurst 1000
(Ford Falcon)

Frank Gardner wins Australian GT/Sports Sedan Championship
(Chevrolet Corvair)

Tim Schenken, with Rolf Stommelen and Toine Hezeman wins
Nurburgring 1000km Sports Car Race (Porsche 935GT)

1978: Peter Brock becomes first driver to win ATCC and (with Jim
Richards) the Sandown 500 and Bathurst 1000 in same year
(Torana A9X)

Alan Jones wins Can-Am Championship, USA
(Lola T333CS Chevrolet)

1979: Alan Jones finishes 3rd in Formula 1 Drivers Championship
(Williams)

Peter Brock and Jim Richards win Bathurst 1000 (Torana A9X)

Peter Brock wins Repco Round Australia Trial (Holden Commodore)

Larry Perkins wins Australian Formula 5000 Championship
(Elfin MR8)

Geoff Brabham wins SCCA Formula Super Vee Championship
(Ralt RT1)

1980: Alan Jones wins Formula 1 Drivers Championship, Australian Grand
Prix (Williams)

Peter Brock wins ATCC and (with Jim Richards) the Sandown 500
and Bathurst in the same year for the second time
(Holden Commodore)

Allan Moffat wins Australian Sports Car Championship
(Porsche 930 Turbo)

1981: Alan Jones finishes 3rd in Formula 1 Drivers Championship
(Williams)

Dick Johnson wins ATCC, Bathurst 1000 (Ford Falcon)

Geoff Brabham wins SCCA Can-Am Championship
(Lola T530 Chevrolet)

1982: Peter Brock and Larry Perkins win Bathurst 1000
(Holden Commodore)

Dick Johnson wins ATCC (Ford Falcon)

Alan Jones, with Frank Gardner as Team Manager, wins Australian
GT/Sports Sedan Championship (BMW)

1983:   Vern Schuppan with Al Holbert and Hurley Haywood wins Le Mans
        24 hour race (Porsche 956) and Japanese Sports Car
        Championship (Porsche 956)

        Peter Brock, John Harvey and Larry Perkins win Bathurst 1000
        (Holden Commodore)

        Allan Moffat wins ATCC (Mazda RX7)

1984:   Peter Brock and Larry Perkins win Bathurst 1000
        (Holden Commodore)

        Dick Johnson wins ATCC (Ford Falcon)

        Tim Schenken appointed Racing Manager, CAMS

        Vern Schuppan wins Japanese Sports Car Championship (Porsche 956)

        Gary Brabham and Tim Lee-Davey win Thundersports Race,
        Snetterton (Tiga TS84)

1986:   Peter Brock, Allan Moffat and John Harvey win Kings Cup at Spa
        24 hour race (Holden Commodore)

1987:   Peter Brock with David Parsons and Peter McLeod wins
        Bathurst 1000 (Holden Commodore)

        Allan Moffat and John Harvey win 1st Round World Touring Car
        Championship at Monza (Holden Commodore)

        David Brabham wins Australian Drivers Championship 'Gold Star'
        (Ralt RT30 VW)

1988:   Geoff Brabham wins IMSA GTP Championship (Nissan GTP ZXT)

        Tony Longhurst and Tomas Mezera, with Frank Gardner as Team
        Manager, win Bathurst 1000 (Ford Sierra)

        Dick Johnson wins ATCC (Ford Sierra)

1989:   David Brabham wins British Formula 3 Championship
        (Bowman Ralt)

        David Brabham wins Macau Grand Prix, Formula 3 (Ralt RT33)

        Gary Brabham wins British Formula 3000 Championship
        (Reynard Cosworth)

        Geoff Brabham wins IMSA GTP Championship (Nissan GTP ZXT)

        Dick Johnson wins ATCC and Bathurst 1000 (Ford Sierra)

        Allan Moffat wins Fuji 500, his final race (Ford Sierra)

1990:   Geoff Brabham wins IMSA GTP Championship (Nissan GTP ZXT)

1991:   David Brabham wins Spa 24- hour race (Nissan GTR)

        David Brabham wins Nurburgring 1000km Race (Jaguar XJR14)

Geoff Brabham wins IMSA GTP Championship, including Sebring 12 hour race, with Gary Brabham and Derek Daly (Nissan NPT–90/91)

Mark Skaife wins Australian Drivers Championship 'Gold Star' (Formula Holden) and Bathurst 1000 (Nissan GTR)

1992: Mark Skaife becomes only driver to win Australian Drivers Championship 'Gold Star' (Formula Holden), ATCC and Bathurst 1000 (Nissan GTR) in same year

Geoff Brabham wins Michigan IROC race (Dodge NASCAR)

1993: Geoff Brabham with Christophe Bouchut and Eric Helary wins Le Mans 24 hour race (Peugeot 905)

Larry Perkins and Gregg Hansford win Bathurst 1000 (Holden Commodore)

Mark Skaife wins Australian Drivers Championship 'Gold Star' (Formula Holden) and ATCC (Nissan GTR)

1994: Dick Johnson and John Bowe win Bathurst 1000 (Ford Falcon)

1995: Larry Perkins and Russell Ingall win Bathurst 1000 (Holden Commodore)

1996: David Brabham wins Japanese GT Championship (McLaren F1)

Craig Lowndes becomes second driver to win ATCC and, with Greg Murphy, the Sandown 500 and Bathurst 1000 in the same year (Holden Commodore)

1997: David and Geoff Brabham win 2 litre Bathurst 1000 (BMW)

Larry Perkins and Russell Ingall win V8 Supercar Bathurst 1000 (Holden Commodore)

1998: David Brabham wins USA Professional Sports Car Championship (Panoz)

Craig Lowndes wins ATCC (Holden Commodore)

1999: Craig Lowndes wins ATCC (Holden Commodore)

2000: Mark Skaife wins ATCC (Holden Commodore)

2001: Mark Skaife wins ATCC and with Tony Longhurst the Bathurst 1000 (Holden Commodore)

2002: Mark Skaife wins ATCC and with Jim Richards the Bathurst 1000 (Holden Commodore)

Mark Webber makes Formula 1 debut, finishing 5th in Australian Grand Prix (Minardi)

2003: Marcus Ambrose wins ATCC (Ford Falcon)

CHAPTER ONE

The Flyer and the Fox

The Rolls Royce engine roared as he banked, stalking the sleek silhouette. Tony Gaze had waited months for this moment, a moment when practice, persistence, perception, speed and courage were focused. His leathered hands gripped the stick with new intensity. His thumb pressed the 'Fire' button.

He heard no sound from the cannon or machine-guns — the engine drowned them — but he felt the plane jerking violently and saw shards of metal exploding off the fuselage of the Messerschmitt 109, which promptly fell off Squadron Leader Ken Holden's tail. The German fighter twisted, breaking up, its pilot preparing to bail out. There was no time to pause and savour the significance of his first 'kill', in the warmth of a June sky above the French town of Lille. Gaze steered his Spitfire towards a formation of 12 more Messerschmitt 109s. He forced one out of its pattern with repeated bursts of fire but was unable to confirm that it crashed. He lost sight of it when others turned to attack.

'They'll be angry with me now,' he thought. 'It's time I went home.' He dived, suddenly aware of the world again when the sea loomed beneath him. As he rode the salt air in escape, exhilaration took hold. It was a feeling that would return many times — in war, and on the world's motor racing circuits.

There would be a rush of adrenaline spurred by the instinct for survival in the face of extreme danger, by the satisfaction of winning a contest, by the feeling of being at one with the awesome power of a dangerous machine.

The pilots of those two Messerschmitts, according to German records, remained alive. In the odd chivalry of the air war at the time, Gaze accepted that. He would later write a simple description of his dogfight that day: 'At last!'

Frederick Anthony Owen Gaze was born in Melbourne on 3 February 1920. His father, Irvine, was a World War I fighter pilot, prisoner of war and explorer, but Tony believes that his driving skills came from his mother. He was a mere 8 years old when he first rode in a Sopwith biplane above the Mornington Peninsula; but his first recollection of motor sport, not long after that day, also left an indelible impression.

Irvine had been asked to drive an Austin 7 in the first Australian Grand Prix, in 1928, his wife, Freda, would not allow it; nevertheless the family travelled to Phillip Island as spectators.

The Gaze family — and about 5000 other people — caught the car ferry from the mainland to Phillip Island and drove for several kilometres before parking beside a desolate, windswept dirt and gravel road that formed the 10.4 kilometre rectangular circuit. There were no concrete and glass towers for race control, no insulated garages to house equipment and service cars, no protective barriers between cars and the crowd.

'It was absolutely crazy,' Gaze recalls. 'There were no safety barriers. The crowd just walked along the edge of the road with people suddenly crying out, "Here comes one! Get out of the way!" There'd be a dirty great cloud of dust. I think the best would do about 160 kilometres an hour, the Bugattis and Lombards. We walked the whole way round the circuit that day ... on the edge of the track. I even remember stopping and having a look at koalas in the trees.'

By 1928 Australian motor racing was already more than two decades old, and the Australian Grand Prix was one of the earliest in the world. Early grands prix were run on a handicap system. The less powerful cars started first; the more powerful cars gave them a start of up to an hour. This led to an often chaotic but no doubt exciting race for the fans, as the faster cars weaved through the field in an effort to catch up. The drivers wore suits, with helmets and goggles (both only optional) the only accessories that made them look like racers. Positions were posted for the fans on a scoreboard much like the scoreboard at a cricket ground. Shell Motor Oils sponsored the sign. Irvine Gaze must have winced as the team he could have driven for won the race easily. The 747cc supercharged Austin driven by Captain Arthur Waite was one of the smallest cars in the field, but it slid and swerved reliably enough to be in front of the others after 160 kilometres.

In 1928, and for many years after, motor racing would be an adventure for daring enthusiasts. Those who owned fast cars wanted to test them against others. They came together at club meetings and other casual get-togethers. Promotion was unheard of, preservation of life rarely thought of. The cars were manned missiles: engine in the front, driver sitting about two-thirds of the way back on a shapeless leather seat, and a mechanic sitting beside to pump air into the fuel tank and oil into the engine. In the few single-seater cars, the driver was positioned astride an exposed drive-shaft, running back from the engine to the rear axle. In most models, the clutch pedal was on the left of the shaft, with the brake and throttle on the far right (Italian-makes positioned the throttle pedal to the immediate right of the shaft). There was no safety belt. The steering wheel was large. Grip was improved by leather gloves, but they were often discarded in wet weather, when they became slippery.

Like most children, Tony Gaze could not see past the glamour. He would carry the memory of grand prix racing with him throughout his schooling — at the highly respected Geelong Grammar. In 1938, at the Rob Roy Hill Climb, the first Australian Hill Climb Championship, he met a driver who would greatly influence his career: 23-year-old Englishman Peter Whitehead. Whitehead was a wealthy and popular entrepreneur who had been visiting Australia to explore some business interests for his wool-growing family and contest a few races. In his black ERA B-type, a dashing motor car in its day, he won not only the Australian Hill Climb Championship at Rob Roy, but also the Australian Grand Prix on the new dirt track at Mt Panorama, Bathurst. His friendship would prove valuable for Tony Gaze.

The Gaze family's English connections enabled Tony to attend Queens College at Cambridge University after he finished school. He began studying natural sciences, switching later to mechanical sciences. He was a member of the famous London Rowing Club, but his passion for driving bubbled to the surface, and he borrowed a Hudson to race at the Brooklands circuit. Brooklands was part-owned by legendary speed record-holder Sir Malcolm Campbell.

Freddie March had also raced there. His full title was Freddie Charles Gordon-Lennox, Duke of Richmond and Gordon. The man who came to be known as Lord March was concentrating more on official motor sport duties when Gaze raced, but their friendship would have a profound effect on world motor sport. Another friend racing there was Prince Birabongse Bhanuban of Thailand — Prince Bira, as he was known in motor racing circles. The Prince was educated at Cambridge and Eton, and joined the wealthy amateurs who sustained top-level motor sport in the 1930s.

When World War II broke out in 1939, Australians studying in England were given the opportunity to sail home, but many didn't go. They were concerned that they might not make it, because the war at sea was intensifying. Some also felt it was the right thing to stay and enlist, for inevitably they would be fighting the Germans somewhere. The Gaze family mobilised quickly at the prospect of action, and it was to the air they turned. Tony's kid brother Scott decided to sail from Australia to join his brother in the RAF, and Irvine enlisted at home in Victoria.

Scott was the showman of the family. If Tony was cheeky, his brother was outrageous. He had nicknamed himself 'the lucky one', and warned Tony not to continue his pilot training because, 'The way the war is going, one of us will get killed, and as I'm the lucky one, it's bound to be you!' Scott borrowed some money from Tony while they were in training at Cambridge, and with it he bought a clapped-out old Austin 7, which he rigged for an elaborate scam. 'At cocktail time every evening, Scott would drive into the wealthier suburbs of Cambridge, search for the richest-looking house in the street, then flick a switch he'd set up in the car to cut out one spark plug. Then he'd knock on the door and ask to borrow a screwdriver because his car was going wrong, knowing bloody well they'd ask him in and offer him a drink.'

The Gaze brothers graduated from pilot training after more than a year, with Tony's papers stamped 'above average'. Their first posting, as requested, was to 610 Squadron at Tangmere, where their father had flown during World War I. Then they were moved to Westhampnett. Tony was on patrol with 'A' flight, Scott with 'B' flight. The early weeks were uneventful, but on 23 March, Tony was back at the airfield when some of the 'B' flight Spitfires returned from patrol. Scott wasn't with them. Tony was told by the returning pilots that some of their planes had peeled off to look for a Junkers 88, a German bomber, in deteriorating weather.

It was a sickening wait. Then a telltale pall of smoke rose from a distant hillside. Word came to the base that a plane had crash-landed in a field near where 'B' flight's chase had begun. It was Scott, slumped in the shattered cockpit, his finger still pressed on the firing button. He was 19 years old. 'He may have found a German. We don't know. He was always trying to outdo me, as brothers usually do, so if he found one he wouldn't have said anything in case he would have had to share it with somebody else. That's the way it was.'

Gaze encountered the frustrating side of military bureaucracy in the days that followed. After Scott's funeral, he received a bill for the blanket which enshrouded his brother. He stormed into the CO's office and threw it on the desk. 'You had better deal with this, sir,' he said, 'because I am going to hit somebody.'

For Tony Gaze, the war was no longer an adventure. He was posted to fly with the famous Douglas Bader on a new type of attack called a 'circus', in which small flights of a dozen or so bombers would be sent on raids to specific targets, at the same time (they hoped) luring German fighters into a battle with the escorting Spitfires and Hurricanes. The first was on 17 April 1941.

Douglas Bader was the flamboyant character who had lost his legs in a pre-war crash then fought the military bureaucracy to return to flying. He was affectionately nicknamed 'Tin Legs'. In private conversation among subordinates he was 'The Legless One'. He was brash, noisy, given to running commentary of dogfights over the radio — and, according to Gaze, 'a bit of a bull artist'. However, Gaze also recalls that Bader's courage and skill were without question. He always encouraged his pilots in battle, and never failed to return to help anyone in trouble. In short, 'We thought he was the best leader we'd ever known. I still do.'

Gaze spent 8 weeks on these circuses, sometimes flying two a day, trying to draw an elusive enemy into battle. He was learning the nuances of his plane, how it slowed considerably when he fired its cannon and machine-guns, due to the recoil. He learnt to unlock his shoulder harness in the cockpit during dogfights so that he could turn to see if there were enemy planes approaching from behind, because that is where the fatal shots almost always came from. His size was really not compatible with the relatively small Spitfire cockpit. His head would jam against the roof, and his shoulders would be squeezed at the sides. 'The good thing was that you were part of the aeroplane. You really felt the wings were coming out of your shoulders.'

When he wasn't peering through the skies for targets to engage, he was feeling the heat and hearing the blasts of German flak stationed in strategic areas of occupied France. In one massive dogfight over St Omer, he engaged a number of Messerschmitt 109s only to discover, on his arrival back in England, 19 holes in his Spitfire's wings as well as an oily windscreen and broken instruments. 'I probably should have been shot down in the early days,' he recalls, 'but the fellow who was shooting at me was a rotten shot. I had no idea anyone was shooting at me. I thought I was the only person shooting at other people.' He found himself chuckling along with everyone else when planes returned shot to pieces. It seemed that the closer a pilot came to death, the more humorous it was for his mates.

Gaze's first 'kill', on that circus to Lille on 26 June, was hardly the watershed he might have expected; it was certainly no substitute for the loss of his brother. The air battle in 1941 was being fought by pilots who were still clinging, albeit tenuously, to principles that had been mercilessly crushed in the shattered Ardennes Forest, the ruins of London, the concentration camps of Germany and the broken borders of Soviet Russia.

By 1941, Tony Gaze had been awarded the Distinguished Flying Cross (DFC), one of the highest honours a pilot could achieve.

Douglas Bader's bravado had been inspirational, so when he was shot down during a sweep over France in August of that year, the squadron was devastated. 'We were like lost kids after he went,' says Gaze. 'We were so used to him that the chap who followed him had a hard time.'

Gaze graduated to Flight Commander, then Squadron Leader, only to lose that rank after an investigation into a failed mission over the Brest Peninsula. He knew he would be made a scapegoat the moment he was greeted by Air Vice-Marshal Broadhurst at Fighter Command Headquarters. 'Ah Gaze,' he said, 'I see you're an Australian. I don't like Australians.'

The only way Gaze would be able to regain his rank would be to return to officer training, which he refused. So it was back to Flight Lieutenant in 616 Squadron at Westhampnett. By November he'd clocked 1000 hours in the air, nearly a third of which were in combat operations.

During bomber escort near Amiens on the morning of 4 September 1943, he single-handedly tangled with a squadron of Focke-Wulfs, shooting down one and damaging another. He called for help on the radio, but no one responded. After a serious of sweeps and attacks towards the pursuing Germans, Gaze's

Spitfire had taken some hits, and as he turned to flee he noticed that the shadow of his plane had changed — a long thin tail was now streaming behind it. He called again on the radio, this time with simple words that have chilled bones since air war began: 'Don't bother. I've had it.'

Fuel was squirting from holes in the fuselage. There were 90 litres left. Other hits had damaged the elevators on his wings. He surveyed the landscape and saw nothing but thick forest. Suddenly a small clearing appeared. He made his descent as shallow as possible, but could not avoid ploughing into the mud at almost full speed. The heavy plane nosed into the field and slowed to a halt, metres from the far edge of the clearing. He would learn after the war that he was the 14th of 48 victims claimed by German ace Gerhard Vogt. None of Gaze's squadron saw what happened to him. He was reported as 'Missing, believed killed', and his family believed they had lost two sons on foreign fields.

The impact of the landing had thrown Gaze's head onto the gunsight. He was feeling dazed, sore and very stupid for not locking his shoulder harness before he crashed. He cursed his old plane, which was no match for a gang of Focke-Wulfs, and cursed himself for 'overconfidence and frustration'. The main thing was to get away before the Germans arrived. He stumbled out, threw his jacket into a bush and headed into the forest. His bloodied eyes searched for shelter as he kept running, through the trees and across a track. He spotted a hut, where an old man waved and shouted at him. Gaze ignored him. A few minutes later, as he paused to rest, a small dog caught up with him. Gaze remembered seeing the dog back at the hut, and sure enough, the old man had caught up too. 'He took me back to the hut and there were others there. They kept asking me if I wanted to surrender to the Germans. I couldn't understand why, but I kept saying no, no, no. Then they produced a mirror, and showed me . . .'

The right side of Gaze's face resembled 'a piece of steak with a pupil stuck on it'. He recalls the horror and disbelief. 'Luckily, I wasn't in that much pain.' The mirrored gunsight had shattered in the crash, its sharp edges slashing his face from one side of his eye down the cheek. There was a similar cut extending across and down from the middle of his eye. A large flap of flesh about 5 centimetres wide had peeled back, exposing the lower eyeball. Blood was crusted around the eye from numerous other small cuts and abrasions.

'Someone crept back to the plane and retrieved the first aid kit. They pushed my face together and wound a tight bandage around my head. Then they sent me off to hide. Not long after that they found a bike for me, and made me follow someone to a nearby schoolhouse. If he hadn't been a lot older than me I might have given up the chase, because my back wasn't feeling too good either. Must have had whiplash. I went up in this loft at the school, and spent three weeks there waiting for my face to heal.' Fortunately for Gaze, he was in the hands of the French Resistance.

He hid for weeks, recovering from his injuries, until he was ready to flee the occupied territories. A local pharmacist visited each day to bathe and re-bandage the wounds, which healed remarkably well without stitching. 'The only problem was, the raw edges of skin were trying to grow over my eye, so we had to keep separating them.'

The Germans foiled one attempt by the Resistance to smuggle Gaze out of the country on a British plane, and he fled to Paris. In a scene reminiscent of the movie *The Great Escape*, he was told to emerge confidently from the train station, look for a man wearing a white hat and smoking a cigarette, and follow him. The man led him to a small flat, where he met a French Canadian, also on the run. After several days of living as a citizen of Paris, Gaze was given a choice: wait for the next full moon, so he could try again to rendezvous somewhere with a British plane, or head 700 kilometres south to the Pyrenees, on the border with neutral Spain. Typically, the impetuous Gaze chose the more active alternative. He would head south, for the mountains, rather than wait in the city and risk capture doing nothing.

There was very little trouble on the first stage of the journey, by train, until Gaze and his guide reached Toulouse, about 90 kilometres from the border, where he had another narrow escape, this time from some Italian guards. Eventually he was taken across the Pyrenees by a Spanish smuggler. Such criminals had become useful to the Allied war effort because they could make more money smuggling people than they could doing anything else. The journey was to have taken 4 days, but with crackdowns on security they diverted to Andorra, which extended the trip to 10 days.

There was no welcoming party when they finally arrived on the other side of the mountains in Spain. It was a further 180 kilometres walk to Barcelona, where Gaze was fitted with a civilian suit, taken to Madrid to a transit camp for escapees, then flown from Gibraltar back home — on 28 October 1943. He had spent 54 days on the run, but the British military bureaucracy still saw fit to interrogate him for 3 more days. 'It was as though I was a crook,' he says.

His wounds kept him from flying for another 6 months, and after that he would be on restricted duties. The British were reluctant for escapees to fly over enemy territory, fearing that if they were shot down again and captured, they might reveal how they had escaped and thus jeopardise the lives of hundreds in the Resistance. Midway through 1944, when the Allies were invading Normandy, he took a chance — by flying, against orders, with a Canadian fighter wing commanded by his old friend Johnny Johnson. 'If anything had happened to me there'd have been a hell of a stink. Officially, I wasn't operational.'

When France belonged to the French again, the regulations allowed Gaze to fly more operations. On 5 August 1944, on patrol over the English Channel, another significant milestone was added to his military career: he found himself being 'chased' by a V–1 flying bomb. This was fortunate, because most V–1s he had seen had been in front of him, and with a head start they were impossible to catch. He quickly banked, and soon was on its tail with time to lock it in his gun sights. Moments later, the V–1 was destroyed.

While the war in Europe ground to its ugly and devastating conclusion, Gaze took over 'B' flight at 610 Squadron and flew a variety of missions. Most of these were against ground targets, but occasionally some of Nazi Germany's more bizarre aerial weapons would show up. On one flight he tackled an Arado Ar234 jet-propelled bomber and a flight of Messerschmitt 262 jet fighters, one of which he shot down. For a Spitfire Mark XIV to shoot down the most hi-tech fighter of its time was a remarkable feat and Tony Gaze was reportedly the only Australian pilot to have achieved it.

In the final weeks of the war, he also flew the Allies' first jet fighter in service, the Gloster Meteor, on six sorties, destroying some ground targets but never having the chance to take on a rival in the air. The war ended before that could happen. In 495 missions and 1636 hours of flight time, Tony Gaze had destroyed 12.5 enemy aircraft, probably destroyed another 4, and damaged 4 more. It was a record good enough to give him the title of 'ace' twice over. He had been awarded two bars to add to his DFC, the equivalent of winning the prestigious award three times. None of that compared with his greatest wartime achievement: 50 pilots trained with him back in 1940, and only two of them were still in the air just 5 years later. He had survived.

Lance Corporal Harry Firth, like so many other Australians thrust unprepared into the mountains of Greece, was wondering if this helter-skelter retreat was going to be a dead-end, literally. For hundreds of kilometres, a trail of vehicles — wheeled, tracked and horse-drawn — wound through mountain passes in a disorganised crawl towards the coast to escape a failed campaign. Firth was sitting forlornly in his truck, occasionally leaning out the window, peering into the distance, where the convoy was little more than a roughly traced line against the rocky Greek hillside. He saw a shadow pass. He heard a familiar droning above him. He saw figures in the distance scrambling off the road, darting for shrubs and rocks to hide behind. Puffs of dust flew from the ground. Some of the figures fell. A truck burst into flames ...

It was in this furnace that one of Australian motor racing's most creative and eccentric characters was forged.

From his early school days in Orbost, a small rural town in Snowy River country, Harry Firth showed a liking for lateral thinking and hard-nosed practicality. The Firth way was not indirect or complicated. He was born on 18 April 1918, and within 8 years was helping his Dad maintain the family car. Before that he had built his own billycart, wisely using his pet dog to pilot the prototype. He laughingly claims that his fascination with mechanics started in primary school, where he removed the wheels from other pupils' bikes to decorate the grounds. 'A few of the older boys had given me a belting, so at lunch time I went down, took all their pushbikes apart and hung the parts in surrounding trees.'

'I was pretty smart in school,' Firth recalls. 'I was up there around the top of my class and very good at perspective and hand drawings. I was also good at language and mathematics.'

By the time he turned 14, Firth had no further need for school. He worked as a mechanic, and his skills became vitally important to the family when his father died in 1933. His personal transport was a motorcycle, but when he worked for his Uncle George in a bigger garage in town the chance came to drive the cars he had worked on. 'I used to use all the back roads,' Firth recalls. 'But you had to know where to go, and when. The farmers whose cars we serviced used to leave them at the garage while they went to the football matches in town on weekends. Now I knew that the police would also be at the football, so I'd hop in these cars, and drive in the other direction ... full chat!'

When he applied for his driver's licence, at the age of 17, the local policeman didn't even bother to test him. 'You can drive all right,' he said, smiling. 'I've been watching you for some time.'

Bikes, mechanics and bravery were to become valuable commodities when Firth was called to war — as a fitter to the Number 1 Despatch Rider Section in the Australian Signals Corp. He trained at RMIT before heading for the Middle East, then North Africa in early 1940.

The despatch riders were among the most courageous, but least celebrated troops of World War II. For a start, there has always been a stigma attached to anyone who dared ride a motorcycle; but in wartime, it was simply the fastest and most convenient way of getting through the lines. There has been, above all, a lack of appreciation for the role they played. When radio or telegraph communications were down, or not able to be used because the enemy had tapped into the system, there was only one way of communicating reports. This meant riders throwing often unreliable machines along broken, potholed tracks at speeds approaching 100 kilometres an hour, swerving and braking through streams of friendly traffic heading in both directions. The weather could be extremely hot, whipping the roads into near-fatal dust clouds. Enemy advance patrols or planes trying to disrupt the lines of communication often shot at the riders, who had no alternative but to press on, sometimes abandoning their machines, at speed, to leap into roadside ditches for cover. If they were lucky, the bike would be still in one piece when they recovered it.

Firth soon discovered that the management of such a vital transport unit would be continuously under threat from the military's own bureaucracy. Punctures, breakdowns, enemy fire and the harsh desert environment were worthy but surmountable challenges for a man like Firth, who could see through a sandstorm of uncertainty to the core of a problem.

'The rule was simple in the army, and everyone knew it. If you couldn't beg, you borrowed, and if all that failed, you stole.' Firth was often forced to steal, usually from captured supply dumps, which were heavily guarded by British MPs but largely unused. He could not understand why the MPs shot at him when he raided the dumps for spare parts.

'No sense of humour, these people,' says Firth, with a fortitude that would bewilder his senior officers, but save his skin — and that of others — time and time again in the desert. From there, his section was transferred to the doomed Balkan campaign. After little more than a token operation, stamped out by the savage onrush of the German invasion, the overwhelmed Allied forces fought a brave and tenacious rearguard action to cover their slow retreat down the Greek peninsula.

During this retreat, through mountainous terrain, Firth would curse the wheels of the military machine that ground so slowly. The bombing and strafing continued. There were many close calls along the potholed roads, and in the paddocks where the trucks were often parked as new headquarters were being set up. One brisk dawn, he had spread a camouflage net over his truck and was preparing for a snooze in the cabin when something, some instinct, shook him alert. 'Something just told me I had to get out of that cabin,' he recalls. He leapt out, slammed the door, and bolted for a ditch several metres away. Within a couple of minutes, he heard a deep, unmistakable 'whoosh' as a German fighter plane swooped, spraying the truck with machine-gun and cannon fire. 'All hell broke loose,' says Firth, 'there must have been incendiary bullets in that lot because ... up she went!' Most people would be relieved to have escaped, but Firth's first responses were anger and dismay, because in that truck were his camera, and £10.

'But the closest I came was when I had a Greek bloke for a passenger. We were under attack, and leapt out of the truck to dig ourselves into the ground as best we could. We watched a plane drop a load of anti-personnel bombs, one at a time, each one closer than the last. There were seven of them. Louder and louder the blasts came until one landed between us and the truck. It blew the back off the Greek's uniform and he took off into the bush. It shook me up a bit, left my ears ringing, but I was okay.'

He made it to the beaches by 25 April 1941, one of the 50,000 Allied troops ready to escape on whatever ships the navy could muster. He embarked at night, to avoid air attack, aboard the *Costa Rica*, a 25,000 tonne passenger liner. He estimates that they were about 50 miles out to sea before daylight and German bombers arrived. The *Costa Rica* was being escorted by four destroyers, with anti-aircraft batteries, and every armed man on the liner raised his rifle when they heard the noise of incoming aircraft. One German pilot came in low, obscured by the blaze of the morning sun, and released two 500 pound bombs, which exploded with a deep, sickening 'boom'. The mighty *Costa Rica* lifted out of the Aegean Sea, fell back, and rapidly began to sink.

Destroyers pulled up on either side, and weary soldiers tried to judge their leaps as the decks of each vessel rose and fell in the ocean swell. Firth realised that the best chance for survival was to wait for the destroyer to fall below the line of the *Costa Rica*'s deck, then jump aboard. He had little time, for the liner was sinking quickly. He took the chance, falling about 5 metres before hitting the steel deck of the destroyer. It was a relatively safe landing, but within seconds, before he could find his footing, someone else jumped from high above ... straight onto his back. He was in acute pain, but alive. Within 20 minutes, the *Costa Rica* was gone.

Firth was stationed briefly in Crete, then Palestine, scrounging and looting to keep his unit in order as the conflict widened to envelop the world. He spent his final weeks of the triumphant Palestinian campaign training the locals to be despatch riders, mapping Lebanon for the army. After a severe bout of dysentery, which kept him from sailing home with the rest of his section, he served as Sergeant with a new section before returning to Australia. In late 1943 he saw action again, in Port Moresby, New Guinea, where Australians found themselves involved in some of the most desperate fighting of the war. His next posting was to Lae, which had been captured by the Australians on 16 September. The frontline would never be far away.

When Harry Firth turned 24, he was a veteran of four campaigns. 'When we got to Lae we set up a whole new base there, and made our runs into the surrounding territory. The conditions in New Guinea were absolutely bloody shithouse. There was no water. The place was rotten. You'd get tinea, sores on your body, dysentery.' It was quite a contrast to the deserts of the Middle East or the mountains of Greece. The jungle was a thick, steamy blanket — opposing troops could creep within metres of each other without being detected. Attacks were at close quarters, and were ferocious. Machine-guns caused devastation at such ranges, but often the fighting would close to the point where bayonets, knives and even fists were used.

The action was rarely visible to the transport units, but they were always armed in case of attack. Firth wore a pistol in a shoulder holster: a 9mm Beretta. 'I wasn't allowed to have it,' he says, 'but I bloody needed it.'

He wasn't in Lae for long before orders came for his return to Australia in early 1944. Firth was one of those soldiers who had slipped through the net a couple of times, and the hierarchy was keen to relieve him of frontline duties. He became a Tour of Duty Instructor at the Bonegilla base just outside Albury. It was a difficult time for him. Even though he was out of the firing line, he would come face to face with the worst of military stubbornness. 'It was back to the land of red tape and bullshit,' he recalls. 'I could teach 'em more than they ever bloody knew.'

That included, on one memorable expedition, the splinting of a broken front fork on a motorcycle with the fork of a tree. Firth bound it with fencing wire stolen from a nearby paddock. Officers were stunned when its rider arrived at the camp, 50 kilometres away.

By the time Harry Firth returned to his unit in New Guinea, the base had shifted again — to Wewak, 500 kilometres northeast of Lae, on the coast. It was late in the war, and the troops were lifted by the fact that it was only a matter of time before the Japanese surrendered.

CHAPTER TWO

Formula 1

Tony Gaze was based on the Continent for some months after the war, but on his return to England, motor racing was re-kindling. His favourite circuit, Brooklands, would never be used again, though, and, his friend, the Duke of Richmond, on behalf of the Junior Car Club, had been searching for an alternative. Gaze and his friend, Dickie Stoop, had also been looking ... for a place to 'test' their MGs for a bit of fun. Wing Commander Douglas Bader had ordered Irish labourers to build a road around their airfield at Westhampnett, on the Duke's estate, so that the RAF could move their fuel tankers around without bogging them down in the soft pastures. Gaze and Stoop had raced their MGs around it. Suddenly, as Gaze laughingly swerved in and out of the corners, it struck him that this would be an ideal circuit. 'I mean, the Duke was looking for one,' Gaze recalls, 'and he already owned one, so I asked him when he would stage a motor race at Westhampnett.' The Duke agreed with that assessment, and thus Goodwood was established. One of the world's most famous circuits, it is still in use today for recreational racing, and is a mecca for motor sport when the famous Festival and Revival meetings are staged.

The circuit opened in 1948, and 19-year-old Stirling Moss won one of the first races there. By then Gaze had returned to Australia, to his father's farm in

Coleraine, Victoria, but before he left he had paid for the making of a memorial trophy for the Scott Gaze handicap race to honour his brother, whose plane had been shot down not far from the circuit. Even when the circuit was deregistered 18 years later following concerns over safety, the Scott Gaze Memorial Trophy would be awarded to the winners of precision flying contests at Goodwood's aviation meetings. It is still awarded today. Tony Gaze cherishes a letter of appreciation sent to him by the Duke, for what turned out to be a significant contribution to motor racing and aviation.

The final days of the war for Harry Firth were uneventful. Three days after victory in the Pacific had been declared he was told bluntly in Wewak that he had served more than his share of months in action and was to leave New Guinea immediately. Within hours, he was rattling around with 11 others in an old DC3 cargo plane, weaving through the steep mountains towards Australia. Ironically, without a parachute, it was one of his most frightening experiences of the war.

'There was no way I was ever going to be associated with the military ever again. I just didn't want to know about it. The bullshit of being told what to do by some bloody nincompoop who didn't have a clue what they were doing.' Like it or not, the war experience had changed him forever. It had taught him resourcefulness, engineering, organisation and administration. It also taught him fear and mistrust. The Beretta he carried under his jacket would stay with him for at least a year after he left active service. Long after he had returned to the family home at Orbost, he kept it under his pillow while he slept. He even drew the gun one night at a local dance, after some youths, disrespectful of his uniform, had given him trouble.

'I didn't stand any bullshit,' Firth recalls. 'Why should I? I'd been overseas fighting for these bastards for 6 years. Having been in the war, where you're expected to shoot people, I didn't see what difference there was when you were back. You went away a meek and mild little boy ... but when you came home ...'

Firth resumed his job as a mechanic in Bairnsdale, near Orbost, before moving 18 months later to Melbourne, where he lived in Brunswick with his brother. He found a job at Preston Motors, then AF Hollins, a renowned workshop which prepared sports cars and racing cars as well as prestige road cars. By this time, Firth had finally said goodbye to his old Beretta, leaving it back in Orbost with his uncle. 'It had to go,' he recalls. 'I would have finished up shooting some bastard with it and I'd be in all sorts of trouble. But I still had my 12-gauge shotgun. It was a hard world in those days.' The 12-gauge would stay beside his bed for another 30 years.

Tony Gaze was feeling the itch at the Coleraine farm and began preparing for serious competition. He left and found a job at reputable Melbourne car dealers Brown and Dureau. With their support, he imported more cars to race, including six single-seater HRG sports cars, which were very popular. One of the buyers was a young car dealer called Stan Jones. He competed against Gaze at Woodside in South Australia and led the race for some time until rolling the HRG, as a result of pushing far too hard far too quickly. Gaze won the race and later went looking for Jones to see how he was. Instead of a sore and disconsolate race driver sitting miserably in a corner, he found a joyous Stan Jones running up to him to exclaim, 'Wasn't that fantastic!'

Harry Firth was a big fan of Jones, whom he regarded as 'a natural'. Jones would go on to not only forge a distinguished racing career, but also father Australia's second Formula 1 World Champion. Another driver who was well known at this time was Lex Davison, who had started his racing in an Alfa Romeo. He was more of the debonair playboy type. Davison applied whatever assets he had at his disposal to orchestrate victory, but his greater wealth was his sportsmanship. Gaze, Davison and Jones would become firm friends, and Harry Firth would be a key player in their early careers.

Australian motor sport was waking up again. In 1947 the first grand prix in 8 years was run, on handicap, over a tarred Mt Panorama circuit. Bill Murray won it in an MGTC, starting 25½ minutes before Alf Barrett's Alfa Romeo, the fastest car in the field. The post-war motor racing world was populated by a mix of affluent adventurers like 'Gelignite' Jack Murray, who would make his name in round-Australia trials. He was also a wrestler, water-skier and lifesaver of some repute. Another was 'Wild Bill' McLachlan, who ran a speedway in Sydney and would later become famous as a national water-skiing champion. Hope Bartlett was another imposing figure in the pits, having forged a career in various action sports. He would later become mentor to an even more famous motor racing figure — his nephew, Frank Gardner. Alec Mildren was another dealer who could not resist the call of competition. These were wild men: mates, rivals, jokers, short on finesse and big on attitude. They drove machinery that had been cobbled together, ranging from awesome to grotesque, defying the lines of modern motoring, in a desperate bid to pack as much power as possible into the chassis: these were the 'specials'.

Gaze brought more than the HRG sports cars to Australia. During the war he also purchased an MG, an Aston Martin and an Alvis Speed 25. In 1946 he approached Geoffrey Taylor, the founder of Alta, to buy a 10-year-old 250 horsepower, supercharged single-seater.

The Alta went straight to the workshops of AF Hollins engineering, to be prepared for the 1948 Australian Grand Prix. Two of the younger staff members were keen to do the job. One was Mick Scott. The other was Harry Firth. The problem was, their employers didn't think that they were up to the task. They were told to instead prepare a BMW 328, which was to be driven by Frank Pratt, who was given little chance of winning the race. Firth was not only annoyed that AF Hollins didn't think him good enough to work with Gaze; he had also developed a rapport with the tall, distinguished driver. They were both ex-servicemen, and they shared a love for motor sport and a dislike of fools. On many mornings they would be deep in conversation over a cup of tea, swapping wartime yarns.

The first major event for Gaze and his Alta in 1948 was the South Australian 100 at Lobethal, in the Adelaide Hills, on New Year's Day. Gaze had an unimpressive race, but witnessed the severe injury of a 14-year-old boy, who was hit by the debris from a crash. The boy had been sitting in a gutter beside the track at the time. The state government promptly banned racing on public roads.

Footage of those early races seems almost barbaric today, with the cars racing tightly packed and seemingly out of control in front of hundreds of blissful spectators standing and sitting in large groups, unprotected by any barriers, just a few metres from the roadside. 'At places like Lobethal you were airborne half the time,' recalls Gaze. 'The dirt at the side of the road was often flicked up at you from people cutting corners, many of them doing it intentionally. You could put your inside wheel through the apex of a corner almost anywhere because there was no load on it. Australian roads mostly had gravel on the inside of those corners, and they were pretty narrow anyway.'

'Someone asked me once,' recalls Gaze, 'what the difference was between driving on the road, and in a race. In a race you just gritted your teeth and drove twice as fast as you dared to do on the road and hoped you could stay in the car when you hit a bump.'

Nearly 4 weeks after Lobethal, Gaze arrived at Point Cook, 20 kilometres southeast of Melbourne, for the Australian Grand Prix, hoping for better luck. The 8.62 kilometre circuit was part of the world's first military airbase: the RAAF had established itself there in February 1914. It featured a fast, wide straight and high-speed corners. The race was held on Australia Day, and Harry Firth, while wishing Gaze all the best, was just as keen to prove his employer AF Hollins wrong by presenting the unheralded BMW 328 in race-winning form. Its owner, Frank Pratt, was a former motorcycle racer from New Zealand, making his first start in a car. He was also injured, having crashed his bike a few weeks before the grand prix.

Gaze's Alta was the fastest car in Australia, capable of covering 400 metres in 14 seconds from a standing start. He had qualified fastest of the 26 cars, putting his Alta on 'scratch' or pole position, which meant that he would be starting the race 14½ minutes after Pratt. It was 110°F (43.3°C); this did not help the Alta, which was notorious for its fickle performance. Its engine overheated on lap 5, causing the magneto to fail. The drivers were also suffering. Even Lex Davison, who had entered a Mercedes, collapsed after bringing his car into the pits on lap 17. Frank Pratt's 'roughie' BMW, prepared by the rookies Firth and Scott, pounded reliably around the circuit to win the race, in a drive that had been hailed as near-perfect in the conditions. Pratt had achieved the rare distinction of winning Australian titles on motorcycle, motorcycle with sidecar and car. That car, a collector's item, is still around today.

For Gaze and his crew it had been a very frustrating start to the year. Once again, the handicap system had proved insurmountable for the faster cars. He couldn't bear to wait around, so as soon as his Alta cooled down, he drove it home.

The 1948 grand prix triggered a running battle between Firth and AF Hollins. 'I had my own ideas on how to do things. I didn't give a stuff what other people thought. It would have to be a very good reason, or some special knowledge, to make me change my mind.'

It wasn't until later in 1948 that Tony Gaze and Harry Firth were able to work together. Gaze had crashed his Alta in practice for the Rob Roy Hill Climb. 'I just went round a right-hand corner, and the car wouldn't straighten. It just kept going to the right. I fell out when it turned upside down, but the throttle had stuck, and when it landed, breaking all the front suspension, the engine was still roaring at full revs, spinning the rear wheels like mad. It was quite an incident. Several people came down to help and one of them pulled the plug wires off to stop the engine. I never found out who it was but since then I've met about three people who said it was them.' To this day, the place where Gaze's car left the road is known as 'Gaze's Gully'.

The following week he walked into AF Hollins and discussed with Firth what he thought should be done with his Alta, which was sitting forlornly in a corner of the workshop, still in pieces. 'Do you mind if I have a go?' asked Firth. Australia's first two legends of motor sport were finally in partnership. Firth worked hard on not only rebuilding the Alta but improving its performance and reliability. For the next year they contested various events, mostly hill climbs, but also circuit races at venues like Fishermens Bend in Victoria.

'He was very courageous,' Firth recalls of Gaze. 'He would have a go at anything, but he also had the brains to work out when he was doing something wrong.'

Gaze saw in Firth an innovative engineer and a perceptive strategist. Firth saw in Gaze a true gentleman; he describes Gaze and his wife, Kay, as 'a wonderful couple'. When the Gazes discussed returning to England, where Gaze planned to race full-time, Firth said he would not be going with them. He was not ready to leave his homeland again so soon after the war. They saddled up the Alta for one last fling, in the 1950 Australian Grand Prix. It was to be held at Nuriootpa, the commercial centre of South Australia's world-famous wine-producing Barossa Valley. The street circuit was 4.8 kilometres long, roughly square with a few kinks in the sides. Thirty-five thousand spectators watched Doug Whiteford's Ford V8 win it. Gaze's only recollection is that, 'I was stupid. I should have won that one.' He dropped a cylinder in a lead-up race.

In a post-war world fast gearing up for an industrial and technological boom, capitalism dictated the politics of what has always been loosely called sport. Almost all the clients Harry Firth came to befriend while he worked for AF Hollins were wealthy. Corporate achievers, socialites, gentry ... they all passed through the workshops, and Firth had their ears. He also learnt from them: free advice from experts on all kinds of financial opportunity, and like everything else of value that crossed Firth's path, it was filed away for later use. 'I could talk to all these people on equal terms because I had a wealth of worldly knowledge that was worth more than money. It was a passport to anywhere.' By 'anywhere', Firth meant anywhere in Melbourne. His future would be as an innovator in his own country; he was a man who would change the course of motor sport history in Australia.

When Tony and Kay Gaze landed in London, motor sport was no longer a game just for enthusiasts. The most daring drivers in the world were gathering, and there would be greater numbers of European events. Momentum was building for a golden age — in the development of machines and the desperation of competitors. The 1950s would give birth to names that would stand in halls of fame forever, names cast in glory ... and tragedy.

The best racing machines in the world were pouring out of workshops and factories and Gaze was eager to jump into them all. His network of contacts was extensive. His plan was to race professionally, returning to Australia every year or so to visit his parents and compete, if possible. His timing was perfect, for 1950 saw the birth of what would become for half a century the premier motor sport: Formula 1. The Federation Internationale de l'Automobile (FIA) announced that Formula 1 (which used to be known as Formula A) was to be for 1500cc supercharged cars or 4500cc cars without supercharging. They would compete in an official World Championship with races conducted over a minimum of 300 kilometres. Until then, races had been 500 kilometres or more.

The 7-race series began with the Grand Prix of Great Britain on 13 May. Giuseppe 'Nino' Farina, who started from pole position, won not only that race, but the first world title for drivers.

Tony Gaze won his final two Australian races in the sports Alta at Balcombe on the Mornington Peninsula in June 1950, then finished the year contesting various European events. His first formal competition was the 1951 World Formula 2 championship, for which he renewed his acquaintance with Alta. Formula 2 was introduced in Europe to provide international competition for drivers who could not find a start in Formula 1. Their engines were restricted to 2000cc, with no supercharging allowed. Australian driver and engineer Jim Gullan prepared the car. They went to a host of exotic locations ... Silverstone, Monza, Rome, Genoa, Naples, the Nurburgring and, of course, Goodwood. His rivals were often factory teams and Formula 1 drivers with far bigger budgets. It was common for a driver to race in one, two or even three different cars at a meeting. 'We all got to know each other. You raced every week, so that on Monday you'd say, "We'll see you down at so and so on Wednesday." And you had to drive to these events. We tried to drive from Nurburgring to Rome in one hit. That's about 1200 kilometres, including crossing the Italian Alps. Eventually we reached Modena, about 300 kilometres short, and I was falling asleep, so we had to stop and wake someone up in the middle of the night to put us up.' Fifty years later, leading race drivers are competing once every two weeks and flying to their events in private jets.

The 1951 campaign ended at Avus, in Berlin, where the Alta 'threw a rod': a piston rod broke and exploded through the engine casing. This was common for Altas in those days. Gaze started the next season competing in the unrestricted Formula Libre class in a Maserati. He was racing against a variety of drivers, including the young Englishman who was forging a very promising future: Stirling Moss. Gaze won at Goodwood and finished 2nd on three other occasions.

He had already competed against the best drivers, but not in the elite category. He was asked in 1952 to drive an HWM car in Formula 1. 'HWM' stood for Hersham and Walton Motors. They were Britain's leading team, and used Alta engines. Even with the new structure of elite racing, the sport was still amateurish. Teams couldn't be certain that they would be ready for the first championship round, even though there were 10 races before it.

Gaze's first starts that year were not with HWM, but in his favourite Alta. His best result was 5th in the Lavant Cup at Goodwood on 14 April. One of Britain's finest drivers, Mike Hawthorn, won the race in a Cooper Bristol. Gaze finally saw action for HWM in round 3 of the championship, at Spa-Francorchamps in Belgium. They prepared five cars for the race. The drivers were Lance Macklin, Peter Collins, Paul Frere, Roger Laurent and the first Australian to compete in the Formula 1 World Championship.

Spa-Francorchamps was a 14 kilometre circuit about 50 kilometres south of Liège. It was designed to be one of the fastest tracks in Europe. Alberto Ascari, in his Ferrari 500, secured pole position with a time of 4 minutes, 37 seconds. On race day, the track was awash with rain. Gaze had qualified 16th, but felt that the car was strong. Shortly after the race was flagged away, he settled in behind Stirling Moss, who was driving his new Bristol-powered ERA. Gaze quickly discovered a problem. The relief valve on his fuel pump had stuck and the engine was getting far more fuel than it needed. The carburettors were flooding, and the excess methanol was spewing into Gaze's face and soaking his clothing. The race had just begun, so Gaze had 10 kilometres or more to go before he could pull into the pits. In a moment, his trepidation turned to outright fear, as Moss's ERA caught fire. Gaze slowed, swerving to avoid the flames as Moss pulled over to the side of the road and leapt free. 'I knew Stirling was an athlete, but he was out of that car so fast ...'

Back in the pits, Gaze's crew made the necessary — but time-consuming — repairs. Few teams carried anything but the most basic spare parts. He returned to the race with no chance of winning and set about making himself familiar with his relatively new car. After several more of the required 36 laps, he noticed that he was passing a lot of cars.

British driver Ken Wharton went off in the Bristol-powered Frazer Nash on lap 10. 'He sailed through a barbed-wire fence,' as Gaze recalls. 'Damned lucky not to cut his head off.'

'About one-third of the distance, I came up rather quickly on Jean Behra in a Gordini, and Piero Taruffi in a Ferrari, and they were bouncing off each other time and again ... in the rain. They were really desperate. The races were so long that they had plenty of time to sort it out, so it was crazy stuff. Eventually they hit for the last time and both went off in front of me.'

Gaze continued to pass other drivers who were either struggling in the wet conditions or fighting some mechanical problem. Seven drivers were out by lap 17, and some of the others were destined to end up 5 or 6 laps down on the leader, Alberto Ascari. He started to think that with the high attrition rate and a little luck he might gain a respectable result. However, Formula 1 was determined to give the Australian a memorable baptism. 'I was driving along at about 200 kilometres per hour, feeling good about myself again, when I copped this tremendous whack in the face.' It was a bird. A bird had flown straight into his face. 'I reached up to feel my face ... touched this horrible mangled mess ... and I thought, "My god, that's my eye." Thankfully, I had double vision, so I realised it couldn't be my eye. It was the bird's guts that I was feeling!' For the next few kilometres, all the drivers Gaze had overtaken passed him, making gestures indicating that they were sorry for what they assumed was a mechanical fault. 'When I got back to the pits, I couldn't even get out of the car. I was absolutely stunned.' Gaze returned to the race and finished 15th, 6 laps behind Ascari.

Gaze's engine failed in the British Grand Prix at Silverstone and his de Dion tube failed in the German Grand Prix at the Nurburgring. He didn't compete again until the final round of the championship, at Monza, where he tried to catch a 'tow' from Ascari in qualifying and almost ran the champion off the road. His punishment was failure to qualify.

Ascari won the race — and another title. Back in the pits, Gaze went looking for the Italian hero and apologised. 'On the track, he'd given me a bit of a look as he went by, but in the pits, he slapped me on the back and in his halting English said, "Forget. We have a cup of tea." He led me off and we had that cup of tea, and from then on, every time he saw me he would say, "Come and have a cup of tea."' The pair became firm friends.

'Tony Gaze was not only the man behind the establishment of Goodwood,' Stirling Moss recalls, 'but like all Australians, he was friendly, easy to get along with, and a quick driver himself. In those days, Formula 1 was not what it is today. I was lucky enough to have a professional career, but really it was about sportsmen doing a sport. Most of the people were like Tony, racing for the same reasons people like playing polo or golf.'

Gaze had learnt much in 1952. Drivers were still living off starting money and thrills. Funding and supply for teams were both inconsistent. When his car broke a crankshaft late in the year, for instance, Alta could not supply a new engine. The deal was over. It had been a sobering welcome to Formula 1.

Late in the 1952 season Gaze had been offered a drive in a 3 litre Maserati. He drove it with success in England and that relationship continued in 1953, along with other adventures, such as the Monte Carlo Rally with Lex Davison and Stan Jones. They had no knowledge of the stages, but competed without incident for every kilometre from Glasgow to Monaco and finished 64th.

When Jones and Davison returned to Australia, Gaze hatched another plan, with Peter Whitehead's brother Graham, to buy two Aston Martin DB3s, one of which almost killed him in the Portuguese Grand Prix at Oporto. He was hit by Pietro Palmieri's Ferrari, and the impact launched the DB3 into the air. It sailed into a tree, broke in half and erupted in flames. Spectators were horrified at what they might find when they ran to the scene. The great irony was that if Gaze had been wearing a safety belt he would have been killed — as it was, he had been thrown out of the cockpit in mid-flight. They found him semi-conscious in the middle of the track and dragged him to safety before the following cars could hit him.

Legend has it that Palmieri was chased from the circuit by officials, and never competed again. Unfortunately, Gaze was unable to replace his car, so he didn't compete for some time. 'We were not rich in those days. For example, a set of tyres would last us half a season. They had a reasonable amount of tread to start with, but after a while it wore right down and we were sliding around quite a lot. But then so was everyone else. Sometimes I think we even went quicker!'

Alberto Ascari won his second Formula 1 championship in 1953. Tony and Kay Gaze were not there. They had gone to New Zealand with Peter Whitehead, searching for a change of luck.

Back in Australia, Harry Firth had left AF Hollins. For 5 years he worked from home in a converted private garage. His fame was spreading, though, thanks to his many contacts in the wealthy world of sports and luxury car ownership. 'They'd all come in their Rolls Royces and Jaguars and all that and we'd sit in the front yard talking about what we were going to do with their cars. The basic wage then was about £8, and in my average week I'd make £45 to £55. My best week? £89 10s. Mind you, you worked. I'd get up at 7 am and go to bed at 2 am the next morning.'

By 1955, Firth had accumulated enough wealth to buy a commercial property to continue his career in engineering and racing, applying his technical skills to the art of driving by competing and winning rallies, hill climbs and circuit events. Hill climbs were lucrative, because Firth turned them into something like a pyramid selling scheme, where he multiplied his purse. He had a Mobil contract that paid him £15 for winning in each class, but he won another £15 if he broke the class record. 'If I took five different cars to each meeting, I could win £30 per event or £150 for the day. I did the whole bloody lot.'

'I built cars, improved cars, prepared them, drove them. I raced an MG; a Sunbeam Alpine; competed in the early Round Australia trials. I was always a little conservative in driving because I wanted to stay alive.'

Tony Gaze, with a Formula 1 HWM with a supercharged 2 litre Alta engine, and Peter Whitehead, with a V12 Ferrari, had put together enough money to race for the summer of 1954–55 in New Zealand. They had technical support from AF Hollins, which Harry Firth had left, and fuel supply from Shell. The latter turned out to be a disastrous deal. The first New Zealand Grand Prix, run at Ardmore airfield, 30 kilometres south of Auckland, on 9 January attracted about 70,000 people. All kinds of cars had been entered under the Formula

Libre category, from the latest designs, driven by the international competitors such as Gaze and Whitehead, to local entries that were built long before the war. The most sophisticated entry was Ken Wharton's high-revving, extremely noisy BRM. Wharton was Britain's best-performed driver at the time. Lex Davison was there in an HWM Jaguar that he had bought from Tony Gaze. Stan Jones brought his Maybach. Also there was a young, lean, raw recruit to the world of international motor sport. His name was Jack Brabham.

Brabham was born in what was then the peaceful outer Sydney suburb of Hurstville on 2 April 1926. He was the only son of a wholesale grocer, whose trucks and cars became a mechanical playground for him. Like most motor sport engineers, Brabham learnt much from experimentation and dismantling. His father taught him to drive when he was 12, in a Chrysler 77. 'Down the bottom end of Hurstville there used to be just paddocks ... and a two-up school. He used to take me down there for a drive on Sunday mornings.'

Three years later Brabham left school to work in Ferguson's Garage, where his father's trucks were maintained. He was studying mechanical engineering at Kogarah Technical College, and bought a Velocette motorcycle, competing with it in scrambles and dirt-track races. Then he bought a Manx Norton, planning to race it at Bathurst, where the Easter bike meetings were held. However, his call-up to the air force came just before the race, in 1943, so he sold the bike. Brabham wanted more than anything to be a pilot, but the war was coming to an end and the RAAF wanted mechanics. He was put to work on Mosquitoes and Beaufighters (twin-engined fighter-bombers that were used with great effect in the Pacific theatre against the Japanese).

When Brabham was released from the armed forces in 1946, he opened a repair shop. One of his first projects was to build a midget racer for an American speedway driver, Johnny Schonberg. They became great friends. 'I was only interested in it from the engineering side, but when Johnny had a couple of shunts, his wife stopped him driving and there I was with a midget on the floor of the workshop and no one to drive it. So I thought I'd have a go at it. Johnny took me down to the mud flats at Tempe, and let me drive it around there to get a feel for it. I started racing at Parramatta Speedway.'

Brabham's first experience of motor racing was quite a shock. 'It was terrible. I got plastered with bricks and stones and couldn't believe how much muck was coming back off the wheels. And being my first time, I had to start right up the back. After two nights of that, they put me up the front. I was still there at the end of the race.' In one season, he had won the New South Wales Championship. It didn't take him long to accumulate more wins, and he soon became the most acclaimed midget racer in Australia. He was Australian Speedway Champion in 1948 and 1949, and South Australian champion in 1949. In 7 years of speedway racing he never turned a car over, which was extraordinary considering the number of meetings he raced at — sometimes three a week — and the high rate of crashes. Every night cars crashed and people were hurt.

'There were a couple killed,' Brabham recalls. 'Kevin Gallagher was one bloke, a friend of mine, who was killed at the Speedway Royal. That was a shock, but it was something I would have to get used to over the years, although I had no idea at the time what I was in for. I was only racing for fun.' Brabham maintained the car in his workshop, not only servicing it, to keep it going through such a busy schedule, but even machining his own parts.

Speedway racing was earning Brabham money, between £50 and £80 a night. No one tried to stop him. His father was his biggest fan. The next step had to be circuit racing. It started with hill climbing in the midget in 1951. The midget was an instant success, but at first organisers refused to award Brabham the victory, claiming that a car with two-wheel brakes was not eligible to win anything. 'That upset me a bit, so I went home, dug up some brakes from a scrapyard somewhere — I think they came off an old jeep or something — and fitted them before going to the Rob Roy Hill Climb and winning the Australian Championship. Then they had to give it to me.' During 1951 he met a young engineer called Ron Tauranac, who had answered his advertisement about selling his old Velocette motorcycle engine. Tauranac proved to be an important contact and Brabham was soon getting regular work from him.

The next step was to prepare a Cooper Mark 4 (Mk4) with a 500cc engine for his first foray into road racing. It was not quick enough, so he planted a 1000cc engine from a HRD (Howard Rice Davies) motorcycle in the Cooper. Then came the revolutionary deal: sponsorship from Redex. With this, Brabham bought the Cooper Bristol which became famous as the 'Redex Special' — because Brabham painted his sponsor's name on the car. It was the first sign of commercialism in Australian motor sport, and the ruling authorities made him remove it, having declared a ban on advertising on race cars. Brabham was entered for the Australian Grand Prix at Albert Park in 1953, but due to the advertising ban he didn't start the race. His first major event against world-class drivers would be across the Tasman.

Brabham claims he fled to New Zealand to escape the conservative Confederation of Australian Motor Sport (CAMS) regulations, and to learn about the wider world of motor racing. 'Going to New Zealand was a big opportunity,' Brabham recalls, 'because it was my first chance to talk to overseas drivers. It was after talking to them that I decided to go to England for a year's experience.'

The organisers of the 1954 New Zealand Grand Prix modified the 3.2 kilometre Ardmore circuit during practice to make it faster and more entertaining. Stan Jones was among the fastest qualifiers, but on the second day a connecting rod burst through the crankcase of his mighty Maybach engine. Parts could not be sent from Australia in time for the race, so the crew began a desperate search of Auckland for anything that might work. They did find similar parts, but had to take them to a machine shop to modify them before patching up the crankcase. It took them all afternoon and late into the night, but by 10.40 the next morning Jones was able to start the engine. After a brief test, the Maybach was taken to Ardmore for the race start. This was typical of racing in those days for all teams.

Tony Gaze and Peter Whitehead had problems of their own. They arrived at the track on race day to find that Shell had not delivered their fuel. All they had was what was left in their tanks after practice. Gaze suggested they drain the fuel from his car into Whitehead's, which had qualified faster. Whitehead said, 'No, we've come this far. We'll start together and just see what happens.' The mechanics went off to try to find some fuel.

There were four cars on each row of the grid. Beside the pole-sitting Ken Wharton were Whitehead, another British driver, Horace Gould, in a Cooper Bristol, then Jones. On the second row of the grid, Lex Davison's HWM Jaguar sat beside a couple of locals: Ron Roycroft in an Alfa Romeo and Allan Freeman in a Cooper Mk4. On the other side of Davison, in eighth spot, was a well-prepared Cooper Bristol Mk2, powered by a 6 cylinder, 1971cc engine. It was more compact in stature than some of the cars surrounding it, but cleverly curved for its day. Only Freeman's little Mk4, with its JAP 2 cylinder motor, looked smaller. The words 'Redex Special' were still painted on the Mk2's flanks, just behind the number 9. The driver didn't have much to say for himself. Jack Brabham rarely had much to say.

It was an incredible race. Whitehead made a fine start and took the early lead before the massive power of Wharton's whining BRM overtook him. Jones, in the patched-up Maybach, gave chase.

Whitehead was out after 13 laps when, at 200 kilometres an hour, there was a blinding flash. Fragments of metal blew out of the front of the cockpit from under his feet, one shard slashing his face just above his eye. His clutch and its housing had shattered with explosive fury. Jones moved to second, Gaze to third — and as he raced past Whitehead and his stricken Ferrari, he noticed his crew running to it to drain the remaining fuel from its tank.

Gaze pulled in to take on the last drops his team had scavenged, then roared off again. He immediately settled into a pace that was 3 seconds a lap faster than Wharton's leading BRM, which had lapped the field but was wearing down its tyres because of the ferocious wheel spin delivered by its aggressive engine. Wharton started to slow. Jones took the lead. The desperate Gaze, having fought through the field, took over. With 92 laps covered, the challenge seemed to over when Gaze finally ran out of fuel — he coasted disconsolately into the pits, waking from self-pity only when he saw his team frantically preparing to refuel again.

'Don't ask!' yelled mechanic Alan Ashton, who must have borrowed from the Harry Firth handbook on crisis situations. Wharton's team hadn't even noticed that several litres of their fuel had gone missing ...

Jones and his team had done the impossible with a car that had been shattered only a day before. Wharton's 2nd place was a fitting reward for his team's persistence, and the guile of Alan Ashton helped Gaze resume the race and finish 3rd. Young Jack Brabham finished 6th ... with an engine on the edge of its life ... holding off eight other drivers. It was a race that not only summed up the extraordinary mechanical challenges of the era, but also signalled the start of a wonderful career.

Tony Gaze looks back fondly on his first meeting with Jack Brabham. 'Well we were all mates in those days. I mean everyone talked to everyone else. I heard he was a damn good driver. He was driving in a dirt-track fashion, which the crowd liked. Everyone said, "Oh if he goes to Europe he'll murder them." I said, "Not if he drives like that, he won't." You had to learn to look after the cars a bit. Driving like that was fine for a short race, but over a long distance ...'

Brabham was well aware that his technique was still taking shape. 'I suppose I was still driving a little bit like I did on the speedway, I hadn't matured yet.' He would, with devastating effect.

After his first excursion to New Zealand in the summer of 1953–54, Gaze spent several months driving a wide variety of cars in an equally wide variety of events. He forged a partnership with Jaguar which brought a win in a C-Type with Peter Whitehead and Alf Barrett in the only Australian 24 hour race at the time, at Mt Druitt. They took one look at the circuit as storm clouds gathered and warned the organisers that a wet surface would not survive the demands of a large field of cars running around at high speed for an entire day.

They were right. A craggy pothole ripped out the rear suspension of the Jaguar when Gaze was at the wheel but the crew refused to give up and welded the rig back onto the car — with little regard for the danger involved in waving a naked flame beneath a full tank of fuel. Gaze won the sports car class. Further back in the field that day was another Jaguar, driven by a young Australian feeling his way around the motor sport world. It was Hope Bartlett's enterprising young nephew Frank Gardner.

Gaze returned to Europe and spent the summer racing his Jaguar-powered HWM sports car. He scored regular wins and placings but then made an unfortunate reacquaintance with the HWM Alta, which was powered with a new Jaguar engine. He had been under medication for a minor illness and was dressing to leave the circuit after practice for a race at Goodwood when he was asked to clamber back into his overalls for another stint. He remembers saying, 'Look, I've finished for the day,' and the mechanic replying, 'No, you're not. They want you to drive the single-seater.' The only other thing Gaze recalls was flashing down the main straight at 210 kilometres an hour and braking for the corner. The medication had clouded his mind. He had put his foot back on the throttle, not the brake. The car shot off an escape road and slammed into a dirt bank. Witnesses later reported that the car turned end over end a few times. A rival team's mechanic later told him, 'It was so bad, I didn't want to look at you. I thought you must be dead.'

Once again, the lack of safety harnesses in the cockpits turned out to be a blessing for Tony Gaze, who was thrown out by the centrifugal force of the spinning, somersaulting car — his body tracing a lazy parabola that ended with a dull thump in the shocked crowd. 'I woke up underneath the X-ray machine in hospital,' he recalls. 'There was sand everywhere.' He was severely concussed. The main problem was a 'wrenched back', according to the hospital, which left him with permanently damaged nerves that would plague him for the rest of his life. 'They said I was very lucky not to have been paralysed. They made me a special harness, with about 16 straps on it, which I was supposed to wear all the time. Of course I took it off the minute I got home and never wore it again. I'm an idiot, but it was so uncomfortable. The main thing I noticed was the loss of sensation in my bum. Every time I went to the loo I had to look in the bowl to see if I'd finished!'

Gaze didn't resume racing until the following summer, when he and Whitehead secured a deal with Ferrari. The long-term plan was to return to Formula 1.

CHAPTER THREE

Brabham

Jack Brabham had decided, following the 1954 New Zealand Grand Prix, that international motor sport was worth a try. It was simply a question of when. He continued racing in Australia, including an educational adventure in the Redex Round Australia Trial, which he contested in a Holden. Country centres greeted the competitors as if they were royal tourists. Brabham, Lex Davison, Stan Jones, David McKay, Tom Sulman, and the specialist endurance man 'Gelignite' Jack Murray were all involved at various times. The reason the event was originally called a 'trial' was that it was not intended to be a race. All drivers had to do was get to a certain place within a certain time, or they would lose points. However, someone noticed that if two contestants were tied, the fastest over the designated distance would win. It was like a gold rush, as word spread that it was really very important to be quickest.

The pressure on the machinery escalated accordingly, and soon the various drivers and co-drivers needed to become expert repairers, shrewd tacticians — and, in some instances, clever salesmen. The trials would become the wellspring of amazing stories of endurance, physical and mechanical, as drivers and teams made remarkable running repairs to major structural damage in outback areas. Occasionally local farmers would be close enough to assist. There were other times when drivers, unaware of their isolation, would walk into life-threatening situations. Brabham himself was almost in serious trouble on one stage where he elected to walk to the nearest town after breaking down, only to be rescued by a passing farmer who informed him that he would never have survived the 100 kilometre journey on foot. Then there were the characters ... like 'Gelignite' Jack.

'The Redex trials were unbelievable,' Brabham recalls. 'Gelignite Jack? Well ... I remember we were camped in a showground in Townsville, and he threw some gelignite outside in the middle of the night. I thought the whole place had gone up.'

'Gelignite' Jack was one of many famous Australian names to arrive at Southport in Queensland for the 1954 Australian Grand Prix. The triangular 9.7 kilometre circuit, bordered on two sides by the Nerang River, used three public roads which provided long, shallow corners and a couple of lengthy straights, but the track was narrow and bumpy. Brabham lasted 1 lap before his engine stopped. Lex Davison won it in the HWM Jaguar. Stan Jones's spectacular crash, his third consecutive failure to finish his home grand prix, earned him the nickname 'Sorrowful'.

The 1955 New Zealand Grand Prix at Ardmore on 8 January, was once again strongly supported by international drivers, including the famous Prince Bira with his Formula 1 Maserati, powered by a 2.5 litre engine. Brabham remembers him as an exotic character. 'He used to travel around with three or four wives and an entourage.'

Brabham had modified his 'Redex Special' Cooper Bristol. Tony Gaze was full of confidence after his Ferrari deal and feared only mechanical failure — these trips were not made with a caravan full of spares, and he wanted to continue his campaign in Australia and South Africa. He and Peter Whitehead chose to run their cars on 100 octane aviation fuel so they would not repeat the shortage they suffered with Shell's methanol the year before. It helped preserve the life of the engines but slowed the performance of the Ferraris, conceding an advantage to Prince Bira, who capitalised on it. He took pole position and won the race, by 23 seconds, from Whitehead. Gaze finished a minute later in 3rd place. Brabham came in convinced by then that he was ready for a trip to Europe.

'After talking to a few of the drivers at the 1954 New Zealand Grand Prix, I thought about spending a year in England,' Brabham recalls, 'and after the 1955 grand prix I made up my mind. I had no idea at the time that it would take me 27 years to come back.'

When Brabham landed in the old world in 1955 he sought out the manufacturers of the car that had made him famous back home. Charles Cooper and his son John ran the Cooper Car Company, maker of the Cooper Bristol. At first, Brabham found a job in their workshop as a mechanic; he was hoping to win their support for his racing career. His persistence was rewarded.

Brabham's first competitive car was a Cooper Alta he bought from Peter Whitehead. 'Peter Whitehead really fixed me up with the wrong car. I had the Cooper Bristol going really well back home and I was going to take that with me to England but he talked me out of it, saying it was too much trouble shipping it over and everything. He told me to flog it, and that he'd sell me a much better car over there. When I got there, the car he sold me was nowhere near the one I wanted.'

He qualified 8th in a competitive field of 20 for the 21 lap Glover Trophy at Goodwood on 11 April 1955. Stirling Moss started from pole in a Maserati but retired after 12 laps with fuel pump problems. Brabham ran out of fuel with 4 laps to go. 'Peter Whitehead's mechanic was servicing the car for me, and gave me the wrong information on how much fuel I'd need. I was running fourth at the time.' The race was won by Maserati driver Roy Salvadori. Brabham raced the Cooper Alta only once more: the engine expired, so he replaced it with a Bristol engine.

Tony Gaze's only problem with the Ferrari was that it was built for a smaller man. His legs bent uncomfortably inside the chassis and his upper body projected awkwardly above the windscreen, which gave him a tremendous buffeting at high speed. He also caught more than his share of debris thrown up by the wheels of the cars ahead of him. In spite of this he won the Rand Grand Prix at the Grand Central circuit in Johannesburg, but when he returned for the European summer, he learnt that Ferrari had not held up their end of the deal they'd struck with him and Whitehead the year before — there would be no rebuilt cars for the Formula 1 season. Without factory support, it was pointless continuing.

While Whitehead returned to self-funded drives, Gaze turned his attention to a new plan, the 'Kangaroo Team'. He figured that promoters of race meetings would pay plenty to have an all-Australian team as an attraction. He had three Aston Martins prepared for the demanding Hyeres 12 hour race in France. That meant recruiting another five drivers. One of them was Jack Brabham.

Tony Gaze remembers Brabham as very much a 'raw' recruit. 'It was funny. It didn't occur to me that he'd never been to Europe. We were scrutineering in Toulon, so we picked him up and took him along. His eyes were popping out of his head at the French girls. He'd say, "Gawd, look at all the sheilas ..." That night we went to a rather flash restaurant. We said, "Now you're in the south of France, what do you want?" He said, "I want a well-done steak." We said, "You can't ... you don't order a well-done steak in a place like this."' A legend had begun. Brabham would become famous in Europe over the years for sending steaks back to the chef repeatedly. European culture was under serious threat.

'I never changed,' says Brabham. 'Years later I was in a fancy restaurant in France and sent the meat back for a third time, when the chef came running out of the kitchen with a big knife in his hand. He leaned over me and said, "I refuse to destroy this piece of meat any more!"'

Gaze was more impressed with Brabham's driving, especially as he had never competed in long-distance events. Brabham was shown how they set rev limits on the cars to preserve the life of the engine, and how to mark conservative braking points — because stopping to change brake linings took far too much time. 'The clutches were also tricky in those cars,' Gaze recalls. 'Jack was still pretty quiet. I tried to impress on him that it was a 12 hour race and if you were running at the end you won. He drove very hard and the brakes did wear out, but I don't think he could have avoided it, you know, the way he drove. He drove very well, though. I always felt that Jack and I should have shared a car because he was the quickest, and I was second-quickest. I drove with David McKay, Jack drove with Tom Sulman, and Dick Cobden and Les Cosh drove the third car.'

Gaze and McKay were poised to win the event. To this day Gaze believes that only the race steward's error in timekeeping stopped them. (Officially, they were a lap behind the leaders but the team's own timekeeping had them on the same lap.) Brabham and Sulman had worked their way to 4th in a car that was losing its brakes. 'Tommy was a bit slow,' Brabham recalls. 'He was pretty old by that time. But we did pretty well as a team.' The Cobden/Cosh car drove into 3rd and they won the trophy for best team. 'Kangaroo Team' was presented on the podium with a bizarre-looking statue of an eagle as a trophy. No one wanted it, so they gave it to Chief Mechanic Jim Roberts.

Sports car racing was at a peak in popularity in 1955. Hyeres was big, but the biggest of them all was the Le Mans 24 hour, a bewildering test of man and machine on a 17.26 kilometre circuit. With the exception of 1936, when the race was cancelled due to strikes, and 8 years surrounding World War II, the Le Mans 24 hour race had been running since 1923, and had built a grand tradition. Virtually all the big names were there, as usual, in 1955, except the great Alberto Ascari, who had been killed earlier in the year while testing a Ferrari sports car at Monza. Gaze and Brabham had signed up as reserve drivers, but only Brabham attended.

The race began at 4 pm on Saturday, 12 June, with the traditional charge of 70 drivers running to leap into their cars and start their engines before driving off. An estimated 250,000 people gathered at spectator points all around the circuit. There were bands playing, carnival rides, sideshows, exhibitions and parties. Spectators wandered all over the massive layout, exploring the vantage points.

After 2 hours and 20 minutes, British driver Lance Macklin, in an Austin Healy, was entering the main straight when he was lapped by Mike Hawthorn in his Jaguar. Frenchman Pierre Levegh, driving a Mercedes, had been pursuing Hawthorn, and was also about to pass Macklin to continue the chase. Juan Manuel Fangio was pursuing Levegh. But up ahead, Hawthorn suddenly slowed down, in order to pull into the pits. Macklin couldn't react quickly enough and pulled out to avoid Hawthorn just as Levegh was attempting to pass. Levegh was reportedly travelling at more than 250 kilometres an hour when he hit the back of Macklin's car. While Macklin was shunted down the straight by the impact, fighting to regain control, the crowd watched in horror as Levegh's Mercedes bounced like a dodgem car across the track.

Fangio, who witnessed the entire incident from behind, reportedly told his crew later that day that Levegh had the presence of mind to throw up his hand, signalling the following drivers to slow down, as his car spun uncontrollably into a 2 metre high earth embankment. The freakish angle of impact launched Levegh's Mercedes skywards. It somersaulted twice before slamming into the crowd and exploding.

The following scenes were the most horrific in motor sport history. Reporters of the time described it as a 'battlefield'. It was claimed by some that the rear axle and engine of the Mercedes sliced through the crowd, decapitating people where they stood. Witnesses spoke of seeing the headless bodies of children, their hands still clasping ice-creams. There were other terrible injuries caused by burning shards of magnesium (magnesium had been built into the engine to save weight). There was a drastic shortage of medical staff and communication was limited. Officials, however, decided not to stop the race. It has been suggested that they were concerned that the flood of people leaving the area would hinder the convoy of ambulances rushing to the scene, but it's also possible that they didn't realise the scale of the disaster.

Jack Brabham had been with the Bristol team, peering down the straight. 'It happened about 300 metres from where I was standing. I saw the car going over the fence. I was absolutely horrified to see that. It stuck in my mind for a long time. There was a lot of talk about whose fault it was, but I dare say it was a racing incident. When that Mercedes hit the crowd it just mowed people down like you wouldn't believe. When I went down later, most of the bodies had been taken away. Others were still there, covered up. There were bits and pieces of the car everywhere.'

When the grim count had finished, 83 spectators and driver Pierre Levegh were dead.

The reaction to Le Mans in 1955 was sudden and drastic. While the race was allowed to continue, with Mike Hawthorn and Ivor Bueb winning by 5 laps from Peter Collins and Paul Frere, the chequered flag that day signalled the end of motor sport in four countries. The French, Swiss, Spanish and Mexican governments simply banned it. Most of the bans were lifted quite soon after, when various organisations proposed alternatives, but the Swiss never relented — and they still haven't. Italy's response was a massive renovation of Monza, where Ascari had died.

For Tony Gaze it was the most tragic definition of a life that had a high level of inherent risk. For Jack Brabham, it was a sobering welcome to big-time motor sport. 'I was there for my first season. It didn't help me much, and a lot of racing was cancelled. It was mainly sports car racing that was affected, which affected the Kangaroo Team more than anything.' The team had limited opportunities in the second half of the year, contesting races in Portugal and Britain before parting amicably.

Kay Gaze, like many drivers' wives, had seen enough. It was time to muster her considerable influence and persuade Tony to settle down. 'Her first husband had been killed when he was a test pilot during the war,' Gaze recalls. 'She'd got him out of the fleet-air arm and into this job testing Spitfires, because she didn't want him killed ... and he was killed. She was more or less suicidal. When I started racing again I said, "Look, if it really worries you at any time, let me know and I'll pack it in." After the second shunt she did get a bit worried. Then you realise that instead of getting "faster" signals from the pits you're getting this worried face looking at you. I asked her what she wanted. She said she wanted me to pack it in.' Gaze planned one final trip to New Zealand with his old mate Peter Whitehead. After that, he promised Kay, he would sell his racing cars and quit.

Jack Brabham returned to England to continue building his career, and contributing to the design and development of the Cooper race cars. He was showing great promise as an engineer. The British Grand Prix of 1955 was his first Formula 1 race. By this time he had switched to a Cooper Bristol T40 — and he persuaded the company to allow him to put the engine in the back, which was revolutionary. Until then, the driver sat behind the engine and in front of the fuel tank. The response to his request was 'There's the workshop. Go and build one.' The Coopers had been heavily involved in Formula 1 when it switched to Formula 2 specifications, but when the regulations changed in 1954 to allow 2.5 litre engines, their influence waned. A few made appearances in various British grands prix, but Brabham's radical T40 was the only entrant in 1955.

'We made two cars, actually,' he recalls, 'One was a sports car, the other a single-seat racing car. The sports car won first time out, at Goodwood. Then it crashed and killed the driver, which didn't help things. I got my car finished just in time for the grand prix.'

The French Grand Prix had been cancelled after the Le Mans disaster, so the British Grand Prix at Aintree became round 6 of the World Championship. Brabham hauled his Cooper around the circuit slower than anyone else in qualifying. With 25 cars in the field, and three cars per row in those days, the Australian suffered the ignominy of being alone on the last row.

Pole-sitter Stirling Moss and Juan Manuel Fangio, in a Mercedes, staged a sizzling contest in wet conditions, and after more than 3 hours of racing, almost always side by side or nose to tail and switching the lead, they finished within 2 seconds of each other ... Moss was the victor. Brabham completed 30 laps before he entered the pits with engine trouble. 'The clutch started slipping. I couldn't go all that hard. But it was a big occasion for Coopers, and we did enough to carry us quite a bit.'

After the British Grand Prix, Brabham trialled the Cooper in a number of races, with very little success initially, mostly due to mechanical failures. In August he finished 4th in the 20 lap *Daily Record* Trophy at Charterhall in Scotland, but he did have the lead for several laps. He was 4th again in the 25 lap Redex Trophy at Snetterton, finishing closely behind Moss who had qualified on pole in a Maserati. 'I had a good dice with Stirling, and probably would have done better if it had kept raining. He was the best driver there at the time, and I learnt a lot from Stirling. He was a terrific bloke to race against ... quick, aggressive, but fair.'

In the Italian Grand Prix at Monza, Fangio lead Piero Taruffi home to clinch his second world title. Jack Brabham was already on his way home for another summer, ready to show his local supporters what he had learnt ... and what he had built.

Port Wakefield was a flat 2 kilometre permanent road course built in 1953, about 60 kilometres north of Adelaide. It was the first purpose-built road racing circuit in Australia, and the highlight of its brief life was the 1955 Australian Grand Prix. A field of 22 cars qualified, and among them was a rare animal of world motor sport. Young Jack Brabham's Cooper Bristol with its rear-engined configuration had been the subject of much debate since its arrival in Australia. Typically, Brabham carted his creation to a variety of events before the grand prix, giving scribes and fans plenty of opportunities to give the 'thing' a good old going over. Jack had a 2 litre engine in the Cooper for his Australian campaign, but it seemed as troublesome there as it had been early on in England. It broke down hopelessly at Bathurst in October and again at Orange, which made the 1360 kilometre journey to Adelaide a potentially humiliating risk.

The favourite at Port Wakefield that year was Reg Hunt in his Maserati, powered by the formidable 250F engine. He took pole position. Lex Davison had withdrawn with pneumonia but Stan Jones, in the Maybach 2, and Doug Whiteford, in the Lago Talbot, would once again be contenders.

Hunt opened up a lead of more than 20 seconds in the first 4 laps of the 80 lap race. It appeared that Brabham and Jones would be fighting for the crumbs, but suddenly they were back in the contest, with a bang. At least that was the sound everyone heard when Hunt's engine broke a cam follower, reducing him to five cylinders. Brabham took the lead among lapped traffic about a third of the way through the race, prompting a roar from the 30,000 spectators packed around the tight course — on a variety of makeshift grandstands, including vehicles and hay bales. He was never headed. It was his first major road course victory in Australia and his first win in any grand prix. Hunt came in 3 seconds behind, and only 1 second in front of a charging Whiteford.

'The track was pretty rough and bumpy, which sort of suited my car a bit,' Brabham recalls. 'I was able to keep up there. When Reg Hunt broke down, it left me without any trouble.'

The Cooper Bristol had lasted longer than ever before, and the victory lap seemed to last longer again as the crowd closed in. Brabham returned to Sydney and won a minor event at Mt Druitt, then broke down at the Queensland Grand Prix after leading the race. The jury was still out on Brabham's automotive experimentation.

The third New Zealand Grand Prix at Ardmore, on 7 January 1956, was the first journey down under for Stirling Moss. Now 25, he was runner-up in the World Championship, and one of the world's most celebrated motor sport personalities. Moss left his factory Mercedes in Europe and brought a Maserati 250S. It had the new disc brakes, and they were far more effective than the drums which were more common then. Moss had such an imposing presence that his rivals were almost 'psyched out' before he turned a wheel.

Tony Gaze, making his final trip to New Zealand, was an exception. He knew Moss as more than just an athlete. 'Stirling was an academic, you see. He worked everything out. I mean, if you wanted to know something about a circuit, you would go to him, because he knew everything. He did his homework.'

Gaze and Peter Whitehead brought the Ferraris they had campaigned for the previous summer — the cars had finally been rebuilt, and were fitted with 750S engines running on alcohol — but knew that they would probably be chasing Moss, who was in ominous form in qualifying. Brabham's Cooper completed the top four.

The fans were hoping for another classic race as the heats began, but they were almost silenced by a crunching sound — the motor sport equivalent of someone running their fingernails across a blackboard. Brabham's gearbox had split. 'We used to use Citroen gearboxes,' he recalls, 'which weren't strong enough. They used to give us a lot of trouble.'

There was no time for him to make repairs, so the race began with a three-car front row, which broke away early to sort out the placings. Moss took the lead, with Gaze hammering away, lap after lap, well behind but hoping for a slice of luck that would enable him to stop the unstoppable. Eighty of the scheduled 100 laps passed before his chance came. Moss was about a lap in front when his face was suddenly splattered with fuel — it smeared his goggles and sickened him with fumes. A hose had broken. He continued until there were only 8 laps to go and he felt his lead was big enough to make a pit stop. They filled his tank, plugged the hose and waved him out. Gaze had been closing on him, but knew he couldn't get there when Moss set a new lap record with only 2 laps to go. The final margin was less than a minute. Peter Whitehead was 3rd.

Finishing 2nd to one of the greatest race drivers of all time was a more than respectable result, and proof that Tony Gaze could have extended his grand prix career. However, he had made a promise to his wife. Following New Zealand he returned to Australia to sell his Ferrari to Lex Davison, after a slight detour in his HWM Jaguar to win the Melbourne Tourist Trophy, remarkably, after running out of oil long before the finish. He forgot to check it because he had spent all his time preparing the Ferrari for Lex.

The Gaze career faded gently, with a few 'fun' drives here and there, but he would never be far from the raucous sounds of straining engines and the sharp smell of fuel, never more than a dream away. Nor could he escape the cold touch of tragedy, reminding him that staying out of the driver's seat was a good way to stay alive.

CHAPTER FOUR

World Champion

Jack Brabham's Cooper T40 had not convinced the critics. In spite of his Australian Grand Prix win, it failed in subsequent races — none of his rivals, who always sought to buy the best cars of the day, were stampeding to the Cooper factory. Lex Davison had the Tony Gaze Ferrari, and Stan Jones bought a Maserati 250F. Even Brabham sold his Cooper and competed in several races in a Maserati 250F in 1956; he also turned down an offer to drive for BRM. Reg Tanner, from Esso, persuaded him to get rid of the Maserati and become a factory driver. 'He told me, "You'll never be able to afford to run this Maserati. Why don't you drive for Coopers?"'

That is how Brabham was offered a full-time drive in September 1956, with Esso support, just in time to sort out a competitive team for the following season. 'It was the best thing that ever happened to me.' His team-mate would be Roy Salvadori.

Brabham's first 'works' drive was not in a car. He drove the team transporter to Goodwood for the Sussex Trophy on 8 September, and was booked for speeding on the way. The citation was sent to the Cooper Factory, which was the address Brabham gave to police. John Cooper discussed the matter with Brabham before marking on the envelope, 'Mr Brabham has returned to Australia ... forwarding address unknown'. Roy Salvadori won for Cooper at Goodwood that weekend. Jack finished 4th, 27 seconds behind.

John Cooper would become one of the great allies in Brabham's career. His sense of humour was typically British. He quickly gave his new driver the nickname 'Black Jack' because of his hair colour and the almost constant 'five o'clock shadow' on his face. 'He always had some funny comment,' Brabham recalls, 'such as, "Do you use knives and forks out there in Australia?" John was a real character and helped me a lot when I was in England, in spite of poor old Charlie, his father, who was really negative about everything. John and I got on very well together.'

Brabham's factory commitments meant that he could not prepare a car in time for the 1956 Australian Grand Prix, which was run at Albert Park in conjunction with the Olympic Games. He did, however, drive a sports car in one of the many support races in the 2 week carnival. 'It was a big occasion for Australian motor racing,' Brabham recalls, 'probably the biggest meeting ever at that time.'

Stirling Moss and Jean Behra teamed to win the sports car race, then finished 1st and 2nd for Ferrari in the grand prix. It was the first factory-backed incursion into Australian motor racing, and an education for the public, who would appreciate the exploits of home-grown drivers even more having sampled the European manufacturer muscle.

Ardmore, New Zealand provided a stark contrast. The 1957 grand prix was run under a shroud of gloom cast by the death of Ken Wharton in the sports car race which preceded it. Wharton had the best car, a 3 litre Ferrari, and was overtaking a slower car when he crashed. According to Jack Brabham, Wharton had been sternly warning other drivers in the pre-race meeting to stick to international rules and overtake on the left. In this case, he did the opposite, driving to the right just as the car in front was doing the right thing and giving way by moving in exactly the same direction. Wharton swerved into loose gravel to avoid a collision. After a long struggle to regain control he struck a pylon. The car turned end over end and he was thrown out. He suffered massive head injuries, and died later in hospital. He was the only driver killed in the circuit's 8 year history.

Brabham was right behind Wharton when it happened. 'I actually feel responsible for that crash. I was trying to get by him, so I was right up with him, going very well. He went in there too fast, trying to get away from me. He went through the straw bales. It was a horrifying accident.'

Brabham, by then armed with a Cooper T41, qualified on the second row for the grand prix and was dicing with Stan Jones for 3rd place when suddenly his car began to struggle. After 100 of the scheduled 120 laps, he limped back to his crew with a burst radiator hose and a blown gasket, losing valuable time. Reg Parnell frustrated Peter Whitehead's fourth and most promising attempt to win the New Zealand Grand Prix. Jones held 3rd, and Brabham came in 10th.

The 1957 Australian Grand Prix was suddenly moved back to March, just 4 months after the 1956 classic in Melbourne. It also moved west — to Caversham, an airfield in Western Australia. Like Point Cook and Ardmore, it was a mixture of runway and roadway. Brabham, Jones and Davison were the headliners, Jones having pumped up his Maserati with a 3 litre engine.

Temperatures climbed to stifling levels. Suburban Perth was threatened by bushfires. 'The problem with race cars in the early days, when it was really hot, was overheating,' says Brabham. 'It was hard to keep the engines and the cockpit cool. The early Coopers were very hard to drive in hot conditions. The pedals got so hot you couldn't touch them without burning your feet. There was no protective footwear. You had to wear light shoes so they could fit among the pedals.'

'I pulled into the pits at one stage,' Brabham recalls, 'coasted in, because the car had petered out. I thought we had run out of fuel. I undid the cap on the fuel tank and the petrol was boiling inside, just like a kettle. It was vapourising. Unbelievable.'

Lex Davison won a controversial race, with the results finalised only after a dispute over lap counting. An exhausted Stan Jones finished 2nd, with Brabham 3rd, a lap down following problems with his fuel pump. The system of lap counting used was to be changed forever after this race — the hapless Western Australian Sporting Car Club, which had done such a wonderful job in preparing the circuit and officiating, took a long time and plenty of beers to get over the 1957 Australian Grand Prix. Brabham held no grudges. 'The only thing I really remember about that race,' he says dryly, 'was that all the flies in Western Australian were there.'

The European summer in 1957 was filled with promise for Cooper, as they rolled out the Brabham-inspired Climaxes for a full season. Brabham finished 6th at Syracuse in Italy and 4th at Goodwood. Then it was time to fit the larger 2.5 litre engine to the rear of the cars and unleash the team on round 2 of the

World Championship, the most famous and exotic round in world motor sport: the Monaco Grand Prix.

Brabham didn't have a good start. He was late for practice, so Peter Collins, who was driving a Ferrari, gave the Cooper a workout for him. When he did get in the car, it was soon obvious to the cultured crowd that he was somehow out of place. The glamorous and historic buildings flanking tight tarmac streets were light years from the Parramatta Speedway, but Brabham gave the people in them a show that they would not forget in a hurry, taking wide lines on the breathtaking hairpins, sliding the rear of the car around at every opportunity. It was stirring, and ultimately costly. Brabham crashed. He salvaged the engine and John Cooper struck a deal with rival owner Rob Walker to take over Les Leston's Cooper. They dropped Brabham's engine into that car and he qualified 15th.

He had not run out of luck yet. On lap 4, three of the best — Collins, Moss and Hawthorn — were caught up in a confusing collision; their races were over. Fangio, who was among them at the time, somehow squirmed through. So did Tony Brooks. In all the confusion, Brabham, for the first time that weekend, stayed out of trouble. He moved up to 3rd.

It wasn't until the closing laps that luck finally turned against him. The fuel pump failed. With the crowd urging on its new favourite, Jack Brabham pushed his car across the line, salvaging 6th place. It wasn't his first grand prix, but it was seen as a historic debut for the man and the car he had almost single-handedly developed. Fangio won from Brooks. It was already an exciting championship. Brabham had just made it even better.

That year, Brabham would not regain the high ground he seized at Monaco, but his first factory-backed season of Formula 1 gave him a wealth of educational experiences and the final, non-championship round in Casablanca was one of them. Fangio, who had beaten Moss for the world title, was leading the race. Brabham had been running his Formula 2 car for Cooper's customer team, Rob Walker Racing, and was forced out with the usual gearbox trouble. He pulled into the pits and the crew took it behind the garages, which technically meant that the car was ruled out and could not resume racing. That's when John Cooper had an idea. 'He came up,' says Brabham, 'and suggested we fix the car and get back in the race, because there had been so many cars dropping out that we might get a result. They worked really hard, changed the gearbox, and I got back in and drove onto the track.

'After a few laps, the Chief Steward sent a message to the team to bring me in or I would be black-flagged. Rob Walker went down to talk to him, and every time I was due to come round, Rob would distract him so he couldn't black-flag me. The steward soon caught on to this, lost his head, saw a car coming round the corner and rushed out, waving the black flag like mad. Trouble was, the car he black-flagged was Fangio's! Now poor old Fangio had spun early in the race and got a push, so he thought that was why he was black-flagged, and he came in. His team went mad at him and sent him out again.

'Fangio was a great bloke. The biggest snag for him was that he couldn't speak English.'

Brabham demonstrated in the 1958 New Zealand Grand Prix at Ardmore that even as he ascended the ladder he could still make time for others in need. Twenty-year-old Bruce McLaren had bought his first serious race car from Brabham, a 1500cc Cooper Climax, and competed successfully throughout 1957. Brabham recognised McLaren's potential and urged Cooper to give him a full-time drive in his first European season. 'New Zealand had a Driver to Europe scheme and Bruce won that, but it only gave him an air fare. When you get there you've got to get in somewhere to drive. I helped him because his family was fantastic to me when I raced in New Zealand. I stayed with them. His mother was like a second mother to me and I used his father's workshop.'

Brabham had bulked up his own Cooper Climax with a 2.2 litre engine. He was joined by team-mate Roy Salvadori and 28-year-old Stuart Lewis-Evans, both driving Alta-powered Connaughts supplied by young British entrepreneur Bernie Ecclestone, who was trying his hand at team ownership. Ecclestone was a go-getter from Ipswich in Suffolk who had made his money in spare parts, motorcycle sales, car auctions, finance and property. He also managed Lewis-Evans. Brabham had no idea that Ecclestone was destined to be the most powerful man in Formula 1 history. 'To me, he was just a used-car dealer, another enthusiast. I knew Stuart very well, though, because I was racing with him.'

Brabham took pole position and dominated the race. The rear-engined Cooper had performed with great composure this time, unlike on its previous visit. 'It was a big thrill,' Brabham recalls, 'and it was the first time there that I was using a Cooper works car. That was important too.' Bruce McLaren didn't finish the race, but his international career had just begun.

Despite all Brabham's hard work developing the rear-engined Cooper, it was Stirling Moss, driving for Cooper's customer Rob Walker, who gave the manufacturer its first World Championship victory — in round 1, Argentina. It was also the first victory for a rear-engined car since the 1930s. 'It was a bit annoying,' Brabham admits, 'but I made up for it later.'

It would have to be much later — the factory team fought with technical problems throughout the season. Apart from a 4th in Monte Carlo, it was a season littered with problems, and with some shattering visions for Jack Brabham. The crowd at Reims for the French Grand Prix was disturbed by the death of one-time championship leader Luigi Musso. Young Brabham was right behind Musso, who was bearing down on leader Mike Hawthorn early in the race, approaching the Muizon corner at full throttle, approximately 250 kilometres per hour, before he lost it. 'I just saw this huge cloud of dust, as he went off,' Brabham recalls. The car slid across the track, hit a ditch, and flipped over and over before coming to rest. Musso had been flung clear, but was fatally injured.

In the German Grand Prix at the Nurburgring on 4 August, the glorious era of British driving domination was dealt a shocking blow by the death of Peter Collins, whose Ferrari veered into a trackside ditch at Pflanzgarten, flipped, and flung him into a tree. He died from severe head injuries. The mounting death toll had called the morality of motor racing into question yet again. 'That one really upset me,' says Brabham, 'because I was very close to him. Peter was one of the few people who gave me a lot of help when I first went over there. He used to give me a lot of advice. The other key person was Ron Flockhart. He was very generous too.'

At the Ain Diab circuit near Casablanca, Morocco's championship debut was ruined when Stuart Lewis-Evans's Vanwall broke down on lap 42. Lewis-Evans steered his crippled car off the circuit, but oil had been spraying from the broken engine, and it caught fire. In moments, he was also engulfed in flames, leaping out of the car. Jack Brabham once again saw the entire awful episode. 'He went running down the road, a human torch, with people chasing him. There were flames everywhere. People were trying to save him but he kept running away from them.' Marshals did catch him and stifle the fire, but not before Lewis-Evans had been horribly burned. Officials chartered a jet to fly him back to Britain; he died 6 days later in the specialist burns unit at East Grinstead.

Mike Hawthorn retired at 29, apparently satisfied with a close championship win over Stirling Moss. Within 3 months he too was dead, crashing his Jaguar while racing Rob Walker's Mercedes on the Guildford bypass in England. 'That was really unfortunate,' Brabham recalls, 'because Mike lived near where two roads used to join in a Y-shape and it was just coincidence that Rob and he should have come together from two sides at the same time. When they saw each other, they decided to have a race. It was raining. Mike lost it, spun off and hit a tree right on the driver's side door. It hit his head. If one of them hadn't turned up at that junction at that second, it wouldn't have happened.'

Roy Salvadori ended the season 5th in the championship, on 15 points. He wanted to move on to a new Aston Martin team and take Brabham with him. Brabham once again refused, and stayed with Cooper. It wasn't just about loyalty; the team was starting to weld into a powerful force. Brabham was proving to the world that a driver was capable of setting up his car and performing on the track in the same weekend — and he had been preparing Salvadori's car as well. He was driving a lot of cars at a lot of meetings. 'It wasn't unusual to drive Formula 1, Formula 2, sports cars and saloon cars in the same year. Sometimes it was all four in the one weekend. You'd be jumping out of one car and into the next.'

Lex Davison won the 1958 Australian Grand Prix at Mt Panorama, following another heartbreaking mechanical failure for Stan Jones with only 4 laps to go. Jones was beginning to think he would never win the race he held so dear. Both drivers would fade into the background again in New Zealand, as Brabham and Moss staged one of the great grands prix down under.

Moss was back in a Rob Walker-prepared 2015cc Cooper Climax. Brabham brought with him a new team-mate: Bruce McLaren. He had persuaded Cooper to use McLaren in place of the defecting Roy Salvadori. McLaren had shown form, almost beating Brabham for the 1958 European Formula 2 championship. Ron Flockhart was also there in a BRM, along with the Maseratis of Frenchman Harry Schell, Swede Joakim (Jo) Bonnier and American Carroll Shelby.

Five thousand fans turned up for practice, in defiance of warnings from race organisers. Moss was a second faster than Brabham in the early practice laps, but more significantly, he sent the timekeepers into convulsions by wiping 5 seconds from the lap record, held by Ross Jensen. Those who saw him were in awe at his car control. Moss was driving at the peak of his powers and proved it in his heat — until the final lap, when he slowed considerably, then stopped. His rear transmission was broken. With all the verve of a consummate showman, he leapt from the car, white overalls gleaming in the New Zealand sun, threw his helmet back into the seat and waved confidently to the crowd with one gloved hand as he pushed his stricken car with the other for approximately 400 metres to the finish line. He was struggling for traction in his slip-on dress shoes, and rivals flashed past, one by one. It meant that he would qualify last, but it never seemed to faze him. 'Starting from the back wasn't so bad, because passing all the slow cars made you look good. The reason I waved to the crowd? Well I must say, I learnt very early on in my career that if you wave at people, even if they aren't waving at you, they'll start waving back and so on. The next year, the promoter will say, "Well he's a popular guy, we'll have him back," and you might get another hundred quid start money! It's showbiz.'

There was another problem facing the Moss team. They needed to replace the car's offside half-shaft and there were no spares available. Jack Brabham had one and there was no hesitation. 'Yes, that was motor racing in those days. Win the race if you could, but if someone needed help, give it to them. We were good mates,' Brabham recalls. It was a mutual respect that grew not just from observation and friendship, but partnership. Moss and Brabham had had the chance to team up for Aston Martin at the 1958 Le Mans 24 hour race, where they stopped after 3½ hours with a broken conrod, but it was one of very few occasions in their careers where they were on the same side. Theirs was a friendship that grew almost entirely out of pure sporting rivalry.

'I'll never forget that gesture in New Zealand,' says Stirling Moss. 'Jack coming up to me and offering me the drive-shaft from his spare car, knowing that I was very likely to beat him. That's the sort of guy that he was, but then, that's what it was about in those days. Competing, but helping each other out as much as we could.'

A crowd of 80,000 — a record at the time — for any sporting event in New Zealand watched Moss become the first driver to win their grand prix twice. He did it with top speeds of up to 250 kilometres an hour and an average speed nearly 5 kilometres an hour faster than Brabham's in his win the year before. 'He came up and thanked me and all the rest of it,' Brabham recalls, 'and I can tell you ... we've been teasing one another about that race ever since.'

Bruce McLaren finished 3rd, which was a good springboard for his coming European season.

The Australian Grand Prix in 1959 swung back to March and across Bass Strait to Longford, Tasmania. Stan Jones, having dragged his ageing Maserati

250F into battle once more, looked at the cute little kid who had been tagging him since the 1952 grand prix and realised that he wasn't such a little kid any more. His son Alan was 12, and still he had not seen his dad lift that trophy. Stan had endured as race after race collapsed underneath him, as if a black hole appeared whenever the end was in sight. He had even sat grimacing in the heat at Caversham, the wreath sitting on his tired shoulders, only to see it taken off and thrown onto his mate Lex Davison after a countback.

The Longford roads were fast. The local fans were fanatical. They worked hard to win the right to stage the event. They deserved a contest and they got one. Jones outmanoeuvred Len Lukey's Cooper, with 6 laps remaining, to finally break through. A monkey was seen rising from his broad frame to sail into the heavens, never to return.

Jack Brabham was one of many who were very happy to learn of Jones's victory. 'Stan was one of the top drivers of his time, probably the best ... a bit of a larrikin. He liked the odd beer occasionally; he was not someone I could really get close to, because of that. But he was very down to earth. In those days, you just did it for fun. It was Stan, Tony, Lex Davison, all very experienced. It was good to drive with them. The thing that made a driver in those days was what car they had. How they went depended on what they turned up in and the rivalry wasn't so much about how well they drove but who could afford to buy the best car. Like Lex, Stan was the playboy driver, turning up with the best car in the best outfit and that sort of thing because he could afford to do it.'

A photograph taken later that day shows Stan sitting oily-faced and exhausted in his cockpit, posing grim-faced with the pit crew surrounding him, and a beaming Alan Jones, dressed in striped shirt and shorts, sitting on the right rear tyre of the Maserati. Alan's right arm is resting on his knee and his left arm is on his dad's shoulders, gently touching the laurel wreath, as if to make sure that this time it wasn't going anywhere.

One of the reasons for Jack Brabham's absence from his home grand prix was the accelerating development of his Cooper Formula 1 car. He had become almost obsessive about preparing a car that could win the World Championship. 'We had a lot of trouble, like we did in New Zealand in 1956, with finding a gearbox that was suitable for the rear-engined car. You couldn't find one that could take the horsepower.'

Brabham had ventured to Paris late in 1958 to explore the modification of a Citroen gearbox that would do the job, and with the enthusiastic assistance of the factory foreman, he modified their castings. It was a classic case of Brabham creativity, with a mix of Harry Firth-style ingenuity. 'They machined 20 gearboxes, which were ready within 2 weeks. They would last for three seasons of racing. If it hadn't been for that, and a new 2.5 litre engine which Coventry Climax had built for the season, we would never have won the World Championship.'

The 1959 season began under the cloud of depression cast by the previous year's catastrophes. The Vanwall team had withdrawn from the championship following Stuart Lewis-Evans's death. So had Bernie Ecclestone, but he was destined to return, first as manager of another promising driver and ultimately as much, much more.

The growing death toll was also raising concerns about the safety of drivers, marshals and spectators. 'Everybody talked about it,' recalls Brabham, 'but nobody did anything about it. The first person who would do something was Jackie Stewart, and that was a few years away yet. Anyway, it was nice to be a survivor.'

Safety might have been in the back of their minds on the track, but putting race drivers in new cars was always a recipe for trouble, as Brabham discovered before the season began. He had been lent a prototype Mini with a 1000cc engine, which he spent the weekend thrashing as he attended a British Racing Drivers Club (BRDC) meeting in London. On one particularly fast street, Brabham noticed (in his mirrors) a police motorcycle in vigorous pursuit. 'There were sparks coming off his footrests as he went around the corners. So I pulled over. He came up alongside, looked in the window and said, "Who the hell do you think you are? Stirling Moss?" I said, "No. But I really enjoy beating him."' When the identity problem had been sorted, Brabham enjoyed an escort to the circuit from a new fan.

Every driver wants to win at Monte Carlo. Few can boast that they took their first championship race win there. In the 1959 grand prix, Stirling Moss took the lead on lap 22 of the scheduled 100 and Brabham followed him, but it looked as if he would be chasing the devastating Englishman to the finish one more time. It took until lap 81 for a chink to appear in the great man's armour. He made a pit stop to check out a transmission problem and returned only briefly before giving up the race. It was Jack Brabham's turn to be left alone in front there, his maturity emerged. This was not the carefree sidewinder that Tony Gaze cautioned in the 1954 New Zealand Grand Prix. This driver was welded to his car as strongly as any other component he had built in his workshop. Brabham had learnt to hone his skills to a fine point: the meeting place of speed, care and caution. It was also a triumph for Brabham the engineer, because the rear-engined car was still unique to Cooper.

'The engine proved itself, the car proved itself and I proved myself,' Brabham recalls. 'The rear engine had been looked upon for a long time as a gimmick. People like Denis Jenkinson, the journalist who co-drove with Stirling to win the Mille Miglia, was a real nut on Ferraris and Maseratis. It was more than he could take when the Coopers were beating them.'

Round 2, the Indianapolis 500, was considered to be a useless component of the 9-round championship. Due to the different specification required for cars to run on the banked oval circuit, European teams had largely ignored the event since 1950. Round 3 was at Zandvoort, Holland, on 31 May. At this circuit, which had been carved out of sand dunes by the Dutch while they were under the rule of Nazis during the war, Brabham could not match Jo Bonnier's pace in an upgraded BRM, and finished 2nd by 15 seconds.

Tony Gaze visited Le Mans in 1959 on one of many journeys back to the circuit as a spectator. Less than a year earlier he had heard the numbing news that his old mate Peter Whitehead had been killed in the Tour De France rally. Whitehead had been navigating for his brother Graham when their Jaguar ran off a bridge and over a cliff. On the suggestion of his old friend, Prince Bira, Gaze had turned his attention to competitive gliding, a perfect marriage of his talents. He would go on to represent Australia in the World Championships in 1960 and set all kinds of records in another 8 years of top-level competition.

But there was nostalgia and a sense of history on his mind as he watched the Le Mans' pit lane in 1959. 'I remember seeing Jack Brabham at Le Mans, when we knew that he was ready for the World Championship. I said to him, "It looks like you're going to win" and he replied, "Wouldn't that be something?"' The laconic Brabham, barely smiling, had changed so much since Gaze first equipped him in Europe, but his reluctance to say too much was still painfully apparent.

'I didn't have much to say because I used to focus on driving the car and preparing it as well,' says Brabham. 'My job was to get that car in shape to win races and it was really a full-time job. That was all I concentrated on. The driving was pleasure. The rest of it was all work.' It would be hard work at the next round.

To the surprise of many, Jack Brabham was leading the championship when the circus arrived at Reims for the French Grand Prix. It was one of the hottest grand prix days on record. 'It was so hot that the tarmac melted,' Brabham recalls. 'Drivers were pulling into the pits and just passing out, unable to go further. I remember having blisters on my feet for weeks after, just from working the pedals. Trying to stop at the end of the straight was absolute agony.'

This was a race with the unenviable reputation for debris damage. Several drivers complained of being hit by rocks flung from the cars in front of them as the track surface crumbled. Cooper's 3rd factory driver, Masten Gregory, was hit in the face. Others suffered mechanical problems from the stones lodging in their engines or chassis. Tony Brooks in a Ferrari, stayed in front all the way, chased by various drivers. Only Phil Hill, in the other Ferrari, could get near him. Brabham's 3rd kept him in the championship lead by 5 points from Brooks, with Hill next on 9 points.

The British Grand Prix at Aintree on 18 July would prove decisive. Tony Brooks's championship threat was diminished when news came through that Ferrari would not be bringing their team to Britain because of strikes back in Italy. Brooks picked up a drive in a Vanwall to keep his hopes alive. The grid was all British machinery. Brabham started from pole and it was his race all the way. 'Well, that was really a fantastic win for me. Stirling Moss, everybody was there. It was Coopers' home grand prix and it was a race of tactics as well, because tyre wear was horrific. Dunlop didn't have the best tyre by any means and it was a battle against the tyres over that distance. I could see my front tyres wearing out very quickly, so I changed my driving style a bit and managed to get to the end without changing those tyres.'

Jack Brabham held a 13 point championship lead after 5 of the 9 rounds.

The next round was in Germany, but not at the Nurburgring. It had been moved to one of Tony Gaze's old stomping grounds: Avus. By then, it didn't seem to matter if they ran the event at the local greyhound track, Gaze's Le Mans prediction was looking better by the minute. However, no one could have predicted the disaster that would precede the Formula 1 event. Jean Behra, who had left Ferrari after a dispute with the team, was killed driving a Porsche in the sports car race supporting the main event. 'Avus was as slippery as buggery round the banking when it rained,' Brabham recalls. 'Just like a skating rink. I was following Behra when his car just went up the wall and over the top. Unfortunately, his car hit a post at the top and that's what killed him. Later on, another driver, De Beaufort, also went over the top in a Porsche, but he missed the post, went down the bank on the other side and landed in the pits. He went through the pits and tried to drive back out on the track. They wouldn't let him.'

Tony Brooks obviously did not agree with those who thought Brabham had the title covered: he won the German Grand Prix. Brabham was into the pits for good on lap 15. With 3 rounds remaining, including a new event, the United States Grand Prix at Sebring, the rear-engine phenomenon and its Australian jockey were not the red-hot favourites anymore.

As if there had not been enough excitement in Brabham's life, 1959 was also the year in which he acquired his pilot's licence. 'Ron Flockhart introduced me to flying. He had a little Auster and we went to a few meetings in that plane. He got me interested in flying. It wasn't long before I started flying myself. I bought a Cessna 180. You had to fly for 40 hours to get your licence. I'd done 30 hours ... and did the last 10 in my own plane. I got my licence and flew to Portugal for a race meeting the next day.'

The next race in the series, the Portuguese Grand Prix was held on 23 August, and Stirling Moss was poised for a long-awaited strike. He was not using the more reliable gearboxes that Brabham had developed, but after a troubled season, he romped away with the race, while Brabham, the only driver who looked capable of catching him, was out on lap 23, less than half the distance. He was caught up in every driver's nightmare: an unnecessary crash that could easily have killed him. 'It was probably the biggest one I did have in my whole career. I was very lucky,' he says.

The organisers of the grand prix had wanted a local driver in the race. Mario Araujo de Cabral, driving a Cooper Maserati T51, qualified 14th of the 16 cars, and his race pace was even less impressive. 'He was driving around getting in everybody's way,' explains Brabham. 'Stirling Moss and I were having a great old dice and we came across Cabral for about the third time. I was right up Stirling's exhaust pipe, ready to out-brake him into the hairpin, where I'd got him once before. Cabral must have looked in his mirrors and thought it was only Stirling behind him, because I was that close to the back of Stirling. So as soon as Stirling went past, Cabral swung back to follow him and didn't see me ... he knocked me straight off the road. I went over the straw bales and headed for a 30 foot [9 metre] drop into some trees. Two things saved me. One, I hit a telegraph post. That stopped the car from going over the edge. I bounced back, upside down, across the track. That was the other thing that saved me. While the car was upside down, I fell out. I had no seatbelt. Then the car hit the track again, still upside down. It made an absolute mess of the car. If I'd had a seatbelt, I wouldn't be talking to you today. The post I hit fell over, bringing wires down onto the track.'

Brabham's team-mate, Masten Gregory, came scorching through at that moment, narrowly missing the scrambling driver. 'When I fell on the track, I sat up, and wondered for a second where I was — I'd been convinced I was heading for those trees in the gully. I suddenly realised I was on the track, looked around, and here's Masten coming at me at about a hundred miles an hour. I rolled out of the way and he went WHOOOSH! I thought he was going to have me.' Brabham walked away with just a few bruises and cuts, but there was worse to come.

'The ride in the ambulance was the most frightening part of all. Bloody sirens screaming all the way, the driver screeching around all the corners. Somehow we made it to the hospital and I only had a bit of skin off so they let me go. I went back to the pits and saw Masten. I said, "Hey! Didn't you see me lying on the track back there? I thought you were going to run over me!" He said, "All I saw was the wires across the track so I took my hands off the wheels, my feet off the pedals and hoped I wouldn't get electrocuted." That was all the apology I got from Masten!'

Tony Brooks failed to capitalise on Brabham's misfortune, finishing 9th, but he was still within 4 points of the championship leader. Stirling Moss's victory over Gregory and Dan Gurney brought him to within 10 points. With two rounds left, it had become a three-way contest. Only a driver's five best results would count towards the title.

Ferrari would traditionally take the fight to their British rivals at their home event, the Italian Grand Prix. They entered five cars to assist Brooks. Moss was becoming the wildest of wild cards in the game. He qualified his by now reliable Cooper on pole. To make it more interesting, Brooks qualified 2nd, ahead of Brabham. It was a mouth-watering front row for the many thousands who jammed themselves into Monza. There were three more Ferraris behind them on row 2, including Phil Hill in one of them. Brabham was ready for the battle. 'To us, it just made the race potentially more satisfying, because we loved beating Ferraris, and there were more Ferraris to beat!'

Just as in Portugal, Brooks would lament a missed opportunity, leaving the race after only 2 laps with engine failure. It was now up to the remaining Ferraris to ensure that Brabham left Monza with as few points as possible.

Moss, Hill, Brabham and Gurney would get the championship points. A technical advantage was what decided it. All the Ferraris pitted for tyres midway through the race, while Moss and Brabham were able to stay out. Moss was in a devastating mood, winning by a margin of 46 seconds from Hill, who made the most of his fresh tyres to overhaul Brabham. Moss needed 7 points more than Brabham in the final race to win the title; Brooks's chances were even slimmer.

Moss applied the pressure by qualifying on pole again at Sebring, for the US Grand Prix. Brabham made sure he would be starting beside his great rival. It was such a regular occurrence that they often joked about it, threatening each other as they sat in their cars, waiting for the race to start. Brooks had to start from row 2, and Ferrari protested, claiming that the driver who qualified ahead of him, Harry Schell, had been granted an incorrect time. Officials threw out the protest.

Brabham did his best to snuff out the Moss menace by jumping him at the start. He couldn't hold him off for long, though, and Moss was soon in familiar territory: clear track and clean air. But 5 laps later, it was over. The unfortunate cause of Moss's failure at the final hurdle was his Cooper's gearbox ... it was the same problem that had hamstrung his early races. A relieved Brabham had to worry only about Brooks, whom he had nicely covered as he circulated in the lead, with Bruce McLaren riding shotgun in his mirrors. As long as he kept a steady pace and stayed in the race, it wouldn't even matter if Brooks passed them all. The excitement escalated when, with just a few hundred metres to go, Brabham ran out of fuel. McLaren seized a rare chance for glory, knowing that Brabham could not lose the title. He whipped his car out from behind Brabham's and made a dive for the finish line, just as Moss's team-mate, Maurice Trintignant, attempted the same manoeuvre from third place. They both speared towards the chequered flag, but McLaren got there first, by 0.6 of a second.

Bruce McLaren was 22 years and 104 days old — the youngest driver to win a Formula 1 Grand Prix. This was a record that would not be broken until the 2003 Hungarian Grand Prix, won by Spain's Fernando Alonso. Troy Ruttman, the winner of the 1952 Indianapolis 500, was 24 days younger than McLaren, but that race, while a round of the championship, was not considered to be a grand prix.

What McLaren and Trintignant had not seen was Jack Brabham's car stopping before the finish line, out of petrol. He was faced with the extraordinary task of pushing his car to a championship win. Brooks could not take enough points to catch him, but Brabham dearly wanted to finish. Step by step, he leaned into his Cooper Climax T51. 'It was a bit of a shock when the car stopped. John Cooper got the number of churns mixed up and there was one less went in my car than went in Bruce's car. I was aware of how close the championship was, but I knew by the time the car had stopped that I only had to finish. I coasted as far as I could, but it was uphill ... enough to make me grunt, I tell you. Everyone was keeping the crowd back in case someone tried to help. If any of them had pushed that car, I'd have been disqualified.'

Brooks flashed past to take 3rd. Brabham, sweating it out behind the Cooper, crossed the line like an exhausted marathon runner in 4th position, a couple of minutes later. He was the new world champion of Formula 1, by just 4 points. 'It was close. I just got over the line, then collapsed. It wasn't easy.

'The next thing that happened was my trip to the caravan that had been set up there for the press. All the motoring writers from London were on the phones. I had to talk to them all. I also had to pass the message to my wife, because she wasn't there. It was chaotic, but it finished up as a big party. Stirling congratulated me, of course, and I felt sorry for him, because really he should have won that championship. Unfortunately, he chose the wrong gearboxes. I went to Citroen and got the right ones, but Stirling persevered with the Calotti box that I used to have. I knew his gears wouldn't last the distance.'

At the start of the new decade, New Zealand was fortunate enough to once again host a world-class field for its non-championship grand prix. Moss, Brabham and McLaren were all welcomed as heroes. There was also another exciting young New Zealander, Dennis Hulme.

In a mirror image of the previous year, Brabham was the tortoise charging from the back of the grid — thanks to an engine fire that ruined his heat — while Moss was the hare. They were together by lap 3, disputing the lead at a reported 200 kilometres per hour. McLaren was right behind them. Dennis Hulme was providing the crowd with a special brand of thrill by starting 5 laps late because his team hadn't finished preparing the car. He cut through the field with such ferocity that if he had started when everyone else did, he would have driven onto the podium.

The duel for the lead intensified, with a mixture of speed, courage and cunning employed by both drivers to contrive a decisive move. It was Brabham who produced it, putting his foot down and driving powerfully out of College Corner to pass Moss for the final time. Moss broke down, and thus, so did his challenge. McLaren caught up to Brabham and the fans were treated to an entertaining, if staged, battle to the finish, due to team orders. The elder team-mate won by 0.6 of a second. Bib Stillwell brought his Cooper in 3rd, ahead of Stan Jones. Denny Hulme finished an astonishing 10th, which did not go unnoticed by the wily Jack Brabham. New Zealand was proving a fertile ground for racing talent.

There is danger on the other side of every uncharted island in the world of Formula 1, as Cooper found out in 1960. Lotus had produced, for the first time, a rear-engined car which was lighter and faster than the Cooper. That was clear after the first round of the season in Argentina, even though Bruce McLaren gave Cooper the win there.

Brabham and John Cooper began their counterattack with a series of sketches they produced on the plane returning from South America. They planned a lower, more streamlined T53. 'When you sit down to redesign a car you have to think about the areas where you need to improve, and the 1959 car wasn't all that good, actually. It used to lift its inside front wheel under throttle in the corners. There were a lot of things wrong with it. We changed the suspension for a start, and went to double wishbones and coil springs all round.'

'By the time we got to London,' Brabham recalls, 'we had it all worked out. Then we proceeded to build it. We finished the car on a Sunday morning, stood back and admired it. It looked fantastic. I couldn't help it. I said, "John, how about I go round the block in it ... see what it's like." I got in it, roared up the Kingston bypass and round the Tolworth roundabout, down to the Hook roundabout. On the way back I passed a police car going the other way. Of course he turned around and chased me. I got back to Coopers, going through all the back streets, and through the front door, where John was waiting. As I drove inside I screamed at him, "Shut the bloody door!" He pulled the door down. We hid the car. The cops pulled up, got out, had a look inside, then just drove off.'

'That's what you call enthusiasm,' Brabham recalls, of a team he was very proud of.

The team was buoyant: not only at the prospect of a car that could beat Lotus, but also at the speed and precision with which they had constructed it. There was sad news, however, before the time the team arrived in Monaco: Harry Schell had been killed in a crash in practice at Silverstone on 13 May. Brabham happened to be practising on the same day. 'What he did was hit the wall, and the car turned over and rolled on him. When I came around the next lap, he was lying on the track, obviously dead. It killed him straight away.'

In Monte Carlo Brabham took the lead after rain fell and stayed there for 6 laps, before spinning off on lap 40. He would be disqualified for receiving assistance to restart. Moss took the win. McLaren was 2nd, retaining his championship lead.

Four drivers, including Roy Salvadori and Masten Gregory, withdrew from the fourth championship round, at Zandvoort (Holland), after qualifying, following an argument over payment of starting money. Moss and Brabham, from the front row, resumed their familiar duel, and on lap 17, the Australian's car appeared to deviate to the fringe of the track, throwing up some debris which gave the chasing Moss a puncture.

'He reminds me of that regularly,' says Brabham with a wry smile. 'You have to remember, there was loose kerbing on the corners. I just clipped it as I went by and a chunk rolled out. Stirling hit it, the tyre went flat and he had to pit. He reckoned I did it on purpose. No way I did that. I really enjoyed racing against Stirling. We had some fantastic dices together.'

According to Moss, Brabham 'was a tough competitor ... I mean he was a good friend of mine, but he wouldn't think twice about pulling across in front of you. If you look at pictures of Jack in the old days, he's sort of looking down at his feet. He's got this sort of crouch, whereas I was very much laid-back. I saw Dr Farina in the late 1940s and I thought his style looked good — leaning back, very nonchalant. I thought that was a good look so I modelled my straight-arm driving position on him. It did make my style and Jack's very different. His style was also much more dirt-track than mine, with understeering, while I was more comfortable with oversteering.'

Moss rejoined the race and chased hard for a point-scoring result, but the horse had bolted. McLaren's failure to finish, due to mechanical problems, left him with only a 3 point lead over Moss in the championship. Brabham moved up to third, another 3 points away. There was one more notable landmark at the

1960 Dutch Grand Prix: the Formula 1 debut of brilliant young Scottish driver Jim Clark. He retired with transmission failure.

Round 5 of the 10 scheduled rounds was the Belgian Grand Prix at Spa, on 19 June. It would become the pivotal motor racing event in 1960 and one of the most infamous of grands prix in a season that would take 'infamy' in motor sport to catastrophic lows. As early as Friday, the smell of blood pervaded the circuit. The axle on Moss's fragile Lotus broke and sent the car rocketing off the circuit. He was thrown clear, but broke both legs on impact. Brabham was one of the first cars on the scene. 'We tried to help him. It was a typical Lotus problem. They used to break fairly regularly. The car rolled a few times and he was lucky to get away with it, really.' Another Lotus failure, this time in the steering, seriously injured Mike Taylor in his Formula 1 debut. He crashed into trees, and would never race again.

It may have been the absence of Moss, or the disturbing crashes. Something drained adrenaline from Brabham's rivals — he finished qualifying a demoralising 2.5 seconds faster than Brooks's BRP Cooper, setting the pattern for a processional race. After 17 laps, Brooks's team-mate, Chris Bristow, was dicing with Ferrari driver Willy Mairesse at the Malmedy corner when he lost control. Like Moss, Bristow was thrown from the car. Unlike Moss, he didn't survive. Five laps later, Lotus driver Alan Stacey suffered the same incredible misfortune that had hampered Tony Gaze at this circuit 8 years earlier: he was struck in the face by a bird. He crashed, was thrown out, and died. 'Where he went off,' says Brabham, 'was a fast part of the circuit, about 160 miles an hour [250 km/h]. Birds were always a problem there. It must have either knocked him out or stunned him, because he just speared off. Horrific accident. Bristow's crash was awful too. He was an up and coming driver, looked like he was going places.'

The clearing of wreckage and removal of bodies made a sobering spectacle, and even though the developmental and indifferent 1950s were over, it was a reminder that world motor sport had not learnt anything from the carnage of that decade. With Schell's death back in May, this round brought the Formula 1 toll to three dead in 5 weeks. There was more to come.

The only good news was for the Cooper crew. Brabham's win (by more than a minute) from Bruce McLaren brought him to within 4 points of his team-mate in the championship. 'The Cooper really shone on fast circuits, and was more aerodynamic than the Lotus, which was nowhere near the size. We could outpace the Lotus without any trouble.'

Reims was the venue for the French Grand Prix, just 3 weeks after the tragedy of Belgium, and this time it was Phil Hill, in a Ferrari, who took the fight to Brabham. Brabham had once again qualified well clear of the field, and won by nearly a minute. 'Reims that year was one of the more satisfying wins of my career,' Brabham recalls, 'because all the publicity had been about Ferrari. It was a Ferrari circuit. They said that I might beat Ferrari elsewhere, but not at Reims. It was absolutely fantastic. We had a wonderful dice and beat them. During the race, I managed to get a break on the Ferraris, a couple of lengths in front. Eventually, Phil Hill caught me up and we were going down to the end of the straight into a right-hander to the pit straight. Luckily, I glanced in the rear vision mirror. There was this cloud of smoke behind me, so instead of turning into the corner I just straightened up a little bit, and Hill went past me with all four wheels locked. He kept going in the direction of Reims. If I had turned in, he would have gone straight over the top of me. It was unbelievably satisfying.'

After Reims, Brabham and McLaren were tied for the championship lead on 24 points, 13 ahead of the injured Moss.

It wasn't just the carnage, the deaths, or the dominance of Brabham's factory team that gave the 1960 season a surreal sense of destructive inevitability — the Cooper team was like an out-of-control locomotive gathering pace on a dead-end line — it was also the tight spacing of events. 'What made it easier, though,' says Brabham, 'was having the right car. The 1960 model was a good car straight out of the box, at every round, whereas the previous year's car was harder to get right.'

Two weeks after France, it was Brabham again at Silverstone for the British Grand Prix. In the following month he rode a wave of victories, including the Silver City Trophy at Brands Hatch on 1 August. In the Portuguese Grand Prix, Brabham's fifth consecutive win made him world champion for the second consecutive year — he had amassed enough points with 2 rounds and 3 months still remaining. 'It was not only a fantastic feeling, but more satisfying than the first one. We really felt that we'd done a job with the car. We were on a roll. We also had the time to plan an even bigger party than the first one. We had Tony Gaze, Lex Davison and Bib Stillwell over from Australia just for the celebrations. It was a truly Australian victory.'

CHAPTER FIVE

The Mountain

Harry Firth had been fishing for business. He had outgrown his space at the Marne Garage in Melbourne, then moved to his own premises in Auburn, Victoria. He had also outgrown his reputation for carving dirt on the rally trails and hill climbs the way a world-class skier carves lines in virgin snow. He broke all kinds of records in all kinds of cars in all kinds of events. Among his favourites was a TR2 special which he flipped with spectacular success after clipping some straw bales at Fishermens Bend. He was thrown out of the car, dazed, grazed and sickened. The car landed upside down. There would be other races, other cars, other challenges. In 1956 the great Maserati driver Jean Behra and test driver Guerino Bertocchi approached Firth at Albert Park during the famous Australian Grand Prix meeting, enquiring about the TR2.

'They offered me a job,' he claims, 'after they'd seen what I did with it. I refused, of course. I found it very amusing that years later, Ferrari was using similar innovations to those that I used on the Triumph back in 1956. Just little things. Must have been a coincidence.'

It was during support races at the big open-wheel events that other greats: Brabham, Salvadori and Gurney, had run a respectful eye over Firth's innovations and adaptations of current model cars. Gurney, in particular, had been curious as to how Firth had overcome the Porsche's inherent understeer, enabling the car to slide around corners. Firth's on-track success with the Porsche won factory recognition in the form of a plaque, sent from Germany.

Ford, however, was Firth's most curious and willing customer. The relationship began with the development, racing and rallying of the Anglia. The contract gave Firth free rein to do his best with whatever the factory wanted to improve, including their new Falcon introduced in 1960 but those results would not, at first, be impressive.

The post-war era in Australia was nurturing a new breed of motor racing hero. These were not men of royalty whose finesse guided grand cars on the world stage. They did not race on tracks that stirred imagination and awe. These were down-to-earth blokes with a means and a yen for racing, men of courage and action whose passion for the raw excitement of their sport might have been confused with oafishness, except that most of them went on to become highly successful businessmen.

Norm Beechey was one of these men. He was also, unwittingly, one of the role models for half a century's worth of iconic Australian characters who would inspire the worship of millions.

'Stormin'' Norm was a used-car dealer who loved to race. He was a big man with a cherubic face and the imposing presence of a front row forward. He had the kind of blustery enthusiasm that overwhelms you ... in a nice way. His love of racing started when he was a kid growing up in Brunswick, Melbourne. Norm met another reckless character, Bob Jane. 'Any motor car we got, we were always trying them out with a zoom off at the traffic lights. So it was only natural that we went on from there.' Beechey has been reluctant to give away details of those 'tests', but when you suggest that he might have driven at 100 kilometres per hour, his reply is: 'It was 100 MILES per hour in those days.'

Beechey started buying and selling cars at the age of 13. He used to drive to Brunswick Technical School via the back streets, sometimes passing the teachers peddling to school on their bikes. Later on he would buy cars in country areas, bring them back to Melbourne, tidy them up and sell them. 'So I had plenty of high speed practice on dirt roads to learn how to drive quickly. By then I was 17 or 18.'

Jane also remembers the street racing very well. 'Norm and I were the same age. His father Dick was a car dealer. He would drive something different every night, something from the car yard. I had whatever I had ... might be an Oldsmobile. Norm used to drive to Collins Street, where *The Age* newspaper was based, to put his ads in the paper. You couldn't do it any other way in those days, so we would race our cars all the way to Collins Street and back again. We would race anything, anywhere. We raced to parties across town. We took some nurses from Melbourne hospital with us once, and it wasn't long before they were screaming at the top of their voices that we were lunatics and demanding to be let out of the cars.'

It was on a bicycle that Bob Jane made his first racing prize-money. He started as a track cyclist, competing at first as an amateur, taking on and beating greats like Russel Mockridge, who went on to win gold for Australia at the 1952 Olympic Games. 'I made a lot of good friends there. I still have friends from those days.' Jane became more and more famous, and at one stage he won seven consecutive events from increasingly larger handicaps. 'I was so good at winning that I took all the bookmakers' money. They got so angry with me that when I was racing they wouldn't show up. I was pretty much forced to quit. Besides, by that stage bike riding was starting to take up a lot of my time, more time than I could afford. I used to train every night from 5 pm to 7 pm to get miles in the legs, and all day Sunday. I had just enough money by then to go motor racing, which had really taken my interest.

'You wouldn't call it racing in those days but we'd go to Calder or somewhere like that and just drive ... it was club racing.'

Beechey started on the track when he was 22, in a new Ford Customline which he drove to the few events that were available for sedan cars in the 1950s. His first major meeting was a strange one for a race driver: the 1956 Olympic Games in Melbourne. Baron de Coubertin did not have Australian touring cars in mind when he established the modern games before the turn of the 20th century, but a special meeting was staged to coincide with those Games and Norm made a special contribution, throwing his Ford around Albert Park ahead of the best touring car drivers of the day. At the same meeting, which was one of the biggest-ever staged in Australia, Stirling Moss won the main event in a Maserati. 'I was lucky to get the drive,' Beechey says. 'Entries had closed but I noticed that Basil Rice had entered a twin-spinner side-valve Ford and I arranged to meet him. He showed me his car. Then I took him for a fast ride in my new OHV Ford. He quickly realised that he would have run very poorly so he kindly offered me his entry.'

There were three distinct stripes down the rear of the car; this meant the car had a driver with a provisional racing licence. 'My technique wasn't very good in those days. I hardly even knew what a braking marker was ... 400, 300 ... I didn't take any notice. I'd just look and say, "Well I'll have to slow it down shortly", and I would start braking well past where you were supposed to brake, so there'd be this big slide, but I'd get around okay. I had little experience. I was in front early but my gearbox jammed in second. I dropped back, and for a lap and a half was trailing Len Lukey's Customline in second position, trying to get the gears to work again. Finally I got it into top gear — it was working, but with no synchromesh — and I chased him until the last corner, where I passed him. I was nearly black-flagged in that race for hitting the straw bales. One caught underneath the car at the first corner and I was going down the road at about 130 miles an hour [208 km/h] with all the straw flying out the back. It looked like a barnyard scene. Fortunately, one of the two officials there was our local spare parts dealer, and he stopped the other one from black-flagging me. He said, "These blokes can really drive. Give 'em a bit of a go!"'

Like most racers, Beechey found money a tougher obstacle than straw bales. 'I was in no financial position to go racing full-time in anything but the car I was driving. I did a few hill climbs and things like that.' He ran the Customline for a few more years until it simply became too expensive to maintain. That's when he ran into the love of his early life. It was a black Holden FX which carried the number plate that was to be its eternal name: PK. Its first race was its first win: the Victorian Touring Car Championship. Harry Firth finished 2nd and John Raeburn 3rd. The crowds were relishing these gladiatorial contests, which seemed to be far more in tune with suburban garages than the more sophisticated open-wheel events of the day. They could not spark the same parochial fires that this domestic disturbance aroused. Touring car racing had arrived.

The trademark for Beechey was his so-called 'out of control' style, which in fact was not out of control at all once he learnt the lessons of that first Albert Park excursion. 'It was the style of car in particular. It had drum brakes, which were very inefficient because it weighed nearly 2 tons. It was a learnt technique to drive a car like that. Part of the technique was to arrive at a corner a bit too fast, turn it in a bit too deep, and get it sliding sideways to grind some of the speed off it; otherwise you wouldn't get round.'

Bob Jane's early forays in motor sport were adventurous at best, impetuous at worst. Like Beechey, his dealership aided car supply. Their yards were about 300 metres apart. Like Beechey, he drove in the 1956 grand prix meeting in a Ford Customline. Unlike Beechey, it clearly didn't inspire him because he took a break from serious competition for a couple of years. He returned in a Maserati 300S — which, according to everyone who saw him, was a little beyond his capability. He slid and spun around the circuit until it crashed. 'It scared the shit out of me,' he recalls.

Later that year he bought a hot Holden from Harry Firth — again, to match his great mate Norm. He crashed that too. 'It was at Phillip Island, middle of 1959. It was monumental. I completely lost control in this race. The car went end over end. I was thrown out, broke both arms, a leg, a wrist, an elbow ... had four skull fractures. It took me 6 months to rebuild myself and the car.' In that time, Jane sought the advice of a mentor, someone who would steer him away from oblivion and into the record books.

Jane and Beechey were protégés of Harry Firth. 'Harry had a workshop in Camberwell,' Jane recalls, 'which coincidentally in later years became the CAMS head office, which is pretty funny really! My brother went there one day, got talking to Harry and on other occasions I'd go with him. We'd talk about cars, you know. The relationship just sort of drifted together. Harry fixed up my driving. I was a lunatic ... drove too fast, tried too hard. When I spun, I'd think, "Shit. I've got to try harder." Harry tempered me, told me to calm down, try different things.'

Beechey believes Firth was one of the biggest influences on his early driving days as well. 'He tutored me. He did a lot of work to improve my driving approach. I took him for a drive around Phillip Island one time and frightened the life out of him with my rough technique. I was most fortunate to have Harry Firth as a tutor.'

While Beechey and Jane were terrifying Firth and lighting up the Victorian circuits, a new concept was born at Phillip Island in 1960: the Armstrong 500 (as in 500 miles [800 km]), named after its first sponsor, and conceived as a race for production cars only, with no modification allowed. This was a race that had Harry Firth written all over it. The tougher the rules, the more fun Firth would have bending them. The island circuit had been coated in bitumen since it hosted the 1928 Australian Grand Prix, but that had only enhanced its reputation as a mixture of high-speed straights and variable-speed corners and undulations. There was also its exposure to the elements. Harsh weather patterns would attack like barbarians from the vast expanses of Bass Strait.

The paring of motor sport back to this production car level produced a grand variety of approaches. For many, the Armstrong 500 was little more than a paddock bash, despite the many billboards of oil companies which saw a great marketing opportunity. Then there were the professional drivers, who saw it as just another paid drive. None of those motives collided with the overall belief that this was a special contest which generated exceptional camaraderie among the competitors. It seemed everyone was there in 1960: Lex Davison and Doug Whiteford, winners of six Australian grands prix between them, teamed up to drive an NSU Prinz in Class A.

Leo and Ian Geoghegan were driving Renault Dauphines. The Geoghegans were from New South Wales, and were recognised as one of the biggest crowd-pulling combinations in their state. It wasn't just that they were brothers and managed by their father Tom. It was their endearing personalities and their performance as a pair. While they went on to pursue quite different career paths, they were best known in the early 1960s as a touring car team at these endurance events. Leo was the front man, the spruiker; he was slender in build and clever in phrase. Ian was just as likeable, but in an entirely different way. He was bigger in build and not the polished performer in front of the media or in public, due to a stutter. However, this did not impair his sociable manner or his popularity.

Tom had them driving jeeps in their early teens. He put Leo, who was three years older than Ian, in a Holden and Ian in a Standard Ten for their racing debuts. Leo had started racing at club level in the early 1950s, taking over his father's car. Ian followed shortly after — being the little brother he usually drove the 'hand-me-down' models. Like their Victorian counterparts Beechey and Jane, the Geoghegans initially raced in modified touring cars, although Leo was already starting his love affair with open-wheel racing; this would take him in a different direction.

Tom dressed them in black overalls, driving black cars. The 'team' fielded a variety of models in different classes, from a Jaguar sedan to a Lotus Elite, Lotus 18, Lotus 23, Daimler sports car ... even a Mini Cooper. They would race primarily in their home state, but they also contested events at Lowood and Lakeside in Queensland. This was their first journey to compete in Victoria. 'I remember it well,' says Leo. 'We had the slowest car in the race. There were three, actually. Jim Leighton and Alan Ling drove one. Ian and Des West drove another and I teamed with Bill Pitt. All the manufacturers took it very seriously because of the concept. The old man had done some sort of a deal with Renault.'

There were rally and trial and hill climb and circuit racers. There were factory and dealer teams. Even journalists competed. It was a who's who of motor sport, gathered as if for a party. Firth drove a Singer Gazelle, which he shared with John Raeburn, but he prepared 5 cars for other drivers. Jane teamed with Lou Molina in a Firth-prepared Falcon, one of the first to race in Australia. 'The '60 model Falcon,' Firth recalls, 'was terrible, a complete dog. I knew Bob and Lou were headed for trouble.' Beechey entered class D with John French in a factory sponsored Vanguard also prepared by Firth.

Firth's great advantage was that he could take his cars to the very track on which they were to race and make sure they stood up to the demands of 500 miles [800 km]. 'When the front wheel passes you going down the main straight,' he recalls, with a touch of understatement, 'it's not too good.' Parts broke with spectacular regularity and were quickly taken back to the workshop for 'improvement', but of course it was against the rules to modify them beyond production standard. It wasn't just a matter of tinkering with the mechanics, either. Firth would study the nuances of each car, then relay the character of the vehicle to the driver, explaining where and how to use throttle and brakes around the circuit. One thing that was difficult to correct was the flex in the chassis. There were no roll cages in those days, and such modification would not have been allowed anyway. Vehicle manufacturers were not as safety conscious as they are now, nor were they as familiar with the physics involved in chassis construction. The more rigid the construction, the safer the car was and the more predictable it was in its handling, but in 1960 it was not unusual for a car under stressful cornering to twist so much that its windshield would pop out.

Firth would also train the mechanics. They performed pit stop drills, rehearsing tyre changes and other technical necessities. Beechey recalls the professionalism of the Firth teams. 'They were all beautifully trained and expertly prepared — and not only that, but I got paid to drive the car. Accommodation was paid. I think it was £250 or something. I thought it was enormous.'

Forty-five cars started the first Armstrong 500, sent off in intervals, with class E going first, and class A last. Thirty-five finished the 167 laps, surviving 8½ hours. The race was won outright by John Roxburgh and Frank Coad in a Vauxhall Cresta, although there was no prize for outright victory at that stage.

Leo Geoghegan recalls his experience in the Renault, an experience that cured him of his interest in Phillip Island's unique endurance contest. 'About halfway through, the race turned into a rally. The surface was breaking up badly. It was only cold mix, because they could never get the heavy machinery across the old wooden bridge to use hot mix. Quite frankly, those first few Armstrong 500s buggered Phillip Island as a track.' The Geoghegans would not return until the circuit was resurfaced in the '70s.

Jane's fate in that first race was a typical mixture of the kind of circumstances that would make the endurance test famous. True to Harry Firth's prediction, Molina rolled the Falcon near the end, but luckily it landed on its wheels and he limped back to the pits, where scrutineers allowed him to complete the event. 'Lou Molina was my best friend,' Jane recalls. 'We had homes together at Yarrawonga. Our families did things together. There were no hard feelings or anything … but he cried. He apologised. I said, "Forget it, mate!" We finished the race with no windscreen and the roof all crushed in, but we raced for fun, not sheep stations.'

Leo Geoghegan recalls the Bob Jane style in 1960. 'Bob in those days was pretty hairy. We were surprised that he survived his early motor racing years, but as he went along he got better and better, and he gathered a good group of people around him. He was a bloody good opponent.'

Davison and Whiteford won class A. Beechey and French were 2nd in their class and 7th overall. Beechey admits that in those days he had no idea of what the race would eventually become. 'I had no idea at all. The type of racing that I was involved in, I think, was the most highly respected and interesting racing. My racing was called"'improved production racing", where you could make improvements and modifications. But as the factories came back into it, more so in the late 1960s and early 1970s, it was all about production cars. It's quite interesting that today it's turned around completely again, and the cars they race at Bathurst are just a shell compared with the production models.'

Firth and Raeburn were 7th in their class and 12th outright, after breaking two separate rocker arms and being stuck for 22 minutes while they repaired them.

In 1961 Firth and Jane decided to team up. 'After the first race,' Jane recalls, 'we realised these production cars had significant weaknesses — you had to look at those and work on them if you wanted to win the race. That first year helped Harry and I figure out what was required.'

Jane was 31 years old in 1961, but he was still a relative newcomer. He bought a 3.8 litre Jaguar to contest the regular meetings. He took on a full-time mechanic, John Sawyer, who would stay with him for years. Firth oversaw the preparation. Jane found Bill Pitt, David McKay and Ian Geoghegan too good in his first Australian Touring Car Championship at Lowood, but after that, he would assert himself.

The late-season mission, however, was the Armstrong 500, for which the Jaguar was not eligible. In one of their casual conversations at the Camberwell workshop Jane and Firth agreed that the Mercedes 220SE was the best car for the job, and Jane bought one, for about £2000. This was relatively expensive in those days, though not in motor racing terms. 'It was a low-mileage demo, from a Mercedes dealer,' he recalls. 'It sounds like a big deal — buying just the car you want — but it wasn't, really.'

Neither had a clue that it would be the start of a history-making relationship that would still be celebrated 40 years later. 'We were chalk and cheese, really,' Jane recalls. 'I don't mean that in any derogatory way at all. Harry was, and is, quite eccentric, you know. He was an improviser. He didn't spend money ... didn't have money to spend. I had the ability to get the right car.'

'I had the ideas, but just didn't have the money to implement them,' Firth recalls. 'Bob had a used-car dealership, therefore he could buy the right car and put it on the showroom floor. We could race it on weekends, then he could put it back in the showroom with the slogan, "Only used on weekends, just like brand new". Of course we wouldn't tell them how it was used on weekends.'

Firth asked Olympic for special tyres which were nylon-cased and made in a compound of his choosing. In return, he would conduct all their testing for them. He found some quick-action jacks to speed up wheel changes at pit stops. He also sourced two electric nut runners (impact wrenches). 'I can get these electric guns,' he told Jane in the workshop one day, 'and they'll cost a couple of hundred bucks each, but we will have two of 'em and that's two more than anyone else. That means we can change the wheels in about the same time it takes to refuel: two and a half minutes. Now ... not a word to any bastard, understand?' Jane could only smile when Firth was so fired with enthusiasm. The electric guns would later make headlines as, 'Firth's Secret Wrench'. There were more secrets in the kit bag.

'Olympic had put all their resources into making the best tyre of that era, for that purpose, and they did a very good job. An interesting aspect was that it was the first German car in the world to race without German tyres. Harry also bought a new set of spark plugs from Bosch,' Jane recalls.

They conducted 500 mile tests. 'There would be a spy in the hills, watching us,' Firth recalls, 'so we'd bait him, go slow or something to give him false information, but we'd know exactly what the car could do.'

'One of the things we learnt,' says Firth, 'was that you gained time by taking the Southern Loop full chat.' The Southern Loop is the fast sweeping corner at the lower end of the circuit. After you drive off the start line there is a long run into a right-hand turn, then Southern Loop carries you in a semicircle around to your left. It is not usually a corner you can take without your brain automatically ordering your right foot to press the brake pedal. 'What we realised is that by kicking the car around the corners, bouncing almost sideways, you could get around them in top gear. The experts were changing down ... these were very clever people ... changing down to second gear, and losing 2 seconds in that section alone.'

'The car would be shaking and shuddering,' Jane recalls, 'and we had a couple of mates from Wangaratta, Ron Phillips and Ern Seeliger, who were testing with us one day. They asked us why we were so quick and we said we were going flat around the loop. They said, "You can't do that." I said, "Yes you can." So they asked us to show them. Anyway, Ernie and Ron tried to do it. I think they did it once ... or nearly did it ... but when they got back to the pits, they were physically sick. The car was shaking and lurching so much, they pulled in and vomited.'

Pit straight in 1961 looked like gasoline alley, flanking the smallest field in the event's history. For many, the novelty had already worn off. There was also a crisis in the car industry. Very few dealers or suppliers could afford to race. However, the 26 entries were of high quality and there was still strong commercial support. 'Armstrong Shock Absorbers ... for comfort and safety', said the race sponsor's signs. BP and Shell logos sat on top of poles towering above crowds of pit crews and officials on one side and eager fans on the other. Almost all were, in fact, in extreme danger, leaning over the verge of the road as the cars streaked past. Some of the onlookers stuck their hands nonchalantly in their pockets, others rested the edges of clipboards on their stomachs. Hats, cardigans, jackets and overalls ... it could have been peak hour in any major city, with pedestrians waiting to cross.

The race didn't go well at first for Jane and Firth. Jane took the wheel for the opening stint and was back in the pits within 2 laps to change a flat tyre, but the Mercedes purred along, covering lap after lap at a consistent tyre-saving pace. Firth's new jacks and other time-saving tactics during pit stops were also taking minutes away from their rivals. They overtook the faster Studebakers and the Vauxhall, and won in 8 hours, 31 minutes.

Norm Beechey had been teamed with Bill March in a Renault Gordini; he finished 2nd in class D and 10th overall. In 1962 David Mckay ushered him into the Scuderia Veloce fold for the modified touring car racing season. It was just in time, because his old Holden, 'PK', was finding the going a little tough.

The move to McKay's team allowed some money to flow into the garage, and Beechey set about trying to find a solution to the growing dominance of Jaguars: they were blasting his Holden off the track, and the meanest of them all belonged to Bob Jane. Since the opening round at the new Calder Park circuit in January, Jane had been on top.

Beechey needed something big to counter the Jaguar power, and by July he found it — the Chevrolet Impala. This was a classic 'Yank tank'. It was broad, long, heavy and noisy. Beechey drove it from the left side, which was quite a novelty, though the manner in which he threw the V8-powered muscle car around the circuits made you wonder which side of the car he ended up sitting on. He won the New South Wales and Victorian Touring Car Championships, setting lap records in both. The colourful and increasingly popular combination of Beechey and the Chevy won 70 per cent of their starts in 1962, but at Longford Jane won the big one — the Australian Touring Car Championship — having stretched his 3.8 litre engine to a handy 4.2 litres.

Jane's Jaguar, supplied from Britain, had caught the attention of British promoters and he was invited to compete against the likes of Roy Salvadori, then busy as a semi-works Jaguar sedan driver along with driving Formula 1. The clash took place at Aintree, during the British Grand Prix meeting. Jane had a few problems at first, but stunned the crowd by taking pole position. What happened next, however, was headline-making stuff in Britain. 'I just did what I would normally do back home: took off at the flag and proceeded to weave all over the track so that they couldn't pass me.' The British fans, unused to such barbaric tactics, were horrified. Jane held them off for 5 laps before spinning and losing several positions. Later in the race he overheated — his British mechanics had ignored his instructions during practice on how to solve the problem.

Firth and Jane returned to Phillip Island in 1962 with a Ford Falcon and repeated their victory, using the same careful preparation and time-saving strategies. They would become enduring forces in production car racing. The Phillip Island circuit, however, could endure no more. It had been broken into pieces.

There would be two big changes for the Armstrong 500 in 1963: the release on the Australian market of the first Ford Cortina; and the move of the Armstrong 500 to Bathurst in New South Wales.

Firth had finally mastered the Falcon, following its inauspicious debut in the 1960 race, and taken it to distinguished results in various events, just as he had done with the Anglia. One of those events was the African Safari, in which he ran as high as 7th against world-class rally teams. The Cortina, however, attracted his attention immediately when he first saw it in the factory. Basically, it cornered and stopped like nothing he had ever seen in a touring car. He showed a doubtful Jane just what it could do at a Sandown test and Jane agreed that the Cortina's brakes and handling would be even more potent when the 500 was held at its new venue.

Bob Jane's Mk2 Jaguar was good for 38 straight wins in 1963. Beechey traded his Chevy Impala for a Ford Galaxie, owned by Lukey Mufflers, but it continued to struggle. 'Norm and I had the most amazing … "clashes" they used to call them,' recalls Jane. 'CAMS had three or four inquiries into the conduct of Jane and Beechey … judicial inquiries. We really tried very hard. He'd hit me and I'd hit him back. We'd go through a corner taking each other out and the crowd would go berserk. The *Sun* newspaper would write about Bob Jane and Norm Beechey and my poor mother would say, "Son, this has got to stop. This is terrible." People believed it. I used to say, "Mum, it's all right. Norm and I are good mates." One of Norm's funniest tricks was telling the newspaper, "Bob Jane hit me up the arse, so I'm gonna put a tow bar on my car." The reporters would come running to me and say, "What are you gonna do, Bob?" And I would say, "I'm gonna buy five grilles." I went to the Jaguar dealer and bought five grilles for the front of my car to punch the shit out of his tow bar. And I did. More headlines. The grandstands would be full.'

Jane, however, would not have Beechey to contend with when he turned his attention to the Armstrong 500. Something far more sinister awaited him.

* * *

Mt Panorama on the misty morning of race day ... Australia's drivers came to revere and relish it. There were bigger mountains — taller, wider, more imposing — but they didn't have a 6.2 kilometre circuit coiled menacingly around them. It cut, turned, banked, dipped and flew. It could launch them like a rocket at the most innocent mistake on the pedals, or churn their stomachs like a roller-coaster, daring them to defy logic as they crested the summit, or it could heave them from side to side like a pitcher feeling the weight of the ball before he threw it angrily at his opponent. It could rain, hail, snow and shine within a day.

The circuit was spawned by the Great Depression and completed in 1938, just in time for the Australian Grand Prix won by Peter Whitehead. Weeks later, the road was sealed. However, sealing the Mt Panorama circuit was like clumsily wiping the fingerprints from a murder weapon. You could never hide the truth of this place with a layer of bitumen.

It was at Mt Panorama in 1963 that Harry Firth and Bob Jane cemented their place, and the Ford Cortina's, in the history of Australian motor sport. Firth built a strong campaign. 'We had two cars for the race, a practice one and a spare. We had to drive them from Melbourne to Bathurst, almost the race distance, before we even started. The police chased us for about 80 kilometres. We just kept at the speed limit until they gave up. It was great fun. then we went to Blayney and tested on a road at the same altitude as Bathurst, so we could set the car up right.'

'I'm not kidding,' says Jane, 'but that Cortina of ours had 93 horsepower. The Geoghegans had 92. I remember it well. You're not talking Ferraris here. But we set it up as accurately and scientifically as we possibly could. We did timing tests up the hill. We'd adjust the distributor with each run to tune the engine to its peak. Then there were tappet clearances. We'd adjust those to see which gave us maximum power. I used to say Harry was so secretive about his tappet clearances that he'd file the numbers off his bloody feeler gauges then forget which was which! But you know they were the little things that won.'

'Before we even got to New South Wales,' Jane continues, 'we had conducted extensive rolling resistance tests on hills to get the best tyres. We'd do a few runs with each tyre just to make sure we were accurate. We'd also experiment with the different pressures. Today you'd use a computer, which would tell you in a flash.'

Another stunt that Firth became famous for was the thorough scanning of every available part that could possibly influence the performance of the

Cortina. The rules dictated that the cars could not be modified, but he knew that even standard production parts had variations. Some came off the line better than others. Jane remembers Firth going to the Ford factory on secret visits, doing what he always did best: scrounging. 'He'd go through all the boxes where they kept the various parts,' says Jane, 'to find, for example, the thickest wheel hub casting, because that was a weakness the car had. He'd look for a manifold that was bigger: more air, more gas, more power. The security guards would be told, as Harry drove out with all these parts in the boot, "You didn't see him, and you don't look in his car." That's how we built the Cortina.'

Then there was the strategy of walking the circuit to research the nuances of each corner. 'During practice,' says Firth, 'I told Bob that when he reached the top of the mountain, he should keep going full chat. When he came back he said, "Rubbish! You bastard, you're trying to kill me!" I said, "You're still here, aren't you?" he said "Yeah, but..." I said, "Well go and do it again."' Firth not only had a plan for every corner, but a plan for every possible scenario in the race. He had also conducted the usual time and motion studies for pit stop efficiency.

Interstate rivalry in 1963 was astonishing. Motor sport is thought of in the new millennium as international and national. In the days when distance was still tyrannical, it was state-based and parochial. 'These people thought they were pretty good,' Firth recalls of his NSW counterparts. 'They used to say, "You're on our turf now, we'll fix you Victorians." They didn't think we knew what we were doing. We let them think that.'

'It was quite amazing, when you look back,' recalls Jane. 'Racing really was just starting. Calder Park and Sandown in Melbourne, and Warwick Farm in Sydney, were all built in the early 1960s. There wasn't much movement from state to state. The NSW drivers didn't know what to make of us. I had a couple of guys working for me. One of them was an ex-sailor, one an ex-boxer. They reckoned we had these two guys to crunch people. Quite untrue, actually, but it looked that way. Sam, the boxer, had a big nose, all bent up, like they do. The other guy, Bobby, was big and mean-looking. If anyone touched the cars they used to scare them off, you know. The locals thought we were the Mafia.'

There were 57 cars entered for the first 500 at Mt Panorama, featuring 16 different models across four classes.

Norm Beechey decided not to compete. He had spent the year trying to improve the V8-powered Ford Galaxie enough to top Jane's Jaguar, and he had an aggressive, race-prepared unit straight from the garage of American engineers Holman and Moody. In one memorable fight at Sandown, in the Victorian Touring Car Championship, he smashed the lap record before losing by half a length. The Galaxie was not quite right for the rough and tumble of the Australian scene, but it was typical of Beechey's character that he managed to overcome its inadequacies by adapting his driving style.

The Geoghegans, however, were more than pleased to see the battle joined at a place they knew well. 'My first recollection of the place,' says Leo, 'was when Mum and Dad took me there in 1938 for the Australian Grand Prix. I was just a child and they later told me that my only words were, "More coat", which just about sums up the place, doesn't it? I had been there when it was pelting sleet on Saturday and then girls would be walking around in swimsuits on Sunday.'

'I remember in October 1956, I was racing down Conrod,' he recalls, 'and reached 104 miles an hour [165 km/h]. It was the first time I'd ever been over 100 miles an hour. I didn't know what to expect. I was watching the speedo going up and up and wondering whether I was going to turn blue or green or something. To me it was like breaking the sound barrier ... unknown territory. I broke the lap record by 3 seconds in one race and that was regarded as sensational at the time. The lap took 3 minutes 36 seconds. Now if ever you've seen a photograph of a road tyre in those days doing a hundred miles an hour, you'll know that it grows. It distorts. The centrifugal force pulls it away from the rim. If we had been able to see what was going on under that mudguard we would have lifted our foot off the throttle.'

Like Firth and Jane, the Geoghegans were armed with a Cortina GT. 'Ford gave us a Cortina and asked us to drive it,' says Leo. 'The factories tended to have their own teams in each state in those days. That was the beginning of a very good relationship with the Ford company. By then we were also importing and racing the Lotus.'

Leo and Ian had not changed their attitude towards the 500, even though it had landed in their state. They still didn't regard it as highly as other forms of racing. 'We said it was going to be a boring weekend because the cars were so slow, and a bit of a pain in the bum because it interfered with our normal racing program. We were heavily committed to the modified cars we had in the stable. There wasn't much money in it, either. But the public was so interested in it. You could see it on TV, and you couldn't see the other races on TV. That's why the sponsors wanted us to go and they looked after us with all our other racing, so we had to go.'

The dress code at the first Bathurst 500 was very much in keeping with the style of the racing. You might describe it as 'smart casual'. Fans could identify with drivers in everything from slacks and polo shirts to overalls. Open-face helmets were the norm, with driving gloves useful because the steering wheels were the showroom standard bakelite, which was quite slippery in sweaty palms.

There was an international decree from General Motors at the time banning factory-supported racing but six S4 Holdens made it to Bathurst to take on the four Cortinas. Among the drivers lining up in the S4s was a 23-year-old called Kevin Bartlett.

Bartlett, originally from Coffs Harbour in New South Wales, had had a yen for motor sport since the 1950s. His father was always enthusiastic about driving. 'He was quite a mean driver in his own right,' Kevin recalls, 'and he used to take me to Mt Druitt. One of the best I ever saw there was Jack Brabham in a Cooper Bristol. Jack would always have the boot right up it . . . he still does. He was outstanding. The difference between him and everyone else was huge. I always thought that if I could ever do that I'd be pretty pleased. Frank Gardner was there, but he wasn't the stand-out driver in those days . . . it was before he went to Europe. Leo Geoghegan was also there, at the forefront of the touring car events. Bill Ford was a foreman at the garage where I worked for Frank Kleinig. He used to race a Monoposto powered by a Hudson engine in open-wheeler races. Bill put a canvas body on it. It didn't look like canvas, because it was painted a vivid red, but it made the car lighter, of course. Basically it was a seat with an engine, four wheels and a gearbox with a layer of paint over it all! With Bill, who eventually became president of the Australian Racing Drivers Club, there was no tomorrow. It was absolutely balls out everywhere. I'll never forget the cars and the way those blokes drove. They were all young in those days and they spurred me on to do the same thing.'

Bartlett's first road car was an 8-year-old MGTC. He used it for his first race, which was at Schofields Aerodrome, against MG Specials which lapped him within 3 laps. 'I realised then that they had done things to their cars that I couldn't afford to do.' This would come to characterise the Bartlett career.

He moved on, to his mother's Morris Minor convertible, which he would race without her knowledge. 'Are you driving it along dirt roads?' she would ask after seeing stone chips and scratches on the paintwork. It was not a dirt road, just the rough race track at Schofields. He got away with it every weekend for about 6 months until the racing became officially sanctioned by his parents. His style had not changed. 'I had been pretty crazy in the Morris Minor. I had done some things out on the track that were pretty stupid. Gee it was enjoyable, though. Of course the car was terribly under-powered. You know I never, ever, lost it in that Morris Minor, which, to me, meant that I wasn't trying hard enough.'

Lynx Engineering had set about building a Ron Tauranac-designed car, and they employed young Bartlett to work as test driver and assistant in their garage. 'That got me into open-wheelers, and once I landed there, I knew that's where I wanted to be. My first drive of the car was at Warwick Farm, and I can remember to this day sitting in it, ready to go out. The promoter at Warwick Farm, Geoff Sykes, walked out to me, knelt down and said, "Now this is where you can go forward, instead of that nonsense you used to do. You'll be good in this." To me, at 21, that was very important. It meant so much to me.'

He raced the Lynx Formula Junior for a couple of years before they pulled out of the operation. Then he became a driver for hire, firstly in a TVR with an MG engine, then in an Elfin with an 857cc Hillman Imp engine, which further developed his on-the-edge style. 'It never occurred to me that you could crash and hurt yourself. That happened to other people.' He also drove a Lotus Super Seven and sports cars in various other events before taking the S4 Holden drive at Bathurst. Bathurst had little significance for him other than being a chance to do even more laps than usual around a circuit famous for its high speeds.

One of the light-hearted entries in class B in 1963 was a Renault R8 driven by another of the emerging talents in Australian motor sport, Frank Matich. By this time, Matich had already competed in an Australian Grand Prix, finishing 8th in a 1.5 litre Elfin Ford. The Renault drive was part of his deal with Total. This race at Bathurst was not as successful. His antics with co-driver George Murray indicated that he wasn't driving with quite the level of ferocity he needed. They had made fun of each other by highlighting, in paint, a couple of dents that they accused each other of causing during practice. Matich still recalls the incident. 'I wrote on the dents, "George did this", with an arrow pointing to them. I can assure you it wasn't me who made them!' Matich and Murray would finish 7th in their class.

The tight regulation of practice, for the sake of the local residents, highlighted the careful, crafty preparation of Harry Firth and Bob Jane. There were teething problems all over pit lane as cars and drivers struggled to come to terms with the demanding circuit. There was the not-so-small matter of the mountain's menacing elevation — it was considerably higher than it looked. Brakes and gearboxes were crying out for mercy. Some were driven too hard. Others were never ready. Later in the race, it was wheels. The forces exerted by the constant changes of camber and hard cornering and braking were actually tearing steel. Kevin Bartlett was one victim, losing a wheel in the Dipper and scraping metal as he drove all the way back to the pits. That was the second wheel they had lost that day. His co-driver, Bill Reynolds, had lost one down Conrod Straight. They would finish 8th in their class.

The competitive nature of the Bathurst event showed, especially for those drivers more familiar with open-wheel racing, just how unnerving sedan racing could be. Unlike the purpose-built race cars, where the springs were stiff and the driver sat lower down, the average sedan was unfamiliar with being stretched and squeezed for 800 kilometres. This was like training a Shetland pony to win the Melbourne Cup. 'A lot of drivers,' recalls Firth, 'felt as if the thing was going to tip over all the time.'

'You didn't have safety glass,' recalls Leo Geoghegan. 'You covered your headlights with masking tape in case they were broken by a flying stone or something. You couldn't have one shatter and leave shards on the track. You put a sheet of Perspex over the driver's window in case you broke that, because windscreen glass at the time went opaque if it was shattered by a stone and you couldn't see a bloody thing.'

After the prescribed 130 laps, Firth and Jane had done it again. It was easy in the end. They were outpaced down the straights by the Studebakers, which were capable of more than 200 kilometres per hour. But when the bigger cars braked early to wash off enough speed to negotiate the corners, Firth and Jane would whip through on the inside with their lighter car and disc brakes.

The heated rivalry with the Geoghegans once again went the Victorians' way, when the Sydneysiders blew a head gasket after 105 laps. 'We all got on well eventually,' recalls Leo, 'but Harry was ostensibly behind the Cortina project. We were technically factory-supported drivers too, but he gave us as little information as he could. He was supposed to be representing Ford! For example, he came along after our generator bracket had broken and said,

"Oh I meant to tell you about that ... we've broken a few of those." I thought, you old bastard ... He was a cunning old bugger.'

In the opinion of Firth and Jane, they had selected the parts, done the testing, formed the strategy. The rest could please themselves. 'It took the Geoghegans and us a couple of years, I guess, to get to know each other,' Jane recalls. 'We soon became good friends and I finished up going to Ian Geoghegan's wedding, but initially it was quite a phenomenon; not really a rivalry, more like distaste for "those Victorians".'

Respect came faster than friendship. Firth remembers Tom Geoghegan coming up to him after Bathurst in 1963 and saying, 'You out-thought us, you out-drove us and you out-pitted us.'

Stunning as it had been for the uninitiated who took up the challenge in 1963, Mt Panorama showed in October 1964 that it could be every bit as virulent as its predecessor, Phillip Island. While much of Australia bathed in spring weather, the mountain turned on its tormentors like a vengeful god, spitting bitterly cold rain on angry winds.

Harry Firth had become world famous among Ford proprietors for his success with the Cortina. In early 1964 he was presented with a watch by Jim Clark at a special ceremony in the Italian town that gave the car its name. Both Clark and his Lotus boss Colin Chapman were fascinated with the Australian's modifications. It was still the car to have.

Bob Jane, having left the Firth stable with no hard feelings, had won the support of Shell for his bid with George Reynolds in a Cortina. Firth drove his Cortina with the experienced John Raeburn, for BP. The Geoghegans were still driving for Total. Ian had won the Australian Touring Car Championship at Lakeside in a GT Cortina which his team built themselves. He had beaten the best Holdens of the day, and Bob Jane's Jaguar.

In a race that never seemed to lose its intensity, the Studebakers again dropped back with fading brakes. Even Firth's Cortina was suffering from the extreme pace. Jane wasn't without problems himself, but he solved them a little faster — and won the race. Bob Jane had now won his fourth consecutive Armstrong 500, including the first two to be held at Bathurst. He could have retired right there and been assured of immortality. He had also done it for the first time without Harry Firth. 'I was very fast, in that time, in a production car. When I was with Harry he used to work me to death because I could pick up time. I could drive. To win without Harry meant that I won it on those driving skills.'

Leo and Ian Geoghegan closed to within 3 laps of the winners with some fine driving, and finished 5th in the class behind Roy Hodgson and John French. For Leo, it was the same old story: 'We were mostly the quickest driver pairing at Bathurst and were always going to win the race, but where you are halfway through the race counts for nothing. It's where you are at the finish.'

Norm Beechey would not follow the trail to Mt Panorama in 1964. He had been blazing a trail of his own, anchoring the first sponsored Australian touring car team. Shell Oil's retail franchise, Neptune, spent almost all of its marketing dollars on the team and it was called Neptune Racing. It featured five cars. Norm drove his Lukey's Ford Galaxie, a Holden sedan wearing the plate PK752 and a new Holden S4 with PK751 on the plate, staying true to the now famous nickname. Jim McKeown drove a Ford Lotus Cortina and Peter Manton was in a Mini Cooper S. While the Armstrong 500 revolutionised big-time events, Neptune Racing revolutionised the concept of team and driver promotion. Norm Beechey was just the front man they needed. He would be stranded on the roof of his car in a flood of fans after his races, pen in hand, signing the photos, programs and posters thrust at him from dozens of outstretched arms.

'We were very well promoted. They even put out special Neptune stickers, with the trident shape, and deliberately under-supplied them to create demand. Service stations had to be rationed!'

The aspect of the Neptune years that Beechey recalls with less affection was the constant changing of cars. 'That was very difficult, because it meant I was forever in a development program, but my sponsors were very keen to bring in a new car each year to attract more fans or purchasers of petrol back into the Neptune brand.' Another problem was the increasing pressures of mixing business with racing. Beechey continued to do this because he enjoyed it. 'There were some weekends when I found I could handle the driving easily, but on others ... well I remember once going out to Calder and getting a phone call from the bank manager saying, "Look Norm, you're a couple of hundred thousand dollars over your overdraft. Would you be able to straighten it up on Monday?" I told him it depended how I went that weekend. I wasn't talking about how we were going to perform on the track — I meant how many cars we'd sell at the dealership. That wasn't very good for your lap times, I can tell you! Really, I was only a part-time racer.'

In 1964 Norm contested 23 meetings across five states at seven venues. He would drive in up to four races at each meeting. The S4 Holden was clearly his favourite at the time, reaching speeds of up to 210 kilometres an hour.

CHAPTER SIX

To be Frank . . .

Frank Matich was born on 25 January 1935 and was brought up on a farming property at Engadine, in Sydney's southern suburbs. His first experience of machinery was driving a Howard tractor with a rotary hoe attached. His interest in driving was a product of his interest in machines, rather than the other way around, and his first drive came after he persuaded his father that the best way to dry the car after washing it was to fling it down the old Warragamba Dam pipeline road near his house.

'To me, working on a motor car was about measuring performance, making the car better. I very quickly came to understand that you could profit as much from handling as you could from the engine. On that dirt road, I learnt that shock absorber control and ride height, the things that go on around the engine, were just as critical as the power output itself, because you needed to maximise the use of that power.'

Matich became a diesel apprentice, aircraft apprentice and automotive apprentice before blending all three. His first racing came from his job with Selective Sports Cars at Tempe, where he set up a workshop to repair and modify sports cars for sale. One customer, an Englishman, crashed an MGTC at a hill climb, abandoned it and fled to England, leaving a bemused Matich to buy it from the finance company. He raced the MG at hill climbs and the Mt Druitt circuit, which he recalls as being crudely cut into an airstrip which the owner, Beilf Jones, also used to graze his cows. 'Now and then you'd tickle one cow's bum and kiss the other's nose as you went through the sweeper. You had to be very careful. A few people had been killed hitting cows.'

From the MGTC he progressed to an Austin Healy, expanding his racing to Bathurst and Orange. Then, there were a few forays at Schofields, where he met a young Kevin Bartlett doing similar things. 'What I want to know is, if Kevin's as young as he tells everyone, what was he doing driving around in those days against me! Frank Gardner, the White Knight, was racing there too, in his C-type and then later in his D-type Jaguars.'

Matich moved on to a sales job at Leaton Motors, persuading them to expand their market into sports and modified cars. 'The principle was to buy a good straight car, take it into the workshop, make it into a near-perfect car, and resell it. It was a principle that suited the era, when acceptance of used cars was far more prevalent than today. I'd buy a Healy for about £600 and we'd totally do it up and sell it, with a warranty, which was novel in those days, for about £1050 to £1080. We were going so well we had a waiting list with deposits paid for cars. Sometimes I'd have 20 deposits. We'd buy cars from all over the country, but you never sold a car in the same suburb you bought it in. Although, having said that, I once sold a car back to the bloke I bought it from, 6 weeks later, and all I'd done really was put a new coat of paint on it, a wheel alignment and tune. I made a profit on it too.'

'People were coming in to buy a "Matich" Austin Healy. I was top dog in the state, in my Healy, and the only person who could knock me off was Frank Gardner in his D-type Jag.'

Frank Gardner was born in Sydney on 1 October 1930, the son of a fisherman who was forced in hard times to sell his trawler and work as a timber cutter. If a Depression-era childhood had not hardened Frank, then the tragic death of his father — crushed against the wall of a shop at Narooma by a drunken driver who'd lost it in the wet — would make certain of it. Gardner went to live with his Uncle Hope Bartlett, who'd worked hard to start the Katoomba–Jenolan Caves bus run in the early 1920s. Hope was a character of great renown who played tennis for NSW, but really made his reputation in a variety of pursuits on water and road, especially the dreaded Maroubra

Speedway. 'It was an unkind place for drivers and got rid of several great names — Charlie East and Phil Garlick among them.' Hope's garage was always full of exotic vehicles, and Gardner spent hours there, gaining his first driving experience at the wheel of a 5 ton paper truck and backing the buses out of the shed.

Gardner, then moved with his uncle, first to Sydney's Cronulla, then on to Palm Beach, where he became an all-round athlete — sailing, shooting, running and swimming. He was a prominent surf lifesaver, sweeping the Championship-winning Whale Beach Surf Club boats and competing in early forms of international iron-man events. While training for these competitions in the local gym he discovered a penchant for boxing, and won every amateur bout he contested. He also took up golf, quickly reducing his handicap to 4, then briefly off scratch. But it was boxing that got the nod and by the time he was 22 he was earning far more as a professional boxer than he could in his day time work as an apprentice mechanic. His considerable intelligence told him, however, that boxing had its limitations. 'Boxing is controlled by a dubious element of society, making some decisions difficult to understand. I saw it as not being a great environment to grow up in, whether at the Don King level or downwards, people you are not quite sure you want to be rubbing shoulders with.'

The next chapter of his life is one that, for his sake, is better left wedged in the creases of age. Gardner found himself on an unenviable list that was to prove far more dangerous than anything he could have faced in the ring or the grimy back rooms of boxing administration: national service. At the time, Australia was fighting a war in Korea. Whatever happened there has been filed away by Frank Gardner in a place he will never admit to visiting. 'It was not my choice. It is behind me. It was a set of circumstances where you wound up in these places you didn't want to be ... but you went. It was a shocking experience. I don't go to any of the marches. It affects different people in different ways. Motor racing I'll talk about.'

On his return to Australia, Gardner picked up all the diverse threads of his civilian life, competing in professional speedway motorcycle racing and in surf boats as captain of the Whale Beach Surf Club. It was there that he suffered his first 'racing' accident — in practice one day the sweep oar broke as the boat dumped off a large wave. Gardner's legs were driven through the timber floor of the hull. His ankles were smashed, and in spite of the best efforts of surgeons armed with a collection of pins and screws, the incident would forever remain with him in the form of a slightly awkward gait, known thereafter on race circuits around the world.

The Sydney Sports Ground and Showground were the main venues for speedway racing, but the finish line for many competitors was much further away, somewhere beyond mortality. Gardner's higher sense of self-preservation took him in a different direction again. He had seen much in his tinkering at Uncle Hope's garage and around the various workshops and it was proving useful at Ultimo Technical College, where he was completing his diploma in metallurgy and engineering. He hit the road circuits in an MG in 1953 and won his first race at Marsden Park airstrip, near Windsor. But he could see that there was room for improvement, in terms of safety, in the motor racing business.

'They had straw bales on the edge of the tracks. If you had an accident and set them alight they would burn for days. You had helmets which had side straps and earpieces missing so you could listen to your engine — how else could you go deaf quickly? You had metal-rimmed goggles with glass in them, so if the glass didn't go through your eyes in an accident the metal would go through your brain. Then you had no overalls as such. I used to drive in a shirt and a pair of pants. There were no flame-proof shoes available, no flame-proof socks, and metal pedals. You sat astride the drive-shaft and if that broke, that was the end of the family jewels. You also had to have a supplementary fuel tank which went over the top of the family jewels to supply two aluminium tanks on either side, and they were only in the space frame, then you had a pick-up tank under your arse. If you hit anything, you attended your own barbecue. The steering wheel was made of wood, which broke up and you ended up with a handful of splinters. The gloves were of no use at all. Of course they could always pull the splinters out in hospital ... if you were still alive.'

Gardner made two key purchases in 1953 with the money he had saved mostly from the sweat of the boxing ring. The first was the Whale Beach Service Station, which set him up in his own engineering business. The second buy was his uncle's Jaguar XK120, regarded by many as the world's fastest production car in its day. He joined the North Shore Sporting and Manly Warringah car clubs, trained five nights a week with his surf boat crew and prepared his new race car with the love of the ultimate enthusiast. One of his early events in the

Jaguar was the 24 hour race at Mt Druitt, which was also contested by Australia's great international journeyman at the time, Tony Gaze.

Gardner compiled a startling record of 29 wins from his first 32 starts in the Jaguar. In 1956 he turned heads again by building a new XK120 body from fibreglass. After weeks of detailed and exacting work, the lightest XK120 in the world started to take shape. He made the mould from plaster of paris and wax reinforced by electrical conduit. Even the grille was made from fibreglass. The windscreen was perspex. All up, the 'Frank'-enstein Jag was 370 kilograms lighter than a regular XK120, a power-to-weight ratio that nothing in the sports car racing world could match, and it showed: Gardner had an incredible sequence of 25 wins from 26 starts all over Australia. Through 1956–57 the wins kept coming and the prestige kept growing, from Mt Druitt to the Silverdale Hill Climb to Bathurst, all the time under the tutelage of the retired Uncle Hope, who was a lively figure in the pits and paddock.

Gardner found it was very satisfying to construct or modify a revolutionary car; it was quite another thing to drive it well enough to justify his work in the garage. He also drove, in early 1957, a C-type Jaguar, and recalls a race at the 1957 Australian Grand Prix meeting when he was in command until a lead came loose on the fuel pump. 'You're more interested, a lot of the time, in getting your car ready, in following your schedule. Making sure you have the car at a certain place by a certain time. Then the unfortunate thing about progress is that once you get there, it's obsolete. All the work has gone into it and as you're driving home you realise you have to get a new car because the bugger you just won in is going to be beaten by someone else's improvements next time.'

Like Brabham before him, Gardner challenged authority by acquiring sponsorship, first from Vacuum oil and Messe batteries, then from James Hardie and Company, an association that gave the company a taste for motor racing and ultimately led to their sponsorship of the Bathurst 1000. Gardner's association with Jaguar continued to the end of the 1958 season — he raced at all the major circuits in the C-type, D-type and the famous XK120. But something had been biting him and he could not ignore it. It was the call of the unknown, the same yearning that made Gaze and Brabham itchy and ambitious. He had been afflicted by the need to test himself against the best in the world, and the best in the world were in Europe.

*   *   *

With backing from Leaton Motors, Frank Matich bought Frank Gardner's C-type Jag, which was on sale pending his trip to Europe. 'It was a big aluminium thing that he had crashed and repaired. But it was a pretty good motor car. I sold my Healy and started racing for Leatons with the C-type.'

Matich's first race in the C-type was at Bathurst in the 1958 Tourist Trophy. He finished 4th. 'It was around this time that handicap racing was being phased out and scratch racing becoming the vogue. My race was one of the earliest scratch races.'

Motor racing in Sydney was growing like Frank Matich's career. The key was the opening of Warwick Farm racecourse to a new kind of horsepower. Aintree promoter Geoff Sykes was asked by the Australian Jockey Club to run the circuit.

'My timing was impeccable,' Matich recalls. 'Warwick Farm was a respectable racing circuit in the Sydney district. You could take your bank manager to Warwick Farm. I can't stress enough that during this period, David McKay was an enormous influence on Australian motor sport. He competed in 14 Australian grands prix you know. But along with McKay the driver, there was McKay the journalist, the team manager and the promoter. He helped bring Geoff Sykes over here and Sykes was one of the true professionals in the sport. David's columns and stories in Sydney's *Daily Telegraph* were not only influential, but pretty much the only mainstream coverage of motor racing in the press. It helped that he was married to one of Frank Packer's daughters at the time, but you can't deny the great things he did for us all.

'David was the guy who brought Ferrari out here. He founded the Scuderia Veloce Team, which eventually became a leading car dealership. He even approached me at one stage to join him, but I was going well enough as I was.'

With Warwick Farm setting such a splendid example, there was talk of more racing circuits coming in. 'I was focused on sports cars,' says Matich, 'because they were tied to my business with Leaton Motors. I was sourcing a Tojeiro Jaguar, a really special Jag that I thought would beat everything out here but I also put in a call to Lotus and a few weeks later got a call back from Colin Chapman himself. He offered to sell me a car, and for £2750 I got a 2.5 litre Lotus 15.'

Matich was about to write a new chapter in sports car racing in Australia.

Frank Gardner's first impressions of England, at the end of 1958, were the same as those of many Australians who have ventured there from a lifestyle of beaches and baking. It was like leaving a cosy little study with a bright blazing open fire and walking downstairs to a bitterly cold, damp basement with a single dull light bulb flickering weakly in its centre.

His first call was to Jaguar headquarters in Coventry; he was searching for a link with the manufacturer he had competed with back home. However, Jaguar had decided to withdraw from competition. He returned to London, where he found work with Aston Martin, helping shape their campaign to win Le Mans. There, in a factory at Feltham, he worked under a General Manager who came to be known, in one of the classical Frank Gardner witticisms, as 'Death Ray', because of his stern discipline. His real name was John Wyer. Racing Manager Reg Parnell quickly recognised Gardner's talents and he was promoted from fitter to fabricator, working for drivers like Stirling Moss, Roy Salvadori and Carroll Shelby at circuits from Silverstone to Zandvoort.

Another of his great moments came in the 1959 Le Mans 24 hour race, where he was involved in John Wyer's decision to replace the regular Aston Martin gearboxes with those from Maserati. Gardner had argued that they were much stronger. It was typically bold and decisive — and Shelby and Salvadori won the race from the second team car, driven by Maurice Trintignant and Paul Frere. Gardner's affair with one of the world's greatest motor races would be like that between Liz Taylor and Richard Burton. He summed it up in his famous line: 'It's a race between the French ... and a bunch of other mugs.' Gardner would not abandon Le Mans, but he would be forever wary of it.

Frank Matich continued his pursuit of sports car titles in various Australian states, with the occasional sortie in open-wheel events. During this time, he secured sponsorship from Total Oil. He also encouraged Total to embrace the Geoghegan brothers in an expanded team. He took his Lotus 15 to Lowood, Queensland for the 1960 Australian Grand Prix and showed great speed against an array of local talent including: Lex Davison, who was never one to miss out on advancing technology had emerged from retirement with an upgraded 3 litre Aston Martin which Frank Gardner had played a leading role in developing; Alec Mildren, who had packed a 2.5 litre Maserati motor into his Cooper chassis; and Stan Jones, who started in a Maybach Corvette, just to name a few.

Matich was in a four-car second row; his was the only sports car in the top eight. 'With the Lotus 15 I was able to run with the best of them, even beat them, on certain circuits, like Warwick Farm, for example.' Not at Lowood. He was out of the race with steering failure. Jones also failed to finish. Mildren finally beat Davison in one of the classic Australian grands prix. The margin, after numerous lead changes, was .05 of a second.

'Unfortunately, I was out of contention,' Matich recalls, 'but I'll never forget it. That was one hell of a race between those two.'

Jack Brabham hadn't been able to bring his cars back to Australia in time for his home grand prix, but he staged yet another memorable contest with Stirling Moss in the 1961 New Zealand Grand Prix. Moss had come from a devastating tour of South Africa, where he had won the Cape and South African Grand Prix in December. It was their fifth consecutive January meeting in New Zealand and the score so far was even: 2–2. The supporting cast numbered 38, including Bruce McLaren, Dennis Hulme, Ron Flockhart, Innes Ireland, Jim Clark, John Surtees and Roy Salvadori. Dan Gurney replaced Graham Hill's BRM team-mate Harry Schell, who had been killed at Silverstone. Stan Jones, Bib Stillwell and David McKay were the leading Australian-based contenders.

An estimated 65,000 fans settled around a sun-baked Ardmore. It may have been the temperature, or it may have been the intensity of competition, but whatever the cause, a trail of lifeless machines began to litter the course, lap after lap, including Moss's Lotus, which had been 15 seconds clear of a despairing Brabham when it died. McLaren became Brabham's only threat, and in the shimmering heat he scraped and clawed fractions of seconds from the champion's lead.

Brabham entered the main straight for the last time, at the limit, squirming into controlled acceleration towards the flag. When it waved excitedly he was 1.7 seconds ahead. Graham Hill took 3rd from Flockhart, Hulme and Clark. 'That was one of the more memorable wins we had,' Brabham recalls. 'Stirling and I had some great times together, but that one felt pretty good. The best part of that era, though, having races in Australia and New Zealand, was that you could keep going for the entire year, and that really helped by the time you started each Formula 1 championship season. You were right on the ball.'

For the new Formula 1 season of 1961, the FIA had decreed that the 2.5 litre engines would be replaced by the Formula 2-standard 1.5 litre engines. It was, in part, a safety measure. Officials blamed the excessive power of the bigger engines for the spate of deaths in 1960. Jack Brabham had another, more cynical theory. 'The crux of the problem in 1961 was Ferrari. They hadn't been able to win any races, so they persuaded the FIA to change the format to 1500cc. Ferrari had a very good 1500cc engine. We didn't have any.'

The Indianapolis 500 was also gone from the schedule. Brabham, however, decided to have a try at America's sacred event. Only Alberto Ascari before him had bothered. 'We were well accepted there. The Americans were good people to race with, actually. They were more generous in the way they treated people, which we would find out much later when my sons started their careers.'

His Cooper T54, with a 2.7 litre, 4 cylinder engine bemused the conservative Americans with their massive front-engined cars. Their opinion changed when Brabham finished a competitive 9th with his much weaker but also much lighter machine. He might have even won if he had used Firestone tyres. Brabham had made extra pit stops solely for tyre changes, because the Dunlops he had brought from Europe were not tough enough for the punishing surface of the brickyard. Heads were turned, and so was the tide. The insular approach of the US was soon to be torn apart by the rear-engine revolution. 'They've been reminding me for years since how much bloody money I cost them,' he laughs, 'because they had to throw all their cars away and start again!'

There would be nothing to laugh about, however, in the year that followed in Formula 1. The Brabham ingenuity would be strangled by regulation, and rival factories such as Ferrari would prove vengeful opponents. It seemed that the only thing that had not changed was the appalling death toll.

On 15 June, 3 days before the next championship round in Belgium, Guilo Cabianca was killed, with three others, during Ferrari testing at Modena. His throttle had jammed open. To buy some time as he frantically tried to rein in the car, he had steered through the open gates of the track, but he couldn't stop before hitting a passing taxi with two passengers aboard.

With 2 rounds left, Brabham realised that not even Cooper's switch to an 8 cylinder engine was going to change the championship results. He had become a spectator as Ferrari drivers Wolfgang Von Trips and Phil Hill decided the title. Moss, in a Lotus 21, could still beat both but only if he won the remaining races and other results fell in his favour.

For the penultimate round, at Monza, Italian officials again insisted on using their banked section of the oval track as part of the main circuit. The race was little more than 1 lap old when pole-sitter Von Trips swept into the Curva Parabolica, locked with Jim Clark in his Lotus. They braked together and collided. Von Trips caught the worst of the moment, and tipped into a vicious somersault that turned the car into a wild, malevolent catherine wheel that followed the line of a trackside fence, threatening scores of spectators who had nowhere to run. It landed among them, killing 14. Von Trips was also dead. Brabham narrowly missed being caught up in another of the world's worst motor racing disasters.

'I was in amongst them. We were all dicing together. Jimmy and Von Trips were just in front of me and I was looking for a way through. The next thing I knew, the two of them just peeled off, bouncing off each other. Jimmy managed to stay on the track. Von Trips launched, rolling over the crash barrier and into the crowd.' The race was allowed to continue. Brabham's engine overheated after 8 laps. Phil Hill won, and sealed the championship, but motor racing had been dragged back to the horrors of Le Mans, as officials and teams scrambled for an appropriate response.

Jim Clark was in a lot of trouble. 'The first thing that happens when you have a crash and someone gets killed in Italy is that they confiscate everything and lock your people up,' Brabham recalls. 'Colin Chapman, who ran Lotus, knew this, and had been hiding Jimmy. He then approached me and asked if I could smuggle Jimmy to England in my plane. I took him out with me onto the tarmac. Customs let us through because I said we were only going to refuel. While we were out there, we hid Jimmy in the back of the plane. Then I went back, got the rest of the family, and flew back to England.'

Motor sport had serious problems. So did Jack Brabham. Unlike the FIA, though, he had a solution.

When Aston Martin had decided to withdraw from Formula 1 — again — at the end of 1960, Frank Gardner went to work for the Jim Russell Racing School. He gained experience working on Lotus and Cooper cars which were used to train potential drivers. This was also a fine place for Gardner to hone his own driving skills. The only plus in the bitter cold of the east coast moors where he worked was that the puddles couldn't wet his feet: they were already frozen. Russell saw what Reg Parnell had seen and promoted Gardner to leading student driver, which gave him the chance to race a Lotus in competition. In effect, he was a living billboard, because the school used his prowess to show off the kind of driver they could produce. In that 1961 season, from March to December, he gave the Russell School team six wins and six other top-five finishes in an estimated 20 starts in Lotus 18s and 20s in Formula Junior, including heats.

'When blokes got to this level,' Gardner recalls, 'they got paid to drive instead of putting their own money into it — it was the changeover from the gentleman drivers to the professionals. It was a bit like the surfing movement. If you had told me those layabout bludgers were actually going to earn a living surfing I would have said you had a kaleidoscope for a mind, but I could see that there was going to be a professional world in motor racing.'

One of Frank Matich's most satisfying wins came in the Australian Tourist Trophy at Phillip Island in the spring of 1960, following his unsuccessful Australian Grand Prix attempt at Lowood. He fuelled a very strong interstate rivalry by beating local favourite Doug Whiteford in a Maserati 300S.

'The interstate rivalry was so intense,' Matich recalls, 'that someone had cut the ropes tying my car to its trailer, while it was parked in a motel car park at Phillip Island the night before the event. Luckily we noticed it moving around a bit as we drove off to the track. We never found out who cut the ropes. I guess it was just an enthusiastic Victorian fan who'd had too much to drink.'

Matich didn't contest the 1961 Australian Grand Prix, run at Mallala, South Australia, in October. Lex Davison won a controversial race — he took the chequered flag after crossing the line behind David McKay, who had been penalised one minute for breaking the start.

Matich was keeping his racing mainly in the Sydney area after Leaton Motors, his primary backer, went bankrupt. The Lotus 15 was owned by Leaton Motors, so it disappeared in the collapse. Matich was back on the phone to Colin Chapman, who put him in touch with the United Dominion Trust racing team, which offered to sell him a second-hand Lotus 19 which Stirling Moss had been racing in the United States. They agreed to bring the car back to the UK for an overhaul before shipping it to Australia.

'I was broke as buggery, but my sponsor, Total, put together a whole new contract, directly with me, so I could fund the deal. The new Lotus cost me £2800, but I was dudded. Fortunately, Mossy was in the country and he checked it out for me. He told me that it was not the car he drove. He got on to his mechanics and they tracked down the people who had organised for the car to be shipped to Australia. Apparently they had flogged off all the parts, replacing them with crook ones. To their credit, UDT refunded virtually all the money, which enabled me to rebuild the car and buy another motor from Reg Parnell, who was very helpful.'

Matich's Lotus 19 was one of the most exciting race cars Australia had seen and won all of its races, with Bib Stillwell's Cooper Monaco the only car capable of challenging him. It was widely accepted that each driver had the best performed examples of their cars in the world. They raced up to four times a month, the rivalry intense.

'It made a huge difference responding to Bib's challenge,' Matich recalls, 'because Total paid me only for a win! £300. So if you look at the records that show more than 60 wins a year ... work it out for yourself.'

It was the drivers lining up for the 1962 New Zealand Grand Prix who delivered the flavour of Formula 1, but their cars were far more powerful. The race did not have to conform to the latest Formula 1 regulations restricting engine capacity because it was not a championship round. Stirling Moss, Jack Brabham and Bruce McLaren provided the punters with a choice of favourites. John Surtees, Roy Salvadori, Lex Davison and Bib Stillwell were also there. Denny Hulme was not, preferring the cheaper option of remaining in Europe. The race start coincided with a flooding downpour, which suited the risk-taking bravado of Moss. He slithered around Ardmore like an antelope on ice, never losing more than he could regain with his uncanny skills. He was so entertaining that 45,000 people stayed on through the rain to watch in awe. Surtees doggedly paced him, a lap behind — he was the best of a beaten pack. McLaren finished 3rd. Brabham stubbornly stayed with dry weather tyres, which almost sent him off track several times before a jammed gear selector made the decision for him. So now it was Moss 3, Brabham 3 — and six unforgettable grands prix for New Zealand. An era was over, though they didn't know it at the time.

As if 1961 hadn't been difficult enough for Brabham, the defending Formula 1 champion, the following years opened the eyes of a driver–engineer who may have thought he had seen it all. Brabham made the fateful decision to quit Cooper and go it alone. 'Coopers weren't keeping up with what had to happen to stay in front. I had a few run-ins with Charlie [Cooper], because they really didn't want to change anything. His statement was always, "Why change when we're winning?" I had already had some assistance from Ron Tauranac, from Australia, so at the end of 1961 I got Ron to come over and we started our own company.'

As John Cooper told the documentary *Champions*, he was greatly disappointed. 'Of course I was, but you know that's motor racing, isn't it, really? I think in his heart he wanted to go and build his own car, which was fair enough, and I have great respect for him.'

Bruce McLaren stayed with Cooper. His new team-mate would be Tony Maggs.

Frank Gardner found out that Brabham would be forming his own team, and he wanted to be in it. 'Frank had come to us for a job,' Brabham recalls. 'He was bloody funny. He used to keep everybody amused. He was a character all right, telling fantastic yarns. You name it, he had it.' A new partnership was forged, and it would put springs on the heels of yet another emerging Australian champion. Gardner and another Australian, Peter Wilkinson, were given the job of building the first Brabham race car. The various designs of the new Brabham would be given the prefix 'BT', which stood for Brabham and Tauranac.

The Brabham team was never going to be a threat to its rivals on the Formula 1 stage in 1962. What Brabham couldn't have taken into account was the sudden loss to the championship of his great sparring partner, Stirling Moss. Moss suffered serious head injuries in a crash during the pre-season Glover Trophy, at Goodwood. He would never race again. 'It was a tremendous shock,' recalls Brabham. 'It wasn't the sort of accident that Stirling would normally have. Even now we don't really know what caused it. He was dicing with Graham Hill at the time. Somehow he got off the edge of the track in the wrong place, and just couldn't recover it.'

The first Brabham race car, the BT3, was not ready for the early rounds of the world championship, in which Brabham used a Lotus Climax 24. His best result in five starts was his last: a 5th at Aintree in the British Grand Prix. The BT3 debuted in the following round, at the Nurburgring, where Brabham eased out with a throttle problem after 9 of the scheduled 15 laps.

Brabham raced the car again back in the UK at Oulton Park's Gold Cup, finishing 3rd behind Jim Clark and Graham Hill, then unveiled a better version for the US Grand Prix at Watkins Glen on 7 October. He qualified 5th and carved through the field with speed and reliability to finish 4th, 1 lap behind the winner, Jim Clark. Before he left for Europe, Brabham drove his car to 2nd place behind a Lotus shared by Clark and Trevor Taylor in the non-championship Mexican Grand Prix. The pieces were starting to come together in this engineering puzzle.

Graham Hill won a close Formula 1 championship in the final round in South Africa, beating Jim Clark. Brabham finished the season with a point-scoring 4th — and faith in the future.

'At the time, the state of the art meant you had to have a Cooper to beat a Cooper. In time, you would have to have a Brabham to beat a Brabham. I was very fortunate in sitting in one of the few cars that was capable of winning, and Jack was the ideal person to be mixed up with. It wasn't big-time racing, either. I remember being at a couple of race meetings with nobody to change gear ratios except myself, nobody to change engines except myself, nobody to give pit signals except myself ... and nobody to drive, except myself.' The lines flow from Frank Gardner like an ice-cold mountain stream, cutting through the steep banks of hyperbole that have been methodically stacked on Formula 1 history.

Gardner had expanded his duties in 1962, taking on the building and preparation of Brabham Formula Junior cars and spending a season in England driving them in various events. Tasmanian Gavin Youl had also been employed to drive the smaller Brabham cars.

The problem was that Gardner was in demand elsewhere, and could not clearly differentiate between his roles as driver and engineer — at least not while he was an employee and unable to delegate an in-tray the size of a small building. The combination was simply too demanding. He competed in approximately 14 events including two sports car races, one of which was the Le Mans 24 hour, where he picked up a drive with Briton David Hobbs in a Lotus Elite Mk14 with a Coventry Climax engine. Hobbs's co-driver was supposed to be Jim Clark, but Clark was unable to race on the Continent because an inquest was under way into his involvement with the crash that had killed Wolfgang Von Trips and 14 spectators the previous September at Monza.

The Le Mans event was run in atrocious conditions, and Gardner was almost in shock when he discovered that they were 3rd outright after a night of teeming rain. The track dried, freeing the more powerful Ferraris from their leashes, and the smaller-engined Lotus was elbowed back to 8th at the finish. They won not only their class, thanks to the 1500cc engine, but also awards for Thermal Efficiency and Index of Performance. The total prize money handed to Lotus was £20,000. For all their hard work, Hobbs and Gardner shared £1000 between them. Big money!

The best result he managed in a Brabham car that season was a heat win at Reims a week before the French Grand Prix. His workshop schedule with the team was exhausting, as Brabham and Ron Tauranac talked and sketched and hammered and welded new versions of the BT in a never-ending cycle of development. Gardner told Les Hughes, of *Historic Motor Racing*: 'They broke the mould with Jack, and Ron must have come out of the same cradle. Ron could survive on cigarettes and coffee, they both needed little sleep, and Jack would insist we go testing when we were all knackered.'

'We worked for every possible hour we could,' Brabham recalls, without a tinge of regret.

Frank Matich had stepped up in 1962. Not only had the Lotus 19 taken him to many wins but Garrie Cooper of Elfin Sports Cars also wanted him to drive for them in three classes, which greatly improved his versatility. Matich encouraged the Geoghegans to come under his sponsorship umbrella. Frank, Leo and Ian became stars of the 'Total Fan Club'.

'Nobody had ever heard of Elfins,' says Matich. 'I remember we beat Gavin Youl in a race when he was out here from England and his mechanics sent Ron Tauranac a telegram of the result. Ron sent a telegram back which read: "What's an Elfin?" They sent another telegram saying: "A quick pixie." They were a beautifully balanced little car and spot on for the races they did. I didn't have to do much with them except set them up for the circuits.'

Typical of his meetings was one at Catalina Park, where he won in Formula Junior in an Elfin 1100, won his class in an Elfin Clubman, won again in an Elfin 1500 and again in the Lotus 19, setting a lap record in the latter. At Warwick Farm in October he dominated the classes and took the fight to the bigger cars in outright contests. He would qualify his Elfin 1500 with its primitive Ford engine amongst 2.5 litre cars. He won the Formula Junior Championship.

'Tom Geoghegan actually complained about the Elfins, saying that I was ruining his Lotus franchise. He also complained to Total that he wasn't getting fair treatment. Well, for a start, I had allowed him to have the Lotus franchise anyway, because it was mine originally, through Leaton Motors. I also helped him with the Total deal. He was just bitter because I'd won a few races. It put a sour note on a great meeting. It was a shame, because Leo and Pete [Ian] were great blokes. I never had any problems with either of them. They were real gentlemen.'

With such a busy schedule in sports cars Matich did not bother contesting the 1962 Australian Grand Prix at Caversham in Western Australia.

Western Australia had won the bid to host the Grand Prix: like the 1956 Olympic Games event, it was to coincide with another international meeting, the Commonwealth Games. The Caversham circuit which had baked the best of them in 1957 was ready to soak up the sweat again. Gold Star winner Stillwell, Davison, Patterson, John Youl and others stood in the shadows of Brabham and McLaren, whose breadth of popularity and achievement was more than adequate to shade the sweltering circuit.

It was McLaren in command from the start. Brabham had his hands full with the plucky Stillwell, who gnawed on him for a while before letting the big players settle it like a couple of Hollywood leads. Brabham had told the media how much he wanted to win. The cut and thrust that followed was evidence of that. Every time he found something more from the car or himself, McLaren would respond. The margin was rarely more than 3 seconds. Their fastest laps were separated by little more than a couple of tenths of a second as they searched for the outer limits. It was sheer, unforgiving determination. Each time the pit boards went up, relaying the situation in basic numbers, they would grit their teeth and go harder again.

McLaren gave Brabham a chance to make the knockout blow. He had lapped Arnold Glass for the second time when he lost concentration and ran off the road. His car control and recovery were such that he turned and resumed full speed before losing the lead, but the shark-like Brabham had closed in for the kill. Glass was still between them. Brabham steadied and made a dive. Glass carried him off the circuit, where Brabham's car helplessly hit some tyres and shot across the slippery, close-cut grass of the infield. One of the great grand prix fights was over. 'I wasn't too happy,' Brabham recalls. 'I can't remember what I said to him after the race but we often have a joke about it.' Brabham had enough grip on the car to drag it back to the pits, where he watched Bruce McLaren win.

No one was more pleased for McLaren than Frank Matich, who had formed a close friendship with the New Zealander and was looking forward to racing him again when the big events moved east. 'We actually met back at Warwick Farm when I ran my Lotus 19. My wife Joan and Bruce's wife Pat were often mistaken for each other. People would be talking to my wife about Bruce and vice versa so we got to be mates — and after that, inseparable. I helped talk him into leaving Coopers and putting his own name on his cars. He was a fabulous talent — even more as a maker of cars than he was driving them. He could bring people together. Bruce was a great guy and a good friend.'

McLaren and Brabham drew swords again at the 1963 New Zealand Grand Prix, which moved to Pukekohe, a new 3.5 kilometre purpose-built circuit about 60 kilometres south of Auckland. It was another sweltering January day when 43,000 people made use of the facilities at a venue that had been handed over for operations only a week before.

It was to be an unhappy race for most of the top drivers, who suffered various mechanical problems and had very little practice time available to iron them out. The only untroubled visitor was John Surtees, who lapped the entire field while his rivals limped in and out of the pits. At the end of a boring 75 laps, Surtees took the chequered flag. Six other cars finished, none of them on the same lap as the winner. World Champion Graham Hill lasted until the final lap before his crunching gearbox finally died. He walked back to the pits. Brabham's BT4 blew a head gasket.

On 10 February they moved to Warwick Farm for another Australian Grand Prix, where some great names were lined up against them. It was the circuit's first staging of the event and drew a large crowd: it was close to the huge population base of Sydney, it was purpose-built, and it rewarded tenacity as well as speed.

Leo Geoghegan brought the Lotus 20B. He had won the Australian Formula Junior Championship in a Lotus 22. The 1960 GT Champion loved open-wheel racing more than anything. 'The question was,' he recalls, 'what did you do next after racing sedans? The only thing you could do, if you weren't a Stan Jones or a Lex Davison, was take on Formula Junior. This was the formula for those blokes like me who couldn't make that impossible leap from sedans to real racing and sports cars. The track itself was great too. At Warwick Farm a good driver in a lesser car always had a chance of beating a lesser driver in a good car. It was a great leveller.'

'Leo's father Tom ruled the boys with an iron hand,' Frank Gardner recalls. 'Great presentation. Well organised. That discipline and formal training stayed with them. Ian [Pete] was nicely balanced in the car. He had a low centre of gravity, mainly because he had a big arse, I suppose. Leo was pretty polished. Good-looking, presentable. He could talk. Of course Pete had a bad speech impediment, but I think back at the yard he sold more cars. People would buy one just to stop the conversation.'

Gardner's summer had been packed with racing for Alec Mildren's team: from Catalina Park to Warwick Farm to Lakeside to Longford to Sandown Park, in a Brabham 1500, a Lotus 23, a Cooper Maserati, a Brabham Ford, and a Cooper Climax. He scored wins at Lakeside and Longford in the Lotus. 'It was a mixture of youthful enthusiasm tempered by commonsense. The main aim all the time was looking for comfort ... comfort in the car, comfort in thinking. They were the prerequisites. Always in your mind in those days was some fresh tragedy; it doesn't matter how much you push those things into the back of your mind, they come forward occasionally. Providing commonsense prevailed, jumping from one person's car to the other was just like going from one golf course to the other. You keep it on the black bits and bring it home without destroying anything.' He would drive the Cooper Maserati for the grand prix.

Frank Matich, in his Elfin 1.5, was part of a small but tenacious band of drivers in the smaller-capacity cars. Most observers discounted them, but Matich would catch their eyes before the meeting was over.

There was one poignant appearance at this race. The great Stirling Moss had been invited to be official starter, as a tribute to his previous appearances in Australia and New Zealand. He had recovered from his injuries, but wasn't yet the statuesque figure that everyone remembered from his previous visits.

Once again, heat became a vital factor. John Surtees took pole comfortably. Frank Matich stunned them all by landing beside David McKay on the second row. Matich's contemporaries would tell you that he was a ruggedly single-minded character and, in his own sphere of influence, an extension of the Brabham philosophy of absolute, uninviting control. The problem, if you could call it that, was his talent and dedication. He would supervise all the work on his car. He knew what he wanted regarding geometry, weight distribution, brakes, tyre pressure. 'He might take pole position or close to it,' recalls one of his rivals in those days, 'but he would still pull the car apart one more time just to make sure everything was right, which used to drive the mechanics crazy.'

Brabham was having suspension problems, and couldn't qualify any higher than row 5, 13th fastest. Only Frank Gardner, who was struggling to come to terms with his 2.9 litre Cooper Maserati, Jim Palmer and Bob Holden were slower.

Drivers put ice in their cockpits for the start of the race as temperatures soared to 38°C. They had already taken off sections of the car bodies to improve air flow. 'Track temperature would have been in the fifties,' Gardner recalls. 'I must say, though, your job was to be fit to drive in whatever conditions. We operated in the days before trainers and managers and fancy liquids. You drank either water or water, so you evaluated what needed to be done and you allowed for it. You paced yourself accordingly.'

On that day, he needn't have worried about being fit to race. Moss waved the flag, and arguably the strongest field in the 28 year history of the grand prix was away. When the smoke cleared and the roar of the engines had shifted down the short straight and into the first right-hand corner, heads turned back to the grid, where Frank Gardner sat idle with a broken axle.

Whatever problems Brabham had been suffering from in qualifying, he seemed to have found some answers, as he pushed forward through the pack, moving up to sixth with a series of slick passes.

After only 10 of the scheduled 45 laps, two important factors had become clear. One was the pace of Brabham, who had moved past McKay to take the challenge to Surtees. The other was the heat, which was starting to tell on concentration levels and equipment. Lex Davison spent several minutes in the pits recovering. Hands and feet were blistering. Engine cooling systems were tested. The pace of the racing suffered, not that anyone outside the pits really noticed — the fans were just willing a local victory.

Frank Matich who finished 8th, remembers seeing Leo Geoghegan in all kinds of trouble. 'Leo had a case of "drop foot". The heat near his feet from the water pipes had deadened his foot. Everyone was worried what to do about it, but it came good, somehow.

'It's hard to believe that in a motor race the drivers were sometimes slowing down in the pit straight, swerving towards their crews, who were throwing water over them from various containers. It was so hot.'

Brabham, in spite of a mid-race spin on John Youl's oil, overtook Surtees after 31 laps. It was an amazing drive from the second-last row of the grid, and the crowd was in raptures. Surtees kept up the pressure for a while, but in the later laps he seemed resigned to 2nd place. Brabham's second Australian Grand Prix win had come 8 years after the first.

The Brabham development continued apace in the 1963 Formula 1 championship, with American Dan Gurney recruited to drive a second car. On

28 July in Stuttgart, Germany, in the Solitude Grand Prix, Jack drove his BT7 to a 24 second victory over Peter Arundell and Innes Ireland. It wasn't a championship race, but it was historic: it was the first time any such event had been won by a driver who had built his own race car.

Like most promising young drivers, Denny Hulme had worked as a mechanic in the Brabham garage while he tried to work his way through the driving ranks. He and Frank Gardner became good mates, and Denny would often ask Gardner if he could help him secure a regular place in the team. Typically, Gardner offered encouragement. In fact, he suggested to Brabham that Hulme be given the chance to drive a Brabham car full-time. It started with some Formula Junior races, and at Brands Hatch on a snowy Boxing Day in 1963 it was Hulme who gave the Brabham Junior its first race win. By the time the Formula 1 team arrived in Sweden, on 1 August, Hulme seized his greatest opportunity, replacing an injured Dan Gurney. He finished a promising 4th.

Brabham himself finished 3rd behind Jim Clark, who was on his way to seven victories in a season and one of the most convincing championship wins of all time.

'Jimmy Clark was obviously a fantastic driver, but you couldn't have a joke with him on the grid,' Brabham recalls. 'He was so uptight before the start of a race it was unbelievable. You couldn't talk to him. Most of us used to have a joke with each other, egg each other on a bit, but not Jim. That used to get me going too, of course. If I was alongside him, just before the start, I'd point to his tyre, as if I'd seen something wrong with it. Then the flag would drop and off we'd go. I used to do that to him pretty regularly. He'd be shaking his fist at me.'

Gardner, meantime, had put together one of the busiest seasons of any engineer–driver. After his hectic schedule with Alec Mildren's team in the Australian summer he returned to England to race the BT2 in Formula Junior for Ian Walker Racing, where his team-mate was another promising young Australian driver, Paul 'Hawkeye' Hawkins. Gardner laughs at the mention of Hawkins, whom he describes as 'a bloody villain'. Gardner's lasting memory of Hawkins was of a very hard driver. 'Ford loaned him motor cars in South Africa. I think he returned them a little worse for wear. Paul liked to get from A to B very quickly, so most trips were an adventure, to say the least, but the bloke could drive. He was a worker. If it was possible to have a go, he would. He had some odd mates though. You'd have to kick them out of the workshop. He liked a drink, but kept himself fit. He put his car into Monaco harbour once. He was never going to die in bed.'

Gardner won the Chichester Cup at Goodwood on 15 April and won again at Montlhery in France on 19 May, where 'Hawkeye' almost brought them both undone. 'We had the race sewn up, a 1–2 finish. All we needed was to ease up, save the mechanicals and the tyres. But Paul, on the last corner of the last lap, decided he wanted to win the race and had a big go to overtake me. I didn't even see him setting it all up but he did it too early in the corner and disappeared into the wall backwards. Unnecessary. Adventureland.' Paul Hawkins would remain one of Australia's most colourful motor racing exports until his death at Island Bend in the 1969 Tourist Trophy race.

Gardner also won a heat at Rouen on 23 June and the Martini International Club Trophy at Silverstone on 6 July — and on the same day, at the same venue, he finished 2nd in class in the sports car event. He then won the Twenty Guards Trophy at Brands Hatch and another round of the regular season at Zandvoort. There were 10 other podium finishes. One of those podiums was in the final race of the international season, at Kyalami in South Africa: the *Rand Daily Mail* 9 Hour race. It was his first drive for John Willment, who was developing an AC Cobra Coupé. The great American Carroll Shelby had a plan to sink a big V8 engine into a small car; this idea, coincidentally, came from Shelby's visit to the Brabham garage, where he spotted a similar transformation that Brabham had completed with a Sunbeam Alpine. Shelby teamed with Willment because he was the biggest Ford dealer in Britain. They employed Frank Gardner because he was one of the smartest engineer–drivers. A mighty combination was emerging from its cocoon, and Ford was about to become Gardner's greatest ally.

'It was an unlikely combination, really. AC made wheelchairs,' Gardner recalls. 'Ford was often in and out of motor sport, but when they decided to do something on an international scale it was obvious they were serious about it. They had a pretty good team around them. They were going to find the money.'

The Australian summer of 1964 was to come alive like never before following an initiative from CAMS, the Association of New Zealand Car Clubs and international promoters and their agents. They agreed to form a second international series to showcase the best drivers in the European off-season.

There would be four events in each country, starting from early in the new year and using the same point-scoring system as the Formula 1 championship. The three best results in each country would count towards a driver's series total, with the winner receiving the Tasman Cup.

Given the restricted transport options of the time, the Tasman series was an extraordinary achievement for Australian and New Zealand motor sport: it not only reflected the great talent both nations had produced, commanding the respect of their international peers, but also helped to make sure that the flow of talent continued, by providing local drivers with the very best competition at least once every year.

The first Tasman series, in 1964, attracted expatriates Jack Brabham, Bruce McLaren, Denny Hulme and Chris Amon, with 1962 World Champion Graham Hill also returning. American Tim Mayer, having tasted Formula 1 in the 1962 US Grand Prix, was another featured driver.

Frank Matich was waiting for them; he had a new Brabham BT7, with a 2.5 litre engine. 'I went overseas to buy the Brabham. I had originally planned to get a Lotus, but Brabham were pushing their cars, and their offer was that if I brought their car to Australia, tested it, refined it and shared the information, they would share all the improvements they had come up with overseas. I stayed for 3 months actually, with Bruce and Pat McLaren, did my research and worked for a while with Ron Tauranac on the design elements of the car as I wanted it. Between us we put together a prototype for the BT7. I also had to source gearboxes from Hewland and tyres from Dunlop. The deal also involved Repco, who had an international deal with Jack but needed to establish an Australian-based racing activity. My problem was, I had lent my best Climax engines to Repco for testing and they didn't return them in time for the New Zealand races, so I was left with none of my best parts such as forged true pistons and Carillo rods — I had to acquire second-hand parts which were out of time.'

Matich and the Geoghegans were still under Total sponsorship. Leo had won the 1963 Formula Junior Championship in his Lotus 22 and the deal was booming. 'The Total Fan Club had many thousands of members,' Matich recalls. 'I remember Leo and I having to go in for days on end just to sign bloody Christmas cards ... someone had had the great idea to send every member an autographed card ...'

Frank Gardner, driving with Alec Mildren Racing again, was armed with

A tightly packed crowd watches Harry Firth in his MG 'P' in the Bairnsdale Hill Climb in the late 1940s. He was also preparing cars for other drivers.

The A.F. Hollins Motors team in 1951 flanking a proud Tony Gaze between the trophy-laden Altas, both of which are road-registered. The sports car is on the left and the cantankerous thoroughbred racer is on the right. Harry Firth is standing in the back row, third from the right. Alan Ashton stands at Gaze's right shoulder.

Top: The *Ecurie Australie* team: Tony Gaze, Lex Davison and Stan Jones in an FX
Holden in the 1953 Monte Carlo Rally.
Bottom: The Gaze Formula 2 schedule for 1951. This was about as formal as it got
in those days and his actual campaign was quite different.

Frank Gardner calls this 'keep in one piece concentration', not wanting to be the quickest ... just the oldest.

How to crash at 100 m.p.h.—AND LIVE!

This remarkable photo came from *The Sun* newspaper on 3 October 1955. It's Harry Firth hanging from the cockpit of his Triumph TR2 at Fishermen's Bend. He managed to stay inside for this roll, but when the car flipped again after hitting hay bales, he was thrown out. Moments later he was sitting up on the road, dazed and cut, but otherwise unhurt.

It was a popular post-war trend to race at airfields and this was a rare sight for Scottish fans in 1952: the only Formula 1 race held at Turnberry, right next to the world famous golf course. The drivers used the clubhouse as a change room. Tony Gaze, in the number 51 HWM Alta, finished 4th to Mike Hawthorn in a Connaught. Note how close the crowd is, swarming all over a flimsy wire fence, largely unprotected.

The remains of Tony Gaze's Aston Martin DB3 at Porto. If he had not been thrown clear...

Harry Firth leading a Phillip Island handicap race in his TR Special, from Allan Jack in a TR2 and Neville Norway Shute, the writer, who at the time was researching his novel *On The Beach*.

Firth, left, and Bob Jane in hostile territory at Bathurst. The partly obscured caption reads: 'Stuff the ARDC, we're doing it our way.'

Tony Gaze cuts a dashing figure in his 2-litre Sports Alta during the Rob Roy hill climb. Drivers tended not to wear helmets or goggles in hill climbs.

A typical race start at Silverstone, 1951, the crowd closing in on the roadway on the left. In those days they swarmed onto the circuit, retreating only far enough to allow the cars to pass, much like today's European rally crowds. This race started in rain and was called off after five laps following a hail storm. Tony Gaze is in car number 6, part of his radiator taped over to retain heat in the extreme cold.

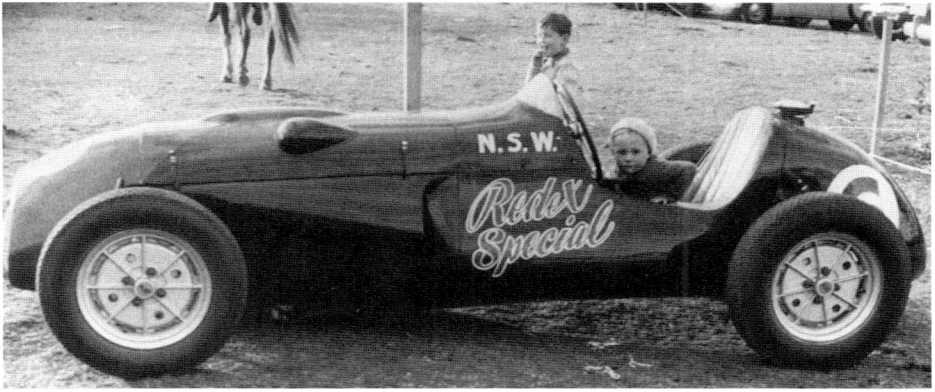

Jack Brabham's famous 'Redex Special', with oldest son, Geoffrey, making one of his earliest appearances behind the wheel.

The side of Brabham only his rivals knew.

The 'Kangaroo Team' at the Hyeres 12-hour race, 27 May 1955. Gaze in the Aston Martin DB3S in the crudest of pit lanes, where mechanics wore beanies and dress shoes to go with their overalls.

Kevin Bartlett in the 2.5-litre Mildren Alfa in the 1969 Japanese Grand Prix, won by Leo Geoghegan. Note the early experimentation with wings. The struts were fragile, and were attached to the moving suspension, which produced variable effects.

the 1500cc Brabham which he had driven with some success the previous year. He recalls the series not being appreciated, at the time, in terms of how special it really was. 'To start with, there wasn't the depth of media coverage that there is today. If you won the New Zealand Grand Prix or something you might get onto page 2 of the sports section, along with a photograph. It wasn't the sort of thing that was going to remain indelible.'

Gardner enjoyed driving for Mildren. 'You never really raced for Alec. He was more of a friend. I wasn't top of the pops as a driver, but technically, I was light years ahead. I'd decide the gear ratios, roll bars and springs, but Alec would be in on the meetings then show up with the pit board and make the signals. It was just like a family day out. It wasn't Ford Motor Company. The series was there strictly for the enthusiasts, and there were plenty of them. But if we had the PR then that we have today ...'

The first event of the historic Tasman series was the Levin International, on 4 January. Denny Hulme turned up in his 2.5 litre Brabham BT4, fresh from a European season where he had finally broken through to race Formula 1. He had also won seven Formula Junior races. Brabham, unable to contest all the 1964 Tasman series events, showed his support by entering Hulme for all of them. 'I just didn't have the time to drive in all the races,' Brabham recalls, 'because I had too much going on in England.'

Bruce McLaren and Tim Mayer raced as team-mates in Cooper T70s at Levin, and Chris Amon drove a Lola T4: there was a strong New Zealand presence at the round. Hulme upstaged them, setting qualifying and race lap records. Mayer finished 2nd.

It had been 7 years of bad luck for Bruce McLaren at his home grand prix, which was the next event of the series. There, at Pukekohe, it was punch and counter-punch again with Brabham, but this time Matich was the big mover. On lap 13, he boldly challenged Brabham, took the lead and equalled Hulme's lap record, set in a preliminary race that morning. By lap 26 his engine gave out and he crawled back to the pits, leaving a trail of oil which Tim Mayer later found, spinning off. 'It blew a gudgeon pin, which actually hit a lady in the crowd. Luckily she wasn't seriously hurt,' Matich recalls.

McLaren was freed from pressure when, approaching the Elbow, Brabham's wheel touched that of New Zealander Tony Shelly and the champion was flipped into the air. It was a safe landing. Shelly finished the race; Brabham didn't.

McLaren struck again in the following race, at Wigram Airfield, beating Brabham by 8 seconds and taking a commanding lead in the series from Hulme.

Frank Matich didn't contest the final round in New Zealand that year. He had run out of engines, having blown one at Pukekohe. 'Repco had the job of supplying parts and service to Jack, Denny and me. I needed parts after Pukekohe but wasn't getting any. The other blokes were. Now remember, Repco had two of my engines which I had lent them. Jack, Denny and Bib Stillwell were getting their parts from those engines! I was pissed off. This was a side of motor racing that I had not experienced. It caused a major problem for me for the entire series.'

At Teretonga, Bruce McLaren, in the absence of Brabham or Hulme, made it three wins from four starts.

The next round, on 9 February, saw the series cross to Melbourne's Sandown Park for the 29th Australian Grand Prix. Here the field would be beefed up as the might of Australia's considerable driving talent was assembled. It was a grid of golden hue: Bruce McLaren and Frank Matich on row one, then Denny Hulme and Tim Mayer; Lex Davison, Bib Stillwell and Bill Patterson; Gavin Youl and Tony Shelly; Jim Palmer, the irrepressible Doug Whiteford and Frank Gardner in the first of the 1500cc cars; David Walker and Charlie Smith; Arnold Glass, Tony Osborne and Keith Rilstone; Mel McEwin and David Fletcher. The crowd was more than 70,000.

There was a late scare as the field gridded up: McLaren had scraped a bump on the way from the pits to the circuit and split a seam on his radiator. The hastily prepared Cooper rejoined the field on their warm-up lap. Perhaps the surge of adrenaline from that panic-stricken start made the difference — but McLaren took the lead. There was a sequence of bold overtakings throughout the field as the cars sorted themselves out. Brabham attacked Matich for second place and passed him. Matich then beautifully defended his position from Mayer, until engine trouble resurfaced and he fell back. 'I was using a shit motor that I had cobbled together,' Matich recalls, 'because supply was blocked from Repco. It was what they call a "green" motor, and it was the last desperate spare that I had left. It used to twist and grow when hot. We had a meeting with Repco about it later and they apologised, but all their supply had gone to other people.'

Brabham and McLaren were in familiar territory, trading the lead, hammering at lap times until they were in the 1 minute 9 second range, a pace too fast to maintain without risking damage to the cars. Others were bled dry just keeping up. Davison's engine gave out. The red-hot racing continued, though, with Brabham upping the ante on lap 31, out-braking McLaren for the last time. The ensuing chase proved too much for McLaren. His Cooper engine cried 'enough' 8 laps later, with a con rod smashing a 10 centimetre hole in the engine block. Brabham eased up, adding 4 seconds to his lap times to save his car from a similar fate.

It was not just the victory that was important; the race was the start of a revolution. There had been seven Brabham-made cars in the event, nearly a third of the field. 'It wasn't the kind of business that would make you millions,' says Brabham, 'but it was profitable. It was helping to keep our racing going.' Fifteen of 24 starters retired, among them Frank Gardner, whose gearbox failed on lap 54.

Graham Hill, driving for David McKay's Scuderia Veloce team, joined them at Warwick Farm, where Brabham beat McLaren by less than a length, officially 0.4 of a second. He made it three in a row at Lakeside, although Matich had had the lead there until his usual engine trouble caned him again.

Brabham's winning streak could not stop Bruce McLaren from taking home the first Tasman Cup, due to his wins in New Zealand and his consistent placings in Australia. The final round in Longford, Tasmania would count only as a tragedy.

Longford made use of public roads and drew a massive crowd of appreciative Tasmanians who pressed up against flimsy barricades and paddock fences within centimetres of the circuit in some places. Poles, trees, even buildings sat in places where cars were likely to exit the track if anything went wrong. In some spots, a couple of straw bales would be stacked against a tree trunk as a safety barrier, but the only thing separating the cars from the corner of Longford's famous pub was a 3-metre deep cushion of spectators peering through chicken wire.

'The whole idea of the circuit was extraordinary,' says Frank Matich. 'You'd come to the big, long Kings Bridge and you'd see frogmen sitting there, waiting to go and pluck people out of the river. It was a typical country bridge, about 100 metres long, big timber boards, so loose they went boonk-a-boonk-a-boonk when you drove over them. Big, thick bolts protruding from them, huge gaps between them, two wooden rails on either side, and when it got wet . . . ohhhhh . . . '

With another 1 week turnaround, there was little time to prepare for this event, especially for drivers like Matich, whose shattered engine was rapidly rebuilt while his car was flown from Queensland. None of this seemed to affect the ferocity of the competition. Lap times were hotly contested.

Practice at Longford in 1964, however, would be remembered for something else. Despite all the horror that international motor sport had thrown onto the pages of Australian newspapers in the past 14 years, the local scene had been largely free of trackside tragedy until this day.

The ever-popular and outstandingly talented Tim Mayer had launched his car at King's Bridge and exited at 170 kilometres per hour. The car hit a bump and became airborne — only briefly, but it landed slightly sideways. Mayer applied the brakes, regaining control, but as he straightened, the two left-side wheels caught the slippery gravel on the shoulder of the road and the undertray of the Cooper scraped on the edge of the bitumen. Reports conflict as to what happened next, but the car slammed into a tree. The impact was just behind the cockpit and it disintegrated. Mayer was thrown clear, but died in the ambulance as it sped towards Launceston Hospital. He had been described as quiet, charming and destined for greatness.

Frank Gardner summed it up like this: 'Prior to the hotel, there was a bump in the road and you had to take your foot off the throttle or even brake in the quickest cars. Otherwise you'd get airborne and couldn't stop before the junction, where the pub was on the corner. I think Timmy had his foot flat and launched it. It was an instant dismissal.'

A shattered Bruce McLaren, who was to have been Mayer's Formula 1 team-mate that year, declined further practice but agreed to race on Monday. For Frank Matich, it was another blow in an already tough series. 'Timmy was a very talented driver and a lovely bloke. He stayed with me a couple of times during that trip. One problem was, the car was a very skinny thing and he never quite fitted it comfortably. He was a vastly different person from his brother Teddy, who was a ruthless wheeler-dealer type — Teddy went on to become Bruce's partner in the McLaren team, which was quite incongruous. I was convinced that Timmy and Teddy must have had different fathers.'

In keeping with the other Australian-based events, the race was demanding and aggressively close. Graham Hill had the last word in this first Tasman series. With Brabham retiring with engine trouble, McLaren took 2nd and Matich kept Bib Stillwell off the podium by less than a tenth of a second, in arguably the best finish of the entire series. 'I was nursing that motor,' says Matich. 'Really, it was hopeless. The thing I was good at was getting the best out of the motor, gearing the car, setting it up to suit the way the motor worked. I remember, for example, at a meeting in the early days when I lost a cylinder during the race and still won — with three cylinders — because I had the car set up so well that the loss of speed was largely accounted for. My theory in those days was a little unusual. It was not so much about maximum power, but maximum use of power — efficiency.'

Frank Matich would have bittersweet memories from the first Tasman series. He had learnt so much about the wider conflict that surrounded the on-track events, issues of politics and management. He laughs about it now. 'You have to understand, Jack was an old bastard, and I mean that in a competitive sense. I'm not putting Jack down. He had offered me a drive in Formula Junior a year earlier. We also discussed a Formula 1 drive involving my Total sponsorship, but Total Australia wanted me to race here, not in Europe. Rob Walker also offered me a drive in Formula 1, following a recommendation from Stirling Moss, but I wasn't interested in going overseas, because it would have meant severing all ties here — including that Total sponsorship.

'I have the greatest respect for Jack, but he was from that rough-and-tumble speedway background, and that was no gentleman's sport. He was the first of the really hard-nosed competitors, and the attitude was: do whatever it took, get away with whatever you could. Who was it started blocking? Jack Brabham. He was the first person to block, and cover position. Once upon a time that was considered unsportsmanlike. Today it's standard practice. He was also famous for throwing up rocks and dust from the edge of the circuit, even overfilling his oil tank so the excess would spew out behind him at his rivals. At the same time, you would never for a moment, have any fear of him bumping you off or running into you. He was just ruthless, a phenomenal competitor.'

Hard driving was one thing, but off the circuit itself, there was the occasional dirty trick, and in most cases, the culprits were never found. 'Bruce McLaren,' Matich recalls, 'spoke of one time he ran out of fuel in a race and later found that someone had put ping pong balls in his fuel tank, reducing its capacity. These were the kind of tricks that went on. I have to say you wouldn't get that kind of behaviour from Bruce. He was exceptional, for the era that was beginning to take over Formula 1.'

* * *

Australia's motor racing heroes were flying in different directions at the start of the 1964 European season. Frank Gardner, who had consistently produced class-winning performances in the Tasman series, was still campaigning Brabham-built Formula 2 cars for John Willment Racing, while developing the AC Cobra for the same team in sports car events. He was to take an important step into the saloon or touring car arena through his warming relationship with Ford. There would also be a rare moment on the Formula 1 stage. Gardner would never lose touch with the team or his friendship with Brabham, which would last a lifetime. He simply couldn't bring himself to 'engineer' the one thing that many other men in his situation would have readily attempted. 'Racing was sport, but it was also my job. I could make much more money driving a sports car or sedan than I could in F1. I was good, but I wasn't world champion material, so I had to decide where my priorities lay. That was with Ford.'

Brabham, meanwhile, was planning the next evolution of his cars for 1964. Dan Gurney had scored 19 championship points in the previous season and the team had finished 3rd in the Constructors Championship, behind Jim Clark's Lotus and the well-established BRM. They would continue to use Coventry Climax engines, constantly working on chassis improvement with designer Ron Tauranac. Four of the first 5 non-championship rounds were in Britain and Brabham won two of them: Silverstone and Aintree. The regular season races, however, proved difficult.

The breakthrough came in the French Grand Prix at Rouen, where Gurney took the win by 24 seconds from Graham Hill, with Brabham 3rd. Brabham could proudly boast his first championship win as a constructor — but he wasn't behind the wheel of the winning car.

The 1964 British Grand Prix at Brands Hatch saw Frank Gardner called up to make his Formula 1 debut, and it was not pleasant. Gardner had already won the touring car race that day, but his Ford-powered Brabham was trapped on the start line and hit from behind. 'The car,' Gardner recalls, 'was in perfect nick. I think it was Chris Amon who stalled in front of me. I moved forward as much as I could and the car behind me got around, but the next car went straight into me.'

The start line collision was typical in a season fraught with problems for the team, but Gardner was thrilled to be part of it. 'There was nothing wrong with the cars. They were the best of that era. They were easy cars to drive in the wet, which there was plenty of in that part of the world. The only failures were driver failures — putting your helmet on and leaving your brains in the pit and stuff like that were the main bloody causes of retirements.'

It was a different situation in Formula 2, where Gardner finished 4th, kept off the podium by Denny Hulme, in the German round at Avus. He did beat the talented young Austrian, Jochen Rindt. He finished 2nd at Enna Pergusa and 2nd again in the Vanwall Trophy at Snetterton which was won by another exciting new driver, Scotsman Jackie Stewart.

'Stewart was always professional,' says Gardner. 'I remember occasionally knocking wheels, which Jackie did in a fair type of way; he'd never deliberately endanger anybody's wellbeing. That was the thing to know when you were approaching a corner.'

There was a host of Formula 2 races in a season, over a great variety of distances at all the leading circuits — and most of the top drivers were there. Brabham won the French series, and in the entire 18 race European Formula 2 season finished with five wins to Clark's four. There were eight other winners and 20 different drivers on the podium. Gardner enjoyed it immensely. 'They had put together a reasonable prize money structure. The meetings were well run and promoters could see, with the names that were appearing, that they had a good product. It was a bit like going to Warwick Farm after all the other Australian circuits: very professional. When that happens, it's worth doing. You're also driving with the better people.'

John Surtees became the first man to win a World Championship on two wheels and four, after Ferrari team orders conspired to trump a luckless Jim Clark in the final Formula 1 round in Mexico. It had been another demanding year for Jack Brabham, whose retirement with electrical failure was his fifth DNF (Did Not Finish) of the championship. It seemed he had spent more time sitting back in the cockpit discussing where everything went wrong than he did racing. He was yet to savour a victory in his own car.

Frank Gardner finished 1964 with a retirement, due to a blown head gasket, driving with Paul Hawkins in a Ford Galaxie in the *Rand Daily Mail* 9 hour race in South Africa. They stayed on for the South African Grand Prix on New Year's Day, 1965. Gardner had the rare opportunity to contest a full championship round again, while Hawkins made his Formula 1 debut. Hawkins was the surprise of the race, qualifying his Ford-powered Brabham 16th but finishing 9th, just behind the man who built the car. Gardner finished

12th, in a BT11. It was the first time three Australians had competed in the same Formula 1 race, and all three finished in the top half of the field.

Within a week, Gardner was back in New Zealand for the second Tasman series. 'Graham Hill wanted to do the Formula 1 race at Kyalami. It wasn't a championship round. Alan Challis, who was later to become chief mechanic at Williams, and I were recruited to help out. Graham could only drive the Brabham if it had a BRM engine in it, so the chassis and everything arrived in South Africa and the BRM engine came out later. Alan and I installed the engine and then were Graham's mechanics for the race, which we won. Then the same car went to East London [South Africa] for the first round of the championship, with the same engine, same gearbox, of which not a great deal was left! I patched it up and drove it there. I had one mechanic in the pit — the other was me! Nevertheless, we got it home in one piece. Graham had driven the team BRM car. Then we drove to Johannesburg, to the airport, and flew Mauritius, Cocos Islands, Perth, Adelaide, Melbourne, Sydney then hooked up with a flight across to Auckland, then drove to Pukekohe for practice on Thursday for the New Zealand Grand Prix drive on the Saturday. You hadn't been to bed or anything. You just had to get yourself ready. All those blokes were on the plane ... Jimmy Clark and others.

'It was bloody dangerous really. But no one really thought it was. No one actually said, "This is dangerous." The money you had in your pocket certainly didn't make it worthwhile. It was a few rand ... it was all pennies.'

In 1965, the rule makers who changed the format of the Tasman series could afford to smile, because their falling in with Formula 1 specifications attracted a brilliant array of drivers, though Jack Brabham and Frank Matich were absent for the early races. In Matich's case, it was disillusionment, again; this time with promoters in New Zealand. 'They were notoriously poor payers. I hadn't been paid for the previous year's trip. There was also the risk to supply lines — we still didn't have great quantities of spares for motors. It was better to consolidate back home where my sponsors were. I wasn't the only one in that situation. It just wasn't worth our while sometimes, going over there.' Matich was still making big money out of his sports car racing.

Leo Geoghegan was yet to experience that. He recalls great excitement at receiving his first invitation from the promoters, following his success back in Australia. 'We took the Lotus Cortina for the support races and I drove the

Lotus 32 in the New Zealand Grand Prix. That was the only event we contested, but it was unique because the Lotus was the first racing car to be airlifted across the Tasman. Qantas gave us a certificate to commemorate the occasion. It was taken in a specially constructed Boeing 707 with a massive hinged door. We strapped the car on its side, against the bulkhead. It wouldn't fit in the hold. Until then, the cars had to be sent by sea, and it required numerous cartons of beer to be distributed to every wharfie involved to make sure they got there, tied down properly, in time for the race.' Geoghegan would later have the same problems with promoters that Matich faced.

In the grand prix at Pukekohe, Graham Hill took out his frustration at losing the world title. He was in command from the start. Frank Gardner finished 2nd after a close fight with New Zealander Jim Palmer. Leo Geoghegan finished 6th, 3 laps down, but the first of the 1.5 litre entries. 'It was a big deal,' Leo recalls, of his first Tasman series event, 'but we thought we were a big deal ourselves — until we got beaten!'

In the following round Gardner proved that in a competitive car he could match it with the world's best. Clark beat him by 11 seconds, with Palmer 3rd. 'Those blokes were formidable drivers and they were in open-wheelers all year. I was chopping and changing from touring cars to sports cars, and doing a fair amount of engineering work as well. I had to stay within my limits in those circumstances.

'As for beating local drivers like Jimmy Palmer, that was always very hard. You also have to remember that we weren't local drivers any more. We had to stop and think which part of the world we were in that weekend, which way the water was running down the plug hole. For the blokes who were on their home tracks, well it was like taking their dog for a walk. We'd come in on a plane. They'd get out of their own beds. I'd no sooner got there than I'd be with Alec checking the gear, off to crack test a crankshaft or something. Glen Abbey, who ran the team for Alec, was the mainstay, backed up by the iron-clad Bob Grange and with them alongside you, you knew you had the best car possible from the parts that were available.'

Clark made it a hat-trick of wins before the series turned to Australia, where Brabham, Matich, Stillwell, Gardner, Leo Geoghegan, Davison, McLaren, Phil Hill, Graham Hill and Palmer brought another massive crowd to Warwick Farm. Once again Matich would prove to be a match for them. In 1964, following that first eye-opening Tasman series, he had continued to race sports cars with great success, but he still felt the sting of what he believed was betrayal. He had decided to go it alone and not stay under the Brabham team umbrella. He knew that he was well down the pecking order, so he determined to make his Brabham the best. 'I tried as best I could to improve the car, stiffening the chassis and other things, but this time I kept it to myself. Ron Tauranac was a nice guy, but everything I had given him the previous year had gone to Jack and I was going to be racing Jack again early in 1965. I was learning, by then, to look after myself. But … you know it might be a bit strange to say this … our priority was still the sports cars. We were developing a new version of the Lotus 19, the 19B, after one of our mechanics, Bruce Richardson, wrote off the first one on a test day at Warwick Farm, while I tested one of the Elfins.'

Matich had carved 3 seconds from his own lap record when taking pole position and jumped them at the start. It was crowded, though, with Clark and Hill soon returning the favour, and by lap 9 Brabham found a way past Matich as well. Davison, Phil Hill, McLaren and Gardner were forced out with various problems. Clark was on a streak that only he could sustain in the face of such a challenge. The real fight was Brabham's defence of 2nd place as his tyres faded and Matich attacked. Clark won by more than a minute, but Brabham's lead on Matich as they crossed the line was only 5.4 seconds. 'My steering locked up in that race,' says Matich. 'It got tighter and tighter until it took the skin off my hands towards the end. They were bleeding. I don't know how I finished. But everybody's got a story. Very rarely did you have a race where nothing went wrong. The trouble is, some blokes work out their excuses before the race.'

Stillwell was 4th, beating Graham Hill and Palmer, with Geoghegan 8th, ahead of newcomer Rocky Tresise. What a race for such a driver to contest. Like the pioneers who preceded him, Tresise must have wandered the friendly pit lane and paddock in awe of the faces he had previously seen only in newspapers and magazines. Tresise was a neighbour, a protégé of Lex Davison, and drove with him in the 1964 Armstrong 500. For him, the Tasman series was a gift. You cannot take moments like that and set them aside for later use; it was time to be spent the way you'd spend your last dollar. The circus travelled to Melbourne again for the 54 lap Sandown 100.

Lex Davison had remained firm friends with Tony Gaze after Gaze retired. In spite of his new career in gliding Gaze kept in touch with the world of motor sport and would not miss the grand prix if he was in Australia when it was on.

It was practice day for the Sandown 100. The cars were out, roaring around the circuit, sharpening their lap times for qualifying, ironing out any wrinkles in their systems. 'I was just on my way to the pits, actually. I had offered to help with the timekeeping for Lex's team,' Gaze recalls. 'When I arrived at the pit area, there was a phone call for the team. I answered it. Someone at the other end said, "Don't come out here. Go and look after Di. Lex has been killed."'

The back straight at Sandown started with a short dash from the right-angled Peters Corner and cars were accelerating fiercely to gain maximum speed in the straight. Davison's Brabham, only recently purchased, slewed off the track, onto the grass and fired into the running rails of the horse racing circuit which runs inside the car racing track. The wooden railing pierced Davison's helmet. It was never determined if he died on impact, or perhaps a fraction of a second before.

'They say he had a heart attack, but I was never sure of that,' recalls Gaze. 'We'd had glider pilots come in to land, suddenly spin into the ground, and they would say it was a heart attack, but I wasn't sure if the pilot hadn't suffered the heart attack because he suddenly realised he was going to die. I don't know, but I think if you were in Lex's position, seeing that you are about to go crashing through the rails at Sandown, the shock might bring on a heart attack.' Others have different opinions.

'It was an absolute mystery,' says Brabham, 'because where he went off was a corner you just didn't go off. There was no way. Obviously he had a problem, with his heart or something, collapsed at the wheel and ran into the fence.'

'The gentlemen racers,' Gardner recalls. 'There was Bib Stillwell with dealerships. With Lex it was shoes. They were a special breed. Irrespective of whether the bloke made a mistake, had a heart attack or what, it was a great loss. To go off where he was, he must have had a heart attack, I'd say. It's always a shock to the system when you see those things. No matter how strongly you try to erase them, they come back to you, some days, with a rush.'

Whatever happened that day, motor sport had lost one of its most adventurous and admired competitors, one of the last swashbuckling lairs of the old school. Davison had been a popular, inspirational figure who lived in a world that few people could ever have access to, though many no doubt aspired to it. He was part of the fantasy of top-level sport. Manufacturers and money were slowly changing priorities in the mid-1960s, laying the foundations for the cold-hearted competition of later eras. Lex Davison was the one of the last links to a glorious past, where money was certainly the means, but never the end. Australia loves its battlers. It also loves its elite, when the elite show a sense of spirit, sportsmanship and character.

Leo Geoghegan had competed in a support race at that meeting. 'I got on very well with Lex because as I was coming up through my apprenticeship from Formula Junior to one and a half litres, aiming for two and a half litre cars, he used to say, "You haven't driven in a real man's race until you've driven in the Australian Grand Prix." When I finally did, in 1963, I finished two places ahead of him and he slowed down and waited for me on the cool-down lap, then stuck his arm out and shook hands with me. He also brought through a lot of young drivers. I didn't find out until many years later at a reunion that Lex had plans to put me in a good car and send me overseas to race. Of course he never got the chance. He was a top man.'

For so many drivers, Davison was a father figure, and his death was a great shock — most Australians involved in motor racing had come to believe that it was the younger, less experienced drivers who were more likely to die. The entire weekend had a surreal feeling.

'People used to refer to him as "old Lex",' says Matich. 'He was only 42. He was a gentleman, a thorough gentleman. But the real tragedy of the whole saga was what was still to come.'

As if celebrating the traditions that Davison had helped foster, the modern-day heroes staged an entertaining race at Sandown, although the crowd figures were well down on previous events. Jack Brabham prevailed by less than 5 seconds from Clark. It wasn't a happy win. 'Lex's death took the shine off everything for the weekend,' Brabham recalls. 'Lex was an icon. He was motor racing as far as Australia was concerned. Unbelievable.'

The Davison name would live on in Australian motor sport for decades, with grandsons Will and Alex forging promising careers in the new millennium, but Tony Gaze, in 1965, was unaware that his future would also be tied to the dynasty. In 1976, his wife Kay would die of cancer, and he would marry Davison's widow Diana, a year later.

The next round, scheduled for Lakeside in Queensland, was excluded from the points system because few drivers were prepared to transport their cars and equipment from Melbourne to Queensland then back to Tasmania, where the Australian Grand Prix was scheduled, just 1 week later. However, Jim Clark, Frank Gardner and Frank Matich joined Spencer Martin and others to turn on a great contest, which Clark won, but only after Matich dropped out with a faulty spark plug. 'I remember losing a few laps making the repairs,' Matich recalls, 'but Jim Clark had enjoyed our dice so much that when I came out of the pits again he not only waited for me but waved me past so that we could resume the battle! We finished together, but of course I was about 3 laps down.' It was a great race and a great gesture. Gardner and Martin made up the rest of the podium.

The Australian Grand Prix of 1965 was held at Longford, the fast but awkward circuit with two wooden bridges that spelt danger to the onlookers but were little more than a blur for drivers — certainly for Brabham, who reportedly reached a speed of 300 kilometres per hour there. Rocky Tresise had missed the Sandown race following Davison's death but returned in his Cooper and qualified on the fourth row of a grid that was as packed with talent as any other round of the series had been. He was starting alongside Jim Palmer and in front of Bob Jane, who had decided in a rare open-wheel excursion, to race an Elfin with a 1500cc Ford engine. By that time, the 1500s were hopelessly outclassed, but Jane was keen to beat similarly equipped rivals.

Frank Matich recalls a special ceremony held before the start of the race. 'It was a minute's silence, with the presentation of a special trophy. Rocky Tresise, the poor bloody kid, was just standing there with tears streaming down his face. Then everybody said, "Right, 2 minutes to go." That kid was crying when he got in the car. He was last away, behind all the 1500s which he should have been in front of, and tried to pass them all.'

Bruce McLaren roared off from pole position to secure the lead. Graham Hill and Brabham diced for second. Clark, who had suffered from a misfire, Matich, Phil Hill and Stillwell were also right up there. One of the drivers in front of Tresise as he tried to recapture those lost positions was Bob Jane, who also had his hands full. Jane passed New Zealand driver Roly Levis. Tresise moved to follow him. Just as Tresise emerged from behind Levis, his car veered out of control and left the track. He was killed on impact.

'The car went through a wire fence,' says Matich, 'a four-strand barbed-wire fence, not even a metre from the road. A photographer was also killed. Hell of a waste.'

Frank Gardner agreed. 'He hadn't worked his way through the ranks. He came from a very wealthy family. He was part of the social set. In those early days it was mostly the upper class who got to drive race cars, and at the time he wasn't a lad that most of the people knew. With some of those blokes you often asked, "Are you serious?" It was like Bob Jane in that Maserati in the early days. I think he went off on every corner. Mind you, while Bob might have called himself a lunatic, he became a very successful lunatic.'

'You have to understand that in that period,' says Matich, 'Melbourne was the home of racing, the home of CAMS, the home of the grand prix scene. The Melbourne teams decided what they were going to do and sometimes didn't look very deeply into it. The kid was Lex's protégé, like his own son. There was lots of talk about the importance of the Lex Davison team continuing. Rocky shouldn't have been in that race, at that time, after that episode. It upset everybody. Shocking.'

Bob Jane lasted only another few laps, as the race was whittled down to a handful of the world's finest exponents of Formula 1 racing. At half distance the plague of mechanical failures struck Matich again, and he pulled his car to an uneasy halt with broken suspension. 'It was very, very scary. I was flat out at the time, about 270 kilometres an hour, when the wheel just folded back on the front and the car just wanted to pull into the trees. It took a long while to stop it.'

At the finish, McLaren had just 3.3 seconds on Brabham, who crossed barely a second ahead of Phil Hill. Graham Hill, Clark, Stillwell and Palmer were all on the same lap — it had been a memorable race. Frank Gardner didn't finish, which turned out to be a costly result after a blazing start of 3 point-scoring rounds. In the final tally, Jim Clark, with 35 points, had won the second Tasman Cup by 11 points from McLaren, with Brabham another 3 points away in 3rd. Gardner, after 5 consecutive pointless rounds, finished tied for 4th with Hill and Palmer, only 6 points behind Brabham.

John Willment had decided to put in a more consistent effort in Formula 1, so Gardner rushed back to England. He finished 4th in the BT11 behind Mike Spence, Jackie Stewart and Jo Bonnier in the Race of Champions at Brands Hatch on 13 March. He then struggled on the Monaco streets for 29 laps before the engine gave out. It was the first of a series of disappointing finishes for the under-funded team.

Frank Gardner's best result in Formula 1 in 1965 was not only outside the confines of the championship, but part of a rare defeat for Jim Clark, who was again dominating Formula 1. In the Mediterranean Grand Prix at Enna-Pergusa, Sicily on 15 August, Jo Siffert in a Brabham BRM beat Clark in a mighty finish, with 0.3 of a second separating them at the flag. Gardner was a distant but impressive 3rd, beating Denny Hulme, Innes Ireland and Jack Brabham. He barely remembers the race, but he does remember what Mike Hailwood did with his car. 'He was driving for Tim Parnell, and put his car into Lake Pergusa. The lake was full of snakes. Now the team wanted to recapture the car, and I was the only bloke around who could swim. I said, "You give me £100 Tim, if you value the car that much, and I'll swim out with a rope and hook it up to the car." Tim said, in his Yorkshire accent, "I'll give you yer bloody 'undred." I said, "Right, then give it to me now." He said, "Can't yer bloomin' wait?" I said, "Look, I might get bitten by a snake out there and die." We haggled and he gave me the money. I gave it to one of the mechanics, stripped to my underpants, tied the rope to my body and dived into this polluted, acid-type lake, chock-a-block full of snakes, dived down about 25 feet, tied the rope to the car and came back up. I was reasonably fit, and it wasn't much of a problem. Tim said, "Bugger that. That was too easy. I want half my 'undred back." He never got it back.'

Jack Brabham endured another troubled season, contesting only 7 of the remaining 10 races. His best finish was 3rd in the final round at Watkins Glen. '1964 and 1965 were really bad years for us. Building cars, racing, it wasn't easy. I even thought about giving up the driving, but really, that's the only part I enjoyed. That was my relaxation. The engine rules in the championship didn't help us. We had our hands tied, because we just didn't have an engine. But I knew in 1965 that the rule change was coming in 1966 and was able to do something about it.'

What Brabham did, from early in 1965, was lay the foundations of a far better car, working with Repco in Australia to head off the next technical change in Formula 1: engine capacity up to 3 litres. Generally, all parties were enthusiastic about the change. There had been a theory that reducing the size of engines made racing safer but it hadn't made any difference to the death or injury rate, and sports car series and open-wheel series in the US had continued to use larger-capacity motors with no notable increase in fatalities. It made for a busy and distracting season in which Brabham's focus on driving would be tested.

Frank Gardner at the end of 1965 would be heading back to Australia for another summer season. He had tested himself again in Formula 1, and his highlights had been high enough to satisfy any doubts about his ability. But the experience also resigned him to the fact that unless he had a competitive drive, he was better off seeking fame and fortune elsewhere. He certainly did that, contesting such a variety of events in such an array of cars that it was a wonder he knew which levers and switches to reach for when he sat behind a wheel.

'Formula 2 or Le Mans cars ... you had to know the art of the situation. You couldn't drive cars like these if your technique wasn't right,' recalls Gardner. 'Those open-wheelers didn't have wings on them at that stage. They were quite quick in a straight line because there was no drag or down force affecting any wings. Cars like this were extremely slippery: 250 kilometres an hour or more down the Le Mans straight.

'The technique came in around the corners. You had to work your feet and your hands, otherwise you were working against the car. I'll give you some basics about driving. You wouldn't stand on the deck of a ship with your legs together — the first thing you do is space them. Same in a car. Second thing is, get your centre of gravity down. Third, keep your shoulders square — the more square you are in the car the better your intake of information. Balance.'

Gardner was in Europe until late October, completing the 4 rounds of the French Formula 2 championship, part of a 16 race calendar. He drove a Lola T60 powered by a BRM engine to finish 2nd behind Jochen Rindt at Reims, and on the same day drove a Cobra with Innes Ireland in a 12 hour sports car race. That car didn't finish. There were 16 major Formula 2 races in Europe in 1965, starting in March and featuring the usual collection of top drivers. There were 11 different winners, including Brabham. Jim Clark was the only driver to win more than once, though — he took out five races.

Frank Matich was hoping that 1966 would be a turning point; everything had gone wrong in 1965. In the wake of a successful Tasman series he resumed his multi-car attack on the major meetings with the Lotus sports car, and the Brabham BT7. He was also to fly to England to test a sports car which Bruce McLaren had invited him to drive at Le Mans. There were also fresh talks with Rob Walker about a Formula 1 drive. But in June at Lakeside, it all came undone. The schedule of the meeting dictated that Matich practise both of his cars in the same 20 minute session. 'I went out in the Brabham for a few laps, and didn't really have time to put on my overalls; I was just wearing jeans and a nylon shirt. I qualified the Brabham. Then I hopped into the Lotus, and as I was warming up to a fast lap, the throttle jammed open in the straight, at full stick. I steered through the kink and into the Armco to wash off speed, but the impact ruptured the fuel tank and splashed petrol over me and along the road. It caught fire, and the fire caught me.

'Now in those days the safety marshals had this strange idea that if they directed fire retardant onto a burning person, it could kill him. They weren't well trained. So here I am, on fire in a nylon shirt, and running towards two marshals, screaming at them to put the fire out, and they were running away from me. I'll never forget it. Cars were still whizzing past through the black smoke around me. I don't know how I wasn't hit. So I ran towards the pits, where I knew there was an ambulance. The two ambulance men ran away too! They had a blanket, and just dropped it on the ground. To this day I don't know why they ran. I should have asked them, but I was too busy. Thankfully, Bobby O'Neill, Laurie's brother, cleared a fence, ran up to me, and as I bent over to pick up the blanket he knocked me over and rolled me up in it.'

Matich was rushed to the newly constructed Redcliffe Hospital before being transferred to Randwick Hospital in Sydney, where he almost lost his arm to gangrene. An astute nursing sister who had had experience in burns cases overseas called in a specialist surgeon. Matich was out of action for more than 6 months. He later discovered that a silly mechanical error had caused the crash. One of his crew had incorrectly fitted the return spring on the throttle.

In a bizarre coincidence, following the crash, Total's parent company sold their Australian operation to Boral, which then withdrew sponsorship from the Matich team. Matich's injury had given them the opportunity. The Brabham race car, owned by Total, was sold. 'I had nothing,' says Matich. 'By that time my dealership interests had been sold. Everything was in my motor racing. Of course the Lotus had been wrecked.' The row over settlement of the contract and expenses would drag on for 3 years.

Jack Brabham's support for the Tasman series in 1966 would be limited to the final couple of rounds. There was massive change taking place in Formula 1 following the new engine rules. It was testing enough for the factory teams, but for the operation run by Brabham and Ron Tauranac it would be far more exhausting. Repco's 3 litre V8 engine would be ready long before the first championship round in Monaco but it needed testing and development. On New Year's Day Brabham gave it a stern trial in the South African Grand Prix, where it led for 52 of 60 laps before breaking down.

The Tasman series still attracted a powerful international field, including a new face: the cheeky, grinning 26-year-old Scot, Jackie Stewart. Joining Stewart were Jim Clark, Graham Hill and Richard Attwood.

Frank Gardner resumed his deal with Alec Mildren and raced in the southern hemisphere events, winning a 6 hour race at Sandown with new young team-mate Kevin Bartlett in an Alfa Romeo Giulia Ti. Then he was into a Maserati sports car at Lakeside, where he qualified first but retired from the race.

Gardner's frustration would build. He failed to finish the New Zealand Grand Prix, in which Leo Geoghegan finished a credible 5th in his Lotus 32. In race two, at Levin, Gardner led — but his car broke down with just 2 laps remaining, handing Attwood the win from Clark. At Wigram his brakes failed and he collided with Clark; both were unable to restart. Jackie Stewart took his first victory down under, then won again at Teretonga, this time with Gardner chasing hard all the way — he was the only other driver to finish on the same lap, with Palmer 3rd.

For the first Australian round, at Warwick Farm, Alec Mildren produced a new car for Gardner, a Brabham with a V12 Maserati engine fitted instead of the 4 cylinder Coventry Climax he had been using. It was discarded after practice in favour of the spare car, an ex-Bib Stillwell Brabham Climax. Bob Jane turned up in the Ford-powered Elfin he had campaigned in 1965, and Leo Geoghegan also competed in a Lotus 32. Another notable entry was Bartlett, making his debut in the series in a Brabham Ford with 1.5 litre engine. Bartlett had driven in the 1963 Armstrong 500 but it was no secret that his first love was open-wheel racing, and he had pursued that with fierce determination in the past three years. This 'works' drive was his reward.

A newcomer to the series was 2 years older, but had seen less circuit racing. He was the 1966 Australian Formula 2 champion, John Harvey.

The Harvey story is rooted in the blood-stained dirt of Sydney's version of the Roman Colosseum: the Showground Speedway. He watched, a wide-eyed teenager, with his enthusiastic dad, as these malevolent machines roared with rib-rattling menace around a tight circular track, drivers bouncing and twisting as they fought the loose controls. It was an exhibition of tenuous mastery over excessive horsepower. The cars in those days were primitive, brutish animals that threatened at any moment to break loose and wreak destruction among the spectators. And they often did.

Harvey would return to his home in suburban Haberfield dreaming of being part of that Colosseum. His love of engines developed into an apprenticeship in the garage of HW Crouch in Sydney. By the age of 17 he was hanging around sporting car clubs. He went to Bathurst for the Easter meetings in the 1950s to help out various teams and watch the wealth of car and motorcycle racing. He remembers watching Gardner and Brabham competing. At first he was happy to be an observer, but then he met some club members who drove speedway cars, and they offered him a drive. 'I soon made it known,' he recalls, 'that I'd like to have a full-time go at it. So they gave me a competitive drive at Windsor Speedway in 1957. It was a scratch race, about 5 laps, involving new drivers like myself and a couple of guys who had to test their cars after repair work. I didn't know much, so I just got to the front and kept going!'

He had natural speed and an affinity with his equipment that took him to the NSW title at his first attempt in 1958 and in the next 5 years as well, along with the Australian title in 1960. He had progressed to a Kurtis Offenhauser, the car you had to have. 'All motor sport in those days was dangerous, of course, but speedway was raced in close quarters, with fences all around the track. They were made of wood, with large uprights and palings or planks nailed to them. The uprights stuck out from the top a couple of feet, and when cars went over the top or along the top, the drivers got knocked around. A lot of them died. It was a young man's sport. You drove by intuition and reflex for 20 or 25 laps and there was no strategy other than getting to the front as quickly as you possibly could. If you were a back marker, as I was for most of my career, you had to pass 20 or 25 cars . . . sometimes 30 on the bigger tracks. The thing that I attempted to do, and I only ever pulled it off twice, once at the Showground and once at Westmead, was to start at the back and hit the lead on the first lap.'

There were crashes that were heart-pounding in their ferocity. Cars would flick into the air and roll, spin and pirouette up and over the fence. 'Horrible crashes. They were a tough lot. I raced for about 7 years on the east coast and in New Zealand and never got a scratch. I ended up upside down once: crawled out, not a scratch. But during that period a lot of people were killed or injured, two or three a year. Mind you, there were a lot of meetings, summer and winter. We were at it all the time.' In the early days drivers were strapped in by a primitive lap safety belt. They changed to shoulder harnesses, but those were anchored on one side only, on the theory that the car would only turn to one side in an accident. Eventually they progressed to a full harness, with roll bars and compulsory helmets.

One of the most frightening crashes Harvey was involved in also became one of his more amusing memories of speedway. He was racing at Sydney Showground one night and found Bob Holt a particularly tough opponent — in more ways than one. They came together as Harvey tried to pass and the result was one of the most spectacular crashes seen at the venue. Holt's car launched so high that it touched the overhead lights and broke the arm of a spectator sitting in the grandstand above the pits. Still photographs show the car vertical, its nose 3 metres above ground. Somehow, Holt survived uninjured. Harvey was also lucky, saved from Holt's vengeful crew only by the presence of a good friend who happened to be a middleweight boxing champion.

'I never saw Bob Holt after that. But many years later, I think it was 1987, I was testing a solar car for General Motors, USA, just north of Alice Springs. We'd pulled over to the side of the road for some adjustments. Then I saw a gravel truck pulling up just ahead and its driver got out to see if we needed any help. As he came towards us he said, "What kind of car is that?" Without looking up I told him. Then we looked at each other. He said, "You're John Harvey aren't you?" I said, "You're Bob Holt!" Bugger me. We had a chat about the speedway incident and a good laugh, on the side of the road, in the middle of nowhere, about 30 years after it happened.'

Harvey rates his greatest dirt-track achievement as a win in the first 50 lap race at Sydney Showground, the KLG Derby in November 1963. 'I set a track record that stood for something like 12 years. They also staged a 100 lapper in Brisbane the following May. It was called the "Marathon". I won that too. Those were tough races. The car had to be good. You were so busy. Over that distance you'd be lapping a lot of cars. You were concentrating so hard you rarely had a chance to check your oil pressure, fuel pressure or water temperature gauges. If you had to look at a gauge for some problem, you were history.'

Another highlight of the extremely popular speedway racing in those days was match-racing. Promoters were always coming up with concepts to make the most of the personalities and their skills, especially when visiting legends such as Bob Tattersall were available. Harvey was pitted against Tattersall in one such event in Sydney and beat the American in three out of three races.

'I think it was the first time he'd ever been beaten in Australia,' recalls Harvey. 'He didn't like it much. But he was a good guy and a very good racer. We had a chat about it and he said, "You'll never do that again." I said, "That's okay. I've done it once. I don't need to do it again!"'

Harvey switched to circuit racing at the end of the 1964–65 season. It was safety — or lack of it — that triggered his move. He was working as a car salesman for his sponsor, Ron Phillips. Phillips had little interest in motor racing at the time, but after watching a few speedway meetings he said, 'This is the most dangerous thing I've ever seen. We've got to get you out of this!' Phillips offered to support a touring car campaign. John chose a Mini Cooper S.

'The Mini used to flex when cornering,' Harvey recalls, 'and the doors would fly open as we were driving. So we used to get a leather strap out of the boot and tie it around the door and the B-pillar when it was closed. It made it hard to get out of the car.' He won his first race, from the rear of the grid. Nothing had changed. The quality of the opposition, however, improved as more and more cars disappeared past Harvey's driver's side window. The highlight of his Mini racing was winning a Lowood 4 hour race in 1965. Soon the touring car titans of the day — Beechey, Jane and Geoghegan — were among his opponents. There was also a firm friendship forged with another young driver. 'One of the first people to come along and welcome me and offer me help if I needed it was Kevin Bartlett.'

In mid-1965 Harvey, with Ron Phillips's backing, turned to open-wheelers, buying a BT14 from Bib Stillwell. He was still racing the Mini, but the BT14 delivered his first dry mouth, high blood pressure special at Bathurst. He knew the circuit, but not at such speed. 'The race was a combination of sports cars and open-wheelers. Frank Matich won easily in a sports car. Jim Palmer finished second in a BT11 Climax and I finished 3rd. It was beautiful to drive, but as you travelled down the main straight, 150 miles an hour, 160, you could see the tyres growing, lifting from the wheel with centrifugal force, the side walls shrinking away from the rim.' It was just as Leo Geoghegan had described it when he first raced on the mountain: exploration, pushing the boundaries in every direction, pressing dangerously into the unknown.

With the BT14 Harvey finished 2nd to Spencer Martin in the 1966 Gold Star series after winning the NSW Road Racing Championship and the national Formula 2 title. 'My race with Spencer for the Gold Star was a classic. It had come down to the final round at Warwick Farm. Kev Bartlett and Frank Gardner had shot away from us but they weren't eligible to win the Gold Star at the time, so we let them go. I stuck on Spencer's tail, just waiting for a mistake, but when we struck lapped traffic he got past them and I was held up. That left me half a dozen car lengths behind. I had one more crack at him late in the race and nearly got past, but he squeezed me out and went on to win by a couple of lengths.

'I had a determination to do well. I had to learn new strategies, but I picked that up as I went along. I beat Leo a couple of times at Oran Park. It was good training for the Tasman series. Leo was good. Very smooth. Very quick. He had really good equipment. To beat Leo was a feather in your cap because he was the top man.'

Kevin Bartlett was stepping up again in the Tasman series, but not quite high enough. Like Harvey, he would be condemned to a 1.5 litre car, which made him part of the second tier in each race. 'I always maintained that you had to have the 2.5 litre car to be competitive, but we weren't a big operation. I was the chief mechanic, I drove the truck. The only thing I didn't do was hang out the pit board when I drove past. That was a bit beyond me. But I got to drive a racing car and got paid for it. I wasn't overawed by the international drivers. They were only a couple of years older than me, if that, and we all became friends, but I learnt a lot from them because they had all the latest gear and knew the latest trends.'

'Kevin had been around the circuits a bit longer than Harvey,' recalls Leo Geoghegan. 'Harvey had been doing speedway. They were both good steerers. Kevin was pretty hairy in those days. I had to give him an extra foot of space, because he didn't realise he was going to need it, but I did. That's what you always have to remember: the difference between the experienced and inexperienced blokes. The experienced drivers could go around 6 inches apart. The inexperienced don't know how close they are to losing control.'

The Australians were enraptured spectators as the 1966 Tasman series hit Warwick Farm. Jim Clark enjoyed a trouble-free race for a change, winning easily from Graham Hill, who had returned to replace Richard Attwood. Frank Gardner chased Hill home to take 3rd, a satisfying result because it was his second consecutive podium finish and he beat the impressive Stewart by nearly 16 seconds. Geoghegan finished 7th, Harvey 8th, Jane 9th. Bartlett retired after 25 laps.

In the Australian Grand Prix it was Graham Hill's turn. Frank Gardner duelled for 2nd place with Clark, who had some mechanical trouble. Gardner was able to beat him by 43 seconds. Once again, Kevin Bartlett and John Harvey acquitted themselves with distinction, finishing 5th and 8th respectively.

'I remember thinking at the time,' says Harvey, 'that this was absolutely sensational. It was my first Australian Grand Prix, and to finish 8th in the 1.5 litre car was just amazing. I'd been racing for about a year in single-seaters and I was stoked with that.'

Despite all the excitement produced by former world champions, future world champions and exciting young Australians at the Australian Grand Prix, the Sandown Park International 500 managed to upstage it in 1966 because Brabham was back — 55,000 people swarmed around the circuit to see him.

To John Harvey's great surprise, the attitude of the world's great drivers was refreshing. 'Jimmy Clark was so friendly, I couldn't believe it. I had the impression that you wouldn't be able to talk to those guys, but he was terrific. The funny thing was that Jack was our hero — he was everyone's hero — and yet he was the hardest to talk to. It wasn't his fault. When he was back home he was so incredibly busy attending to everything, and everywhere he went he was surrounded by people, from Repco to all the other associates.'

Brabham was not using the Repco V8 that he had prepared for the Formula 1 season, but he staged a fine fight from pole, launching clear of Stewart at the start, only to lose his lead 2 laps later. Hill and Clark were behind them. Jim Palmer and Frank Gardner renewed their acquaintance. The field was reduced to five after 6 laps, when Brabham stopped on the back of the circuit. Stewart increased his lead.

It was developing into two races in one, because further back, in the lesser-powered cars, Geoghegan, Bartlett, Greg Cusack, Harvey and Les Howard were staging a terrific contest for the fans. Harvey was out on lap 7, and he wasn't the only driver of a 1.5 litre car to have problems. Geoghegan was gone on lap 17. They were cutting each other up with their pace. 'The five cars were nose to tail,' recalls Geoghegan. 'It was very interesting, because Kevin and Les were young and driving a bit over their heads. Greg and I were behind them, looking at each other, shaking our heads and saying, "Look at these silly buggers". I wondered how we were going to get past them, because they were at the limit. It didn't matter, because I was out pretty soon after that, but it would have looked good while it lasted. I think if it had kept going it would have ended up in tears.'

Stewart won, from Clark, Hill, Palmer and Gardner. Howard, 6th, won the small car struggle.

By this time Leo Geoghegan was starting to familiarise himself with the top drivers, but more importantly, with their technical staff. 'From them,' he says, 'you could really learn.' He chose not to go to Longford for the final round; this turned out to be a wise decision.

The final round of the 1966 series at Longford, scene of so much excitement and tragedy, was a BRM demonstration. Stewart and Hill dominated an eight-car field that included Brabham, Clark and Gardner. In his first series down under, Jackie Stewart had danced a highland jig through 8 rounds, scoring 45 points, 15 more than his team-mate Graham Hill, and 20 more than Jim Clark. It was debatable which driver went home happiest, though, because while Stewart had won four races, Hill's two victories were both in grands prix. Frank Gardner took home 18 points, and was the highest-placed Australian.

'They paid us start money. I think it was a thousand quid a race,' recalls Gardner. 'Alec Mildren's car that I drove, with the two engines, would have cost about £8000. We were the best-finishing privateers and one of the most successful local teams in the history of the series. I knew I could run up the front with those people, which was what it was all about. I mean, if you've got a hard luck story and you want someone to listen, get a Labrador.'

Bartlett remembers Gardner as a great team-mate, but tough. 'He had his own plans and ideas, which he didn't always disclose to me, but he didn't step in my way either. Frank was a mentor to me because the machine he left at the end of the series would be the machine that I would drive in Australia for the rest of the year. He would not only leave all the little adjustments that he had made, but explain them all to me. I learnt a lot about set-up from Frank. During a race, he didn't worry about me because he knew I wouldn't punt him off.'

'Frank Gardner spent more time in Europe and worked on a higher level of technology and a wider spread of cars,' says John Harvey, 'but I think Frank Matich was his match behind the steering wheel and with his use of what technology he had. I mean, he was smart.'

'They went in different directions,' says Kevin Bartlett. 'Matich, I feel, did himself a disservice during the era of the Tasman series. The main attraction was open-wheelers. Matich went the way of sports cars, which were far more popular than they are these days, but I think he was influenced by Bruce McLaren, who was a good friend of Frank's, and Denny Hulme, who were slaying 'em in the American sports car series. Matich built superb sports cars and went down that path, and when he did it, he went very commercial. He'd make one for himself and one for sale to somebody else. It's a shame he didn't stick with open-wheelers, but he would have had good reason not to. Of course, that would change in the Formula 5000 era.'

CHAPTER SEVEN

The Man, the Car, the Moment

When it comes to Jack Brabham, there is no greater fan than Frank Gardner. 'I've never run into a thick champion in my life; they don't exist. The bloke is a champion because he's thought and worked his way there. It doesn't happen the way the storybooks would have you believe. He was probably before his time, and he was the best lateral thinker I've ever run into. Talent-wise, as a driver, on his day he could beat anybody. I mean, I have seen Moss and everybody else of that era, but out of all the mist and shit it was Brabham who saw the chequered flag first.'

1966 was the year Australia changed to decimal currency. Formula 1 was changing its currency too: the wins would now be traded in 3 litre engines. Ferrari was the favourite, given the team's vast experience, the availability of suitable engines and their renowned reliability. Jack Brabham was the unknown quantity. He and Ron Tauranac had constructed a space-frame chassis, and he fitted a five-speed Hewland gearbox and the Repco V8 engine that had been coming together since 1964. The beauty of the Repco-Brabham project was its simplicity and affordability. It's first win was by 7 seconds in the

BRDC International Trophy. The championship would prove a little tougher than that.

'Jack could run away from them in a race, provided the car was right and he'd been to bed. You see, you never knew if Jack had been to bed or spent the night in the workshop,' recalls Frank Gardner.

While watching the Brabham phenomenon continue, Gardner was forging a special place of his own; he was driving a Lola T61 Cosworth in Formula 2 for the Midlands team, a sports car for Sid Taylor and a McLaren Elva Mk2 for Alan Brown Racing. His first big international race, however, was at Sebring in the US, where his Ford partners, Alan Mann Racing, were continuing their development of the GT40. He was competing so often that extreme weather simply became part of the business.

'It snowed on occasions. At the Nurburgring it could be snowing on one side of the circuit and not on the other. That was quite exciting,' he says, tongue in cheek. 'It was always a case of just doing the job, not trying to do the impossible — the pearly gates were jammed with people who'd tried that. Most blokes in those days did it because they chose to. Had there been a war on, they probably would have been fighter pilots, like Tony Gaze, but there was no war on, so they raced cars.'

The Ford connection was growing stronger, and would soon include saloon or touring cars, which was fine with Gardner. 'Well Brabham's first World Championship was worth under $100,000. Until Bernie Ecclestone came along and made it professional, Formula 1 was as amateurish as anything else. The money just wasn't there. I could have gone to Formula 1 with BRMs or Coopers or with Jack and the best signing on fee was £8000. Then, if you were lucky, you got 25 per cent of the prize money. You paid your own way around. You may have got a little bit extra from sponsors. The tyre companies hadn't come into it with big money at that stage. Ford chose to run a touring car program. The reason was that every time Jimmy Clark won a Formula 1 race in the Lotus Cosworth they would say, 'Clark wins', not 'Ford wins'. So touring cars were better value for them.

'I was told, "Swallow your pride. Don't take Formula 1. Drive touring cars. The whole thing will be organised by Alan Mann. We will pay you £15,000 and give you a couple of cars to drive around in, pay all your expenses, international flights or whatever. Here's a five year contract with an option for five more."

'Frank didn't have a good Formula 1 team to go to, otherwise he would have handled himself very well in that area,' Brabham recalls. 'When I had Dan Gurney, there wasn't a place for Frank. The other problem we had was that Ron Tauranac didn't rate Frank, unfortunately. They didn't see eye to eye. I reckon if they had, Frank could have continued driving for us.'

Gardner describes the touring car of 1966: 'They were compromises. An open-wheeler was made around you to fit and balance and get all the frequencies happening together. The touring car didn't have torsional rigidity. Tyres were not appropriate. You would use the same tyres for wet and dry tracks sometimes. You could alter springs, roll bars and things, but it was totally insensitive to change because of the chassis flexing. I preferred the car to be set up soft so you could transfer the weight and put less strain on some of the parts over the race distance, which was 75 to 100 kilometres. You needed to be reasonably fit, and you had to look after your gear.' He was still swapping cars one or two times during the course of a meeting, having gained permission to drive anything, basically, provided it wasn't Formula 1 and didn't compete with Ford.

It had been a shaky start to the Formula 1 championship for Brabham. Jackie Stewart and John Surtees won the first 2 rounds but in round 3, in France, he capitalised on problems suffered by John Surtees in a Cooper Maserati and Lorenzo Bandini in a Ferrari and took over on lap 32 of 48, holding on to beat new Ferrari driver Mike Parkes by only 9 seconds. Brabham was the first man to win a Formula 1 championship round in a car of his own construction. 'It was one of the great wins of my life. After all the work we'd put in over the years, to win like that was very encouraging. We did to Ferrari with the Brabham what we'd done to them with the Cooper at the same track back in 1960. My team-mate Denny Hulme finished 3rd. We won everything. The Formula 2 race as well, with a Honda engine.'

It was also a triumph for a great partnership, with Ron Tauranac, and yet theirs was not the kind of relationship many people imagined. 'It wasn't a personal thing,' says Brabham. 'It was an engineering thing. His engineering and mine, what we were aiming to do, was compatible. We clicked in that area, but socially we didn't click.'

Ferrari kept away from the following round, at Brands Hatch. Brabham and Hulme qualified 1 and 2 on the grid. That's how they finished. 'By that stage,' says Brabham, 'we felt we had the measure of the Ferraris. The Coopers and

Lotuses were coming on strong but they had quite a bit of trouble with reliability. We knew that in the long run they would be hard to beat.'

The only concern for the Brabham team when they arrived at Zandvoort late in July for the Dutch Grand Prix, was talk in the media about Brabham's age. He responded to that by emerging from the garage, stooped, wearing a false beard and using a walking stick. 'The press had been giving me a hard time because I turned 40. They called me the "old man of motor racing", so I figured if that's what they thought, I'd show them. Luckily for me, I won — if I hadn't, the press would have murdered me.' He now led the championship by 16 points from Graham Hill; then it was 2 points to Jackie Stewart, 1 point to Bandini and Jochen Rindt and another 1 point to Denny Hulme.

Neither of the Brabham team cars could make the four-car front row for the German Grand Prix, but Brabham remembers it as a very important win. 'Everyone wants to win at the Nurburgring because it's such a special track, but to win it that year, the first year of the 3 litre cars, and in the rain, which made it very difficult, that was a great feeling.'

Brabham entered round 7 at Monza, with 39 championship points to Hill's 17. In the month between the German and Italian grands prix the other teams had worked hard to prepare themselves for one late lunge at the title. Richie Ginther turned up as Honda declared its hand. Dan Gurney finally had the V12 engine he wanted. BRM had sorted out its troublesome H16 engines and fitted those. So did Lotus. Even Ferrari and Maserati had not been idle, upgrading their engines to combat the rock-solid Brabham-Repco combination. Bruce McLaren was still not ready to return to racing, having experimented with different engines in early rounds, then taken a break to re-group in his first season as manufacturer.

Monza was to be a better test for Brabham, who couldn't muster enough speed to go higher than a third row start. He fought with three Ferraris until lap 8, when he discovered the hard way that a screw had not been tightened before the race, and an oil leak was about to claim him. Ludovico Scarfiotti and Mike Spence gave Ferrari a 1–2 finish. Of all the factory drivers capable of winning, Scarfiotti would have been Brabham's choice, because he was no threat for the title. Graham Hill and John Surtees had been the only drivers who could have made a challenge for the title, and they too, had dropped out of the race. That result had given Brabham his third World Championship, with 2 rounds remaining.

The final rounds in the US and Mexico were an anti-climax to a feat that, in those times, was outstanding. It would become clear decades later that this feat would probably never be achieved again. Formula 1 would never allow the individual, however great his intellect or wealth, to combine the demanding tasks of designing, building, preparing and driving in the same team in the same season, let alone win the championship.

The Brabham superiority was only enforced by that year's Formula 2 results. In many cases, those events were run in conjunction with Formula 1, emphasising the demands on Brabham, who won 10 of 16 Formula 2 races. The Formula 2 championship in 1966 was as powerful as ever, attracting the usual influx of Formula 1 greats along with a host of would-be champions like Jacky Ickx and Jean-Pierre Beltoise. 'We'd do 53 races a year, week to week, in all kinds of cars,' Brabham recalls. 'It was physically demanding but enjoyable. Winning in other cars was a lot of fun. For example, winning the British Touring Car championship in a Mustang in 1965 was very satisfying, especially when I was racing against Jimmy Clark and people like that.'

After a slow start to the year, Frank Gardner ended 1966 with a remarkable string of consistently strong results in sports, saloon and Formula 2 cars. From May onwards, he drove for four different teams all over Europe, over all kinds of distances. He was on the podium three times in 13 top–five finishes, and had only four retirements. His main employer was Alan Mann, who virtually was Ford, organising, making decisions, with occasional fatherly advice from Ford Managing Director Walter Hayes. That year at Le Mans, three teams with GT40s were pressed into action. New Zealanders Bruce McLaren and Chris Amon drove the Shelby factory team GT40 to victory ahead of team-mates Denny Hulme and Ken Miles, with the Holman-Moody Ford team providing the third-placed car, driven by Ronnie Bucknum and Dick Hutcherson. Gardner and Sir John Whitmore retired with transmission failure in the Alan Mann entry after 6½ hours.

But the year wasn't over until Gardner had returned to Australia to race for Alec Mildren, and he won the Hordern trophy at Warwick Farm on 4 December.

Frank Matich had returned to racing in a Mini Cooper at Bathurst in October 1966. It had taken him nearly 18 months to recover from burns suffered in the

1965 Lotus crash, months which reduced him once more to subsistence level, economically speaking. Sponsorship and car supply had vanished in the fire at Lakeside. The break, however, did give him plenty of time to think about his next step and plan its execution. Garrie Cooper, from Elfin, proposed that if Matich designed a sports car, he would build it for a good price, provided he could duplicate the chassis for his own cars. They also shared a contract with BP. The first of the Matich sports cars was born, though it was referred to as a 'Traco'. The engine was a 4.5 litre Oldsmobile. The car, built in Laurie O'Neill's Sydney workshop, from leftover Lotus 19 parts and new components from Elfin, would dominate Australian sports car racing for the remainder of the season. 'I was pretty serious,' he says. 'There was talk about dropping the 2.5 litre formula in open-wheel racing, and engines were hard to get. It wasn't worth getting into it when they were going to change it.' The Traco would also be the start of an evolutionary period, the first in a series of Matich masterpieces, another of which was in the pipeline for 1967.

The 1967 season would be a helter-skelter ride for everyone in Formula 1. The South African Grand Prix was back on the calendar, and that meant a 2 January start — just 5 days before the start of the Tasman series, to which many of the top drivers had also committed. The Brabham team-mates were on the front row, but after encountering problems, Hulme finished 3rd and Brabham 5th behind Pedro Rodriguez in a Cooper Maserati. Their next mission was the Tasman series.

BRM was there in force, with Jackie Stewart, Chris Irwin, Piers Courage and Richard Attwood. Jim Clark returned in his V8-powered Lotus, and Brabham provided 2.5 litre Repco V8s for himself and Denny Hulme. The battlers would be drivers like Alec Mildren, racing team-mates Frank Gardner and Kevin Bartlett, along with Leo Geoghegan, in 4 cylinder cars.

Clark won three races to Stewart's one in New Zealand, where the Australians were mostly beset with breakdowns, but there was far more to this series than results. Bartlett said it for everyone when he explained how much fun it was just being part of the circus. 'Frank Gardner and Jimmy Clark were good mates. They both loved golf and waterskiing and I used to be the boy hanging around trying to get a free ski. It was the sort of series where everyone was friends with everyone else. We all attended the same functions together. In a small country like New Zealand, everyone was part of the same big travelling circus as we rolled from event to event. You'd be driving along to the next meeting and all of a sudden you'd notice one of the fellas pull alongside, and there'd be a race on. I tell you, the term 'rent-a-wreck' was invented in those days. The rental cars would get wrecked. There were some blinding chases, some of which involved the local police. There was one particular instance when two or three of us were observed in a 40 mile an hour zone doing 90. I can't mention the two world champions who were involved, but we outran the police. It wasn't out and out hooliganism, but ... you'd think we'd have had enough on the track, wouldn't you?

'Then there were the food fights and the like. It would all start with just one person throwing a bread roll or something and then it would be on until the place was demolished. But one thing about those blokes, they always put their hands in their pockets at the end of the night and paid for it all.

'I loved the racing in New Zealand. The atmosphere was terrific, because when you went to the tracks you also went to various civic receptions where you had to make speeches. These were formal occasions with local politicians and the like. It was as if you were really wanted there. Of course they wanted to see the world champions, but it was a very pleasant experience for all of us.'

Round 5, in Australia, was the Lakeside International in Queensland, over 66 laps. As usual, Leo Geoghegan, John Harvey in an 1860cc Brabham Ford and Australia's youngest-ever Gold Star winner, 27-year-old Spencer Martin in a Repco-Brabham supplied by Bob Jane, were waiting like gunfighters in the saloon for the arrival of the blow-ins from overseas. Bob Jane had never been content with his prolific success in touring cars, in either national championships with his modified monsters or in the headline-making Armstrong 500, with production cars. He had been asked by Shell's Racing Manager John Mulumby to take on the management of an open-wheel racing team, with Martin driving the Repco-Brabham. He would win two Gold Star championships with Martin, but the team would expand to include sports cars, and foster the careers of some of our greatest drivers.

Jackie Stewart, who had missed the final round in New Zealand to go tyre testing, resumed his duel with Clark — unfortunately, he had to retreat to the pits with 7 laps to go. By the end of the race, Clark had a 14 point series lead.

Graham Hill arrived to drive a Lotus in the 1967 Australian Grand Prix at Warwick Farm. 'Hilly set his Lotus up differently from Clark,' recalls Leo Geoghegan. 'Jim would just drive the car as it was. Graham would be making little tweaks all through practice. He liked an oversteering car, which a Lotus wasn't, so you'd see Graham walking across the paddock with a set of front anti-roll bars in one hand and rear anti-roll bars in the other. The mechanics would look up, see him coming and say, "Oh shit, he's at it again."'

The crowd was close to 40,000 for another 'new-era' Australian Grand Prix. Stewart had set a sizzling pole position pace, well clear of Clark, although the older of the Scots appeared to have been foxing. With dense, rain-filled cloud surrounding the circuit, it looked as though sheer speed would be only a small part of the equation anyway. There were 'Geoghegan' placards and banners set up in various parts of the circuit in response to his grand qualifying drive — which put his little car beside Brabham on the second row. 'It was the first time we'd really got on top of the Climax,' Geoghegan recalls. 'When we bought the car it was ex-Clark, ex-Lotus. The engine in the car was one Clark had won with at Warwick Farm the year before. The car had had a bit of a whack at Teretonga that year, so we pulled it apart and found a crack in the engine block. We rang everywhere to source a new block, including England, America and South Africa, but couldn't find one. The car that season was unreliable.' Geoghegan's defeat by Martin in the domestic series had been considered a little unlucky, given his speed. Martin also had the considerable weight of Bob Jane's team behind him.

John Harvey, however, would never know how strong his race pace would be: he broke a drive-shaft in the warm-up, one of three pre-race retirements. He was gutted.

It was Jackie Stewart, at the end of 45 laps. Clark was 16 seconds behind him. The crowd roared their approval when Frank Gardner crossed the line in 3rd place, his first Australian Grand Prix podium finish. Brabham was a fighting 4th, ahead of Geoghegan and Bartlett. It was quite a day for the Australians, in spite of continued Scottish dominance.

Leo Geoghegan said it took a couple of visits for the foreign drivers to get used to the Australian sense of humour. It was typical of him, and others, to cloak their enormous respect for the international champions with some good old-fashioned 'slinging off'. 'I used to always call Jackie Stewart a little Scottish git. Of course he came to understand it was really a compliment.'

In round 7, at Sandown, a 52 lap race, Brabham was once again foiled by a simple mechanical failure. Some soldering on an ignition pick-up wire had broken, and his car ground to a halt while leading the race from Stewart, who in turn broke down, allowing Clark to take yet another victory and win the Tasman Cup. Gardner and Geoghegan had fought like gladiators almost the entire race distance, Geoghegan getting away in the closing stages, but their 4 cylinder cars filling up the podium was a welcome sight for the fans, who were still to see an Australian victory in the series. Bartlett finished 5th and Harvey 6th.

John Harvey loved Longford, venue for the final round, but was well aware of its villainy. 'When you came to the Longford Hotel, the apex of a 90 degree corner, there were people hanging out of the windows a couple of feet away and you could just about reach out and shake hands with them. But another problem was the railway crossing. One of the local train drivers hated motor racing. The races were always organised in consultation with the local railways, and there was give and take, but I remember one day this bloke must have said to himself, "Stuff you lot, I'm going through," and in the middle of a practice session, the cars have come around a corner, hard on the throttle to accelerate towards the crossing, and the boom gates are coming down! There's the train going past! Hard on the brakes ... wait for it to pass ...'

Jack Brabham would have the last word in this series, winning by more than a minute from Clark, with Chris Irwin holding off Gardner, Bartlett and Harvey for 3rd.

'Kevin was not only a great bloke; he was a great driver,' says Brabham, 'and I was always interested in John Harvey because he came from speedway racing, the same as I did. He was real good.'

While Jim Clark had won the series, Jack Brabham and Frank Gardner had tied with Jackie Stewart, an indication not only of Brabham's strike rate in a limited number of appearances, but also of Gardner's durability and tenacity in locally supplied equipment. Kevin Bartlett was the next highest point-scorer among the Australians, just behind Richard Attwood, and just in front of Leo Geoghegan and Denny Hulme. Then followed Chris Irwin, Jim Palmer and John Harvey.

Bartlett recalls one of the chief lessons learnt in that era, a lesson which never left him. 'Actually, it struck me after a long battle I had with Jackie Stewart in a non-Tasman series race at Surfers Paradise. You had to be courteous to your competitor; hard and fast, but courteous. If the bloke put his nose in front of you, you know he's got you because he's done something better two or three corners back. You might even just put your finger up as if to say,

"Right, you've got me." But then you'd have to get him on the next one, and he'd do exactly the same. I ended up with fastest lap in that race, even though I didn't win, and I got a lot of accolades out of it.'

Alan Mann Racing had mapped out a big 1967 for Frank Gardner. He would continue his sports car campaign and compete in his first British Saloon Car championship, in a Falcon. He had also agreed to drive for Brabham again in the Formula 2 season, in a BT23. That involved no fewer than 14 events. There would even be a one-off Formula 1 drive in a non-championship round. He could have been excused for following Brabham's lead and buying himself a plane, but that did not fit in with Gardner's ideas on self-preservation. 'Jack, who flew a plane the way he drove a car, was a practical bloke, and compared to some other well-known figures I could think of, he was a role model for safety in an aircraft.'

There were close things on many weekends as the aviators — various wealthy entrepreneurs and drivers — literally threw caution to the winds, abandoning flight plans and landing at the wrong places. 'Graham Hill was absolutely bloody dangerous in an aircraft,' Gardner says with wry smile, 'and Colin "Chunky" Chapman wasn't much better. He came in one day, far too quick in his Piper, ran off the end of the paddock, tried to spin the aircraft, but only succeeded in blowing over an entire boy scouts' campsite.'

Jack Brabham, in spite of a solid start to the 1967 season in South Africa with the previous year's engine, had unveiled an upgraded version of his car. It was good enough for pole position in round 2 at Monaco, beside Ferrari driver Lorenzo Bandini, but the 'improved' engine blew up and he spun in front of the charging pack. Drivers throttled back and braked, veering in all directions as they tried to stay in the race. Team-mate Denny Hulme, still using the older version of the BT, was the only driver on the lead lap at the end of the race — it was one of his easiest wins. Bandini chased Hulme until lap 82 of 100. There, at the notorious chicane, he lost control. The car rolled and caught fire, with Bandini pinned underneath. Marshalls extinguished the fire and freed Bandini, who had been severely burned. He died a few days later, in hospital.

Jim Clark and Graham Hill would prove threatening in their Lotus 49s, but Brabham had only to look to the other side of his garage to see the greatest danger to his fourth title. In a season that also featured a bizarre scoring system — drivers could drop the worst of their first six results, then the worst of their last five — it was Denny Hulme who took control. He made his boss chase hard. There were no concessions from either driver and points were hard to come by when the Lotus drivers were also on song.

The Italian Grand Prix turned out to be one of the great races of the season, and pivotal to the championship. Brabham was still trailing Hulme and needed a win. John Surtees, in the Honda, was the unexpected leader after the Lotuses were forced out with problems. Brabham would never forget the intensity of the race, which escalated as he searched for a way past Surtees with only a few corners remaining. The Honda was strong, but there was a chance on the final curve. A trail of cement had been dropped on the inside line to cover an earlier oil spill. Brabham knew that drivers had been avoiding that line all day, for fear of slipping on any residue that hadn't been absorbed. He took the chance and dived on the white trail as Surtees moved slightly wider to avoid it. He found himself in the lead as they exited the corner for the charge to the finish line, but only for fractions of a second, for there had been enough oil in that corner to break the BT24's grip and reduce his acceleration out of it. Surtees was a wheel-width in front when the flag fell.

'That was a fantastic dice,' Brabham recalls. 'I had a few problems with the car to start with but eventually pegged him back. Down the end of the straight, on the inside, I knew that that cement dust was there, and that it was my only chance. I just lost enough momentum for him to out-sprint me to the line. At that stage I still believed that I was going to win the championship. There were no team orders. Denny and I were finishing up the front all the time. I thought I would win.'

Brabham had cut Hulme's lead to just 3 points. The two races remaining were in the US and Mexico. Adding to the tension was the likelihood that Hulme was going to leave Brabham's team at the end of the season. He had been driving in Can-Am races for Bruce McLaren, who was keen to recruit him to his Formula 1 team.

Hulme told the *Champions* documentary, 'The mechanics were even slightly divided within the team. That happens nowadays as well when there are two good guys in one team trying to win the championship. We didn't have so many mechanics, only two for me and two for Jack. Jack once again was still giving himself the best parts, but sometimes they were a bit fragile and weren't properly tested, so I probably had, in the end, the better opportunity to win the championship.'

Brabham believes Hulme had his tongue in his cheek when he said that. 'He used to joke about me getting new parts and that. It's true that I got a different part before the US Grand Prix, but it was the wrong bloody part! They put a cast iron cam follower in the engine by mistake. It cost me a lot of power ... and the race. Denny used to laugh and say I was trying something new, but that wasn't the case.'

The Lotus Cosworth 49s of Jim Clark and Graham Hill dominated the US Grand Prix from qualifying to chequered flag. The race everyone was watching, though, was between the two cars immediately behind. Hulme was beating Brabham, and for the championship ladder to change, it had to be the other way around. It was never going to happen. Brabham punctured, triggering a slow leak which forced him to drop back. Hulme took 3rd. The best Brabham could do was 5th, overtaken by Jo Siffert in a Cooper Maserati.

To win the championship, Brabham would have to beat his team-mate by 8 points in the final round in Mexico, even though Hulme's championship lead was only 5. That was the complexity of the point-scoring rules. It was somewhat ironic that it was Jim Clark's dodgy Lotus, with a clutch problem, that denied Brabham victory — after so many failures in previous rounds. However, it would not have made any difference because as Brabham crossed the line in 2nd place, a conservative Hulme was making certain of his World Championship win by securing 3rd.

There were no hard feelings about the defeat, or about Hulme's pending defection to McLaren. Jack Brabham had completed one of the great decades of achievement in international motor sport. 'It was a victory for the team and the constructors. We had no idea at the time that no one else would be able to do it — I always thought Bruce McLaren could do it. He was the only other one who probably could have. Unfortunately, he died before he could.'

In 1967 Frank Matich's long-time supporter and sponsor Laurie O'Neill sold the Traco sports car to Niel Allen. Matich then built his own car, the SR3, which also had an Oldsmobile engine. He now had a keen rival in a similarly equipped car, and had taken a step further in evolution.

Matich had some powerful allies. Bruce McLaren had spoken to Firestone Director of Racing Bill McClusky, who offered a contract. The Firestone deal was to help with tyre testing and also lead to Matich establishing a sales outlet in Australia. 'The great thing was that they had enthusiasm and commitment but little experience in road racing. This enabled me to play a prominent role. If I wanted to try something, they would build it for me. Repco also came back into the arrangement to supply engines for the SR3, and this time it would be unaffected by the Brabham influence. The situation was so good that if anyone at that stage had asked me to drive open-wheelers again, at any level, I probably would have refused.'

The SR3 would also be tested on the international stage against the finest sports car built by his friend Bruce McLaren, the M6A. McLaren and Hulme had been dominating the Can-Am series in that car.

The SR3 did not bring the results expected in the US. It was not discovered until later, when the cars were back in Australia, that the distributor settings had been faulty, and the engine was retarding at high revs, subtracting power just when it needed to add power. Given that, and the experience gained on the faster, more open circuits of the American heartland, Matich had proved enough to his backers to win their support for a full tilt in 1968. The car had also shown enough promise to attract the interest of Ferrari which, with the beautiful P4, had beaten the SR3 in the US and was keen to do so again, unaware that Matich had problems there. The ever watchful David McKay, keen to promote Australian racing, persuaded them to bring the P4 down under to contest the 1968 Tasman series support races. Chris Amon, who would be driving a Formula 1 Ferrari in that series, would drive the P4 as well.

Frank Gardner in 1967 competed as Jack Brabham's team-mate in a torrid series of 25 Formula 2 races in all the European hot spots; 10 of those races formed the European Championship, in which Gardner finished 2nd, 11 points behind Jacky Ickx. His results included a win and six top-10 finishes in a BT23 FVA. There was also a series for non-graded British Commonwealth drivers: Frank finished 2nd in that, 1 point behind Alan Rees.

When Gardner arrived in South Africa to contest the *Rand Daily Mail* 9 hour sports car race for Alan Mann Racing, on 14 November, he was preparing for his 54th major race start that year. He had pushed the boundaries with Ford's GT40, and suffered the usual hard luck story at Le Mans, but he won at Nuremberg, Crystal Palace and Oulton Park in the Lola T70 for Sid Taylor's team. The big splash, however, had been made in the humble Falcon. Gardner won the British Touring Car Championship in it with eight wins, two 2nds, 1 4th and 1 failure to finish following a puncture and a spin. He amassed

70 points in the series, 8 more than defending champion John Fitzpatrick, driving a Ford Anglia. Touring car racing in Australia was in its infancy, but this was a sophisticated series and in previous years it had been contested, indeed won, by great drivers. Mike Parkes had finished 2nd to John Whitmore in the 1961 series. Graham Hill finished 3rd in the series won by Jack Sears in 1963, Roy Salvadori was 4th. Jim Clark won the series from John Fitzpatrick in 1964. Gardner was becoming recognised as one of the finest all-round driving talents in Europe, to which he responds, with a typically laconic grin, 'I suppose I had a little bit of an advantage in the fact that people knew that if I was in the truck and it broke down, I could fix it.'

It must be said that he did not crave the spotlight, but his reputation for understatement and self-deprecating humour was widespread. A curious example of this was the legendary terry-towelling hat. At first, it was just something to ward off the sun, a throwback to his roots in Australian surfing culture. 'I had worn all kinds of hats around the beaches as a young bloke, so in Europe I just kept wearing it, but as I progressed, people came to expect it.'

The hat rapidly became a symbol of his Australian image. It would not matter if he were at Le Mans, where the fans would catch sight of the hat and scream 'Franko!', or any other sun-baked circuit. It wasn't until his name had become famous in Europe that his motives for wearing it changed. 'It was murder to sit out at a European restaurant, anywhere near places like the Nurburgring or whatever. You might finish up signing 40 or 50 autographs. If you left the track and went to a restaurant or something, or you stopped and talked to somebody in public, you needed something to give you immunity. I found that when I took the hat off, no one would recognise me. It was perfect. You could have half your meal in peace, unless there was some astute individual there.'

Everything would change for the 1968 World Formula 1 championship: aerodynamics, tyres, teams, drivers and the balance of power.

Frank Gardner signalled his intention to make an indelible mark on the Tasman series when he qualified on pole and won the Hordern Trophy, still an important lead-in event at Warwick Farm on 3 December 1967. He had resumed his partnership with Alec Mildren Racing and was driving a Brabham BT23D with a 2.5 litre Alfa Romeo V8 engine. Lotus's Clark and Hill would again be the decisive pairing in the Tasman series, although Clark's late failure in the New Zealand Grand Prix at Pukekohe enabled Chris Amon to take a popular win in his Ferrari. Gardner came in a fighting 2nd. The World Championship competitors had had just 5 days after the South African Grand Prix to prepare for the New Zealand Grand Prix.

Amon won at Levin, Clark at Wigram and McLaren at Teretonga, where Gardner finished 3rd.

Alec Mildren Racing brought Kevin Bartlett back to team with Frank Gardner for the Australian Tasman series rounds. Bartlett had, for the second year in a row, lost a thrilling Gold Star series battle with Spencer Martin. 'One event stuck out,' Bartlett recalls. 'It was at Bathurst, where I competed not only in the Brabham Climax but also in the Alfa Romeo GTA against Bob Jane and those blokes. I won one of the races in the GTA against Bob's Mustang, a 1600 versus a 4.7 litre. He beat me in the second one, but I got a new lap record. When I contested the open-wheel race, in a completely different type of car, Spencer and I had a tremendous dice all the way. I broke lap records on every other lap. At the end of the day I think we won 100 bottles of champagne for the first 100 mile an hour speed, another 100 for the lap record and another 100 for winning the race. We had a big party. I've never been able to drink champagne since. Now I know why they spray it.'

Teaming with Frank Gardner was an important step in Bartlett's development as a driver. 'I learnt so much from Frank. I was driving a year-old car each time, but that was good, because it was well sorted. Frank was a great bloke and one of the best drivers in so many ways. My target was always to beat him, or beat his times. That's what I would aim for. He was my yardstick, that's how much I thought of him. It wasn't the Jochen Rindts or the Jackie Stewarts; it was Frank, and if I could match him on the day I'd be a happy camper.'

'Kev took an unnecessary battering a couple of times,' Gardner recalls. 'But sometimes you have to swallow your pride. If the thing doesn't handle and doesn't stop quite right you've got to work your way around it with a margin for error. Kev was probably brave enough to try to use it to the limit when the limit wasn't there.'

Leo Geoghegan would again be competitive in the Tasman series, but out-gunned by the internationals.

Clark won at Surfers Paradise but Geoghegan finished 4th after a close fight with Piers Courage. Bartlett was 5th, beating Hulme, while Gardner finished 9th.

There were 35,000 people at Warwick Farm on 18 February to see Jack Brabham return for his first Tasman series race for 1968. It had been a great and yet disappointing year for Brabham: he'd lost his world title to Denny Hulme, but won the constructors' title with three 1–2 finishes. He and Hulme were to compete against each other again, this time in rival teams in Australia. Part of the reason Brabham had not made an earlier appearance in the series was that he was deep in development with Ron Tauranac again, trying to find an answer to Lotus. They had come up with a lighter chassis, and were hoping that Repco's newest engine would deliver race-winning power. Leo Geoghegan remembers the champion as one of the quietest drivers in the paddock. 'He would always say g'day to you but you couldn't get much more out of him. He would be very quiet and obviously in total concentration. He was also so bloody busy. He would be doing the work of a mechanic — of course that would have cost him a quid, which was why he was doing it himself!'

It was a disappointing race for the many Brabham fans, as Brabham fought with a car that was leaking oil: he finished 7th. It was doubtful that anyone could have beaten Clark, who won by 11 seconds from Hill and took command of the series. Gardner, Bartlett, Geoghegan and Harvey retired.

Everyone arrived at Sandown for the Australian Grand Prix with Melbourne in the middle of a drought. It was a lean time again for the local fans, who watched the Australian entries retreat to the pits with various problems. While Clark and Amon sorted out the top two spots, Gardner was the only Australian with a chance for a podium position. With 7 laps to go, he was chasing down Graham Hill for 3rd. As the corners disappeared and the crowd started to surge, first to its feet, then to the fences, Amon tried everything in his power to get past the Scot, but Clark was simply out-braking him at every turn. At the same time, Gardner had caught and passed Hill, but Hill soon regained the advantage. When they approached the finish line, Clark and Amon were fighting their cars, regaining control after final corner manoeuvring had left them both out of shape. Clark was just a metre in front when it mattered. Nearly a minute later, it was Hill and Gardner, side by side, in the same kind of finish. The Australian fans groaned with disappointment as Gardner missed the podium by 0.2 of a second. Piers Courage finished 5th, ahead of Attwood, Geoghegan, Bartlett and Hulme. Not since 1960, when Alec Mildren beat Lex Davison, had there been an Australian Grand Prix like this one.

Leo Geoghegan recalls another race at Sandown that weekend which was also a classic, though for different reasons. 'They staged a novelty event over a few laps and all the drivers had to use Cortinas supplied by local Ford dealers. They had a grid, but of course by the time the flag dropped for the start everyone had crept up from the back and the front row was about five cars wide. It stayed like that into the first corner. I was in the middle of it all and thought there was going to be a disaster. We were literally door handle to door handle. Then, as we rounded the corner — not going at normal race speed, thank heavens, because we would have all gone off — I could hear these funny noises. It was a metallic "ping" every now and then. I couldn't work it out. The car seemed to be going all right. Then the race settled down a bit and I couldn't hear the noise anymore. Anyway, Kevin Bartlett won, because when we got to the top of the hill on the final lap he took off across the infield instead of going through the last couple of corners. He won 100 bottles of champagne. I didn't find out until later that the "pinging" sound I could hear on that first lap was all the door handles getting knocked off and bouncing down the track.'

The series decider, at Longford, was in doubt after heavy rain had left pools all over the circuit. Some drivers wanted to compete, others refused — it depended on how capable their wet tyres were. Harvey was keen, Bartlett and Hulme were not.

Frank Gardner was not surprised that Hulme refused to drive, claiming that he was superstitious. 'Denny's old man, Clive, was a Victoria Cross winner, and a psychic. He could divine oil and water and all sorts of things. His favourite party trick was to get a ring off one of the girls, give it to someone to wrap in a handkerchief and plant it somewhere in a 40 acre paddock. Then he'd go and find it. I reckon the bloke really was psychic. He told a council once exactly where to find water, and how deep down it was. He sometimes asked me if I wanted to hear my future. I told him, "Not particularly. I don't want to hear it. Thank you kindly for the offer." He'd say, "No, come on, I'll tell you." I'd say, "No. Forget it Clive." I think few of those things rubbed off on Denny.'

The appropriately named Piers Courage won the race. Clark's 5th place won him another series, but he would never return to Australia.

It seemed everyone had a Jim Clark story, even though the Scot was renowned for his quiet, mostly shy nature when in the public eye. Leo Geoghegan used to offer Clark the use of his family's Liverpool workshop when the Tasman series was in Sydney. 'When Jim wasn't in the car, he was usually off learning to fly at Bankstown airport, but occasionally he would hang around our workshop, which we always shared with Team Lotus and a few other strays from New Zealand. I remember one day, when Jim had nothing to do, I asked him to mow my mother's lawn, and he did! She had no idea who he was, just thought he was some gardener I'd hired. It was a big lawn. It would have taken him a couple of hours.'

Clark was not only famous for mowing lawns. He once mowed the carpet at a Travelodge Motel in Chadstone, Melbourne during a social evening following one of the Tasman series rounds at Sandown. The motel was L-shaped and formed a natural outdoor party area, and a lot of the drivers who were staying there decided to have a celebration.

Leo Geoghegan was there. 'Jim had won the 100 bottles of champagne for pole and Kevin had his 100 from winning that Cortina race. Graham Hill was making like a tightrope walker across the peak of the motel roof, with someone trying to knock him off by firing a garden hose at him, full blast. Then we all heard this whirring noise, and Jimmy Clark was in the rooms with the motel's mower, not very successfully clipping the shag pile carpet. Bob Jane turned up later on with my brother Pete in a D-Type Jaguar, and right on their heels was a very irate copper on a motorbike. The copper's got smoke coming out of his ears, so someone comes up straight away, hands him a beer and says, "Here mate, cool down." He did, but he was still keen to get Bob. "I'm going to arrest that man." We said, "Hang on, that's Bob Jane. He's a safe driver." The cop said, "He's been doing 100 miles an hour in the traffic!" We said, "Well, have another beer." Anyway, about an hour later, the copper was placated and we were all getting free rides around the block on the police motorcycle. We sent him back to his station at the end of his shift completely pissed. How he got home after that I will never, ever know.'

Kevin Bartlett remembers that night well. 'There were people on the roof, people jumping naked into the pool. Jackie Stewart was always pretty straight, he didn't drink much, but the others used to imbibe a fair bit, mainly the younger ones. But really, it was all smiles; everyone was happy and just having a great time.'

There were no parties for Frank Matich, but he was a very satisfied man after the summer of 1967–68. His domination of sports car racing in Australia was never going to be tested seriously by a local driver, and he whipped Chris Amon's Ferrari P4 in three out of three races. Lap records tumbled. That series, and the knowledge gained from four races in 1967, encouraged Frank to return to the US for the entire Can-Am series in 1968. 'We were very confident we could beat them, especially with the latest model, the SR4, in the wings. Repco had a four valve per cylinder, 5 litre engine ready to put in the car and Firestone had developed a new tyre for it as well.'

Frank Gardner returned to England in 1968 to resume his rewarding relationship with Alan Mann Racing. He drove a Lotus Cortina in early rounds of the British Touring Car Championship and a twin-cam Escort in a few European rounds. He took the Escort to wins at Aspern and Zolder. He also drove a Cooper with a BRM engine in a Formula 1 race at Silverstone, which he didn't finish. Every time he turned around he was getting into a different car. Gardner had great respect for Alan Mann. 'He was light years ahead of his time. Apart from the F3L, which came later, I've not known him to get involved with a disaster. In his touring and sports cars, it was nothing but professional. We were developing something all the time, thinking about the future.'

Jochen Rindt, who had won the British and French Formula 2 series in 1967 and scored 6 championship points for Cooper's Formula 1 team, replaced Denny Hulme as Jack Brabham's team-mate in 1968. He was in for a tough year, in more ways than one.

The next round of the Formula 1 championship was the Spanish Grand Prix in May, 5 months after the first round. Any excitement at the resumption of racing had been tempered by the news that Jim Clark had been killed, in a Formula 2 race at Hockenheim on 7 April 1968. His rear tyre blew at very high speed on a wet track, and the car hit a tree.

'I couldn't believe it when I heard the news,' says Brabham. 'But when I found out the circumstances, it didn't surprise me. You see, Jimmy had no feel for the motor car whatsoever. He used to be a fantastic driver, but if there was something going wrong, he wouldn't know. It was unbelievable. Just a few months earlier, we had been racing at Rouen in Formula 2 and Jimmy's right rear tyre was deflating. We could all see it as we diced and slipstreamed each other. I just couldn't believe that he was still driving the thing. It got to the stage where he was still leading, heading downhill towards the esses, with Rindt and Hill and me behind him. I thought, it won't happen. He just won't get down there with his tyre deflated. So I backed right off, slowed down. I didn't want to get caught up in the accident. Rindt and Hill followed him down, and sure enough, Jimmy went straight into the barrier ... BANG. But the other two boys got through. By the time I came past, thinking how clever I'd been, Jimmy had bounced back off the barrier and I sliced the entire front of his car off as I went past. Now, how he did not know that car had a puncture that day, I just do not understand. That's what killed him at Hockenheim. He just did not have a feel for the car.'

For Kevin Bartlett, Clark had been a friend and a hero. 'It was a terrible blow. We all looked up to Jimmy. We all knew how good he was. From my point of view, you didn't really compete against Jimmy, you just knew he was better. If you saw Jim Clark in your mirrors, you didn't bother to signal him past, you just let him go! You tried to model yourself on his approach to racing, but my style of driving was nothing like his. Because of the cars I was driving and where they came from, my style was sort of halfway between Frank Gardner and Jack Brabham. Leo's style was more like Jimmy's.'

'We all reckoned he was so good he'd never get hurt,' recalls Leo Geoghegan. 'It was like Bradman getting out for a duck — you didn't expect it to happen.'

Frank Gardner remembers the Flying Scot with great affection. 'Jimmy, he was just a racer, an amazingly gifted individual who could drive anything. He was a bit of an enigma. You would never know that the bloke you were looking at was James Clark, the best driver in the world. Occasionally, when he had a couple of sherbets or something, he might clarify his position in life, but it would be extremely unusual, whereas Jackie Stewart capitalised on the commercialism and what had to be done in the professional world — he was not overpowering, but he was extremely forceful. They were quite different.'

Gardner had taught Clark to body surf at Sydney's Whale Beach. Jackie Stewart and Graham Hill would also be part of the fun. 'They were extremely talented,' Gardner recalls. 'Those sorts of people at that level could pick up something like a golf club and the eye–hand–ball co-ordination was there. Their progress in surfing was remarkable for the short time I was with them. They weren't stupid, but they were fearless. If you told them with conviction that it could be done, they'd do it. It was like on the race track. If they trusted your judgment, and you told them that a car could do 200 around a corner, they'd get in the thing and do 200 around the bloody corner.'

The crowd at Jarama for the Spanish Grand Prix on 12 May was also in mourning over the loss of Mike Spence in a practice crash at Indianapolis, and

Jackie Stewart was out for a month with injuries from a crash in Formula 2. Clark's team-mate, Graham Hill, won the main event. Only 5 cars finished.

Questions about safety were even more intense by the time the teams arrived in Spa for the fourth round. Wings on the cars had begun to proliferate. Some looked like menacing little fins on the nose, while others were rudimentary and gawky, sitting astride fragile-looking struts mounted on the rear suspension of the car, rather like the earliest biplane technology. Teams had at last discovered down force, the opposite of lift, the force that takes planes into the air and keeps them there.

'Our wing,' recalls Brabham, 'was made by Ron Tauranac. It was a lower, smaller wing on the back. When I tested it, it was just as if someone had put their hand on the car to steady it for you. It was pretty obvious that these were going to be a big asset. It all developed from there. But they also caused many accidents.'

There were other experiments too. Jo Schlesser, a talented Frenchman who had fought with all the top drivers in recent years in the Formula 2 championships, was killed driving a new Honda Type RA302, which used the first air-cooled motor since Porsche's 8 cylinder in 1962. Schlesser crashed on lap 3 and died in the inferno. John Surtees had refused to drive the car because he thought it was unsafe. Much of the engine was made of magnesium alloy, which was highly flammable.

Graham Hill, at 39, won the Formula 1 World Championship the way any driver wants to win it: by winning the final round. Dan Gurney's Eagle team retreated across the Atlantic. Honda and Cooper also decided to quit Formula 1. Jack Brabham was considering retirement, but not his. Repco's newest-generation engine had been as much a failure as the previous year's engines had been reliable. They had found, like many other influential players in the game, that the cost of top-level motor sport tends to escalate dramatically. They simply could not keep pace with the giants who were starting to throw their weight behind development. It was time to quit, and Brabham persuaded them to do so.

The fraternity, the sportsmanship, the old world was dying. It was more than time passing. It was people. Frank Gardner still has a photograph of 8 drivers, of whom only he and Graeme Lawrence survived their racing careers. Gardner had been driving an F3L in practice for the 1000 kilometre race at the

Nurburgring on 19 May when he was forced to stop at the wreckage of Chris Irwin's F3L. The 26-year-old Englishman's car had somersaulted at high speed. He was alive, just. 'You've got to be careful they haven't got a broken neck or a broken back,' Gardner recalls, having attended other similar incidents. 'It was always a compromise, moving somebody. You're thinking, "Well shit, if this thing goes up, they're going to die anyway." It's decision time, and you are the bloke. That north to south circuit at the Nurburgring was about 29 kilometres around. That's a long way for medical services to travel. I've said it many times: it was designed by Hitler for Jewish drivers. Anyway, Irwin made it, but he never drove again. He was one of the more promising ones.'

Gardner's insatiable work ethic kept him going, and he piled on the wins in saloon and sports cars for his Ford overseers. He raced the Cortina, then built, tested and won in the new Escorts. The Lola T70 was also proving a winner in the sports car arena.

There was one other car: it was not race-winning material, but Gardner is proud of his leading role in its construction. It was Chitty Chitty Bang Bang, the famous jalopy from the movie of the same name, starring Dick Van Dyke. 'Alan Mann was approached to put it together. We put a Ford Zephyr engine into it. We had wings coming out. It looked the real article, with wooden panels on the back. We also made batmobiles and things like that. It was like designing a Formula 1 car!' Another engineer on that project was Howard Marsden, who would later move to Australia and become a powerful force in touring car success for Nissan and Ford. He was a sad loss to motor sport when he died from cancer in 2003.

Gardner, with Marsden in the team, won his second British Touring Car Championship: 84 points to Brian Muir's 58.

The twin-cam Escort proved even more competitive than the Falcon had the previous season. Gardner's final race in Europe in the Escort was a victory at Brands Hatch in late October, before the call to Australia came again. He had raced 11 different cars that year in approximately 50 events, from January to December in 11 different countries across four continents. 'A lot of races we drove to. A few people had their own aircraft but a lot of them were bloody dangerous. You wouldn't ride with them. Commercial aircraft in those days could be a day late. So driving through Europe was the safest option. You were young. Your brain worked, and you were gifted with good equipment. I never had a road accident in all that time.'

With the South African Grand Prix put back to 1 March, the 1969 Tasman series was no longer interrupting the schedule of the world's best drivers. World Champion Graham Hill returned to take on a batch of drivers in their twenties: Chris Amon, Jochen Rindt, Piers Courage and Derek Bell. They would capture the points while Gardner, Geoghegan and Bartlett, as usual, kept them honest.

John Harvey would not be there. He had joined Bob Jane's racing team, following the withdrawal of his previous sponsor, Ron Phillips. With Jane's backing he would drive in the Gold Star and Tasman series, in sports cars and touring cars.

At Bathurst on the Easter long weekend, Harvey, against his better judgment, decided to practise without seatbelts, simply because the car was so fresh from the factory that they had not been fitted yet. 'It was raining,' he recalls, 'and I remember having a dice with Kevin Bartlett to set the best time. I had gone over the top and was coming down through the Reid Park section when the back of the car just dropped. I'm not sure what broke. I spun around. The wheel dug in, which tripped the car, and over I went. Now without any seatbelts, I've come out of the car but my legs were trapped around the steering wheel as it slid upside down along the road then ended up back on its wheels again. When it stopped I was still caught in the steering wheel, lying on my back across the road. I had some pretty horrendous head injuries and was bleeding from everywhere.'

A nurse who happened to be watching the race that day with her boyfriend ran onto the circuit and turned Harvey's limp body over. Doctors later told him that she had saved his life. He would have drowned in his own blood if not for her. 'I never met her, but I sent her a nice letter.'

The impact had torn the uniform and most of the skin from his body. He had several skull fractures, along with hearing, nasal and eyesight damage, but even though his ankles were caught in the cockpit for the entire time, not one other bone had been broken. 'The *Daily Telegraph* newspaper must have been really worried,' Harvey recalls, 'because they had printed on the Monday that I had died on Sunday night. I had the benefit, before the word got out that I wasn't quite dead, of reading all these lovely letters that had been sent to my wife Beverley saying what a wonderful guy I was. Luckily I never got any crook letters saying what a dickhead I was.'

Harvey would have to sit out the remainder of 1968 and much of the 1969 Tasman series. He recovered from most of his injuries quickly, but it took months to regain his sight completely.

The Formula 1 factories were still very supportive of the series, offering, for the first time, full teams for all the races. Amon and Bell drove Ferraris. Hill and Rindt drove for Lotus. Courage drove for a new team owner on the scene, Frank Williams. Frank Gardner and Kevin Bartlett resumed their deal with Alec Mildren.

Gardner was a popular test driver and engineer. 'There was a lot of development. Some people were looking at body shapes, others at wings. In the early days nobody quite understood what the "centre of pressure" was, but when you got behind a car with the early wings on, the turbulence made it a handful to hang on to. You also had to watch the mountings. If it let go at the wrong time you were hospitalised, especially on high-speed corners.'

There was no way the Australian teams could match the developmental muscle of the factories, even on 'home ground'. 'We tried to do all the events,' recalls Leo Geoghegan. 'We took two mechanics to New Zealand but we ran out of resources — not money: we needed a couple more blokes. We were running on borrowed trailers and parts, and because of that we were always half a race behind.'

Geoghegan at first used no wings, but he discovered that they were the future when Piers Courage passed him on the outside on a corner. He was just as shocked when he caught Courage easily in the next straight. After a few more corners, however, Courage drove away, aided by the superior down force. 'The penny dropped,' Geoghegan recalls. 'We were going home, to build a set of wings.'

The teams had only a week to prepare for the Australian Grand Prix at Lakeside. Kevin Bartlett, fresh from winning the Gold Star series, was ready to take on the big names again, and Max Stewart made it a three-car team for Alec Mildren. 'Our team was the first Australian team with wings,' recalls Bartlett, 'but when we turned up at Lakeside I ran away and hid. I couldn't believe it. We had seen the first wing in an *Autosport* magazine the week before and we said, "That looks like a good idea!" We rang Frank Gardner and he told us how to make them. What he said, basically, was make an aeroplane wing, turn it upside down and bolt it on. So we had a fabricator make them up but I think it was a very ordinary piece of gear. Aerodynamically, it was not all that brilliant.'

Chris Amon won the grand prix from Derek Bell. Bartlett and Gardner were forced out with engine trouble but the crowd lifted when they saw Geoghegan, still without wings on his car, fending off Graham Hill's Ford-powered Lotus in the fight for 3rd. The reason Geoghegan was able to compete with the World Champion was that Hill had had to make an unscheduled stop after his wing collapsed, and he chose to continue without it. Geoghegan held on for a podium finish that had the crowd cheering madly. In that crowd was a young man who was just starting out as a race driver in club events, a man who never missed a meeting at Lakeside. His name was Dick Johnson.

The wings left the circuits littered with debris, but everyone agreed that motor sport had been changed forever. 'It was frightening,' Bartlett remembers, 'but the wings were amazingly effective. I didn't back off into the corners — I just went through. It was like experimenting with a wind tunnel that weekend, except it was a real race. It was bloody dangerous, when you think about it. If they don't break, it's great. If they break, you crash.'

The Geoghegans finally produced wings for the next Tasman series race, at Warwick Farm. It was a wet track though, and there was no stopping the amazing Jochen Rindt, who mesmerised them all with his sliding and squirming at the limit of control. He beat Bell, with Gardner's driving skills bringing him home 3rd. Bartlett and Geoghegan were next. Amon failed to finish there, but his win in the final round at Sandown secured the Tasman Cup. Jack Brabham returned to compete there in his BT31B, with Repco's 2.5 litre V8, and finished 3rd. John Harvey also returned to the fray, for the first time in the Brabham V8, but failed to finish.

'One of the great challenges of the Tasman series,' Bartlett recalls, 'was not just the racing itself, but the lap records which the Clarks, Stewarts, Hills and Rindts would leave behind when they went home. The local blokes would be racing at those circuits two or three times more that season, and it gave us a target to aim for. I'm pleased to say that two or three times we did it. I don't know one bloke who ever resented running 4th, 5th or 6th in the Tasman series. We knew it was, relatively speaking, a great performance.'

After his recovery, John Harvey made the most of the mighty empire that Bob Jane was building. Jane had set up his T-Mart chain of tyre stores and was racing a large and varied team of cars. The boss drove sedans, and left the rest up to Harvey. 'The chain of stores was starting to take off,' recalls Harvey, 'and this team was a great promotion. Bob had the first multi-car transporter, a semi-trailer that carried four cars, when other people were still towing their cars around on open trailers. It would be years before any of the other teams picked up on it. It was this fantastic billboard, driving around Australia, and the T-Mart network just grew and grew. In one year we did something like 32 meetings. We had lots of wins. I was pretty sharp, because I was never out of a race car, especially when you throw in all the testing. I was doing it all the time.'

The news was not always good for the Jane team, though. At the Easter meeting at Bathurst, the invisible edge that drivers live on was crossed yet again. 'Young Bevan Gibson was driving the Elfin sports car,' Harvey recalls, 'and he was doing 300 kilometres an hour when the car got air underneath it going over the hump in Conrod Straight. It just flipped up, landed upside down, burst into flames and slid along the straight for about 200 metres, all the way to Murray's Corner.'

Gibson had been trying to catch Frank Matich in his mighty SR4. Normally it would have been a forlorn attempt, but on this day, to Gibson's great cost, Matich had a problem. 'There would have been probably 10 seconds a lap difference between my car and Bevan's,' says Matich, 'but my throttle was playing up. It obviously encouraged Bevan to get up there. Poor little bastard must have thought it was his big chance. I didn't know it at the time, but I saw the film of it later. I was heading into the corner after Conrod and there's this huge ball of fire catching me. It was spinning. I was totally unaware of it until I turned the corner and went up the main straight. It was just terrible. I stopped on the next lap. So did a few other people. Bevan was a lovely young kid. He was a real trier.'

'He was my team-mate,' says Harvey. 'We had dinner the night before. We had even spoken about the instability of the car over the hump. My advice was, just lift your foot off the throttle to keep the nose down and it won't destabilise.'

Jack Brabham was at that meeting, for an unscheduled race between overseas commitments, and Harvey was to compete against him. 'The start was delayed because Jack wasn't ready! We rushed into turn one and the swarm was heading up mountain straight when BOOM! Jack just flew past us and was off into the distance. That was probably worth waiting for. Anyway, I finished a distant 2nd. Kevin was in that race but I was never in danger from behind. It was a tough one, though, because every time I passed the crash site the fire retardant was still there near the road — and the skid marks.'

Bob Jane was in shock for some time after that day. 'The death of Bevan Gibson was a great shock to me. The sight of the Elfin sports car sliding down Conrod Straight, upside down, with Bevan still in it, is still quite vivid in my mind. I felt close to Bevan's family and felt, to some extent, responsible at the time but the family accepted this accident just as I had to.'

John Harvey had the greatest respect for Frank Matich. Matich offered him a deal at one stage, but he decided to stick with the T-Mart team. 'Frank was one of the best single-seater drivers of all time. Young people today might ask me who he was and why I regard him so highly, and I explain it this way: if an Australian bloke with no international driving experience entered the Australian Grand Prix today with a car that was a year old, did all the work on it himself, got out there, took pole position, then led for about half the race, what would you reckon? Fantastic. Frank did that quite a few times. He was good.'

Matich, meantime, had determined that his SR4 prototype with Repco power and Firestone tyres was ready to ship to the US for that magnetic Can-Am series. He had seen the grand plan rise and fade into oblivion the previous season, 1968, as so many great schemes do in the world of motor racing. There had been a delay in production, and the triumvirate missed its deadline to fully test the car in time for the 1968 series. The decision was taken to stay home and compete locally, sharpen the SR4, and then launch it again for the 1969 series. The car had been devastating against the Australian sports cars; it was like using a sledgehammer to drive in a panel pin. Matich not only won everything; he also slashed track records.

'CAMS got the shits,' says Matich. 'After we hacked 3 seconds off the lap record at Sandown, going about 380 kilometres an hour up the back straight, they weren't happy rewriting the record books with a sports car. It was the only car I was racing at the time. You have to realise that local open-wheel racing was dying out, except for the Tasman series. Leo and Kevin and Spencer Martin and those blokes were still going in the Gold Star, but it didn't have the public image.

'The opposition to the SR4 wasn't that strong, either. Niel Allen was there. Bob Jane ran against me sometimes in a McLaren — and he also gave that drive to Johnny Harvey — but it wasn't about competition or driving. It was the car that the public came to see. They'd be buzzing. "What time will it do today? Will it get the lap record today or tomorrow?" That kind of thing.'

It was time to finally test the car against the best. 'We were technically ready. We sent off our entries for the American events. The whole thing was ready, including transport. Qantas was sponsoring us and were geared up to fly the cars over. There was even a movie being made about the entire campaign.'

The movie makers would not have quite the ending they anticipated.

*　　*　　*

Jack Brabham had been contemplating life after driving. He had a plan, but Jochen Rindt, the young driver he was banking on, would not be around to help, having accepted an offer to drive for Lotus, so the plan sat on the shelf for a while as Brabham cranked up his engineering genius for yet another tilt at the might of the Formula 1 factories. But he was no Don Quixote of motor sport. The grim face of concentration behind the wheel said it all. 'Jack was not then, and never will be, a funny man,' says Frank Gardner. 'He got on with the job. It was typical of him that one of the few times I saw him break up with laughter was when he was telling me about a race at Crystal Palace when Rindt, who he'd been pressuring all the way, suddenly gave in to that pressure and went off in front of him, bits and pieces and wheels and everything flying everywhere! Now as Jack's telling me this he's pissing himself with laughter — not because he thought crashing was funny, but because he had caught out his mate!'

Brabham knew that the first step as he approached the 1970s had to be the acquisition of the latest weaponry, and it didn't take a genius to figure out that the Ford Cosworth engine was going to be the nuclear power of Formula 1.

CHAPTER EIGHT

Local Heroes

While the Tasman series in the mid-1960s brought unprecedented glamour to Australian circuits, linking local fans to the increasingly wealthy world of Formula 1, there had been a seismic shift on the domestic scene. Australia had begun to accept in 1965 that the Bathurst 1000 was going to be the home of 'fair dinkum' motor racing. Organisers decided to formally recognise the outright winners, while maintaining the class structure that had encouraged smaller and cheaper cars into the field. This enabled them to keep it a 'grass roots' production car race, while accepting that to be first across the line was worthy of a formal presentation. There had always been willing competitors, but also a large number of teams more concerned about completing the race than competing. This was changing too. The intensity was building.

Ford wanted to place greater emphasis on the event, so they strengthened their hand by giving control of their factory team to a single, capable engineer–manager who could deliver them the much-needed showroom sparkle of the winning trophy. That man was Harry Firth.

Frank Gardner, by then working with Ford in Europe, described Harry Firth as 'an extremely practical bush engineer with a wonderful feel. He had a feel for people. He had a feel for the business.'

Firth set about turning the locally assembled two-door Cortina into a race-winning production car. That meant the changes had to be made at the factory. He lowered it, stiffened the springs, extracted more power from the 1.5 litre engine, installed a close-ratio gearbox, improved the brakes, increased the fuel tank capacity and made the car generally lighter. The GT500 was born. It went on sale in July, 3 months before the race, and sold like hotcakes. 'I got £110 per car, to make 110 cars for the company. Then I made about 80 more in various shapes and forms for private individuals. It paid off my overdraft, kept Firth Motors in business, and even built some extensions on the premises. I was employing five permanent staff and five casuals.'

Firth had also used versions of the Cortina to win various rallies, and the hugely popular epic of its time: the 11,260 kilometre Round Australia Trial (in this instance, aided by special Kleber rally tyres from the new Bob Jane T-Marts).

There were many kinds of drivers drawn to Bathurst in 1965. Some, like 23-year-old Colin Bond, were a little unsure of what they were in for, and didn't realise that they were starting a relationship that would, in spite of their best endeavours elsewhere, come to define their entire career. Bond teamed with Arthur Treloar in an Isuzu Bellett; it was the only one in the field.

Bond had always been a sportsman, and no arena seemed out of his reach. He was a professional soccer player for Gladesville–Ryde, his home suburb in Sydney. He was also a good golfer. But the call of the screeching wheel was louder than anything else. 'Really, the sport that you could best make a living from seemed to be motor sport. My biggest influence was the Redex Trials, because they got an awful lot of publicity — front page on most of the papers for the weeks they were on.

'I had plenty of practice, even before I qualified for a driver's licence. I used to back Mum and Dad's car up and down the driveway at home when they weren't around, occasionally taking it on the road for a while, but making sure I had it back in the driveway in enough time to cool the engine down before they got home.'

Bond worked as an apprentice mechanic for Grenville Motors after leaving Meadowbank High School and bought a Singer Nine for £950. It was not an exotic race car; it was a mobile classroom for a budding race driver.

The Singer soon gave way to an Austin Healey Sprite and Bond moved up to competition level in the MG Car Club, competing in hill climbs, circuit races, even rallies, for which the car was not well suited — but Bond's skills were. Rally, to the untried enthusiast, can be a nightmare of complications. It depends a lot on the skills of a co-driver to find their way to the various stages using maps. 'I recall getting lost, in my first rally, near Thirlmere, south of Sydney. My co-driver in those days was Andy Frankel. We had already been penalised for getting to the scrutineering late. So I was going pretty hard, but wasn't catching up with anyone, and no one was catching us. We came to a dead-end. I drove back to a nearby farmhouse, produced my map and asked the farmer to show us where we were. He looked at it and said, "Have you got another map?" The event was over by the time we got back.'

The skills improved. The events intensified. The Sprite was tooled and tucked and touched up to go faster and faster. Bond competed in state and national motorkhanas, and more rallies, which in the early 1960s were often contested at night because organisers were unable to ensure road closures. 'It was all based on navigation, not controlled, shorter stages like today. In events like the Southern Cross Rally, staged around Port Macquarie, you'd do 850 kilometres a night for four nights in a row, sleeping during the day. Reading maps was so important. Quite a few of us would be driving through people's properties at three o'clock in the morning, waking up some angry farmer who'd then start shooting at them.'

The Round Australia Rally in 1964 was Bond's first large-scale test. The Sprite was ineligible, so he entered a Volkswagen. Bond's brother Bruce was about to return from an army posting in New Guinea and needed a car. The deal was that he would pay for the car, they would use it in the trial, then hand it over to him. Bond, with George Shepheard co-driving and Andy Frankel navigating, won the under-25 division prize of £250, which just about paid their expenses.

For any race driver with an eye for the big-time, purpose-built race cars are a magnet. Bond bought a Lynx Peugeot from Bob Holden, and started some serious circuit racing and hill climbs. He finished on the podium in his first outing, at Hume Weir in 1964, with Dave Walker and Barry Collerson ahead of him. Both would go on to forge distinguished careers in top-level open-wheel racing, Walker driving for a year in Formula 1 as Emerson Fittipaldi's team-mate at Lotus. Bond would win 80 per cent of his races with the Lynx Peugeot.

The Isuzu Bellett was nothing like the young driver who took it to the Bathurst circuit in 1965: he was to become a prolific winner. 'Arthur Treloar and

I used to take the car in rallies mostly,' Bond recalls. 'Funny thing was, he insisted on taking his girlfriend Josie with us. I didn't mind, but would you believe that for the entire time, as we raced around the bumpy forest roads, she just sat in the middle of the back seat, knitting. The build on Belletts in those days wasn't too good. Quite often we'd hit a bump pretty hard, and when we arrived at a gate and Arthur went to jump out to open the gate, he couldn't get the door open. The bump had bent something. When we hit another bump, it would open again. Sometimes the bonnet, which hinged from the front, would come undone and start to lift as you drove, faster. Like the door, it would take another bump to shut itself.'

In the 1965 Armstrong 500, Harry Firth was not allowed to drive any of the GT500s he built because Ford thought it was inappropriate. Instead, he drove a Cortina 220 with John Raeburn in class A: limited to cars costing up to £900.

John Harvey signed up to drive with John French in a Mini Cooper. It was Harvey's first Bathurst 500, and one of his jobs was to jump in and out of the team cars to set the ignition timing. 'It wasn't very sophisticated in those days,' Harvey recalls. 'You'd have a stopwatch around your neck. You'd go around turn one and start to accelerate up mountain straight, pick a point, change into top gear, press the stop watch and right at the end of the straight you'd hit the watch again. You'd come back to the pits and say, for example, it was 20 seconds. They would then advance or retard the timing, move the distributor a little bit. Then you'd go out, do the same thing over again. If you reached the end of the straight in 19.6 seconds, you'd gained something, so you'd go back and adjust it again. When you started to lose time, you knew you'd gone too far. That's what I did on the Saturday.'

Leo and Ian Geoghegan fronted on the morning of the big day, to everyone's amusement, in business suits. 'We were driving for Total,' recalls Leo, 'who were very good to us, but Hans Tieberman from Gowings suggested we wear suits. He was shocked when we agreed. When he asked us how much money we'd want, I figured I'd make an outrageous claim for an outrageous offer. I told him a grand. He said, "Is that all?" I immediately thought, oh shit, I've undersold us! We were getting 400 quid to drive the car for Ford, so I thought a grand was a lot of dough.'

The sleek black suits, ties, jackets, lightweight leather shoes and pork pie hats were the talk of pit lane. 'We got the lion's share of the pre-race publicity.

We were standing in pit lane like gentlemen in our suits under umbrellas,' Leo remembers. 'It was then — and probably still is — the most valuable advertising time in Australia: the 10 minutes before Bathurst.' They traded the hats for helmets, but kept the suits and ties for the entire race.

It was around this time that Ian acquired the nickname 'Pete', after a journalist dubbed him 'Black Pete' in a story. It was a comparison with a cartoon character and satirised the Geoghegans' trademark black colours. The name would stick. Bob Jane was back, teamed with George Reynolds. Kevin Bartlett drove a Morris de Luxe with Ron Haylen. For years afterwards, most drivers would take various offers to drive in the 500 in a range of cars, some of them frighteningly inadequate, others powerfully prepared. Only the serious touring car contestants would focus each year on Bathurst success as an important means of maintaining their sponsorship.

The heartbreak and the heroics were always evident. Barry 'Bo' Seton and Midge Bosworth won the race in 1965 with a steady pace. There would be famous photographs taken afterwards, of Bo sitting proudly with the winner's trophy, and his young son Glenn bathing in the victory. Glenn would grow up to become a race driver, twice winner of the Australian Touring Car Championship and hopelessly addicted to the punishing mystique of the mountain.

Colin Bond recalls that race, his first Bathurst, finishing 30th overall and 6th in class B. 'We were going all right but the front right wheel fell off and I watched it careering up the road. I pulled over to change it, as the rules decreed, opened the boot, got the jack and the spare and raced around: there was nothing there. The hub and brakes went off with the wheel. So, back to the pits. This was no factory team, just a bunch of mates competing in their car. We had no spare hub. Then we saw a man sitting on his car behind pit lane. The car was a Bellett. We asked him if we could borrow his hub for the rest of the race. He agreed, so we replaced the hub, finished the race, then refitted the hub back on this bloke's car for him. Poor bugger. His brakes must have had grooves in them four mills deep ...'

'The daunting thing about a race like Bathurst,' Bond recalls, 'is that the drum brakes wore out so fast. It wasn't long before you had to approach every corner in the middle of the road because you didn't know which way the car was going to pull when you braked. It would go left one time and right the next.'

The odd thing was that in spite of their cars' superior performance, Ford chose to abandon racing for a couple of years while they focused on the new project with which they hoped to capture the hearts of Australian motorists: the Falcon. The factory's love–hate relationship with the mountain had begun. Harry Firth, however, flew to the US to race a Lotus Cortina in the Trans-Am series with a young Canadian called Allan Moffat. He couldn't have known at the time what role Moffat would play in the history of Australian motor sport.

Firth boasts that in a wet practice session, he lent Moffat more than adequate support by outpacing the European Touring Car Champion, John Whitmore, by several seconds a lap. He also made the most of all the Cortina parts at his disposal, winning the Southern Cross Rally against a strong international field.

In 1966 pounds turned to dollars and dollars were being thrown by various factories, in various ways, at Mt Panorama. Frank Matich was in one of several Mini Coopers. His co-driver was his accountant, Frank Demuth. 'That's the kind of race it was in those days, but it was quasi works-supported. We had dealer support and it was a pretty fast car, which the international entries didn't like, because they had all the good bits. It was a very competitive race that year. It was also my comeback race from the burns I suffered when I crashed the Lotus at Lakeside.' Matich hurled the Mini around the circuit, recording the fastest lap, before a wheel came off in the dipper and he crashed into a tree.

It would be Matich's last race in the Bathurst 1000, even though his career would continue for another 8 years. 'It was a big bloody event, a big deal for the manufacturers, but it was an endurance race for touring cars, something entirely different in its day.'

Harry Firth was in another Mini, with Ern Abbott; finished 6th, 2 laps behind the winners, Raano Altonen and Bob Holden. Altonen was one of a few international rally drivers British Motor Corporation (BMC) had imported to spice up the occasion. The amazing Mini, in spite of eight retirements, still managed to fill the first 10 placings. Colin Bond and Arthur Treloar returned in their trusty Isuzu Bellett, finishing 30th overall and 8th their in class. They would not return in a hurry, preferring to focus on rallies.

* * *

The Geoghegans and Bob Jane, who hadn't made the trip to Bathurst in 1966, were back in force the following year to drive the latest product of Harry Firth's renewed relationship with Ford. The GTXR Falcon had arrived, to disprove the theory that lighter, smaller cars were better suited to the mountain. The Minis were still on top of their game, but this was a new game. The V8 engine was a new species, and it would flourish on the mountain circuit, threatening the extinction of all others. 'That was a revolution in Australian motoring,' recalls Leo Geoghegan. 'You could buy a V8 Ford car off the floor. Prior to that, we were all driving 6 cylinder Holdens or Fords. The Falcon V8 was an excellent car. For a racing driver, all of a sudden, Bathurst wasn't boring any more.'

While the factory focus changed the sharp end of the field, there was still the often absorbing midfield struggle. David McKay had entered a couple of Volvo 122Ss in class D, and he asked Kevin Bartlett and John Harvey to drive one of them. They found it very amusing. 'The Volvo was pretty ordinary in practice,' Harvey recalls, 'but having made the commitment to David we couldn't withdraw, so we decided to give the thing a good thrashing. The plan was that it would blow up and we'd be out of it and get to go home early.'

Car management was the key to the controversial 1967 race. Pete Geoghegan had been mistakenly credited with a lap by the official counters after taking a short-cut through the infield when he ran out of fuel. It proved crucial in the final laps when his brother closed to within 4 seconds of leader Fred Gibson, who was Harry Firth's co-driver in a Falcon. With Firth urging him on, Gibson found some more speed, and won the race by 11 seconds. The man holding the chequered flag, however, started to wave it at Leo Geoghegan, because the Australian Racing Drivers Club (ARDC) had judged that he was almost a lap in front.

Leo Geoghegan remembers it well. His team knew there had been confusion. 'Timing and lap count were always a bone of contention, and what the ARDC said was what counted. They said we were leading, so we went along with that. I could see Freddy at the finish and I wondered if I should pass him, just to be on the safe side, but I would have looked a complete dickhead if I ran out of brakes or ran off the road in doing so. According to the officials, I was about to lap him. The truth was I was still behind him.

'They still hadn't sorted it out before we actually stepped up to receive the trophy. Pete and I were on a podium that was two 44 gallon drums with a couple of planks across them, sitting in the middle of the pits. I remember saying to Pete, "Thank Christ we've won it. Now we don't have to do this race again."' As if the mountain had heard his insult, the result was later reversed, following a protest from Harry Firth. Leo Geoghegan would never go closer to winning the great race.

Amidst all the controversy one of those typically bizarre Bathurst stories went almost unnoticed. It was Harvey and Bartlett's Volvo. 'It just kept on going,' Harvey laughs when he recalls the day, 'and the harder we thrashed it, the better it seemed to go! We ended up receiving the trophy for winning our class!'

'It never surrendered,' says Bartlett. 'I drove a few races with Harvey, but that would have to be one of the funniest. He was a great bloke to drive with. They were good times.'

The Volvo story did not end there. Harvey was driving the car back to Sydney the following morning, with a hung-over Bartlett beside him, when the car overheated. The scrutineers had not refilled the radiator properly after checking the engine. 'We pulled over,' says Harvey, 'and saw a creek at the bottom of a gorge beside the road. Kevin was too sick to move so I had to climb down into this snow-filled gorge with our trophy, which was a crystal jug and some nice cups, as well as our two racing helmets, to fill them all with water and scramble back up the slippery slope. I did that three times. I'd had it by the time I finished, so I flung the trophy and the helmets back in the car, without bothering to repack the crystalware.'

It wasn't until they had arrived back in Sydney that Harvey received a phone call from the race organisers who told him that there had been a mistake. They had not won their class, but finished 3rd. It was another glaring example of that brilliant timing and lap counting. Harvey was asked to return his trophy, so he went to the Volvo's boot to get it, but all he found was a shattered mess of glass that had bounced around among tools and other objects for the entire trip home. He removed the pieces from the car, packed them carefully in their original case and returned it all to the ARDC, collecting his new trophy for 3rd place. It was identical to the first, except for the engraving. 'No one said a word,' recalls Harvey. 'Maybe they thought they had broken it. Anyway, it worked out rather well, didn't it?'

Harry Firth was into everything. In 1968 he prepared three Falcons to win the teams event, and finished 8th in his own entry for the first London to Sydney

Marathon, which was won by Scotsman Andrew Cowan, teamed with Colin Maikin and navigator Brian Coyle in a Hillman Hunter. While Firth had been on the marathon, he had left another team of GT Falcons to be prepared for the Bathurst 500, which had changed its name again thanks to a new sponsor, Hardie-Ferodo.

Holden had been uneasy at Ford's Bathurst success so they offered passive support to David McKay's Scuderia Veloce dealership, for a new breed of car — the Monaro. McKay, like Firth with the Falcons, had prepared and raced Monaros in the London to Sydney Marathon, but not with the same success.

Results at Bathurst by this time depended heavily on reliability married to power. Pit stops and judgment were also crucial, as management and crews tried to preserve their collapsing cars in the pressure-filled environment of pit lane. In 1968, the Ford challenge wilted first, with the Geoghegans retreating to the back of the pits, and the Seton-Gibson car literally blowing up in Conrod Straight. It was Monaro 1–2–3, but McKay's factory team was upstaged by Bruce McPhee and Barry Mulholland.

Kevin Bartlett and Doug Chivas won class E and finished 4th overall in an Alfa. It was a disaster for the Alfa driven by Frank Gardner and John French, however. All the Alfa crews were changing front wheels with disturbing frequency, and there were various other problems resulting in dead cars, but when Gardner's car was brought back to the pits on a truck it was too much for officials, who disqualified him. 'I remember those wheels were a problem,' says Gardner. 'They were inadequate for a race of that distance. It didn't matter that we were disqualified, because it was simply dangerous.'

Gardner knew where Bathurst stood in the scheme of things, even in those days. 'You got used to the Nurburgring and other tracks in Europe, so you knew there were much better tracks around the world. In the early days you'd go to some of those circuits on a gloomy, wet day and you'd find it very daunting. The speeds of the local cars at Bathurst weren't that high, but when they started to move things along a bit it grew into Australia's Indianapolis. Everyone who was anyone on the Australian scene had to have raced at Bathurst or they hadn't raced.'

A notable absentee from the Armstrong 500 once it moved from Victoria to New South Wales was 'Stormin' Norman Beechey. There was still a flourishing series of races in which exotic, imported touring cars which did not fit the

Bathurst regulations could be thrown around at breathtaking speed and, in Beechey's case, breathtaking slides. Other drivers shunned the American cars, but Beechey seemed attracted to them. With Neptune Racing's sponsors demanding a change, he persisted with more big V8s, tempering their raw power with better brakes and various weight-loss programs.

'Neptune wanted me to have a car capable of beating Bob Jane's Jaguar. It had to be a V8 Mustang. When I told them I had to go to America to get this car, I knew that for all their generous support, this would be another step up entirely. They said, "Well go and get one." I just sat there, and there was a very long, pregnant pause. Then they said the magic words, "We will fund it." That really did change it for a young man like me who didn't know where America was or what a passport was ... I had to go and find that out.'

Ford's US racing factory since 1957, Holman and Moody, offered Beechey a Mustang coupé that they had been using as a promotional vehicle for children's charities. He then asked Carroll Shelby to fit a Cobra 289 engine, slipping the builder an extra $500 to make it even better. The result was 375 horsepower. It arrived in December 1964 and was due to race in late January 1965. It had factory-fitted drum brakes, but Beechey was familiar with those, having used them on the Impala. The Mustang was a thoroughbred among hacks. It blew them off the circuit like Phar Lap in a midweek country meeting, sweeping the Australian Touring Car Championship, the South Australian Touring Car Championship and the NSW Touring Car Championship in consecutive months. Then it was the Tasmanian title and anything else he contested. Jane, Geoghegan and company were shaking their heads in wonder, and searching for their chequebooks. They had to get one.

Winning streaks were rare in days when there was no endless supply of spares. The car you had was all you had. 'There were a lot of failures by myself and my competitors,' says Beechey. 'These cars that we raced were nothing more than hotted up road cars and the axles were not exactly strong.'

Ian 'Pete' Geoghegan would always be there, keeping Beechey in sight. The famous brothers had lost their mentor, their father Tom, to kidney failure in 1965. It was a long-term illness, and while devastated, the family kept racing. Beechey had nothing but praise for his long-time rival: 'Pete Geoghegan was one of the best drivers I ever raced against. He was by far the superior driver, in my opinion, in that he was also the safest driver to compete with. We had some very, very tough races from time to time and there was never any indication that he was going to lean on you. When you're teetering around a corner in a racing car, you only need someone to put their hand out, give you a push, and you're gone. It doesn't take much effort when you're on the very edge. Just a touch. Pete wouldn't do that.'

Throughout that time, Beechey insisted that performance was relative to circumstance, and that is why he did not leap as anxiously onto the Bathurst bandwagon as other popular drivers. 'Bathurst was important, but it was still a once a year race. It wasn't, by itself, sustaining motor racing. With Shell, Ford and GM executives living in Melbourne, a win there was very important and still is today. You could win three in New South Wales or Queensland, but the executives went to the meetings in Melbourne.'

Beechey may have borrowed team-mate Jim McKeown's Cortina for a win in the 1966 South Australian Championship, setting a lap record along the way, but sponsor Neptune, in keeping with their policy, urged him to use a V8 Chevy Nova as his main race car. With it he managed to establish a powerful and separate identity from his rivals, who had rushed to acquire Mustangs. They had all subscribed to the adage, 'If you can't beat 'em, join 'em', but Beechey was always loyal to his subsidy from Neptune and slipped out from under the blanket. The Nova had 475 horsepower (compared with the Mustang's 400), and left it behind, but its drum brakes made it a difficult car to stop. He often defied the experts by belting the Mustangs into submission.

'I remember going to the championship race at Bathurst in 1966. It was my first race there. I took the Mustang and the Nova, to see which would be better. I chose the Nova, because I passed Pete Geoghegan going up the hill so easily that I thought he'd missed a gear. But when I went down the hill, I kept my foot into it going over the hump, and nearly flipped the car. The front lifted about two and a half feet. I was doing about 167 miles an hour. Pete, who saw it all, came into the pits afterwards and said to me in his usual stutter, "B ... d ... g ... aaargh!" I just nodded and said, "I know!"' Next time Beechey took that hump he lifted his foot from the throttle — and his heart rate stayed slightly below the rev counter.

Beechey had his chance to beat Geoghegan that year but an oil leak from the gearbox onto the clutch brought him undone. It was Geoghegan 1st, Beechey 2nd, Kevin Bartlett in a GTA Alfa 3rd. In 1967, at Lakeside, Beechey had another chance but failed because he contested a 9 lap warm-up event earlier in the day and it used up the tyres. 'I was comfortably leading but I blew a tyre 5 laps from the end at Lakeside. One race too many on those.' Beechey did win the Queensland, Victorian and South Australian titles to emphasise the point. In 1968 he won the Victorian title and a special event at Bay Park in New Zealand. There was nothing wrong with him or the Nova, but the record books show a clean sweep for Geoghegan in the Australian Championships from 1966 to 1969.

'The thing about Pete,' Leo recalls, 'was that he was a gifted individual. He was naturally lazy. I mean, if you asked him if he'd like to go out and do a few more laps just to make sure the car was okay, he'd almost always just shrug and say "No"! He just didn't need to. He was able to drive fast enough to beat his rivals and save the car at the same time, but when asked for it, he could just step up and break lap records. He was that good.'

A typical 'Pete' story comes from a Warwick Farm meeting in 1968 when the team mechanic, Mick Lambert, greeted him after a practice session.

'How's it handling?' Lambert asked.

'It's, it's, it's too, t-t-too . . . '

'Too much understeer?'

'N-n-no. T-t-too . . . '

'Too much oversteer?'

'N-n-n-n-no . . . '

'Too high in the diff ratio?'

'No-n-n-no . . . it's t-t-t . . . too bloody hot here. Let's go home.'

The production cars may have occupied the high ground but there was no racing more popular in the 1960s than 'Stormin' Norman, 'Black Pete', and their rivals. It was not just about cars. It was theatre. 'I remember driving around in the warm-up lap one day and, for some reason, I looked up at the trees, and there were all these kids hanging off the branches like monkeys because they couldn't see over the people on the ground. I hardly ever raced where there wasn't a top crowd,' says Beechey.

Leo Geoghegan, on the other hand, would never lose his passion for open-wheel racing, but he had to concede that 'tin tops' were the popular category — promoters quickly discovered this too. 'The big three, prior to Moffat's ascendancy, were Pete, Norm and Bob,' he says. 'All a promoter had to do was put those three names on his advertising and they would draw the crowds. It wouldn't matter if the Gold Star Championship was the main event. They came to watch the touring cars. We used to get really good starting money between us. We'd go to Calder and take a beating from Norm — he was always bloody good there — because we were paid so well. Then Norm would come to Warwick Farm and we'd get our own back, because that was our circuit. Queensland was also big money. It was all appearance money. The winning money was token. We all made good dough from each other. It was no good having just one of us there: they needed at least two for a good race. Part of the reason we were well paid was that we always turned up. It didn't matter if we had had a big crash or some other problem. We would get there. Sometimes it cost us more to get there than we made on the weekend, but we dare not let the promoters down.'

The end of 1968 was also the end of Harry Firth's history-making relationship with Ford. After numerous squabbles and successes, the final back-breaking series of disagreements came with a management change in the racing department, as a result of which Firth found himself handcuffed to convention yet again. 'I wanted to do things and they wouldn't let me.' There was also a personality clash with the new American boss Al Turner, a NASCAR exponent from Texas who didn't see things the Firth way. Finally, after lining up a deal with rival General Motors, Firth told Ford the marriage was over.

1969 would also be a pivotal year in the history of the great Bathurst race. Colin Bond would make his return to the event and two new names would appear on the list. Together, they would take touring car racing to a new place in the Australian sporting psyche.

CHAPTER NINE

Right Time, Wrong Place

Tim Schenken was not born to race cars. There was no pedigree, no wall of trophies at home to inspire him, no victory laps to share with any relatives. It just happened. Schenken was born on 26 September 1943 in Gordon, Sydney and spent his early years in the neighbouring suburb of Killara. His father, Hans, was born of German parents in Russia, from where he escaped during the Russian Revolution. Despite having had such dramatic life experiences, Hans Schenken was no daredevil; he was a cautious driver who had no interest in cars. Tim's Australian mother, Shirley, had a number of brothers, one of whom was a yachtsman of some distinction, so he suspects his sense of adventure may have come from her side of the family.

It certainly didn't appear when he first saw race cars, at the Mt Druitt circuit. He can't recall why his family was even there, but he can recall seeing Jack Brabham and Dick Cobden racing. 'Funnily enough, I wasn't hooked on motor sport at that stage. It didn't grab me until I moved to Melbourne in 1955. I was 12. My father was transferred there by Felt and Textiles, the company he worked for. I went to school at Camberwell Grammar. A friend of mine, Paul Bernadou, introduced me to hill climbs and other small events, which his father Leon competed in. It was there that I suddenly decided to become a racing driver.'

Templestowe, Rob Roy, Phillip Island, Fishermens Bend, Albert Park ... wherever there was a race meeting, that's where the obsessed Schenken would be. 'I couldn't see how school could help me become a racing driver. From about the age of 13 my schooling went downhill. The only reason I wanted to go at all was to talk to Paul about motor racing.'

Schenken started collecting any technical magazine he could lay his hands on, and soon he built himself a go-kart from an old steel single-bed frame that he found at the tip. It was powered by a 125cc Villiers 2-stroke engine with a three-speed gearbox and ran on old wheelbarrow wheels. 'It could have been the first go-kart ever built here. I used to drive it at Templestowe, on dirt roads made for a housing estate. My friends started doing much the same, and after a while there were three or four of us. One day we were invited to go to Baxter Park to stage a demonstration race on the speedway circuit. That was my first sort of race.'

It was not widely known that Schenken had a penchant for suburban street tests, which involved courageous unlicensed dashes which lasted as long as his appetite for risk — and the tendency of police to frown on such matters — would allow. He was only 14 when he 'borrowed' his father's car, a Wolseley 4/44. 'I used to carefully open the big steel door on the garage while my parents were asleep in the adjacent room, push the car out into the street, roll it down the road, then start it, and proceed to drive around the suburbs like a complete lunatic, using all the road, like a racing driver. How I never hit anything I'll never know.' He was almost caught by the police once, after leaving tell-tale 'doughnut' trails in a nearby park. His parents were at a loss to explain the mud all over their car.

On the track, he soon outgrew his go-kart. When he was 15, he lobbied his parents, with the skills of a politician, to purchase a Simca Aronde as a second car. 'I used to pinch that car at night too, and thrash it. My parents had no idea at that stage what was going on or where it was leading. They just saw it all as interference with my education, which was rapidly becoming a disaster.'

He left school and started work as an office assistant with car dealers and importers while scanning technical books and racing magazines for anything he could find about motor sport. 'My hero was Stirling Moss. He was right up there. Jack Brabham, Tony Brooks, Stuart Lewis-Evans, Fangio ... but Moss was my idol. We went to a race at Albert Park once and saw his Maserati in the paddock. I took a slice of the paintwork from the front of it, snuck it into my scrapbook, and later got him to sign it.'

Schenken's parents had still not discovered his clandestine relationship with their beloved Simca, even when he qualified for his driver's licence and started racing it. At the Templestowe Hill Climb several years later they decided to watch him racing his newly acquired Austin A30, which he had bought with money borrowed from his father. Circuit announcer Ken McPhail started calling the action. 'Here comes young Tim Schenken, who you'll all be familiar with following his racing exploits in the Simca Aronde.'

Hans and Shirley Schenken looked at each other, puzzled. There must have been some mistake. 'She spoke about it right up until she passed away, at 96 years of age,' Schenken recalls. 'I could never bring myself to tell her.'

An Austin Healey came next, then a Lotus 18, which helped him win the Victorian Formula 2 championship in 1964. In the same year he made the occasional detour into an overgrown go-kart constructed by a friend, Dick White. This was a purpose-built monster with a Speedway JAP engine, capable of up to 120 kilometres an hour. 'I was using it for hill climbs, and in 1965 I finished up winning the Australian Championship, beating, of all people, Colin Bond. He had come down from Sydney in a proper race car — a super-charged Lynx Peugeot — and was beaten by this thing built out of wheelbarrow wheels and metal tubing.'

'I couldn't believe it,' Bond recalls. The friends still joke about it 40 years later — they now work together in race control for the V8 Supercar Championship. 'It certainly made a long trip longer. We drove down from Sydney on the Friday night after work, practised on Saturday, competed on Sunday and drove back Sunday night for work Monday morning. That was the way it was done in those days. Tim will never let me forget it either.'

Schenken's future, however, was linked to the Lotus. It had belonged to Rocky Tresise and that connection brought a phone call from Lex Davison, who offered Schenken a full-time drive for his team in a 1.5 litre Elfin. A couple of weeks later, however, Davison was dead, and two weeks after that, Tresise was dead. 'I have to say my first reaction at the time was a mixture of sorrow at the tragedy of their deaths and a realisation of just what I was getting myself into. I really didn't have anyone to support me. I remember going to the funerals and standing on my own there. It was very emotional. I had only known Lex for a short time, but he was a hero of mine. I had his autograph. I knew Rocky a little better because I had raced against him a few times. It was a very difficult situation.'

Davison's widow, Diana, asked Schenken not to compete in the next scheduled formula junior meeting at Calder Park for which the Davison team had entered him in his own Lotus 18. 'It was all looking very dodgy,' Schenken recalls. 'The press were on to it and it was a big deal. All I ever wanted to do was go motor racing. Here I was on the verge of the big-time and I'm being told not to race.' Schenken decided to drive at Calder. 'I don't know exactly what it is, but you just don't think it's going to happen to you. You think you're immortal. You have confidence in yourself and your car. I have no recollection of that race, but I was up the front somewhere. All I know is that I'm still here today.'

Schenken, having survived the experience, won at Winton before heading for a bout with Kevin Bartlett and Greg Cusack in the Australian Formula 2 championship at Warwick Farm where he failed to finish, but by then he had decided that his future was in Europe.

He waved goodbye to family and friends in December 1965 and within weeks was in London, working with his mate Brian Andrew for the Chequered Flag Racing Team and living at Earls Court, commonly referred to as 'Kangaroo Valley'. He raced a Ford Anglia for a while before borrowing some money from his father to add to his own and buying a Lotus 22 to race in Formula 3. In 1964, the FIA changed Formula Junior, in which drivers like Jim Clark, John Surtees and Denny Hulme had competed, to Formula 3. They retained the specification of 1000cc engines derived from production touring cars. It was a fiercely competitive series.

Schenken had no wins in that car, but he did finish on the podium many times and he beat plenty of other drivers who were in the latest equipment. He had been told by *Autosport* magazine that they would write an article about him arriving in England to follow in Brabham's footsteps. 'They told me that they had written a similar piece for Jochen Rindt the year before and he had immediately been offered a great drive with Roy Winkleman Racing, the team for which he won the Guards 100. I'm still waiting for the phone call ...'

There was a call from the Merlyn team, though, offering Schenken and a few other drivers a test for their Formula Ford works team. Schenken was chosen for a subsidised drive in the 1968 championship, and contested 68 races that year. 'I could do four races a weekend, at two meetings, transporting the race car in an old van.' It was a rewarding year in more ways than one.

He met expatriate Aussies Brian Muir and Paul Hawkins, learning the trade from their advice. 'I remember after my first Formula 3 win at Brands Hatch, I was walking back down the pits when Frank Gardner's wife Gloria called me over and congratulated me. I met Frank then. I had seen him before, watched him racing, but never met him.

'And I remember a Swedish kid came up to me at Brands Hatch. It was his first race in England and he asked me about gear ratios. His name was Ronnie Peterson. In those days people were very secretive about things like gear ratios. I gave him the information, though, and we became very good friends after that.'

Schenken won many races for Merlyn, attracting an offer to compete in a Chevron Ford for Rodney Bloor in Formula 3. He won 15 races for Bloor on top of his 35 Formula Ford wins for Merlyn. He was the British champion in both categories, won the Grovewood Award for being the most promising young driver in the land and appeared on the front page of *Autosport* magazine.

Towards the end of the season, other drives emerged. He competed at Kyalami, South Africa, in a 9 hour race, driving a Chevron BMW with Brian Redman. They finished 4th overall and won their class. Then Jack Brabham and Ron Tauranac offered Schenken help to drive in Formula 3 for a customer team. His meeting with them, during a Formula Ford meeting at Spa, was another exciting step up the ladder and young Schenken was a little full of himself. Brabham glanced at his watch. 'Well, we can talk more about this later. Practice is coming up. Shouldn't you be out there?'

'Oh, don't worry about that,' Schenken replied. 'I can beat them all anyway. I'll go down later on.' What he hadn't accounted for was Spa's fickle weather patterns. While he had been talking to Tauranac and Brabham, his rivals had been putting down some smart times in dry conditions. By the time he got into his car late in the session, it had started raining on the far side of the long circuit. It was impossible for him to beat those times. A bemused Brabham team watched him start from further down the grid than he had promised.

'I was sitting in the cockpit,' Schenken recalls, 'and of course who else but Jack comes wandering over. "Weren't you going to be on pole, Tim?" he asked with a grin. Fortunately, I won the race.'

Two days after Christmas, Schenken competed in the first Brabham BT28 powered by a Ford engine, finishing 2nd in the Formula 3 championship round at Brands Hatch and becoming familiar with the factory. He realised just how significant a step he had taken when he saw Brabham arrive at a test in his private plane. He was also in awe at Brabham's ability to jump into a Formula 3 car and not only match his (Schenken's) times, but also identify problems.

In 18 starts across 1969, Schenken was never out of the top five, winning five times and finishing on the podium on 10 other occasions. 'The two guys I had been dicing with all year were Emerson Fittipaldi and Ronnie Peterson. The other important thing was that we were racing much of the time in conjunction with the larger formula cars, so we were in front of all the right people, the teams that we wanted to get into.' While most Continental rounds were not linked, some, like the French events, were part of their own championships. Schenken became the French Formula 3 champion.

Meanwhile, Jack Brabham had bigger issues, such as developing the Ford's power, and wings, to keep ahead of the game in Formula 1. It wouldn't have been hard to improve on his 2 point 1968 season, in which he finished only 2 of 12 races. His new team-mate was Belgian Jacky Ickx. 'He was a very good driver,' says Brabham, 'but for some reason we never clicked; it was not like with Jochen or Dan Gurney.'

Jochen Rindt had moved to Lotus. 'I would have retired a year earlier if Jochen had stayed with the team,' says Brabham. 'I wanted to have Jochen drive for me again in 1969, and in 1970 take over my drive, so I could just run the team. But then he came to me and said he had a problem: Ford and Colin Chapman had offered him a lot more money to drive for them. I'd have been kidding myself if I had said I could match that. We shook hands on it and I said, "Well if that's what you want to do, it's fine by me." I understood. That's why he went driving for Lotus. I've felt guilty about it ever since.'

The Ford Cosworth engine was not popular with everyone. 'We had a problem getting the right engines from Cosworth for a start,' Brabham recalls. 'We had been beating them with the Repco for so long that they were a bit against our team. We didn't get the best deal on engines. They were also looking after Stewart and Chapman — they got the best equipment.'

Jackie Stewart won six races for Matra, and the title, with 63 points. Jacky Ickx proved that the Brabham package was still competitive, winning two races and coming in second in the championship with 37 points. Piers Courage scored 16 points and Brabham scored 14. The team finished second in the Constructors Championship. Brabham, on a personal level, was only moderately successful. He broke his ankle in a testing crash at Silverstone, and therefore missed three rounds. In the eight races he did contest, there were two poles and two podium finishes.

'My worst moment that year,' Brabham recalls, 'was when a wing came off while I was driving in South Africa. I was heading into the fast corner which you always took flat out, and I just touched the kerb on the way out, as you had to do to keep the car steady. The rear wing collapsed. It wrapped around the wheel, and the wheel just ripped the wing straight off. It was if someone had taken the back wheels off the car. It couldn't have been worse. I was so lucky that I didn't have a huge accident. I was weaving from one side of the track to the other trying to keep the thing under control. Just scraped the wall ... I was so close it wasn't funny. They had to take the wings off to balance the car. The funny thing was, I won a gold watch. They were awarding a gold watch for the fastest speed down the main straight, and without wings that was easy.'

In 1969 Frank Gardner made another uneventful journey for Alan Mann Racing to Le Mans. He was out of the race after 8 hours, but not before he was clocked in the Mulsanne straight at 430 kilometres per hour — faster than anyone had ever driven there before. The rest of the year's racing program went almost as fast. He had eight podium finishes in the twin-cam Escort in the British Touring Car Championship, including three wins. He won four races across three continents in the Lola T70 V8 sports car. He also drove a Formula 5000 Lola in Britain and a Lola Can-Am car in America.

At the end of the season he held 14 lap records in Britain, but his greatest achievement that year was marrying Gloria Hyde, a beautiful Australian model he had met the year before. They were married in Australia and spent their honeymoon in South Africa, where Gardner finished 2nd in a 9 hour race and won three other events in the T70. 'I wasn't in trouble for racing on my honeymoon. It was something we talked about. I said, "This is the deal. If we get married, this is how it has to be." It all fitted in. We're still married, still mates. It obviously couldn't have been that bad. The way to make a marriage work is to let them think they're having their own way ... then let them have it.' Gardner did, however, decide not to compete in the upcoming Tasman series, following the death of a close family friend in a motoring accident.

The cameras were rolling on Frank Matich. A film was being shot of his campaign to take the sleek, aggressive SR4 sports car to the US to compete in the Can-Am series. The preparation had been perfect. With about a week to go before take-off, Matich received a bizarre phone call.

'I had been informed that the promoters in the US, the Sports Car Club of America (SCCA), had decided to exclude the SR4 from their competition that year. Teddy Mayer, running Bruce McLaren's US operations, approached Jim Hall of the Chaparral team and together they appealed to the SCCA to exclude any car with anything other than American stock block engines. Their argument was that the SR4 would have been too good, detracting from the American-engined cars, and the series would lose public support. I was in shock. I went to CAMS straight away and demanded they protest. They were not the slightest bit interested. They not only refused to go into bat for me, but they had actually viewed the whole thing as some sort of desertion or betrayal on my part. Christ, I was only going to take on one series. I was never going to leave Australia permanently. But this was their attitude about people going away. CAMS were in their own world.'

Matich took it as a compliment, that he had frightened his opposition so much. It appears they were also a little afraid of change in Australia where it was not long before CAMS also excluded his SR4 having decided, suspiciously, on a change in the series specifications. He believes their real motive was to prevent him rewriting all the track records. After all, who likes a monopoly, other than the one who is monopolising?

By November 1969 Kevin Bartlett had won his second consecutive Gold Star series and was about to take on his first Macau Grand Prix. His Mildren Alfa, nicknamed 'The Yellow Submarine', was transported to Macau by a ferry which used to be a gambling ship. 'I'd never been to Macau, but it was exactly as you imagined it from the movies. I was expecting to see Humphrey Bogart walk around the corner.' The 8 kilometre circuit was not closed until the race weekend, so Bartlett studied it by hiring a 125cc Yamaha motorcycle, waiting until midnight when the traffic had calmed, and riding the course.

In a couple of days he had become so familiar with it that he could ride it with his eyes closed, and sure enough, he was the first Australian to win the event. 'That was a terrific race. I took a car there that was bigger in capacity than anyone else's, which meant that all I had to do, really, was beat the clock. But Macau was the sort of race that you really had to know. It was a classic street circuit, with no barriers — street lamps, that was about it. A sea wall, in places, but if you ran off there it was like a boat ramp — straight into the water. They used to have frogmen there to get you when you did.'

*   *   *

The 1970 Tasman series was the first which allowed the entry of Formula 5000 cars, and Frank Matich, thanks to the crushing of his SR4 by the establishment, had been ahead of the game, preparing the McLaren M10A, with a Chevrolet 5 litre V8 engine. He finished 3rd in round 1 at Levin, then won the New Zealand Grand Prix at Pukekohe and round 3 at Wigram. 'We made a coffee table out of one of the wheels from the car that won the New Zealand Grand Prix. That was a nice win.'

He missed the final round at Teretonga, and then things went wrong in each of the three Australian races, keeping him off the podium. He lost the series by 5 points to Graeme Lawrence in a 2.5 litre Ferrari. 'I was never worried about losing the series,' he says. 'I was only interested in one meeting at a time. It was a good series.'

Leo Geoghegan was confined to the Australian rounds of the Tasman, more than a little upset that the New Zealand promoters hadn't sent him an invitation, especially after he'd won the 1969 Japanese Grand Prix in a Lotus 39T powered by a Repco 740 engine. He was always going to struggle, though: he was pitting an ageing car against mightier machines.

John Harvey and Kevin Bartlett also contested the series. Bartlett, using a new locally made Waggott engine, enjoyed his dices with team-mate Max Stewart. 'Max had great ability. We raced against each other for so many years we could read each other's minds. We used to practise together, eat together. At the race track, if I was in a position to help him, I would, and vice versa.' They tied for 3rd in the series.

'It wasn't my best chance to win the series,' Bartlett recalls, 'but it was one of them. Graeme Lawrence had a fabulous little car, a few years old, very reliable and under-stressed. I always regretted the Mildren team taking the Alfa 2.5 litre engine out of the "submarine", because that was the sweetest engine I had ever used. I reckon with that engine I would have bolted in. The problem was, the Alfa was a redundant engine, and spare parts were becoming scarce. We moved to the Waggotts because they were a new-generation engine with parts available, and room for development.'

Tim Schenken had taken a working holiday in Kyalami to drive a prototype sports car for Chevron: a B16 with a Cosworth engine aboard. It was there that he received a lesson in aerodynamics from no less a character than Frank Gardner. Schenken's team had been struggling with the Chevron's handling, and no amount of changes made any difference, until Gardner suggested they cut some aluminium strips about an inch wide, and pop rivet them onto the rear bodywork so that they sat almost vertical. Schenken was shocked at the improvement. 'The whole thing had been a simple aerodynamic problem. There were no wind tunnels in those days. Cars were often built the way they were just because they looked nice. That didn't mean they worked efficiently.'

Ferrari in 1970 lured Jacky Ickx away from the Brabham team, which hired Rolf Stommelen. 'He brought sponsorship with him and it helped us through the season,' Brabham recalls. He also had a new monocoque chassis, the BT33. 'It was a bloody good motor car. We should have won the championship in 1970. We had a few problems, though.' It would be a season of mishaps and misery for Brabham, but he would rise above it all to prove something, to the world, and himself.

He believes he could have won the Indianapolis 500. 'The gudgeon pin broke halfway through the race, and cut the engine in half! I had 950 horsepower, good enough for 400 kilometres an hour down the straight. The corners were coming up very quickly, and on every one of them you come out a whisker from the wall. The traffic is something else. It's like racing in a canal. You have to know exactly where you are, and even then you can have an accident. Someone else has one ... and you're just in it. It's very dangerous. I didn't like oval racing at all, but it was one of those things you had to do.'

Kevin Bartlett was also at 'The Brickyard' that season, and it was an emotional, exhausting experience for him. He was there because of an offer from Frank Matich, who had been unable to fulfil a commitment to the United States Auto Club (USAC) series because he was busy developing his Formula 5000 car. USAC was the original Indy car series. Its premier event had always been, and would continue to be, the Indianapolis 500.

Like so many drivers from overseas, Bartlett struggled with the nuances of oval circuits, and the structure of American open-wheel racing. He arrived in March, and found their wingless cars very crude compared with the Formula 1 styles he was used to. 'It was an Eisert — built like a truck.'

He persisted, and within a week raced at Sears Point, which was a tight but interesting circuit with rises and falls. 'I remember it was a very noisy car, and I'm sure it damaged my hearing. I qualified fifth. They all dropped their dacks and wondered what was going on. A fuel problem cost us a podium finish, but I made an impact on the Johnny Rutherfords and Al Unsers. I had more road racing experience than a lot of those speedway guys.' He was invited to continue, so he returned to Australia and mixed local drives with the American series for a while.

At the Indy 500 it was a different story. On the banked corners of oval racing, where the relatively unsafe cars were doing 400 kilometres an hour in a straight line, 250 on the curves, the Americans were in their element. Bartlett qualified 19th, but on the infamous 'bump day', when racers have a last chance to knock other drivers out of the field with a late qualifying effort, he missed out. 'I did about 1500 miles in testing and went through a few engines. The car was just not suited to full-throttle racing and it lacked straight line speed.'

Mario Andretti was helpful. 'Mario was only a year older than me but he had had a few more years' experience. He showed me a few things. I'll never forget him telling me, "You're not using enough road." I said, "Yeah, but I don't want to hit the wall." He said, "You won't hit the wall if you get up to the wall." I was a bit stunned by this. He said, "The closer you are to the wall, the more air pressure there is between you and the wall. What you do is come up to it until you are so close, you can actually feel the car move back again. The aerodynamics of the car create their own cushion of air." These were non ground-effect cars, aerodynamic bricks with at least 700 horsepower. To make it go faster, they just increased the engine output. I had been driving winged cars for 3 years before that. It was great advice.

'I got used to Indy but was very disillusioned with it. When I was bumped I had the opportunity to drive another car. I did get in that car and was much quicker. I was sitting in line to qualify, and it rained, so racing stopped. The system, the weather, beat me. On top of that, my second son was born 6 weeks premature while I was there. The first thing I wanted to do was get home. I could have taken that drive, stayed with that team and probably become a regular competitor with them in USAC, but at the time, I put family first. I have no regrets, of course, but I never went back to USAC.'

1970 was turning out to be a frustrating Formula 1 season for Jack Brabham, and when Denny Hulme burnt his hands severely at Indianapolis, leaping in panic from a flaming car, there was gloom in the garage. The week before the next round at Spa brought even worse news.

'We were at Silverstone,' Schenken recalls. 'Jack had been testing his Formula 1 car and I had been testing the Formula 3. He jumped into my car for a while to sort something out. I asked him why he wasn't going very fast. He explained that there was simply no need to go fast all the time in testing. Then he went off somewhere for a while. It wasn't long after — in fact I'd barely stopped thinking about what he said — when he came back to me, looking absolutely stone-faced. "I've just received a phone call," he said. "Bruce McLaren has been killed, testing his Can-Am car at Goodwood." He looked at me intently and added, "The lesson is, when you're testing, you don't have to go at lap record speed all the time. Do only what you need to do, because what we do is dangerous."'

'What shook me more than anything,' says Brabham, 'was that I had just come back from Indianapolis, sitting next to Bruce in the plane. He said to me then that he was not going racing anymore; he would just be doing a bit of testing. I said to him, "Bruce, the testing is more dangerous than the driving. If you have an accident when you're testing there'll be nobody there, nobody to help you. That's just my opinion." Within seven days, he was dead.'

The Matich family was on the other side of the world when the news came. Matich had woken in the early hours and sat up in bed to make a call to the McLaren factory. 'We used to talk on the phone, or our wives would talk, at least once a week about business and gossip, all kinds of things. When I was put through and asked for Bruce, I could tell from the tone of the bloke's voice that something was wrong. He just said, "Oh dear." I waited and waited before someone came on and told me he had just been killed. It upset us a hell of a lot. Bruce was a very smart, but nice bloke. You wouldn't have an argument with him. You would with me, but not with Bruce.

'You wonder how someone like Bruce would have the tiger in him to be a driver, especially against a tough competitor like Jack. He was a very decent bloke, but smart enough to surround himself with a couple of very tough people, including Teddy Mayer. He had built an empire. His business was the equivalent of Ferrari.'

The death of Bruce McLaren affected Matich so much that the plan to race the M10 in the US that year was shelved. 'To be honest? It would have meant working with Teddy Mayer. I couldn't do it.'

Jack Brabham was still a threat to win title number four when the Formula 1 series reached Holland, where the McLaren team returned to racing. Spectators held their breath as they watched two terrifying practice crashes that could easily have taken two more lives. Pedro Rodriguez was one lucky driver;

Brabham was the other. 'We were tyre testing on the Wednesday before the race. Stommelen was supposed to be driving but he didn't turn up, so at the end of the day Ron asked me to hop into Stommelen's car and do some laps. I must have cut a tyre or something exiting the pits because on an S-bend, going into the right-hander, the outside tyre deflated suddenly. I started to slide off, but the deflated tyre came off the rim, which dug in when it hit the sand. I rolled three or four times into the bank, where I got wrapped up in a wire-mesh fence. I finished upside down, bound tightly inside the car, so I just sat there, with fuel running out of the tank. Thankfully it just soaked into the sand. It was just like I said to Bruce McLaren. There was no one around because it was a practice day. Eventually, when they dragged all the wire away, I unbuckled my seatbelt a bit too quickly and fell out on my head! I had a sore neck for days.'

Championship leader Rindt, armed with a new Lotus 72C, took command of the Dutch Grand Prix. It would have been the talking point of the weekend, except for Piers Courage crashing his De Tomaso Cosworth on lap 22. He bounced into a sandbank, struck a pole, and landed upside down. Courage was killed. It was one of the worst accidents that Jack Brabham had seen, and he had seen plenty. 'It was terrible, dreadful. I can't remember whether I had a problem, but he started in front of me in the race. I was a few cars behind him. I just saw him spear straight off and into a bank. The car exploded. I mean, absolutely exploded. It was like a bomb. I couldn't believe it. As I went past, I felt not only this wave of heat come over me from the fire, but also a massive rush of air, like a shock wave, from the blast itself. It nearly blew me off the circuit. To top it off, I saw his crash helmet rolling along the track. The moment I saw it, I knew who it was.'

'My mother and father happened to be at that race,' continues Brabham, 'and coincidentally, they were in the pits at the time, with Piers's wife. That didn't help.' Courage's small-budget team, run by Frank Williams, had struggled enough in Formula 1. How Williams dealt with the moment would define a large slice of motor racing history.

Tim Schenken had been struggling in the Formula 2 races, due to a mix of mechanical problems and lack of confidence against the top drivers. 'I remember qualifying well at Zolder, sitting on the grid, with Jacky Ickx on one side and Jo Siffert on the other. I couldn't believe it, and actually psyched myself out. It was all too much for me.' He would have to get used to it, though, because he had also tested the Brabham Formula 1 car, and it would not be long before he would be asked to step up. At Zandvoort, following the death of Piers Courage, he would have the opportunity, but where in the malevolent world of motor sport does a driver draw the line between opportunity and civility?

'I took a deep breath,' Schenken recalls, 'and visited Frank Williams's workshop in Slough, not far from where I lived. I asked him if he would consider me for the job of driving the car. It was a very emotional experience. It's not the easiest thing to ask for a drive when the previous driver has just been killed. It took a lot of thinking about. Frank agreed. It was a low-budget team with a car that was in the early stages of design. Frank was really scratching for funding to keep going.'

'Frank Williams in those days was a real go-getter,' says Brabham. 'He didn't have a lot of money, but he was doing a lot for the amount of money he had. He was really scratching, so we used to help him a bit. He had our cars for a while. He used to get our mechanics to make him bits and pieces in the workshop, and slip them to him out the back door. He had to do that sort of thing to keep going.'

Jochen Rindt had won at Zolder, but Brabham's fading chance to win the title could have been rekindled had he not run out of fuel in the following round, in France. 'I was leading the race going into the final corner at the time. It was a mistake from one of the mechanics. He started the car that morning with the engine set on full rich, and they never switched it back. So I was using far more fuel than I realised. Needless to say, I went looking for him when I got back to the pits.' While Brabham coasted towards the line, Rindt flashed past, relegating him to 2nd.

'If I had won all the races that were botched in that season, I would have won the championship easily.' Brabham was asked by a journalist which mechanic had made the mistake with the fuel. Brabham told the journalist that it was Ron Dennis [Brabham was wrong].

The Austrian Grand Prix was staged at a bright new circuit cut into the side of a serene valley. It was an exciting test called the Osterreichring. It would be Tim Schenken's initiation into Formula 1. The designer of the De Tomaso car was Gian Paolo Dallara, whose name is still behind race car designs today. In 1970 his project was in its infancy. 'One of the problems the car had was an incredible kick-back in the steering. On rough circuits it was so bad it wrecked your wrists.' Schenken topped a wet practice session, proving his skills, but in the race he retired with engine trouble after only 25 of the 60 laps. 'I was lapping fairly quickly, I recall, at one stage. This was a car that was consistently at the back of the grid. It was never going to be competitive, but I was pretty happy with what I achieved.

'Frank Williams in those days was … well put it this way, in 1968 he was Frank Williams 1968 Ltd. Then the company went broke. He became Frank Williams 1969 Ltd. That went broke. So it was Frank Williams 1970 Ltd. That's the team I drove for, if you get what I mean.' The team never seemed to make ends meet, Williams annually reinventing it to attract enough support to keep afloat. Racing constantly on a shoestring budget was very demanding.

The Italian Grand Prix at Monza brought the season to a new low. In Friday practice, Schenken's great rival, Emerson Fittipaldi, in his first drive of the Lotus 72C, survived a terrifying crash at the Parabolica, his car climbing a bank of dirt and sailing into a clump of trees, missing all of them. Saturday dawned, and championship leader Rindt, also in the 72C, was practising. Observers saw his car turn left as he braked into a corner. It crashed into the barriers. The car was a mess. Rindt was taken to hospital, but was dead before he arrived.

'It was another very emotional weekend,' Schenken recalls. 'I had known Jochen Rindt. I had met him through Formula 2, raced against him. He was a big hero of mine. A huge star. I remember talking to Jackie Stewart the following morning. He was in quite a state. It was quite strange, though, because there was huge sorrow and yet the next thing you'd all be racing again and everything would be back to normal. It just wasn't spoken about.'

Frank Gardner had great respect for Rindt, against whom he had competed in Formula 2. 'Rindt in his early days had a hell of an accident at the Nurburgring, and knocked himself around pretty badly. From then on he drove with lots of discretion, lots of polish — and he was very quick, in the Ronnie Peterson mould. But you see, in pushing stuff always to the limit, sooner or later something's going to break on the car. Those guys were usually good enough to drive through the Lotus's problems, which were many, and the same with Jimmy Clark.'

Jack Brabham was also critical of Lotus. 'They had been experimenting with in-board disc brakes on the front of the car, to take the weight out of the wheel. There was a shaft running from the in-board brakes to the wheel. The shaft wasn't strong enough. When Jochen got to the end of the straight and put his foot on the brake, the shaft broke. It wrapped around the wheel and took all the suspension, and the whole wheel, off. He was killed at 160 miles an hour with only three wheels and no brakes. They were too near the bone all the time. The cars were just too light. It was another Colin Chapman loss of a driver — and he lost a few, I tell you.

'The worst thing was, there was no doctor there. They reckon that had a doctor got to him early they could have saved him, but by the time they got to a hospital they were too late. There were doctors at circuits in those days, but not at that particular meeting. There was never much in the way of medical support.

'I also feel a bit responsible, you know. I had a contract with Jochen, really. I could have kept him at Brabham if I had made him abide by the contract, but there was so much money involved in the offer from Lotus that I didn't feel it was right to keep him.'

'The Lotus was an exciting car,' says Gardner. 'But Colin Chapman was also a great talker. He could sell anything. He could control a meeting and get that meeting to arrive at a decision, whether that decision was good, bad or indifferent. If he told someone that a steering arm or something else was strong enough to drive with, they would usually go out and drive with it.'

No one could catch Rindt's total in the ensuing rounds, and by the time the series concluded in Mexico, Formula 1 had its first posthumous champion. Jack Brabham's final championship season would be one of sadness and frustration. 'It was another championship that I lost through stupid things. I should have won in 1967 and I should have won in 1970. The last round, in Mexico, was a failure because of another dud engine from Cosworth. I'd already sold the team to Ron Tauranac, in preparation for retirement. I felt bad not only for myself, but also for the team, for all the people who had been involved around me, people who had spent their careers trying to help me build the best car and win races with it.'

For the second time in his career Bernie Ecclestone cut his ties with Formula 1 following the death of a close associate. He had been Jochen Rindt's business partner. He would return for a final time, however, to play a key role in the Brabham story.

Frank Gardner continued his lucrative relationships with Ford and Lola in 1970, preparing Escort rally cars and driving a Mustang 302 to eight wins in the British Touring Car Championship, which he lost to Bill McGovern by just 4 points.

Gardner had also agreed to race for Lola in the British Formula 5000 series, in which he used their Chevrolet V8-powered T190 chassis. 'It was a good formula. You just had to drive the cars. There's no such thing as a bad car or a bad circuit if you drive to the conditions.' The British series was made up of 10 rounds in the UK and 4 rounds on the European Continent. Most consisted of two short races, with the results aggregated to determine the overall winner. In at least two of the meetings Gardner raced both cars on the same weekend. He won the AP trophy at Silverstone on 15 August and finished the season with three podiums out of four starts. The T190 would be upgraded the following year, not once, but twice, in a fascinating development race that would bring substantially better results.

The 1970 Gold Star series came down to the final round at Mallala, South Australia, where John Harvey, still driving the Repco-powered 'Jane', carried a championship lead. All he had to do was finish 6th or better to beat Leo Geoghegan in his Waggott-powered Lotus 59B. 'Leo's 2 litre car wasn't as powerful. I followed him for quite a while but he slowed down a bit with some problem so I passed him. I thought that was it. No pressure. I could just taste this Gold Star ... I wanted it so much. Then I went up the long back straight, only a few laps to go, and the wing broke off just as I entered the long right-hander at full speed. That was it for me. Leo won the championship. I had tried so hard so many times. Bob spent a lot of time and effort on it too, because he had already won two with Spencer Martin and he certainly wanted me to win one.'

The 1970 Australian Grand Prix, run later in the month at Warwick Farm, came nearly 2 years after the previous one, and was the first to embrace the new 'stock-block' V8-powered cars. Once again the story was deeper than the bare statistics indicate. Most drivers had apparently equal cars, but they were in vastly different states of reliability, due to vastly different preparation. When it came to preparation, Frank Matich was supreme. He had bucked the trend, replacing the Chevrolet engine in his McLaren M10B with a Repco V8, and ruled the weekend, with pole, victory and lap record. 'To be honest,' says Matich, 'compared with the American Formula 5000 races, it was a piece of cake. I should have been shot if I hadn't won the Australian races. I had been to the US and conducted extensive tests for Goodyear, following Firestone's withdrawal from motor sport. I wasn't competing regularly every week, but the number of laps I clocked had been invaluable. That was the secret of being able to improve the cars. Everything you learnt you categorised, and used to take the car a step further. The driving became easy when you made the car better.'

Leo Geoghegan was a credible 4th, proving once again that the 2 litre cars were more effective at Warwick Farm, but Kevin Bartlett suffered yet another breakdown.

Formula 5000 cars won all seven races of the 1971 Tasman series, which New Zealander Graham McRae won by 35 points to Matich's 31. It was a fast series, with lap records tumbling. Matich, in the only F5000 car that did not have a Chevrolet engine, finished 2nd in three races before winning at Sandown Park. 'I remember Graham McRae being a very good driver, but a very serious bloke,' says Matich. 'He resented not only my relationship with McLaren, but also my relationship with Goodyear. For some reason he saw it all as a conspiracy against him. I could just walk up, sit down, and stare at the back of his car and he'd get all twitchy. "What's wrong?" he'd ask. I'd say, "Have you still got that same support for the lower wishbone?" He'd panic and say, "Why? What have you got?" He used to go nuts.'

Frank Gardner had returned for the series in his Lola, winning at Warwick Farm and finished 2nd at Sandown; it was a brave effort considering he had injured his back during testing at Levin. For all their friendly jibes, he had this to say on his final series against Matich: 'Frank was smart and had some smart people working for him. He was a very interesting and colourful bloke and above all, probably Australia's best driver; he was extremely talented. I remember winning a Hordern Trophy from him, and I must say, I was pleased when the race was over. I had a better set-up car than he had. I had the edge on him in most places, but he made up for it in driving ability.'

Jack Brabham may have left racing, but his team was still intact — and, with Ron Tauranac at the helm, determined to compete strongly in the 1971 championship. This was an important decision for Tim Schenken, because it gave him a path into Formula 1, where his team-mate would be Graham Hill.

Schenken had befriended the former Brabham mechanic whom Brabham had blamed for the fuel mix-up that cost him the 1970 British Grand Prix: Ron Dennis. Schenken had a lot of time for Dennis. 'Ron was an ambitious young man and wanted to move on. At the end of 1970 he found backing from a Greek shipping magnate and formed a Formula 2 team with Neil Trundle. It was called Rondel — a combination of their two names. I was his first driver, and Graham Hill was my team-mate there as well. So during that year I was racing in both categories.'

'Ron Dennis worked for me for 2 years,' says Brabham. 'It was funny, actually, that I blamed him for what happened at Silverstone. He always denied it. It wasn't until years later that I learnt the truth. I was having dinner with one of my old mechanics from that team and got the shock of my life when he admitted that it was him who made the mistake, not Ron! Well, I had to straight away apologise to Ron.'

'The thing that I remember most about Ron's Formula 2 team,' says Schenken, 'was that not only were the cars beautifully prepared, but his transporters were immaculate. You could eat your dinner off the floor. It was very different from many of the teams, whose cars were well prepared but very grubby. Ron's two nicknames were rather cool, I thought. One was "Team Dream", because he was so ambitious, and the other was "Team Briefcase", because he carried one everywhere.'

After a few rounds of the championship it was clear that the 1971 Brabham car would not be good enough — but neither was the rookie driver. 'I had been having trouble making the most of the car,' says Schenken. 'I was braking too early into the corners. It really clicked at the French Grand Prix, where I started to show more speed.' He qualified 7th at the British Grand Prix, seven positions better than ever before, and was running 3rd, catching Ronnie Peterson, until the gearbox failed. At the German Grand Prix he qualified 9th and finished 6th. 'I was down on power there. I'd be up with them one minute, then they'd just run away from me. One reason was that some of the teams had discovered that the air boxes were having greater effect on the performance of the car than we had previously understood. A better box ensured cleaner air, which increased power. We didn't catch on to that straight away.' On all but one occasion he beat Hill, who by then was in the later model BT34.

Pedro Rodriguez was killed in a sports car race at the Norisring, a few weeks before the Austrian Grand Prix, but for Schenken, the show had to go on if he was to cement his career in Formula 1. He qualified 7th and finished 3rd, behind Jo Siffert and Emerson Fittipaldi. 'I had been running 3rd, catching the second car, at Silverstone, when I had trouble with the transmission. I had also been in position to finish on the podium in France, so Austria was a very satisfying result. I knew that I could do well.'

After 10 starts, Tim Schenken finished the official Formula 1 season with 5 points, equal 14th in the championship. He had the greatest respect for Ron Tauranac, but Tauranac was not at his best as a team manager. 'Ron was a loner,' explains Schenken. 'Those who had been at Brabham long enough knew him well enough. We used to call him "Anorak": you could never get him off your back. When you worked for Ron, you really had to do it his way.'

Jack Brabham, who also had the greatest respect for Tauranac, could not help but agree. 'Everybody found it difficult working for Ron. That was nothing unusual. He just wasn't the easiest person to work with.'

Schenken's Formula 2 season with Rondel was a richer feast, taking him to far-flung places and races where he diced with the best drivers in the world for several top-10 finishes. There were exciting duels with his friends Ronnie Peterson and Emerson Fittipaldi, but he had different problems with his ageing team-mate Graham Hill, who was also a good friend and a continuous source of amusement. 'I'll never forget a race in Rouen,' Schenken says, 'where, just before the start, Graham had to have a pee. The toilets were disgusting and miles away from the pits, so he peed into a soft-drink bottle and just left it in the truck. It was also a very hot day. Sure enough, one of Graham's own mechanics, rushing past, grabbed the bottle and took a swig out of it.'

Hill is the subject of many memorable stories. Schenken and Peterson would often hitch a ride with him in his private plane. On the way to a race at Pau, France, after the plane had reached cruising altitude, Hill switched to automatic pilot and fell asleep. The two passengers looked at each other, shrugged, and tried to relax. They found it increasingly unnerving, however, hearing Hill's snores and watching the fuel gauge fall rapidly. Schenken broke the silence first. 'Should I wake him up?'

Peterson replied, 'Surely he knows ...'

The plane flew on, and two sweating race drivers watched the gauge reach almost zero. Hill was still asleep. Schenken finally lost his cool and shook Hill from his slumber. 'Oh that ...' said Hill, and flicked a switch, changing fuel tanks. They watched the needle on the gauge rise again and breathed a sigh of relief — but wondered what might have happened if they had not been there.

Another of Hill's great flying faux pas was when he landed at a secret military air base in Sweden, thinking it was a local airport. He then berated Schenken for not coming to collect him — Schenken had been at the right airport, waiting, for hours. The Swedish police sorted it out. 'For years after,'

Schenken recalls, 'it became one of Graham's favourite stories, telling everyone about this Swedish military air base that was so secret he managed to land his Piper Aztec there.'

The most significant event of the year for Schenken took place in the paddock during practice for the Italian Grand Prix. He was approached by a mysterious woman who told him that Ferrari wanted to speak to him. He repeatedly ignored her, believing it to be a practical joke, but when he finally submitted and arrived at the Ferrari tent, he discovered, to his embarrassment, that the great man himself, Enzo Ferrari, wanted him to drive their sports cars. 'I asked them for a lot of money, which I thought was pretty bold, and they said "Yes" right away. Perhaps I should have asked for more!' It was a deal that would set up Tim Schenken's career for years to come, and would be far more prosperous than Formula 1.

In 1971 Frank Gardner took his Lola T192 back to Europe, keen to follow up his successful 1970 debut in the British Formula 5000 season. His saloon car racing, however, was to take another turn. 'Stuart Turner came in to run Ford and I lost that friendly atmosphere I'd had with Walter Hayes. Stuart was starting to tell me what I could and couldn't do. I'd never had that with Walter. At the same time, General Motors, of course, offered me more money. They had the Chevy Camaros. They knew we were doing the European Touring Car Championship. So I had to tell Stuart, "I think your ideas are great. The only thing missing here is compatibility between Stuart and Frank, so I'll take my lack of compatibility to General Motors for more money."'

Just as he did in the Ford days, Gardner often raced the Lola and the Camaro at the same meeting. He won the over-2 litre class in the British Saloon Car Championship, winning only one race in five starts, but that win was his 100th in saloon car racing.

The majority of his year was spent in Formula 5000, where the Lola development was intensifying. He started the season in the T192, qualifying second and winning the first round, at Snetterton. He scored two more wins and three podiums, the latest on 4 July at Mallory Park. After that meeting Gardner and Eric Broadley decided that the Surtees and McLaren cars were going to be too strong by the end of the year, so they plotted an astonishing mid-season revamp of the car. Within 2 weeks, the T300 was produced. It was radically different. 'Different chassis, suspension, brakes, everything,' Gardner recalls. 'But there was nothing that we didn't know about. They were all Lola parts. Eric really applied himself to it. We spent a lot of time getting it right. It was just a case of getting it to be quick enough. It was a bit of a handful at first, but we levelled it out.'

He took the car to Thruxton, without any testing, qualified on pole and finished 3rd on aggregate behind Graham McRae. He finished 2nd overall at Silverstone, then a week later won the round at Oulton Park. He won three more rounds and finished 2nd in two others. At Hockenheim, he beat Emerson Fittipaldi in both heats. The championship was his. 'It was always good to run against a bloke like Fittipaldi. He was great. He was a gentleman, but above all, he could drive. It's no good saying this or that bloke's a nice guy ... if he's miscast, I lose interest. But if anyone was ever cast to drive race cars it was Fittipaldi. He really was a real professional.'

It had taken 4 years for the plan to be put into operation, but Frank Matich finally made his way to the US for a serious tilt at a major road racing championship. He had won the Australian and New Zealand grands prix in the Formula 5000 era, and with the Repco-powered McLaren M10 which he had developed himself, it was finally the hour of reckoning: 27 April 1971. After qualifying 3rd, he finished 2nd in both heats before winning the Riverside Grand Prix. He then moved to Laguna Seca, finishing 2nd to David Hobbs in the Monterey Grand Prix. The US campaign was part of a deal with Trojan Industries to further develop McLaren cars and Goodyear tyres. His sponsors believed it was successful. Matich was not finished, though. He skipped the next eight rounds as he worked on an even more exciting project back home.

There was no fanfare about Vern Schuppan's win in the British Formula Atlantic Championship in 1971. People were too busy asking where he had come from. The answer to that question was a tiny town called Booleroo Centre, where he was born on 19 March 1943. He was not there long before his father set up a garage, panelbeating shop and car dealership in Whyalla. That's where the driving bug bit.

'As I grew older I worked in the garage, and I moved cars around for Dad, long before I had a licence. I watched the 1955 Australian Grand Prix at Port Wakefield, which Jack Brabham won, and that really got me interested in racing. I still have a photograph that I took of Jack in the pits, working on that bob-tailed Cooper.'

Schuppan began work in the family garage full-time after leaving school, and collected parts to build his own car, much to his father's annoyance — he considered it dangerous. 'Dad finally gave in and helped me buy a go-kart, but only because he thought it would cure my urge to be a race driver.'

It was like pouring fuel on the flames. A working holiday in Europe as a 22-year-old, taking in events at Goodwood and other major venues, only made Schuppan more determined. He returned home to win the South Australian and Victorian go-kart titles, married his girlfriend Jennifer and then popped an even bigger question: would you return to Europe with me as I pursue a racing career? Jennifer was not keen on the idea but she agreed to the terms, which included a 2 year probationary period, after which they would return if Vern had not succeeded. In May 1969 they packed a campervan, loaded it on a ship, and set sail. They had saved $5000.

'I found work in London with Murray Rainey, whom I'd met in Australia at a go-kart meeting. He was a bit of a wheeler-dealer, buying, restoring and selling old cars, but he was also great mates with Ken Tyrrell, Ron Tauranac and Jack Brabham.'

Schuppan started working his new contacts for advice and help. Tauranac told him how good the drivers were over there and gently advised him to use the money he had saved on a plane ticket home; Tauranac's was not the only wise head that did not want to see Schuppan disappointed. 'I went and saw Tim Schenken at Silverstone. He wasn't stand-offish, but he asked me the same questions as Ron: what have you done and how much have you got? We were watching a Formula Ford race at the time. Tim had won that series the previous year but there were about 80 cars trying to qualify. He turned to his friend, New Zealand Formula 3 driver Howden Ganley and said: "Look at that. I wouldn't want to be in there now ..."'

'Tim told me I should avoid Formula Ford and try Prod-Sports, a strange kind of Formula Libre category; it was a bit of a dead-end if you had a Formula 1 career in mind. I still haven't heard of anyone who's gone anywhere doing that series. So I said I didn't want to do that and he said, "Well, what do you want to do?" I said, "Formula 3." I think that was the end of it for Tim. He shrugged and said, "Well, you do what you like, mate. What are you asking my advice for?"'

'I remember the first time I met Vern,' Schenken recalls. 'I told him to go back to Australia or something. He was very upset. I mean, he was just like me, really. He went over there with nothing and battled away.'

The odd thing was that Schuppan, having made a relatively late start, was 6 months older than Schenken at the time, but had assumed that Tim was older because of his experience. Having settled in a job and home, Schuppan bought an old Alexis Formula Ford — the cheapest he could find, at £950 — and with his few remaining pounds, he set about preparing it to race.

At his first meeting, he ran into Tim Schenken again. 'He shook his head,' Schuppan recalls, 'and said, "Why in the world did you buy that? It's an absolutely terrible car!" Our relationship had started badly and gone downhill from there.'

They would become firm friends in later years. 'We both laugh at it now,' says Schenken, 'but it must have pissed him off at the time!'

Schuppan's simple and somewhat courageous theory was that if he bought a bad car and performed reasonably well he would be noticed more. In those days there were Formula Ford races everywhere, but they were very hard to get into. He would trailer the car behind the campervan from meeting to meeting, twice a weekend, occasionally getting a start. Finally, he drove to 3rd place from the back of the grid in a Formula Libre race, a performance that caught the eye of team owner Tony Maycon. Schuppan quickly sold his old car and used the funds from the sale to finance his first works drive.

Motor sport scribes had also noticed Schuppan, and they compared him with Schenken, which was not well received by either of them. The stairway to success continued, however, deals leading to deals, with Schuppan doing well enough with each offer to keep more offers coming. Finally he secured an engine deal from BRM, along with a place in the Palliser team in Formula Atlantic; he rewarded their faith with a British championship win.

'The BRM wasn't the best engine, but it suited my car very well. I scored a number of pole positions, and about 6 wins from 12 starts. Formula Atlantic was a much more powerful category than Formula Ford. My main rivals, Ray Allen, Sid Williams and Tom Belso, were very hot prospects at the time. I saw that season as a great opportunity to cement a place with BRM that might lead to a test in Formula 1.'

*   *   *

Only Jack Brabham had won the Australian Grand Prix in a car of his own design and construction — and even then the Cooper name was still attached to it. In 1971, Frank Matich had the Australian Grand Prix all to himself with the Repco-powered A50, which had been first tested barely a week before the race. His previous car, the M10, had become more of a Matich than a McLaren thanks to the massive development that he had contributed to it in Australia and the US. The A50, so named because it happened to be Repco's 50th year, was merely the next step. 'We did two days of testing at Warwick Farm,' he recalls, 'before we started formal practice for the event.' Matich was as confident about the A50 as he had been about the SR4 sports car.

Kevin Bartlett had left the Mildren team by then and was driving his own McLaren M10, with backing from Shell. 'It was significant that I had gone out by myself. Alec was scaling back his operation. I could probably have stayed with him a little longer, but I saw what was coming — Formula 5000 would be the premier open-wheel category. So I took the plunge. Max Stewart stayed with Alec. It was an amicable parting, but I wasn't really ready for it, mentally. I bought the car and equipment from Niel Allen, but couldn't afford parts or spares. I then had a crash in practice at Sandown, a nasty one. I fronted for the race with a Rothmans nose and rear wing that I had borrowed from Matich. I didn't have time to change them — all I could do was put a few Shell stickers on! Rothmans got a good deal that weekend. It was a pot-pourri, but you know what? I won that Sandown race.'

Of the 23 starters in the 1971 Australian Grand Prix at Warwick Farm on 21 November, 8 were Formula 5000 cars. They were becoming the most popular car among the leading drivers. Matich had signed up Colin Bond to drive his McLaren M10, Frank Gardner was in a Lola T300, John Surtees in a TS8. John Harvey, still driving for Bob Jane, had won the first of what would be two Australian Sports Car Championships in a McLaren M6 with Repco power, but for the grand prix Jane prepared a BT36 with a Waggott engine. It looked strong.

'We arrived at the meeting, having had a short test at Oran Park the previous day,' Harvey recalls. 'We did a few laps in practice. The engine was fine. All I wanted was a little bit more brake on the front; otherwise it was perfect. We qualified third, but Frank Matich was not very far in front in his F5000.' Bond was on the third row, alongside Bartlett but in front of Surtees. Gardner crashed in practice and didn't start the race.

Matich bounced away and started to build a lead. As his immediate rivals struck trouble, Harvey was looking like the only real chance of causing an upset. 'We followed Frank, in 2nd place, looking good, but the exhaust tailpipe fell off. We had no chance of catching him then.'

Frank Matich had become the first driver since Brabham to win two consecutive Australian grands prix. 'It was after that race that I coined the phrase, "Life wasn't meant to be easy ... Buy Australian", which I think was used again ... a few times. I came up with it because for the first time, the package was all Australian. We had a beautiful car, a very tight team by that time, about 13 people, and we were all very proud.' Typically for the Matich team, there were no parties; it was just back to headquarters to prepare for the next meeting.

The next Australian Grand Prix would be held at Sandown on 20 February 1972, rejoining the Tasman series after another switch from one end of the year to the other. Frank Gardner had finally won the New Zealand Grand Prix after a tense fight with Graham McRae, David Hobbs and Mike Hailwood, but a faulty gearbox cost him the race he really wanted — the Australian Grand Prix. 'I had the measure of the whole race, but a little pin that holds the gear lever in had worked loose, and I was trying to hold the whole thing in with my thumb while I was changing gears. It was just that little thing that took the edge off the performance, so there I was watching the whole race slip away. That was the Australian Grand Prix, which I never managed to win. It was nice winning the New Zealand Grand Prix, but I'd have loved to win the Australian as well. I did manage a podium finish in 1967.'

John Harvey finished 7th, but was thrilled with an achievement that almost made up for his so-near-and-yet-so-far relationship with the coveted Gold Star award. He had been presented with the award for Most Meritorious Performance by an Australian-based driver. 'That car — the BT36 — blew every other 2 litre car into the weeds. It was a sensational car. I've driven plenty of Brabhams, more than most, and that was the best.' Despite all this, he and Bob Jane would soon abandon open-wheel racing altogether and, under pressure from their sponsor, Castrol, concentrate on touring cars, which is where the company felt its marketing would have the most impact. Harvey, like so many others, had to forsake the category he loved and end his career in the sedans he once despised.

There was no despair in the Matich camp after what had been, by his standards, a disappointing series. 'We were not only developing the Matich car,' he explains, 'but conducting vital tests for Goodyear, who were using the data as a springboard for their international season. We had problems here and there, but that happens to everyone at some stage.' In that time, Matich employed Howard Marsden, who had worked with Frank Gardner for Alan Mann Racing in England and with Frank Williams Formula 2 team. It was Marsden's first Australian job, the launching pad for what would be a very influential career in Australian motor sport.

There was one special honour that somehow made up for any on-track failures: Matich had been invited to join the Grand Prix Drivers Association (GPDA). 'I was the only Australian member, other than Jack, and the only driver who hadn't competed in Formula 1. I still have the armband, with No. 29 on it. That was another thing that pissed CAMS off. The GPDA was focusing on track safety, with Jackie Stewart leading the charge. I was asked to do track inspections back here and they had their backs up. They looked on us as if we were a hostile trade union.' Matich decided to turn away from the US to focus on winning the only major Australian title he had yet to claim ... mainly because he had never really tried to win it. In 1972 his target would be the Gold Star series.

Frank Gardner had been asked by Lola to drive its Formula 5000 car in Europe again in 1972, but as things turned out, the 1971 Tasman series was to be his last in open-wheel racing. 'I just decided they were going bloody quick. They were snatching 200 miles an hour, and any shunt at 200 miles an hour is going to be a big one. I was also having a fair amount of back trouble. I had to have some surgery done on that, so it may have been the smart thing to do. I knew that I could win the British Touring Car Championship again without a great deal of trouble, so I told Eric Broadley at Lola that I would only do their test driving. We reached a compromise. If you're uncomfortable in the car, and if you're not 100 per cent fit, you shouldn't be there.'

Vern Schuppan's Formula Atlantic campaign had been renewed in 1972, but most importantly, he had been asked by Louis Stanley, head of the BRM team, to test their Formula 1 cars, and race them in some non-championship rounds. He was told that if he performed well he would be signed up for a full season in 1973.

The Formula 1 scene was heating up, and there was a constant shifting of power in drivers, teams, manufacturers. Ron Tauranac had decided to sell the

Brabham team to Bernie Ecclestone. Jack Brabham was not pleased. Like any businessman whose name is etched on a famous product, but who has no control over its destiny, he was concerned that the right people should be involved. 'No, I didn't like the idea of the Brabham name being sold. It was bad news to me. There was nothing I could do about it. Bernie was only interested in Formula 1, so he got rid of all the production cars, chucked out all the jigs and body moulds, threw them onto the tip. After all the work we'd put in, it upset me a bit.'

He refused to get involved because it had been his decision to leave everything in Tauranac's hands after the 1970 season. At the insistence of his three sons, Geoff, Gary and David, he had bought a farm. 'It wasn't long before Geoff tapped me on the shoulder and wanted to run a Formula Ford. Unfortunately, he did quite well,' Brabham says, tongue in cheek. The world of motor racing would soon be vibrating again with the roar of Brabham-driven cars and Jack Brabham would be inexorably drawn back into the politics and commercialism that only a few years before he had been very pleased to escape.

Bernie Ecclestone, returning from another self-imposed break from Formula 1, was finally in the game for keeps when he bought the Brabham team. Tim Schenken, at the time, was not convinced that Ecclestone was the right man to look after the famous name. 'Bernie,' he recalls, 'had always been a fringe-dweller in Formula 1, not always a visible character. I simply didn't believe the stories I had heard about him buying the team, so eventually I confronted Ron and he admitted that it was true. I was very disappointed in Ron for not telling me what was going on.'

Ecclestone sat down with Schenken and discussed renewing his contract. He wanted Schenken to sign for the next 2 years. Ecclestone's argument was that if he invested in Schenken for 1 year, he wanted to make sure the faith would be repaid with loyalty the following year. 'But I only wanted a 1 year deal, and my argument was that I had no idea how he was going to run the team and if I signed for 2 years and we didn't work out I wouldn't have been free to move on. We couldn't agree. So I made a phone call to John Surtees, and I suppose that really was the turning point of my career.'

'Tim would have been better off staying with Bernie,' says Brabham, 'because Bernie did get the team going and going well. They did win. Tim could have done a lot better with the right teams.'

Ecclestone's return would mark the start of the most dramatic era in Formula 1 history. He was a thinker, as well as a doer. He had grand plans and he took them on with great verve, even if they were occasionally destined for the scrap heap, as Frank Gardner laughingly recalls. 'He came to me one day — I honestly can't remember when it was but it was in the early days, the late 1950s — and he said, "We've got this new sports car we want you to have a look at. Will you come to Brands Hatch and drive it?" It was a little aluminium bloody thing. I think it had a Climax in it. I had a run in it, had a think about it, and said, "Bernie the best thing you could do here is jack up the windscreen wiper and put a new car under it!"'

For Brabham, the evolution of what had been his team would be a hurtful process. He never begrudged Ecclestone his success, or criticised his management skills, but he would like to have seen his name sustained in history the way McLaren and Williams have been. 'Bernie, after a few years, got mixed up with the FIA and everything, and decided he didn't want the team anymore. He finished up selling it three times: once to Alfa Romeo, then he bought it back, once to a bloke in Germany, who went broke. The third owners went broke as well. It all finished up in receivership, disappeared.'

Schenken started brilliantly in his deal with Ferrari to drive the 312B sports car. He teamed with Ronnie Peterson to win the 1000 kilometre race in Buenos Aires on 9 January. 'Ronnie, as well as being a close friend of mine, was an incredibly quick driver in the same style as Jochen Rindt. I'll never forget him driving me through Sweden one night in a blizzard on an icy road, with cars stopping and suddenly slowing in front of us, more weaving towards us, and we're doing over 100 miles an hour! Ronnie was yakking away, all the time guiding the car with his finger as it slid from side to side. His girlfriend was cowering in the front seat, in tears.'

Schenken was to have a tougher time in his Formula 1 career with the Surtees team, which was backed by Rob Walker and using the TS9B cars. They did not look like changing the fortunes of their predecessors.

In the Argentinian Grand Prix, the first round of the championship, Schenken finished a reputable 5th, but realised that he might have a few problems. 'The gear lever knob was made of wood. Surtees had bought it in a speed shop. When you looked at it, it seemed robust enough, but I spoke to the engineer and warned him that it was a bit fragile. He wouldn't change it. Sure enough, during the race it came off, and I was changing gear with this raw steel lever with no knob on it. I was so angry that I kept hold of the knob in the palm of my hand, and when I passed the pits at about 200 kilometres an hour, I threw it at Surtees, barely missing him. I was later told that John kept asking his crew to find the offending missile. Why was I pissed off? Well the scars on my palm have only recently faded away ... more than 30 years after the event.'

That race was the Formula 1 debut of another Australian, Dave Walker, who was driving a better car for a better team: a Lotus 72D, with Emerson Fittipaldi his team-mate. Walker had dominated the 1971 British Formula 3 series and was highly regarded, but life would prove to be difficult in the shadow of the anointed Brazilian.

In the months that followed, Schenken discovered that with the Ferrari sports car, the hours may have been longer but the rewards were greater: he and Ronnie Peterson drove to numerous podium finishes and a win at the Nurburgring. In the unimpressive, often abrasive Formula 1 team, however, his team-mate, former World Motorcycle Champion Mike Hailwood, was outperforming him.

He did finish 3rd to Hulme and Fittipaldi at Oulton Park, in the non-championship International Gold Cup. Vern Schuppan was also there, finally driving the Formula 1 BRM, as Louis Stanley had promised. Schuppan qualified fifth, and was surprised by how much at home he felt in the car, but in the race he was almost taken out in a concertina crash involving Ronnie Peterson and factory BRM driver Reine Wisell. There was no damage to the car. Schuppan resumed the race, and finished 5th. For his first Formula 1 drive, he was very pleased.

It turned out to be a bad news–good news–bad news sequence. Wisell was hurt in that crash, and unable to drive in the next round of the championship in Belgium, so BRM asked Schuppan to take over. He lost the opportunity, however, because the team needed his car for their other team driver Helmut Marko.

Emerson Fittipaldi charged through the final rounds to become the youngest world champion, at 25. Tim Schenken didn't finish higher than his first round 5th in any other race; he netted only two championship points for the year. 'John Surtees was certainly a very odd character,' he recalls, 'and very difficult to get on with. To win world titles on two and four wheels was a fantastic achievement. You can't take that away from him, but with me it was a total clash of personalities. The season was just a disaster ... problem after problem after problem. It was a poor career move. In those days very few people had managers or anything like that. Perhaps if I'd had one, that situation would not have happened. But life goes on.'

In Formula 2 with Rondel and sports cars with Ferrari, Schenken was seeing far more champagne in 1972. Ferrari won the sports car series. There was no title for drivers. 'Ferrari offered all their drivers the chance to buy their race cars at the end of 1972. I could have bought mine for £12,000. Jacky Ickx and Clay Regazzoni were the only two who took up the offer. The rest of us thought, why would we want to buy our race cars? Those cars are worth more than a million dollars today!'

Ron Dennis, buoyant with his success in the Formula 2 arena, had plans to run a team in Formula 1. Schenken hitched his future to that idea, and waited.

Vern Schuppan finished the 1972 season strongly, proving his versatility to BRM with impressive Formula 1 testing and Formula 2 racing. On 16 September at Oulton Park, to the surprise of Schenken, Scheckter, Surtees, Peter Gethin, Peterson, Niki Lauda, Hill and James Hunt, Schuppan qualified on the front row. Peterson and Hunt were beside him. He beat them both off the line, and for just a moment experienced the thrill of leading most of the world's best drivers, and they were not in slow cars. Then, before the end of the first lap, his engine spat a flywheel and it was all over. 'I truly believe I would have won that race. It was only 40 laps.

'I was in good shape again at Hockenheim, where I was dicing with Dave Morgan somewhere midfield. He cut a corner, and I thought that was a good idea, so I did it too. Trouble was, I did it twice and they disqualified me.' Tim Schenken beat Mike Hailwood and Ronnie Peterson for the win, which didn't do anything to warm his frosty relationship with Schuppan. Schuppan closed the European season in Formula 1 again, finishing 4th in the Victory race at Brands Hatch. Jean Pierre Beltoise won it. 'It was quite a weekend. I was replacing Peter Gethin, who refused to drive until he was paid some money they owed him! They didn't have time to fit me for a seat, so I tried Peter's, but it was impossible, so I sat on the floor.'

Louis Stanley, apparently true to his word, offered Schuppan a full-time Formula 1 drive for 1973, alongside Clay Regazzoni. It sounded like a good deal.

By the end of 1972, Leo Geoghegan had quit touring car racing, but there was no path to return to his beloved open-wheelers without massive financial support. 'I announced my retirement at Lakeside and just went home. No sooner did I get there than all these people started ringing up and asking me to drive their cars! I thought, what a dickhead I am, I should have retired years ago!'

The first offer was from Malcolm Ramsey: to drive a Birrana in the 1.6 litre Formula 2 series. Geoghegan tested it, liked it, and approached his old mate Hans Tieberman, by then working for Grace Brothers. Tieberman was the mastermind who had clothed the Geoghegans in suits for the 1965 Bathurst race — and had sponsored them ever since. Geoghegan told him the Birrana was a great little car. He still had support from Firestone tyres and Castrol. An air fare deal was struck. It was back to the track, in a hurry.

Frank Gardner knuckled down on the test track in 1972, strengthening an already solid relationship with Lola boss Eric Broadley and his team of designers and engineers. He was starting to get to know some of the motor racing industry's whiz kids, including Patrick Head, who would become one of the chief designers and most highly regarded names in the modern era. 'Patrick Head was a thinker. He was composed. John Bernard, of the two, was the brighter — brilliant in fact, capable of anything — but he was the ballerina, rising and falling like a barometer, whereas Patrick had the disposition. He was the pressure man. You'd never ruffle him.'

Gardner had helped Lola grow from a very small operation, capable of building only 25 cars a year, to a respected giant building more than 65 a year. They were the largest race car builder in the world and a serious contributor to the British economy. Gardner rates this success as highly as many of his on-track achievements, but he was still attracted to the cruise of a victory lap and the climb to the podium. He and the Chevy Camaro were good for 8 wins and a podium finish in 10 starts in the British Saloon Car Championship. His only retirement was a crash at Silverstone after starting on pole, one of seven pole positions in the series. He finished 3rd in the standings, only 9 points behind the winner, Bill McGovern in a Sunbeam Imp.

One of his most satisfying wins was against young Tim Schenken in the Ford Sport Day on 1 June. 'Tim still has a go at me because it was a production car race just for Ford Capris at Brands Hatch and the prize was a brand new Capri. It was pissing wet and it was a co-driver race, in which you had to use a Formula 1 driver. François Cevert did the first split for me. I drove the second half. François hadn't had much experience in touring cars, so he had slipped back a bit, and when I got hold of this thing I was coming up on this untidy Arab with a couple of laps to run … and it happens to be Tim. I didn't have enough time to buggerise around so I just shoved him off: you know, went through on the inside and won the race. Tim always says that I cost him a Capri. He says, "I've got the photographic evidence … you punted me off the track!" I say, "Well you shouldn't have been holding me up! I'd come from half a lap behind! What makes you think you've got the right to be a mobile chicane!"'

Schenken's 'photographic evidence' is a sequence of still shots depicting the incident. 'Frank used me as a brake going into the final corner,' he recalls. 'I didn't have a lot to do with Frank. We used to see him at Kyalami because he raced sports cars there, but apart from that, we literally ran into each other at Brands!' Both men still have a chuckle about it more than three decades later.

In late October, Gardner relaxed his ban on open-wheel racing and took the Lola T330 to Brands Hatch for the final round of the British Formula 5000 Championship, qualifying 2nd and finishing 3rd to Brian Redman and Graham McRae. There was method in it. 'I needed the points to win the British Drivers Championship,' he explains. 'In those days, to win the championship you had to score points in touring cars, sports cars and open-wheelers. I was in contention for my third championship, and it was the main title to win, very difficult. All I needed was a top-five finish, so there was no point in trying to shuffle people out of the way for no reason. Guys like Redman and Peter Gethin were always hard to beat — they were hard racers and didn't drive rubbish.'

Kevin Bartlett had struck a good deal in 1972 that would enable him to race in two continents for a few years. 'It flowed from my earlier experience in USAC. The same people invited me to drive in Formula 5000. So I took my McLaren over to Laguna Seca. I led that race, I don't know why, for all but the second-last lap. I had a steering problem and was left-foot braking to compensate. I should have pulled over to check it out but I didn't want to lose the lead. I finished up running off the track, got back on and came 4th. I had broken a bolt on the front hub assembly. The brake caliper was all that held the wheel on!

'The bloke who sponsored me to go over there just shook his head and said, "We gotta get you a new car." I sent the McLaren back home and raced a

Lola T300.' Bartlett would be supplied a Lola chassis for the remainder of 1972 and '73 to contest the US F5000 championship. The team would update the car every season. He was sponsored by Shell and still racing in Australia's Gold Star and Tasman series. 'I got to know the flight attendants very well.' What he needed during this exhausting period was a personal sponsor to help subsidise the campaigns, but he 'was too bloody busy racing to go out and chase sponsors! Most of the time I was just hopping on and off aeroplanes.'

'I even had an opportunity once to race Formula 1,' Bartlett recalls. 'I was offered a test with Brabham, when Jack and Ron were in charge. Politically, it was very difficult to get any further than that because there was this sum of $60,000 which I had to find. I went around Australia for weeks and weeks trying to raise the money. In those days I was getting four or five grand a race, US dollars, with all expenses paid. So the $60,000 wasn't too outrageous. I just couldn't raise it at the time. I was talking to people like Shell, and they simply said it wasn't their area. I was most disappointed. Maybe if I had stayed in America in 1971 and 1972, I might have raised the money to race in Formula 1. It was only later that I realised that a former sponsor over there, Chuck Jones, could have got me into Formula 1. He ended up sponsoring Clay Regazzoni!'

While Bartlett was hammering away in the Formula 5000 series in the US, Frank Matich was ticking an empty box on his résumé. He won the Gold Star series for the first time, and the only time until then that he had really concentrated on winning it at all. He won four of the six rounds. 'There had been a fair bit of criticism of me, and it was understandable. I had zipped off to America in the SR3 a few years before. We prepared and sacrificed for a year to go with the SR4 ... and never went. Then we got the M10 and A50 and went to the L and M series. I thought it was politically expedient to settle here for a while, especially with new sponsorship from Shell, who didn't want me to race overseas.'

'I have to say,' he says, 'that while the American series was widely regarded as the best in the world, and the toughest, it was also the craziest. They were big fields and a lot of the blokes were local drivers who you didn't know, and some of them were on dope! That's a fact! So, to race against the guys like Kevin Bartlett back home was a privilege. They were good pedallers, serious drivers, not part-timers. The average talent here was far above the average talent there. It's just that we had small fields. However, we were aiming at setting up a really big effort to tackle the US again in 1973.'

It was another forgettable Tasman series for Kevin Bartlett. He retired after 17 laps of the New Zealand Grand Prix, scored points with a 4th at Levin, finished 7th at Wigram, 8th at Teretonga, 10th at Surfers Paradise, 8th at Warwick Farm, retired at Sandown and was 9th in Adelaide. The Lola was good, but once again he was battling to stay mechanically sound with short supply lines.

Vern Schuppan returned to Australia for Christmas, having been told by BRM that he would be one of two full-time drivers in 1973. 'It wasn't until I arrived back in England and read the *Daily Express* that I discovered that Niki Lauda had bought my drive.' Schuppan became a reserve driver, and after a few strong performances in non-championship races before the season began, he was offered a drive in the Gulf Mirage sports car at Le Mans for John Wyer, the same John Wyer who had once employed Frank Gardner.

Jackie Stewart won 5 of the 15 Formula 1 championship rounds in 1973. Ronnie Peterson won four and Emerson Fittipaldi three. These were drivers Tim Schenken could beat, in the right car. Instead, he was one of several drivers cycled through the Frank Williams garage as team-mates for Howden Ganley. He was still waiting for Rondel to have their Formula 1 car ready, but continued his successful relationship with them in Formula 2. Even the Ferrari sports car deal dried up after a couple of podium finishes. 'Ferrari had realised by the end of the previous year that they had spread themselves too thin, and they decided to concentrate on Formula 1. Ronnie Peterson had moved on to drive for Lotus and Carlos Reutemann and I contested only selected races. I got on well with him, but I thought he was easily psyched out. Funny that — he went on to become Alan Jones's team-mate, very nearly won a world title, and finished up as a very successful politician in Argentina.'

Schenken also drove in a three-car Le Mans team, pairing with Reutemann. 'This was a very important race for Ferrari. Carlos and I were heading for victory until the early hours of the morning, when our engine gave up.'

Vern Schuppan had begun to forge a special relationship with Le Mans in 1973. His co-driver in John Wyer's Mirage GR7 was Mike Hailwood, whom he described as 'a tremendous bloke to drive with. When you're number two driver in sports cars the number one can be notorious — like my good pal Derek Bell, for example — for hogging the car a bit in practice and qualifying.

Mike wasn't like that at all. He'd qualify the car, but give you plenty of time to learn the circuits and get used to the car.

'I was driving in the early hours when I hit some oil from a previous crash, spun off and flipped the car. We were running 3rd at the time. The marshals turned the car back over for me, but they couldn't push start it because that was against the rules. I made it back to the pits, where I told them what happened. Wyer, whose nickname was "Death Ray", glared at me and said, "You didn't ... " I thought that was my last drive for him, but fortunately it wasn't.'

Frank Matich in 1973 had been primed and ready for the US, yet again. 'We were going to clean 'em up, and there's no reason why we shouldn't have. We had the Matich A51, a refined, improved version of the A50, a beautiful motor car. Everything was perfect.' Everything, that is, except a strange fault with oil circulation, caused by the shape of the engine block. It was more of a problem on faster circuits, where it caused severe power loss. The baffled team, with Repco's assistance, changed 13 engines in 3 races in their effort to solve the problem. By the time they reached Watkins Glen, Matich had even employed Vern Schuppan to drive a second car, to speed up the investigation. 'I thought it would be good to have Vern on board because he was a great driver with Formula 1 experience. We could have forged a very strong team together and had a good time, but it was embarrassing, really, because the car just wasn't working properly. At Watkins Glen it was particularly bad, and we didn't at the time know why.'

Neither of them even started the race. Schuppan moved on to drive in a couple of races for Graham McRae, while the Matich expedition returned to Australia mid-year, tails between their legs. Repco came up with a temporary solution after further tests back home but it was all too late. 'We'd used up a lot of money, so I decided to fix the thing properly without spending anymore. I later found out that other engine designers, including Porsche, had had similar problems with the shape of their engine blocks.'

There was one other vital reason why Matich did not return to the US that year. His wife Joan was walking up some stairs when a simple turn of the shoulders wrenched her neck. She collapsed in agony. What might have seemed an average injury that would be solved by a few days' rest became a life-threatening trauma. Joan underwent surgery for spinal fusion, which failed, making the injury worse. When she was released from hospital after months in traction, this vibrant, attractive woman had been reduced to a wreck weighing less than 30 kilograms. Matich quickly put motor sport in its rightful place. 'I let Bobby Muir drive my car. He wrote it off, testing at Warwick Farm.'

The Birrana manufacturing company had sold plenty of race cars to other teams and drivers following the success of Leo Geoghegan at the helm of their Formula 2 model. Suddenly, the 36-year-old was alive again. 'I had a great time, because at a lot of meetings I'd drive a sports sedan as well. I raced at 48 events in my first year of retirement, and had only 2 weeks off.' He won most of his races, and later that year finished his final Bathurst campaign on the podium with Colin Bond, only a metre from his brother Pete, who was celebrating victory with Allan Moffat.

Leo entered the Australian Grand Prix in November 1973, but the little Formula 2 engine was no match for the Formula 5000 beasts. He didn't bother to start after a miserable qualifying session. Graham McRae of New Zealand won the race, for the second consecutive year. It had been an exceptional period for McRae: he had also had three Tasman series wins and victory in the US F5000 series, winning three of eight races.

Kevin Bartlett finished 9th, 9 laps down, in the Lola T330 which he had campaigned in America. 'I was like a gypsy in those days,' he recalls, 'compared with where I wanted to be. I had done some L and M series races again. I bought a brand new car in Los Angeles, but attempted to do it all with very little backing. By the time I got to Watkins Glen I had sold my car — for a profit. I drove Max Stewart's car because he crashed it in practice and broke his wrist. Matich, Max and even Vern Schuppan were over there too for that race. They'd been doing a few events. My wage for driving the car paid for Max's and my hotel bills and bought enough fuel for us to drive back to the west coast. We were living off the smell of an oily rag.'

By early 1974 the Tasman series was clearly not the powerful promotional gold mine that it had been. Peter Gethin and Teddy Pilette came over from Europe in the Formula 5000 Chevron B24s. Gethin ran away with the series, winning only 2 of the 8 rounds but taking points in all the others.

Bartlett, whose dynamic style and enormously popular blue-collar reputation had become integrated with the series' history, would say goodbye after round 2, the Pukekohe International. 'I was trying harder and harder and harder in practice, going fourth or fifth fastest, but the times just weren't coming. Suddenly, my left side rear tyre deflated. Even in Formula 5000 you do get sideways, and I didn't realise what had happened. No brain, no pain. My mechanic, Johnny Anderson, was trying to signal me in. I tucked the wheel into turn 1, hit the horse-racing barrier, ripped the nose off the car and spun across the track. By that time I had no brakes, because they were knocked off on the fence. I kept spinning until I speared under the Armco into an old marshal's barrier, so hard it knocked the dash and the steering wheel off. It didn't get as far as my head before it bounced back again. I had quite a few injuries. All my left side: ankle, tibia, fibula, pelvis.

'My sponsor, Rothmans, was wonderful, paying for everything. I'd only been with them for a year.'

The old marshal's barrier which no one bothered to dismantle may have saved Bartlett from decapitation. However, his injuries were severe, and he would suffer mysterious back pain for many years. It wouldn't be until November 2003 that he would undergo spinal surgery to correct it. 'I remember the doctors telling me that I needed surgery to finally correct my old back injury. My response was, "What old back injury?" They said, "Didn't you know? You broke your back 29 years ago."'

Kevin Bartlett would make his comeback late in 1974, to write another extraordinary chapter in the history of the Bathurst 1000. 'But my biggest problems, quite frankly, were going to be financial.'

It had been his wife's back injury that had kept Frank Matich from the track, but since the middle of 1973 he had been planning his return. Joan Matich had started to recover after months of intensive physiotherapy from close family friend Ron Flint. Matich had, before the crisis, some unfinished business with a car that he had designed and developed, but not fully exploited. He began work again, sporadically at first, honing his A51 until it was the car he wanted it to be. He called this new evolution the A52. 'We were so much faster than the other cars out there, in terms of lap times. We had solved the oil hydraulic situation and proved that we had the best Formula 5000 car in the world. The fact that it ran competitively even with the engine trouble it suffered in America was proof of that. We decided that we were on track again, and ready for one more trip to the US.'

The plan was to return for the round at Oran Park, the first of the Australian events in the 1974 Tasman series. One week before that round, Matich was working on the family boat, which was moored in front of their waterfront property at Clareville. He started the generator, not realising that a mechanic who had worked on it earlier in the day had done some faulty rewiring. The entire boat was live.

Matich leaned over the engine, and suddenly his left arm and chest were pinned to the block, current pouring through him, hugging him to what seemed like certain death. 'I could feel myself dying, my life just draining away. I was there for 11 minutes, getting weaker and weaker. It was the most helpless feeling. I can't begin to describe it. There was tremendous noise in my head, and I was locked onto the metal. I was actually disgusted with myself, and worried about my son Kris or Joan touching the boat too. It was like how they describe drowning ... I could see the light, but couldn't get up there. I passed out at one stage and would have died, but the burn on my chest made such a hole that it actually reduced the current, and it then acted like a pacemaker! What had stopped my heart, started it again! I don't know how long I was out, but suddenly I heard noise again and it wasn't as severe. I rested for a moment or two, then put together a super effort and wrenched myself, with all my strength, off the engine. By this time I was pretty cooked. My hands and feet were curled up. There were flash marks all over me. I was a mess. My chest had this black hole in it and the smell of burning flesh was awful.

'Ambulance and police vehicles arrived. A nearby resident, who was a doctor, rushed over. Neighbours gathered. One smart bloke brought rubber gloves to take me off the boat, but by that time I had turned off the generator myself. My mate Ron Flint was also there and he told Joan, "Trust me, don't let them take Frank to hospital!"'

Joan Matich had been saved by Flint, and she didn't hesitate to order the ambulance away. 'There was hell to pay,' says Matich. 'I had almost died, cooked, in shock, and here we were refusing medical treatment! They all left in disgust. Ron had already filled a bath full of Epsom salts. He treated the wounds and worked on me every day to get my muscles back to life. Within a week I made that drive at Oran Park, but I gave up. I couldn't remember one corner to the next. I had another go a week later at Surfers Paradise, my first race after the accident. I was starting to get my marbles together, but I finished 3rd behind Teddy Pilette and Peter Gethin.'

Matich tried again at Sandown, where an engine blew while he was leading the race. He closed the Australian leg of the series with a fighting 4th in Adelaide. It was one of the most extraordinary comebacks in Australian motor sport, and through the entire ordeal the team said nothing to officials, fans or the media. There was almost no publicity. 'One reason was that CAMS would have gone off! I did disclose it to the track doctors on the day of the races, though.'

There had been two major health scares in the Matich family in 6 months and Matich, approaching his forties, was starting to ponder the broader issues. He had established himself in business with Goodyear Tyres. There were many other avenues to pursue. He sensed that even if he did regain his faculties, it would take months. 'I recovered. I went to work, but I was never going to be the same — not for at least a year. I thought about maintaining the team with Bob Muir or Vern Schuppan driving for me but the circuits wouldn't pay starting money unless I was driving, so I didn't pursue that. It was time to quit.'

There was no fanfare, no monumental statement, no tribute, no pang of regret. It wasn't until months later, when Matich was asked by journalist Mike Kable what he was up to, that he casually admitted it. 'Mate, I've been retired since March.'

CHAPTER TEN

Moffat and Brock

In 1969 Holden decided to take a stand at Bathurst. They channelled the factory funds through their retail outlets, forming the Holden 'Dealer' team. They also recruited the toughest and smartest touring car technician and tactician of the day, a man who had built his reputation on flouting convention and stretching the rules. Harry Firth had taken his 'shopping trolley' to the General Motors factory to evaluate his position in this new deal. 'It was a handshake deal between me and John Bagshaw. No big hullabaloo,' recalls Firth. 'I had final say on everything.' His Monaros would take on the GTHO Falcons, now under the flamboyant Al Turner, whose Stetson hat and cowboy drawl failed to convince the paddock that he was anything but a formidable team boss. The battle lines were drawn.

Norm Beechey had not lost his massive following or his lust for racing, but at the end of 1968 he had lost three consecutive Australian titles to Ian 'Pete' Geoghegan. Neptune had been absorbed by its parent company Shell, and the team colours changed. It was time for another change, too. The much loved and hugely popular Chevy Nova went on to become an icon in American drag racing, but in Australian touring car racing it was losing the key races to Pete Geoghegan's Mustang. After driving a Camaro with some success in three races, Beechey was approached by General Motors to drive their new 327 Monaro. It was an offer too good to refuse.

The Monaro was kept hidden in a garage in North Melbourne. It was on four stands, like a prototype space ship when Beechey first laid eyes on it. His team started working on it, preparing it to beat the Mustang. They tested several types of carburettor at Calder, among other subtle changes, before finally unleashing the monster in their first battle. 'It was a hell of a race, and we finished up beating Pete by 2 feet across the line. If I hadn't done all that testing we would never have won. Years later, someone told me he never thought we would have gone to so much trouble in our type of racing and I replied, "You obviously never raced against Pete Geoghegan."'

The Chevy Camaro which Beechey had shunned for the more lucrative Holden deal was by no means a poor car. It would become a championship winner for Bob Jane. However, Holden was more popular with the fans. Beechey won his share of races, but it was another case of backing the wrong horse when it came to winning the elusive Australian championship. The Monaro proved inferior to the Mustang and Pete Geoghegan won title number five in 1969, his fourth in a row. Holden's locally built coupé was not a spent force, however; Beechey would have a far more competitive car for the following season.

For the Geoghegan brothers, 1969 had been the end of a successful era. Pete Geoghegan was the dominant driver in the Australian Touring Car Championship and Leo had competed with great distinction in largely underpowered cars against the best drivers in the world in the Tasman series. They had not, however, won the great race at Bathurst, and the 500 was about to become 10 years old.

Ford was still keen on the Geoghegans as its stormtroopers, and they were arguably the most potent of 15 pairings aboard new Falcons in the field of 63. Leo remembers the tide turning in the way the motor sport operation was run under Al Turner's leadership. '1969 was the first year when the cars came directly from the factory to the track. They were all pretty equal. Unlike the championship races contested by Norm and Bob and Pete, you were only allowed to do a minimum of modifications.'

Harry Firth, meantime, was working his special brand of magic at the GMH factory. There were three Monaros under his control, to match the three Falcons under Al Turner. Both managers were busy recruiting the best driver combinations. Turner drew his first pairing from his holster: Bo Seton, who had won in 1965 with Midge Bosworth, and Fred Gibson, who had won with Firth in 1967. The next car was to be driven by the Geoghegans, but the final two drivers were pretty much unknown. Alan Hamilton was the son of a Melbourne car dealer. His partner was a Canadian based in Victoria. He was quiet, intense and stunningly aggressive on the track.

Allan Moffat was born in 1939 in Saskatchewan, Canada. The roots were not deep. His father was on the move in the tractor business, up and around. As he progressed through the Massey Fergusson corporate ranks the family put their possessions in the hands of removalists several times. Most of the locations were Canadian or North American, but they also settled for 5 years in South Africa, where Moffat went to high school. He saw his first motor race there, at a circuit called Grand Central, near Johannesburg. It was an early version of the famous Kyalami circuit. There he saw touring cars in action, but there was still no spark of recognition that this was something he might try. He spent much of his spare teenage hours tinkering with a wrecked 1935 Ford that he had bought, learning its inner workings from front to rear in the hot African afternoons. They were hours full of curiosity, not connected to racing. 'I didn't realise it at the time, but that was the beginning of my racing career.'

The family made another move, to Melbourne, but motor sport was still little more than a mild interest for Moffat — until 1962, at Sandown's first meeting. The fanfare, the occasion, the crowd ... it all had an edge that appealed to the young Canadian. That was when he started feeling that motor sport might be in his blood. 'Seeing Moss, Brabham, Clark, Gurney ... they brought the cream of Formula 1 drivers to open the circuit. It was a hell of a step up from what I'd seen on the back blocks of Transvaal. It still hadn't quite dawned on me that I might actually do it, but it looked like something worth doing.'

Moffat became a marketing cadet with Volkswagen Australia, and embarked on a series of club events, winning his share. 'We were all on our own then,' he recalls. 'I had no idea what CAMS was. I stumbled around the circuits of Victoria, ever cautious, because the hire purchase agreement under which I bought my car said that you were not allowed to take it on a racing circuit. So even though they were only club events, for 18 months I never did two meetings in a row in case someone scanned the entry forms!'

Tim Schenken met Moffat in Melbourne when they were starting their racing careers. 'I met Allan before I even got my racing licence. My parents would drop me off at his place and I'd head down the driveway to help him prepare his Triumph. I remember once, he looked to be working hard under the car, his feet protruding from underneath, but when I got there I realised he was fast asleep. I went to some club races with him, and he was embarrassing to be with, because he couldn't do 3 laps without spinning.'

Moffat's recollection was, 'At least I only had to spin once to find out where the limit was, and I never did it in front of him! As for being asleep, well, given the heat of the day, more heat radiating from the engine ... for all he knew I could have been unconscious, having worked myself to a standstill.'

When the jokes are set aside, Schenken has high regard for the Canadian. 'Allan was in the same mould as people like Nigel Mansell and Graham Hill — and even Damon Hill — who were absolutely determined to be successful. That sheer determination overcame any problems he had.'

The next step, however, was massive. The Moffat family moved back to Toronto. This time Moffat was old enough to make his own choices and initially he remained in Australia, but he was still not settled. He opted to go home for Christmas in 1963 to make an informed decision about his future. The trip dragged on as he picked up old threads and pondered whether he might be better off racing in the US. 'It was a scary place in which to try and do something. I felt more comfortable in Australia, but CAMS had a policy of no commercial sponsorship on the cars and I had no real way of setting myself up without that. It wasn't until 1969 that they rescinded that rule.'

The 1964 Indianapolis 500 loomed. Moffat tethered himself in the vast stands with 250,000 others and received a dose of heart-stopping electricity. 'Jimmy Clark and Jackie Stewart were there with Team Lotus. It was the era of AJ Foyt and Parnelli Jones. It truly did electrify me. I went away from that weekend with a view that no matter what I had to do, I would get serious. Professionally, it started in that grandstand at Indianapolis. Five weeks later I was at Watkins Glen watching a sports car race. Unbeknownst to me, Team Lotus had been hired by Ford America to help promote a Cortina team to boost US sales. I hung around the back of the pits drooling over these cars and bumped into one of the mechanics. I asked him where they were going next and he told me it was Des Moines, Iowa, 2000 kilometres from Toronto. I followed them there. The same mechanic recognised me and introduced me to the team manager, who happened to be an Australian called Ray Carson. Ray showed me where a bucket was and told me that if I wanted to wash the cars, "Be my guest!" People like me were a dime a dozen at every race track in the world. Ray expected me to last one weekend, just like all the others. Six months later I was still washing their cars and packing their trucks.'

By season's end, when the cars were to be sold to make way for the new season models, the team co-ordinator, Peter Quenet, agreed to sell one of them to Moffat for $4500, including a new engine and whatever spares he could fit in the car. It was a great deal, and at 25, Moffat could hardly refuse it, but it still took a generous loan from his father to make it happen. 'I had one hell of a job selling the idea to my Dad to lend me $3000 — in those days that was a hell of a lot of money.' He gave himself 2 years in which to set himself up. For most people, the difference between the inside and outside of the spectator fencing at any race circuit was only a couple of centimetres. For Allan Moffat, the difference was $3000.

Peter Quenet's Cortina team headed to the Formula 1 round at Mosport Park, Canada, to catch up with Clark and Stewart, and with their assistance Moffat followed and competed in a support race, where he finished 3rd. The next stop was the New York docks. He had decided to return to Australia; his instincts told him the story would unfold with more speed there. What had been merely an idea at the end of May at Indianapolis would become, by the end of November at Sandown, a full-throttle, roaring reality. It was a 6 hour race, and the Cortina had been tuned for endurance events. Moffat had confidence in the car, providing he could get it to the event.

'The boat was late and I only got the car on the Friday before the race. I elected not to do practice and just use the day to prepare the car. I got to the track at five o'clock on the Saturday afternoon and the clerk of the course let me do 2 laps on my own. I started at the back of the grid, so far back under the Dunlop bridge that I couldn't see the starter. There I was, alone with the seagulls, trying to fix a twist in my seatbelt, when I heard the roar of the leading Ford Galaxie going up the back straight. I thought, I'd better get the hell outa here. Three hours later, I was in the lead.'

Moffat won his class, first time out. The cheque was about £20. He then had a race at Mallala, where a dice with Jim McKeown left them both stranded off the track. 'The next week I got a telegram from Peter Quenet inviting me to race in the US in 1965 with a two-car team in the 12 round Sports Car Club of America championship. It would be fully funded, with appearance money. I kept my Lotus Cortina back here in mothballs, and got on the next plane to Detroit.'

There were three divisions in the SCCA National Sedan Championship. The top three in each division went to the 'run-off' at Riverside to decide the overall champion. Moffat won Central Division, but was narrowly beaten in the final by the man he beat in the preliminary rounds: Horst Kwech, who was driving an Alfa. He had a busy year competing in various other non-championship endurance races, and returned to Australia to compete in the 1965–66 Tasman series support races. He bounced back into North America for a roundabout of one-off drives, mostly in long-distance events, where with passive factory support, as opposed to 100 per cent financial backing, he picked up key victories — and with each one he improved his status. He also crossed paths with a couple of other players who would become legends on the Australian scene — and it wasn't an entirely pleasant experience.

It was in a Trans-Am race at St Louis, Missouri. The Trans-Am series had been devised by the SCCA in 1966 to give American manufacturers a stage on which to run their muscle cars. There were two divisions, for under and over 2 litre engine capacity. The series was so big that Alfa Romeo sent teams to compete, and Jochen Rindt was one of their drivers. Ford also took the events seriously: their official factory team, Alan Mann Racing, had called over some of their gun drivers from Europe, including Jacky Ickx and Frank Gardner and British touring car champion Sir John Whitmore. Howard Marsden was their Team Manager.

The Moffat team, using an ex-Team Lotus Cortina, sister car to the one that he had in Australia, was officially private, but its roots were in the Lotus connection with Ford and it was supported by Peter Quenet. The Mann team, however, was Ford's official team, worldwide. There were raised eyebrows when the Moffat car took pole. That speed impressed Goodyear, who then supported Moffat for the next event, in Bryar, New Hampshire. He won the race, beating V8s, 2 litre cars, everyone. 'It was one of the most significant victories I ever had. I ran into Horst Kweck afterwards and couldn't help but ask, "What did you think the first time I lapped you, Horst?" He said, "Oh, I thought, typical Moffat, you'll go too hard and blow up." Then I said, "And what did you think the second time I lapped you?" He replied with a smile, "I thought I'd better pull my finger out."'

The Mann team immediately went on the attack, demanding to know why Moffat had trumped the factory. 'They claimed they had never seen a Cortina

Tasman Series race at Warwick Farm, 1966. Jim Clark from pole, on the far left, leaps away from Frank Gardner, nearest the photographers. Graham Hill is between them on the front row and Jackie Stewart right behind them in the smoke. Leo Geoghegan is on the far right of row three.   (PHOTO: NIGEL SNOWDON)

Local hero Gardner on a victory parade at Warwick Farm with mechanic and good friend, Glen Abbey.

Gardner … still on top in the early 70s, having beaten Reine Wisell and Dieter Glemser in a Formula 2 race at Hockenheim. It was part of a series dedicated to the late Jochen Rindt.

A collection of greats. Standing casually in front of a packed grandstand at Sandown before the 1964 Australian Grand Prix are, from the left: Tony Shelly, Mel McEwin, Denny Hulme, Lex Davison peeking over Hulme's shoulder, Frank Matich, Jack Brabham, Bib Stillwell, Bruce McLaren, Tim Mayer looking down, Doug Whiteford behind the commentator, and Frank Gardner.

Colin Bond and Fred Gibson, co-drivers at Bathurst in 1978, sharing a laugh. It would be one of few in a tough season for the Moffat team, following the highs of '77.

Ready ... set ... a legendary line-up of Bathurst winners from 1968 to 1977, promoting the 1977 race. From left: Bob Morris, Colin Bond, Peter Brock, Allan Moffat, John Goss and Bruce McPhee.

Stormin' Norman Beechey enjoying victory on the bonnet of his Chevy Impala with a not-too-dejected rival, Bob Jane, after the Half Hour Classic at Calder Park in 1962.

Round one of the Australian Touring Car Championship in 1970, Norm Beechey in the Monaro 350 GTS leading Ian 'Pete' Geoghegan at Calder Park. Beechey won the championship.

John Harvey in the Kurtis Offenhauser that won him so many speedway titles.

Bob Jane's McLaren Repco M6 in which John Harvey won the 1971 and '72 Australian Sports Car Championships. Harvey was unbeaten and set a number of records including the first 100 mile per hour lap of Phillip Island.

Kevin Bartlett in a Lynx Formula Junior in 1962 at Lakeside.

Phillip Island, November 1972, and Kevin Bartlett, buried in his Lola T300 Formula 5000 monster, turning MG Corner on his way to a national Formula 1 lap record of 1:40.7 secs. These cars were deafening and brutally powerful for their flimsy chassis, which gave little protection for the driver sitting in front of that heavy, stock block V8.

Somewhere in front of the Schenken stare would be red mist.

The 1971 British Grand Prix at Silverstone was a typical hard-luck story for Tim Schenken, who had qualified 7th in his BT33 and was heading for 3rd place before gearbox trouble stopped him and Emerson Fittipaldi found the podium instead.

Top: Frank Matich celebrates a victory in comfort after an Australian Formula Junior Championship race at Catalina Park. The lounge chair was his trophy.
Middle: Frank Matich leading John Harvey, Don Sullivan and Niel Allen — Calder, Victoria, 1969.
Bottom: Surfers Paradise, 8 September 1972. The awesome Matich A50 … all power … all his own work.

go so fast, that it must have had some lightning engine in it,' Moffat recalls, 'and I said, "Well, it's got an Australian engine in it." They retorted that they had BRM engines in their cars and suggested a test back in Europe. I agreed, provided I went back to Europe with the engine and they didn't touch it until I got there. Do you think that happened? They had it apart and reassembled before I saw it on the dynamometer. The joke was, they found my engine had less horsepower than theirs. That really had them scratching their heads.' They then suggested that Moffat had somehow switched the engines, at which point he reminded them that they had had complete supervision of the engines. The whole thing left Moffat very disappointed, though. It would be the first time, but not the last, that he would be disillusioned by the politics of motor sport, and the bitterness would never leave him. He described his relationship with Frank Gardner in the following years as 'terse'.

The situation worked in his favour, however, because he inherited full factory support from Quenet to run directly against the Alan Mann team, and in some endurance events in 1967 he enlisted none other than Harry Firth as a co-driver, scoring a podium finish at Green Valley in Texas. 'Harry was superb. He was working with Ford Australia at the time and was very affable. When we got to Riverside for the final of that year, it was a question of him driving or me. He had been so successful in Texas that I felt obliged to ask him to drive the car, but he insisted I drive it. "I'll just give the engine another little workover," he said, which he did, and we were leading the Mann team again, before we lost our fanbelt.'

In December 1967, Moffat was hired as development driver by Kar Kraft, Ford's Advanced Vehicles Division, the group responsible for their Le Mans project. In 1968, their brief was to develop the Mustang as a vehicle to take on the Chevrolet Camaro. 'It was the most significant university I went to,' he says. He gathered further experience driving with Horst Kweck for the Shelby two-car team at the Daytona 24 hour, where they suffered suspension failure, and at the Sebring 12 hour, where they suffered engine failure.

After working with Kar Kraft for 18 months, Moffat returned to Australia to set up his own team. 'Unfortunately for me, my mothballed Cortina had already been superseded by Ford's newest monster, the Trans-Am Mustang.'

His only hope, as he bordered on despair, was a letter sent to Jack Passino, Ford's head of international motor sport, asking if there was any cheap way that he could acquire a Trans-Am Mustang with which to compete in Australia.

Passino had seen Moffat win in New Hampshire. He was a fan. He invited Moffat to Detroit, where the Canadian-born Australian discovered that his best friends in the world were Americans. After 4 uncertain days fidgeting in a motel room, he received a phone call from Passino offering him a new Trans-Am Mustang, for nothing. 'That was really the greatest phone call I ever got in my life. I couldn't believe my ears. Nobody ever believed that that happened to me. That's how rare it is.' The car had been prepared in South Carolina by Bud Moore Engineering, one of two Ford-backed teams running two cars. The other was run by Carroll Shelby. The car was trucked to New York City and flown to Australia in the hold of a Boeing 707. Moffat sat in the passenger section above, never as close as he wanted to be. That car was his whole life.

Moffat and Mustang were more than alliteration in 1969. Like the aligning of planets, sponsorship was also allowed in that Australian season, and his Coca-Cola deal was the first of its kind. Wins flowed like the product and tasted twice as sweet. His first race in the new car was the Sandown Southern Sixty, three races adding up to 60 miles (90 kilometres). It would be one of his finest wins, the first of 101 in that car. But he could not nail the championship he so desperately wanted. That went to Pete Geoghegan. Al Turner had noticed Moffat and invited him to the fold to drive a factory Falcon at Bathurst, where he would be opposed not only to his former co-driver, Harry Firth, who was in his first season of preparing cars for Holden, but also to a young driver who was to become his greatest rival on the track. Together, they would take Australian motor sport to a popularity no one had dreamed of.

Harry Firth's Holden team was a slightly more adventurous blend than Ford's. With Spencer Martin injuring his back and Kevin Bartlett unavailable due to commitments with Alfa Romeo, Firth had to modify his original plans. He chose the brilliant rally driver but relatively inexperienced touring car driver Colin Bond, to partner Tony Roberts, also primarily a rally driver. Henk Woelders, the son of a Queensland Holden dealer, was paired with Peter Macrow. The third car featured veteran Holden driver, Des West and a handsome, knockabout lad with a mess of jet-black hair and a cheeky, endearing smile. He had never driven at Bathurst before, was rough around the edges, but had shown extraordinary bravado in his club racing with a backyard-built Austin A30. Unlike Moffat, who in his first full season had made his presence felt among the elite, few people had even heard of Peter Brock.

* * *

There had been nothing unusual about the Brock beginnings: paddock bashing on the family farm at Diamond Creek in rural Victoria, kinship with things mechanical, a flair for testing his ability against things that can be measured, like distance and time. Bikes, tractors, ploughs and cars all became instruments of that measurement. He was 7 years old in 1952, and already attacking the wheel of his father's Holden. 'I was determined, backing things out of sheds, moving them around the paddock. Anything mechanical, I wanted to know all about it. I was fortunate to have been brought up in a rural atmosphere where you could do those things.' The awkwardness of a Fergusson tractor was transformed into subtle manoeuvrability in the mind of young Brock as he discovered its handling nuances, leaping onto the inside steering brake to lock up the inside back wheel momentarily, causing it to spin wildly when suddenly released on the dewy morning grass. Cows went off their milk as Brock charged among them, unaware that he was testing their reaction times as much as his own. His father was forced to spend so much time repairing broken machinery that he coined the expression 'Peter proof' — except that really, nothing on Earth was.

'I think it taught me something called mechanical sympathy. Unless you were able to form a bit of a bond between yourself and the machine, to learn its limitations, you were in for a bit of grief. My view would be: this car and I are going to do some great things, so maybe we should talk to each other a bit. There are occasions when you simply cannot change the car, so you have to understand it, and change your technique.' Sympathy? Understanding? They are odd expressions coming from someone who would make a career out of the clunking, spinning and friction of motor sport.

Brock's laser-beam mind extended to all forms of conventional pastimes for Victorian children, including Australian Rules football and cricket, but in his teenage years, machinery took charge. The plan was to spend as little money as possible in the backyard construction of something compatible with the awesome performance of the cars he watched with such enthusiasm at the Templestowe and Rob Roy hill climbs, and at the Altona and Albert Park circuits. The solution was an Austin 7, which his father Geoff helped him procure for the princely sum of £5. Geoff was a bush mechanic, as most farmers had to be. 'I couldn't shed this thing of its heavy bodywork, which was the first plan of attack, so I literally took to it with an axe, ' Brock recalls. 'Mum never forgave me for ruining a perfectly good axe that had formerly been used for cutting firewood. But it was effective in the panelbeating game.'

Brock, lean and light as a feather, made maximum use of the power-to-weight advantage gained by a panel-less car that was little more than a frame with wheels and seat bolted to it. 'If anyone saw a thing like that these days they would shudder. There'd probably be a law against it.'

A procession of cheap cars started to parade through the Brock family garage as he bought and modified a number of vehicles, some of them even fit to be registered. At 18, he entered a club race meeting in a '48 series Holden which he had bought and restored. He won a race in his car, then borrowed a friend's Mini and won the main event. 'I don't know how I did it. I just did what came naturally. I started to do more races. But then I got called up for national service.'

Peter Brock, at 20, became a 'Nasho', dragged for 2 years into compulsory military service. There was a war escalating in Vietnam. 'It was very political. I don't think that there was one person from the first intake who actually served in Vietnam. There was thinking at the time that raw recruits from national service wouldn't be fit to fight in a war. By the time they decided that we could, we had less than a year of our term to serve.'

He spent his 2 years at various bases, settling for most of that term at Kapuka, near Wagga Wagga, where he was directed, to his great surprise, to serve in the medical corps, which he and his mates turned into something like the MASH unit in the long-running television series. 'I had no idea how the human body worked but I learnt a lot, and became a doctor's assistant.'

The army's faithfully maintained Land Rovers were given a thrashing. 'It was embarrassing. We were warned by the military police. They wanted to nail us. But it was quid pro quo, because we were the medical guys and we could call them inside for injections for any reason we liked.'

For reasons that escaped his peers, Brock was promoted to running the Regimental Aid Post (RAP), which he found very useful, because the basins used to wash medical instruments were perfect for cleaning spare parts for their cars. He banned uniforms, claiming that overalls were easier to maintain. He also forbade saluting in the RAP, 'because we didn't want saluting and standing to attention to stir up dust on the floor because it might cause infection. For a year, we had every scam going that you could possibly think of.'

It was in this environment that the Brock passion for racing was fuelled. He turned up at Tasman series races, watching the best international drivers doing battle in exotic cars with Australian heroes like Brabham, Gardner, Matich, Leo Geoghegan, Bartlett and Harvey. He watched in wonder as Firth, Pete Geoghegan, Beechey and Jane twisted their touring cars. This was fertile ground in which to plant the seed of yet another wonderful career. 'I thought, "This is me. Somehow I've gotta get out there. I don't know how, but I'm gonna do it."'

His most significant trip was to Sturt Auto Wreckers in Wagga Wagga, where Ted Bartholomew sold him an Austin A30 for $15. He also bought an old HD Holden, purely to obtain the 179 cubic inch motor that sat imposingly within. He used the RAP surgical baths to clean parts for the A30, which he was lovingly restoring and modifying in his father's garage at home. The staff doctor caught them once, recoiled in horror, and retreated, refusing to believe what he had just seen.

By the time Brock was discharged from service, his A30 was ready to race. He had spent every available minute working on it. His father had made the most of his mechanical skills to set up a garage in Melbourne, and a solid base was forged. Brock's first bout was in pouring rain at Winton, in country Victoria, and within a few rounds, he was winning. The first win was at Hume Weir. 'I drove in every little tin-pot race you could think of. I ran it as a sedan, a sports car, anything it qualified for. It didn't cost much to race. I towed the car behind Mum's panel van and we slept in the van if we were away from home. You'd get there, wander around and find someone who was cooking snags or something. I didn't care about eating. I didn't care about winning. I didn't care about anything. I just wanted to be in it.'

The A30 became as famous as the man who drove it. To cope with the nagging problem of air getting underneath the car at the high speed generated by the 179 motor, Brock searched for a crude form of spoiler, which he discovered one day above the windscreen of an FE Holden. It was the sun visor. His father had some old ones in the shed, so Brock welded and shaped the metal along the front of his A30, below the radiator, sweeping back to form the wheel arches. He also installed an aluminium under-tray, an instinctive decision: 'It was 10 seconds a lap faster.'

The next step was a visit to Frank Matich's factory in Sydney, to find some effective tyres. Matich was the Australian importer of Firestone at the time. 'He didn't have much in the size I wanted, but he did have some second-hand tyres off Leo Geoghegan's Lotus 32 which ran in the Tasman series. I didn't pay much more than a hundred bucks for the whole lot but they were weapons, even against the super-lightweight, tricked-up Minis. I cleaned 'em up. I used to put the regular tyres back on for the local events, though.'

The clincher was the Australian Sports Sedan Championship at Hume Weir in 1969. 'It was 30 or 40 laps, and probably one of the pivotal races of my career. I drove the whole race with Glyn Brown in a Mini right up my clacker. I had learnt by then to focus on what I was doing, but I knew he was there. He never got by me. It was then that I changed my opinion about myself.'

After one more race for a local Holden dealer, finishing 3rd to a couple of Mini Cooper Ss at Winton, word of Peter Brock found its way through Bevan Gibson's father, Hoot, to Harry Firth, who was on the lookout for new talent.

'I got a phone call in the workshop. The voice said, "Hello, Harry Firth here. Can I speak to Peter Brock?" I thought it was one of my mates putting on a voice. I didn't even think it was a very good impersonation, actually. But I played the game, and talked to him. He offered me a drive at Bathurst.' Brock must have been convinced at some stage during the call that it was the real deal, because the following day he received a similar call from John Roxburgh offering him a drive in the Datsun team. Brock politely refused. 'I think the message there for young drivers is to take your opportunities. When things are offered to you, take them. You can spend so much time rationalising, justifying, intellectualising that sometimes you miss the opportunity. It was a magic moment in my life.' Brock and Holden were an item.

Colin Bond had been steadily working his way up the motor racing ladder to become the consummate professional driver by the age of 27. He had won 21 of 27 races in his Lynx Peugeot open-wheeler. He was New South Wales Hill Climb Champion three years in a row from 1965. He finished 2nd in the 1965 and 1966 Australian championship. The first of those defeats came against Tim Schenken in that bizarre locally built Dick White special running on wheelbarrow wheels. The second was when Alan Hamilton beat him in a Porsche Spider at Collingrove, South Australia.

Bond held outright records in every hill climb in New South Wales and was the first person to climb Silverdale in less than 35 seconds. Anyone that beat 40 seconds received a special badge. They had to make a new badge for Bond.

The problem, however, was always money. If something broke, he would have to wait until his wages came through to do anything about it.

At the same time, he was employed by Mitsubishi to drive the new Colt in various rallies. 'It was a good little car to drive, very easy to handle. You always felt that however much you lost it, you could always recover. They weren't terribly quick, not quick enough to win, but they never stopped and were a lot of fun. We finished 2nd in New Caledonia, which was a big rally.

'The New Caledonia Rally attracted a lot of international drivers. One of the navigators was a young fella called Jean Todt, who climbed the ladder of success to eventually become manager of the Le Mans-winning Peugeot team and the world's most successful Formula 1 team: Michael Schumacher's Ferrari. In those days he was just another little-known competitor.'

It was on the rally routes that Bond gave Mitsubishi its first international victory: not a true rally, but a navigational event sponsored by KLG. He also met up with Scottish driver Andrew Cowan, who had won the London to Sydney Marathon in which Harry Firth competed for Ford, and they remained good friends. Bond even encouraged Cowan to join the Mitsubishi factory team: Cowan not only took the advice but went on to win many rallies for Mitsubishi and become their Rally Team Manager during Tommi Makinen's 4-year World Championship reign in the 1990s. 'I should have taken a commission for that.'

Bond's most decisive motor racing partnership, the deal that would lift him to immortality, was also forged in the heat of rally competition. 'I had competed in rallies against Harry Firth for years. He had the Cortina, I had the Colt. He asked me to join the Holden Dealer team for Sandown, but I had a commitment to drive in a rally in New Guinea. I think he ran Kevin Bartlett with Spencer Martin in a Monaro but it ran out of brakes on the 3rd or 4th lap, went straight on at the end of the straight, and Spencer hurt his back.'

Firth said to the Sydney-based Bond, 'Take the Monaro to Amaroo Park for the ARDC test the week before Bathurst and familiarise yourself.' Bond methodically did the job, his rally experience having made him a thorough and professional assessor of a car's limitations.

Firth recalls, 'He did exactly what he was told and finished up a second faster than the race-prepared teams that were there on the day. Of course he was a marvellous rally driver. He was a quick thinker. He could read the roads and succeed in all kinds of conditions.'

'We really were "works" drivers in those days,' Bond recalls with a smile, 'We drove the works! The cars, the trucks, everything. This was my first introduction to big-time racing. It was good.'

'In the meantime,' Firth recalls, 'I had Brock. I had him out to Calder and a couple of other places. I thought, "This bloke is going to be bloody good." He had it. It was very obvious.'

Brock recalls the early days as an eye-opening rush. 'Harry might have been out of his depth if thrust into today's racing, but irrespective of the technical side, he was a master motivator, a psychologist in the mould of Percy Cerruty, the eccentric trainer of Herb Elliott and other Olympic athletes. In later years, I spent a bit of time at the Olympics with Herb as part of the Australian motivational team and we'd often discuss those aspects of our lives, in particular these two idiosyncratic old blokes with their quirky ways who had such profound effect on us. It was "Karate Kid"-type stuff. Somehow, you came out the other end digging a bit deeper, having a better idea of who you were, being better at making yourself better. I was very fortunate to have found Harry at that stage of my life.'

The captivating thing for Firth about Brock was that he showed willingness to improve. His talent was not an obstacle, as it can be with more headstrong young drivers. 'He was rough. He was raw. Naïve in the ways of the world, but he could drive, and he would listen to what you told him. You could tell Brock to do something in those days and he would do exactly what he was told. He was precise and could adapt to new ways of doing things. He was a thinker. He'd done well with that Austin A30, but I said, "Get rid of that thing and I'll build you a real car."'

CHAPTER ELEVEN

The Stakes are Raised

'I stood there,' Peter Brock recalls, 'watching as they wrote my name on the car. I just had to see it to believe it.' It was typical of the wide-eyed way in which he embraced his early racing.

In another workshop Allan Moffat was also pondering his new status, with the observations of a race-hardened driver who had already developed some scars. 'To be a factory driver,' he recalls, 'you had to be asked to be factory driver. So my nearest rivals, really, were the other guys in my team.'

The 1969 Hardie-Ferodo 1000 was the seed of an Australian sporting saga, a saga of two drivers and two manufacturers who would etch their names forever in the culture of motoring. In spite of this, the race would be won by another great talent who, because he diversified in his career and was not politically motivated or aggressively ambitious, became type-cast as the all-round nice guy.

'In those days,' Colin Bond recalls, 'It wasn't the highly professional set-up it is today. Sponsorship money was shovelled into the car's development. We were paid a fixed wage to drive and we could also pick up about 20 bucks a day working as mechanics in the team. In fact, quite often Harry would ring up and say, "If you want your car to be ready for the next race you'd better get down to the workshop for the next couple of weeks." We usually drove the cars to and from work, and to the race meetings.'

'We ran our cars in on the highway,' recalls Brock, 'on the road from Melbourne to Bathurst. Simple as that. That was the Harry plan. I was given detailed instructions on how to drive it on the way.'

When the team arrived, Brock learnt what a tough battleground the mountain could be. 'We were still regarded by the New South Wales drivers as foreigners. Things weren't that easy in those days when dealing with officialdom either.'

Ford's opposing line-up was, on paper at least, far superior.

'Pete Geoghegan was an extremely tough driver,' Moffat recalls, 'one that had already won five Australian touring car titles. He had no qualms about throwing the car around if he had to, which was not my idea of driving style, but he had passion. I found him very difficult to beat. I pretty much kept to myself when it came to the social side. I had already formed the opinion that the race weekend was work. The people who were employing you were entitled to your very best endeavours. It was not in my nature to make it a weekend social adventure. That was the way I handled it for my entire career. Don't forget, in those days it was just Saturday practice and race on Sunday. If you didn't make every minute of that Saturday count, you weren't doing your job.'

'We started from pole,' recalls Leo Geoghegan. 'We knew we had to nurse the car, doing 500 miles (800 kilometres) on one set of brake pads because the time taken to change pads was too long. If you nursed them too much you were too slow. If you didn't nurse them enough they wore out. I've always called it a 500 mile guessing competition: "How hard should I drive this car?"'

Harry Firth's Michelin road tyres were less exotic than Turner's racing Goodyears, but proven to last the distance. The problem was, after one of the most memorable first laps in the history of the race, few thought they would have to worry about tyre wear at all. As the massive field of 60, heavy with fuel and pulsating with horsepower, roared up the mountain, snaked across the top and choked up on the dangerously curved descent, Mike Savva's GTHO Falcon moved across unwittingly on Bill Brown's Falcon, which ran out of track and into a bank on the high side. It flipped, landing on its roof in front of the field, as if some mischievous gods were trying to stop the race. The first 15 drivers saw the crash early enough to slow and squeeze through the little space that had been left. However, as the stranded Brown and panicking flag marshals watched in horror, the swarm of smaller cars that made up the bulk of the field ploughed like lemmings into the wreckage. John French, in an Alfa, was one driver who would have cleared the trap had it not been for a car behind him flipping him as it charged in. Now two drivers were trapped upside down, as the concertina carnage continued. Then there was silence.

Back in the main straight, a confused crowd was wondering where three-quarters of the field had gone. There was no radio communication with the cars and no line of sight between race control and the crash. Barely a hundred spectators were in the sector where the pile-up had occurred. Marshals were running frantically back and forth to ensure that the remaining cars did not add to the chaos on their second lap. French and Brown waited nervously for assistance, warning anyone within earshot not to smoke a cigarette. The smell of petrol was overwhelming.

When the track was finally cleared, the race resumed — and Leo Geoghegan discovered that brakes were not his only concern. 'It was tyres. We didn't know how long they would last, and as it turned out, Ian blew the first tyre on lap 40. We knew we had a problem.' Reports suggest that the Falcon was about 3 seconds a lap quicker than the Monaro but lost at least that much time because of the greater frequency of pit stops.

Colin Bond delivered for Harry Firth. 'We won easily in the end,' Bond recalls. 'We had been running up the front all day, looking after the brakes. I remember coming in for a pad change on the second stop, but it was more of a precaution, really, because Harry had noticed Henk's pads were wearing fast. My pads were fine. We only got out on our final stop about 14 seconds ahead of Bruce McPhee, after leading by more than a minute. He was our only threat. In traffic it got down to 8 seconds, and we got a little jerky, but we stayed out of trouble and had figured that he had to make another stop for fuel, which he did. It was quite a day, winning at Bathurst in my first full-time professional drive.'

Peter Brock brought his car across the line 3rd, in a display that impressed everyone. 'The thing I remember most about that first experience,' says Brock, 'was how demanding it was on the body. I had bruises in all kinds of places where I was bracing myself against the car. We had a four-point harness but the seats, which were referred to as buckets, were more like bench seats cut in half. You moved around a bit. The cars were quite heavily sprung, even by today's standards, but we still used the old radial tyres, so the cars didn't dig in with grip. They would slide and squirm around a lot, with a minimum of body roll. The body shells were flexing like buggery with bolt-in roll cages made of aluminium. Basically, all they did was stop the roof from caving in when you tipped over. Brakes were like an emergency device: you used them only when you had to!'

Bond walked up to Des West for a chat during the rowdy Holden celebrations. West was shaking his head. 'What's up?' Bond asked.

'This race is getting so tough,' West replied. 'I'm flat out having a smoke on my way around these days.'

Brock enjoyed driving with West. 'He was so cool. He knew what to do. He knew what he could do. Sure, he had the packet of fags under the dashboard. To this day, I don't know how he could have done it. It was staggering.'

'Some of the cars were still very slow, and therefore not overly taxing, although they didn't have power steering,' says Bond. 'A lot of weird stuff did go on. It certainly wasn't unusual in those days to eat something while you were competing. Some people would eat lollies. Others had sandwiches. I know of one bloke who peed in his suit. That was okay, except for the bloke who had to get in the car after him! It may have been because of those long nights I spent rallying, but I didn't need anything . . . or need to do anything.'

Allan Moffat had made a lucky diversion from the early race carnage. He steered his Falcon into a run-off area on lap 1 to sort out a faulty gearbox, missed the mass collision, returned to the race and paced himself through that destructive day to finish his first Bathurst in 4th place. Ford also had the makings of a hero. 'I was appreciative that Al called me into the pits, worried about the tyres blowing, the way they had on the others. But I knew the corner, the anti-camber turn two, where the wear was occurring, and I adjusted my speed to counter that. Had I been left alone to look after the tyres the way I could, and go through to the first pit stop at maximum distance, I have no doubt that I could have won Bathurst in my first attempt.'

Turner would later admit that he need not have called Moffat in for what turned out to be an unnecessary 4-minute pit stop. He was only 2 minutes behind Bond at the finish.

Bond almost immediately won at Lakeside, followed by a series race at Warwick Farm and the 1970 Surfers Paradise 12 hour, and finished 2nd to Moffat in the Tasman series for sedans. 'After winning Bathurst,' he recalls, 'The wheels started turning for Harry and Holden. Brocky and I were signed up as full-time HDT drivers. I was also signed to do rallies. The funny thing was, GMH was still refusing to let Holden officially support circuit racing, but they allowed them to support rallies. So we had to run rallies in order to get funding from the factory. They didn't quite understand things too well back in Detroit. When there was any official visit from the Americans, suddenly Harry's workshop was full of rally cars!'

Brock was taking to Firth's flick-it-in and get-it-around style like a dog to an old bone. It was straight from the Diamond Creek paddocks. 'Harry often spoke in another language, gesturing as he went. He would say, "Listen cock, I want you to … huh … then ugh … then huh …" After he finished you'd wonder if maybe you'd missed out on a key "ugh" but I kind of knew what he was thinking. It was special.'

1970 was a comeback of sorts for Stormin' Norm Beechey. Over Christmas in 1969 he built, with his team of mechanics, a 350 Monaro at his workshop in Coburg. It took 5 weeks. The plan was to take on the successful Bob Jane and Allan Moffat, in their Trans-Am Mustangs. They had indirect help from CAMS, which altered regulations to allow Beechey to make competitive modifications. Pete Geoghegan in his regular Mustang and Bill Brown, Jim McKeown and Brian Foley in Porsches were other keen rivals. The factory ingredients in the 350 were good, but the trick was in bigger tyres and wide, flared guards, modifications which would not have been allowed on the Bathurst cars but were essential for winning the various touring car championship rounds. Armed with this car, Beechey finally regained the national championship he had previously won 5 years earlier. It was a worthy title to win, too, because the opposition had rarely been so strong for so long. The meetings were regular and intense.

While Beechey was asserting his imposing frame in yet another muscular V8, Harry Firth was already searching for a new challenge with which to mastermind a famous Bathurst win. That challenge was a new Holden car, the Torana. He had seen the shell in the factory and hand-picked the components so that Holden could provide him with a winning power-to-weight ratio.

Colin Bond was sceptical at first. 'We were to use the GTR Torana for rallies. Brian Hope was my co-driver. That was a simpler version of the XU1, and it replaced the Monaro, which had been great to rally with, although a little big and hard on tyres. We finished 2nd in the Ampol Bi-Centenary Trial with a

Monaro and won our class. I really liked the Monaro in rallies, but in the end, the Toranas were faster all round. I even won the first circuit race at Warwick Farm in the XU1. I passed Monaro after Monaro and finally caught Bob Jane on the last lap. Janey tried to punt me off a few times but we won it.' Bond would drive alone at Bathurst in 1970, while Brock was given Bob Morris as co-driver.

The Sandown 3 hour race was the Torana's first endurance test on a circuit, and it was given a pasting by the beefy Falcons. Firth was far from deterred, though, because he knew how effective a light, powerful car could be on the mountain; after all, he built the Cortina. Falcons and Toranas were in separate classes, but each group thought they could win outright.

Leo Geoghegan was recruited to drive a 6 cylinder Valiant Pacer with Nick Ledingham. The Geoghegan team had been relatively successful in the Tasman series, but the food on the table was supplied by touring cars. That is why Leo developed the Pacer and Charger cars for the championship and Bathurst. This was not the way he wanted his career to go, but progress was tugging at his shirt sleeves. 'It was back into touring cars, which gave me the shits, quite frankly, especially the production cars. It was all the wannabes saying, "There's Geoghegan, I'm better than him" and driving into your door, wanting to become instant heroes.'

Norm Beechey was finally lured to Bathurst for the 500 in 1970 to pair with Bruce Hindhaugh. Beechey had run some races in the car, and had almost beaten John Harvey in a Monaro at Lakeside, but that was over 15 laps. 'In practice, I came into the pits and said, "If we don't change the head gasket on this car, it will boil tomorrow in no time." They just looked at me. I said, "Well are we going to change the head gasket?" and they said they just couldn't do that. So I left my road car on the other side of the main straight, ready for an early exit on race day.'

In total there were five manufacturers directly supporting entries across the classes, with more than 30 dealers subsidising cars. It was the strongest field in the 10 year history of the 500. Moffat qualified better than any of them, ahead of two other Falcons and Bond's Torana.

'I had been elevated to the number one car,' Moffat recalls, 'and all the duties that went with it: testing and the like. We were keen to wipe the slate after 1969. It had been devastating for Al Turner on his first attempt. Remember, the project in 1969 did not start on the first of January. Al wasn't even in the country then. We had the full year to prepare in 1970.'

Bond showed the other Torana drivers what to do when the race started, using the smaller car's nimble handling to outmanoeuvre the Falcons. He led for 5 laps. Moffat refused to be baited and drove his own race. When Bond pitted with carburettor problems, Moffat took charge, nursing the larger car through lap after lap to win by 39 seconds. 'I was absolutely delighted. I was aware of the significance of the race long before I ever got there. It was still early in my career. I had plenty of DNFs — too many to win the Touring Car Championship that year — so Bathurst was of tremendous importance for me. With Holden running Brock in one car and Bond in the other, they were fast, and there were plenty of other Fords quite capable of winning if we had screwed up.'

Leo Geoghegan finished 5th in the Pacer, 2 laps down. Norm Beechey had been right about his car. 'Sure enough, I brought it in during the race after 39 laps, boiling its head off. They asked me if I was going to hang around for the rest of the day and I told them I was going off to West Wyalong with my wife to shoot rabbits.'

Allan Moffat polarised the public in the following season of 1971. The diehard fans loved him more and the other camp hated him more. His rivals often did not know what to make of him. His approach was gentlemanly at any of the off-track activities. On track he was still urbane and quietly spoken when approached, but he was a cold, clinical operator in the car. Having dined on the 'fair dinkum' band of Australian-bred predecessors, the grass roots supporters took a while to come to terms with their latest champion. They had feasted on the cherubic enthusiasm of Stormin' Norman, the tough, laconic Jane and the stuttering innocence of 'Black Pete'. Then they were served up the smiling, jovial Bond and the handsome young knockabout Brock. 'While Brock was the true blue Aussie,' Moffat recalls, 'I was the convenient anti-hero, being a foreigner. My true Australian status hadn't rubbed off.

'It didn't worry me because it was my nature,' he continues. 'I was the only one who could lead my life. I had no other job, no commercial interests. I just had to make what I did behind the wheel count. I never refused to say hello to anyone, but being affable to the extent of roaming around the pits having a chat to everyone for the sake of passing the time of day just wasn't me. I spent my time with the people I worked with, being a part of every bit of development on the car.'

He was beaten, arguably, by his own aggression when he lost the 1971 championship to Bob Jane in the Chevrolet Camaro. 'From the moment they left the format of a single-race championship and made it a proper series, every race had to count, so the DNFs were costly. With the Mustang, there was no compromise. I could have played it super-cool and collected a bunch of 2nd or 3rd places to get the points, but for me it was win or nothing, and I drove it to win all the time.'

Jane recalls clashes that got out of hand. 'The racing had been very hairy between Moffat and me. He was a very serious guy. He wanted to win. In fact Allan said to me, even though we were mates, "I can't like you. If I like you, I can't race against you 'cause I can't run into you." I had some physicals with him, actually.' It would become very physical, but not until the following year.

Endurance races leading up to Bathurst in 1971 revealed the same old drama for Ford's Falcon. It was still destroying brakes. The Torana was looking more and more like a winning car, with Colin Bond going close before failing at Oran Park, then winning at Sandown. He also won the Australian Rally Championship and the Southern Cross Rally. 'By that time,' he recalls. 'I was very involved in both rally and circuit races in Toranas. The busy schedule hurt me at Oran Park. I'd competed in a Queensland rally overnight, flown back the next morning and started at the back of the grid because I'd missed qualifying! I got to the lead before breaking down.'

Only Moffat could have cuddled the Falcon to a record-breaking lap of Mt Panorama. He peaked at 240 kilometres per hour down Conrod, but drove with calculated precision where necessary. Kevin Bartlett was finally armed with race-winning potential, a GTHO Falcon. Bond and Brock were the solo drivers for Harry Firth's Holden Dealer team. Bob Jane and John Harvey combined in a non-factory Torana. Leo Geoghegan had been expecting great things at Bathurst in Valiant's Charger, which he had tested extensively; he drove with Peter Brown. Norm Beechey teamed with his old Neptune Racing team-mate Jim McKeown in another Charger. None of them could get close to Moffat, though.

He won by a lap. 'That made it a very satisfying double. It removed any illusions. Detractors always like to imply that when you do have some success that you'd been lucky.'

By the end of 1971, Norm Beechey was starting to realise that there was more to life than motor sport. His two final flings at Mt Panorama had been dogged by misfortune. He had noticed that with the growing stature of the Bathurst race, the emphasis in touring car racing was slowly changing from the modified category to the production categories that characterised the 500. 'I still liked Bathurst. It was a magnificent circuit. I won a round of the championship there in the 350 Monaro, and I felt I was pretty good around there. I had no fear of the track, just respect for it. I think with the speeds that you were travelling you had to. I used to go down the main straight with my foot poised above the clutch, in case anything went wrong. Once I went down there in the Monaro, the tacho on 7500, she hit a bump and it jumped to 8500 and POONG! There'd be two clouds of smoke come out the back as the rear tyres spun.' He chuckles, almost breathlessly, at the memory.

Beechey had established successful business interests in the motoring world that were becoming increasingly demanding. Full-time drivers like Brock and Moffat were taking over the arena. One meeting at Lakeside hammered it home. 'I had arrived there on the Friday, in what I considered to be plenty of time to practise, only to find that Moffat had been there since Tuesday.' Even if he had been inclined to redefine his career, he could not escape the fact that he was earning a lot more money outside the realm of motor sport. Unlike so many sporting heroes, Norm Beechey found the ultimate decision easy and he stuck with it.

His final race was in September 1972, winning the Western Australian Touring Car Championship at Wanneroo. It was a fitting way to finish for a man who, with a little help from his rivals, established the personality of Australian touring car racing, an image that has defined it for more than 40 years: raw, but professional; extroverted, but humble. When you examine the cult heroes of today, there's always a lot of Norm Beechey in that image.

'I rarely raced against Norm,' recalls Leo Geoghegan. 'He was mostly against Pete, but he was a bloody good driver. He was underestimated by a lot of people because he was a showman extraordinaire. He was brilliant at that. In fact they could use a few of them now. He was great value to his sponsors and followers. Norm, Bob Jane, and Moffat, who was coming through the ranks then, would have won more championships if they hadn't run into Pete in his heyday. I'm glad they went on to win a few, because they were great drivers and that's a better reflection of their ability. In those early days it wasn't always a series, and you had only one chance sometimes to win it or lose it.'

*   *   *

In 1972, for the third year in a row, factory support intensified for the Bathurst 1000. So did the rivalry among drivers. Bob Jane had won his second consecutive Australian Touring Car Championship in the Chevy Camaro.

If Moffat and Jane simmered in 1971, they boiled in 1972. Their most famous clash followed a touring car race at Warwick Farm. 'He hit me up the arse. I spun off the track and nearly killed two track marshals,' Jane recalls. 'So I drove back on and chased him but couldn't catch him. He knew what was going to happen if I did,' says Jane.

John Harvey was Jane's team-mate, driving in the open-wheel category, and remembers it as a humorous incident even if Jane and Moffat saw it differently at the time. 'When Bob came back onto the track he aimed his car straight for Allan as he accelerated up the straight. He was going to T-bone him, but he missed. So Bob's really fuming. Allan won the race and pulled back into the pits. Of course he sees Bob coming for him so he keeps his seatbelt on and his helmet and just stays in the car. Bob's going off his head at him through the window. Allan's just sitting there. The next thing I know Bob's punching shit out of him through the window. Allan's still got his helmet on so the punches are just bouncing off. Anyway, they dragged Bob off and that was the end of that.'

'Everyone at Warwick Farm understood my personality at the time,' said Jane. 'I grabbed hold of him to drag him out of the car, but in my anger, I didn't see that he was still strapped in. So I, regretfully in some ways, gave him a decent whack.'

Moffat remembers his passing move as a legitimate opportunity. 'I went through the hole he left! He didn't like it much and he demonstrated that to me in the pits afterwards. But it wasn't all that which bothered me as much as his political influence with CAMS.'

Jane did not leave his anger on the track. He protested. Officials imposed a fine of $50, but Jane appealed against the fine, claiming that it was inadequate. 'I wanted to stop such actions, because all I could think of was those two marshals I was sliding towards, who were running and running. I was convinced I was going to hit them. How I didn't, I don't know.'

It escalated, finishing at a judicial hearing at Sydney's Wentworth Hotel. The hearing went from 7 pm to 2 am, CAMS officials presiding, with lawyers drawn up on both sides. There were floods of questions. Jane's lawyer cross-examined Moffat. 'I put it to you, Mr Moffat, that you deliberately shoved Bob Jane off the track during that race.'

According to reports at the time, Moffat coolly replied, 'No, I couldn't have done that.' There was a long pause during which only nervous coughing and shuffling of papers could be heard. 'I couldn't have done that, because every time I have, I've come off second-best.'

Moffat does not recall making that statement, but he does recall being very disillusioned with the judicial process, which he saw as more political than legal. He was also disappointed that solicitors had been involved; CAMS later decided not to allow them to become involved in appeals.

The hearing was adjourned. Ten minutes later, the judiciary disqualified Moffat, and handed the race to Jane. Jane went on to win the final round, and the 1972 championship.

The acrimony lasted a long time, and Moffat learnt another lesson: that motor sport was not just about racing. It was about winning. 'Well it cost me the championship. It had been deemed a racing incident by the stewards after the race. I was exonerated on the track. A month later, at a tribunal, I went from being exonerated by stewards who were privy to all the information they needed to make a judgment, to being excluded from the race, losing all the prize money and 9 valuable points. It made me aware that the governing body was going to be difficult to work with. I drove for the factory at Bathurst, but for the rest of the year I was a one-man show with my Mustang, trying to keep the wolf from the door. The tribunal incident left me a little bit cold, I have to tell you. I realised I still had a long way to go on the political stage.'

John Harvey recalls that the 1972 incident provoked the great irony of motor racing: it is sport *and* business, which are not always compatible. 'You have to remember that in the late 1960s it was Bob who helped Allan when he needed to sell his TR3 to raise enough money to buy a ticket to the United States. Coca-Cola had given him enough money to buy the Mustang but he had nothing left to pay for his air fare. It was only when he got on the track that they became competitors in the '70s and, you know, business is business and friendship is friendship. The two didn't mix as far as Bob was concerned.'

Moffat found that a little harder to swallow. 'I have great respect for everything Bob did, and over the years that hasn't changed, except for that one incident involving CAMS at Warwick Farm.' Nevertheless, between 1968 and 1972, Moffat had won 101 of his 151 races in the Mustang.

Bob Jane's four ATCC titles spanned 9 years, in which time racing had become far more serious and professional, and the focus on the production car epic at Bathurst had become intense. Brock and Bond were again driving for Harry Firth, and by then were arguably the best combination in the land. Bond had won his second Australian Rally Championship.

'The key,' Brock recalls, 'was the Torana's horsepower. Between 1969 and 1972 we were just not quick enough. When we got hold of the 202 engine, we had the zip that we needed. We had a scare, though, when the very first couple we received at Auburn from the Fishermens Bend factory were faulty. Dad and my brother Phil had delivered these brand new, unpainted Toranas with these new engines we'd been waiting for — but all the pistons were cracked. We were in shock. Then, after a bit of interrogation, we realised Dad and Phil had got all excited and decided to have a race. Wrecked the bloody brand new engines. The Brock factor strikes again.'

The new cars which housed those engines were bright silver, adorned with a little signwriting. 'We raced them fairly unsuccessfully for about 6 months in the Touring Car Championship. They were all right, but not beating the Fords. Then, some guru down at George Pattersons, the advertising agency that worked for Holden, came up with an idea for a new colour scheme. When my car came back from being repainted in the now-famous black, white and red, it just looked hot. It looked lower, leaner, faster ... like a winner. I have to tell you, from that day on, those cars went a second a lap faster. We went to Calder and we won — and we kept winning. Of course we did a few other things, and it depended on the type of circuits we were on, but that paint job transformed the focus of the team onto the car, and I went to Bathurst that year thinking I could win.'

For the first time in the history of the race, it rained, and Firth produced another master stroke from his deep bag of tricks, using Goodyear wet race tyres, and they went to Brock. Bond was given a set of Dunlop intermediates. Brock made the most of his full wet tyres and his new-found 202 zip, trailing Moffat who was on imported American tyres, for some time in blinding rain. He felt safe in the knowledge that his arch rival would not put a foot wrong. 'I chased him and chased him and chased him.'

Behind them was carnage, including Colin Bond's worst crash on the mountain. On the third lap, it became clear his intermediates did not have enough grip. He aquaplaned on standing water at McPhillamy, bounced into a bank and rolled down a hill. He was unhurt. 'I had had a "moment" on every lap prior to that. I was a fraction wider than the racing lines, didn't turn in tightly enough, and suddenly the car's on its roof. There I was, sliding down the road, upside down and all you can do is look out the front window, watching the road shooting past. I've got my foot hard on the brakes, hard as I can, as you do, but — funny about this — I wasn't slowing down! Then I did another twist and turn, finishing back on my wheels in the infield. I tried to drive it out but the right front wheel was missing.'

The Brock pressure resulted in a Moffat spin just beyond the Reid Park gates at about quarter distance. The Torana was through. Brock recalls the moment vividly. 'I remember, momentarily, our eyes locked. I could see them in the rear vision mirror of his car. In that nanosecond, he just drifted a fraction wide, maybe only a tyre width, into the sheet of water, and spun. As he's gone around, his right rear has just missed my right-hand side. You could have put a cigarette paper between us ... it all seemed to happen in slow motion.'

'That little puddle of water had grown bigger with every lap,' Moffat recalls. 'Like a clever little beaver — I won't get too cute about it! — Peter got through, but it was his good driving that stopped me taking him with me. It was that close. I never saw him again for the rest of the day. In the rain you have to be somewhat cautious, but Peter was simply brilliant in those conditions.'

Brilliant, and thirsty, as Brock recalls an era when no one could even spell rehydration, let alone do it. 'I had been in that car six and a half hours and Harry had not given me a drink. He wouldn't, because he believed that I would then need a toilet break and lose my concentration. I was young and fit and coped with it all right but my kidneys would have been screaming. Then, to make it worse, I had a couple of beers afterwards! That was the last time we drove alone at Bathurst.'

Harry Firth regarded it as his most satisfying win. 'We walked it in. It was a joke and no one had believed we could do it. We proved them absolutely wrong.'

The celebrations that night were also foundation hours for the legend behind the legend, the life of the race driver that is rarely discussed these days without prior consultation with legal experts. When it came to that life, Brock was without peer. 'Let's just say that my biggest problem that night was which girl to go with. Hell of a decision to make for a young bloke. Was it worth it? Yep! That day changed my life.'

The Moffat–Brock rivalry had been cemented. Australia had their motor sport version of Ali and Frasier. If you weren't a Brock supporter you were a Moffat supporter. That was it. 'At that stage,' Brock recalls, 'the focus was right on the Ford–Holden thing. Moffat was great. He was the black hat really. He would get out there and say and do the things to incite people. He had a turn of phrase that was always going to be inflammatory and controversial. We barely spoke to each other. I might have run into him and said, "Hello", or "How are you Al?" and he would look daggers at me. Barely anything was said. We went on for about 10 years like that. That's the truth. I admired him, but at the time thought we had nothing in common. I later learnt we had a similar sense of humour and got on very well.'

It was Brock, however, who would reap the most from the era, as the factory and sponsors milked his charisma to the max. It made him think about open-wheel racing. He had tinkered with some Formula 2 races.

'I was having a chat with Jack Brabham at Oran Park one day,' he recalls, 'before I won Bathurst. I idolised Jack and I asked him about going to Europe. To be quite honest, he poured cold water on the idea. But I think he was just being realistic. I still thought that if I got that Formula 2 car going successfully I might have been able to do something, but quite frankly, Holden came to me with an offer too good to refuse. In their eyes, Formula 2 was an indulgence. They let me get it out of my system. I chose to focus then on touring cars and never had any regrets.'

The Brock win in 1972 was not only the start of his extraordinary relationship with one of the world's most famous circuits. It was also the first sign of the fraying of the Holden Dealer team's (HDT's) internal structure. 'I was still the number one driver,' recalls Colin Bond, 'but the big difference was, I was based in Sydney, and Brock was in Melbourne. He was at the workshop all the time. When it came to status in the team, this was to be the biggest problem for me. Before the 1972 Bathurst race we only had one set of wet tyres and one set of intermediates. Harry asked me what I wanted and I told him the wets. I went to the toilet, and when I came out, the wet tyres were on Brocky's car. We joke about it today, but it happened all right.' Firth denies it, claiming that Bond always had a choice.

Motor sport is certainly about performance, but it is also about politics. The Brock–Bond situation was not new, and is still typical of almost every relationship between team drivers all over the world. 'The greatest asset I had as a kid,' Brock recalls, 'was that I was totally besotted with motor racing. I would crawl over 10 miles of broken beer bottles to get my hands on a car and go for a drive, to the point of being totally selfish. I didn't care what else was happening. I just wanted to drive a race car. Bondy obviously had other priorities and it was reflected in his overall results. If you're there every day running around doing jobs, helping them take an engine out or whatever, working with the team, it makes an enormous difference.'

The following year, the championship and the great race were brought into line: modifications were allowed, but the cars still had to be locally sold models, which meant the popular Mustang and Camaro were banished to a separate category. Moffat in the Falcon and Brock in the Torana staged an epic championship fight from Symmons Plains to Calder to Sandown to Wanneroo. Moffat won all four. They resumed the battle at Surfers Paradise and Adelaide. Brock won those. He also won the seventh round, at Oran Park, but was later disqualified because of an oversized exhaust manifold. Moffat won that round, and with it the title.

Howard Marsden was appointed to replace Al Turner, who went on to other projects for Ford in Asia. Moffat had been offered the job, but convinced Ford that he would be more valuable behind a wheel than a desk, and recommended Marsden. The Falcon became the year-round focus of attention, because by then it was eligible for the touring car championship. 'Howard and his team did a great job,' recalls Moffat. 'It was almost a photo finish with the XU1, which was very aggressive around Oran Park. My Bathurst car in '73 was the first of the two-door hard-tops, the XA GT.'

Brock remembers the intensity. 'There were spies! People would be peeking into each other's garages, checking to see what they were doing to the cars and how long they were working on them. It was full on, even down to the airlines we flew. We flew Qantas and they flew Ansett. We just didn't want to be in the same part of the world as them. They were the enemy.'

John Harvey had not raced in the 1972 Bathurst 500, but for 1973 he teamed again with his boss Bob Jane in a Torana. 'To be honest, in the early days even though Bathurst was on television, I wouldn't even be bothered watching it. I'd be out mowing the lawn. I was a single-seater driver. Normally at those meetings the touring cars were a secondary category, but in the early 1970s they really took over.'

Another interesting pairing was Leo Geoghegan and Colin Bond in a factory Torana. It did not matter to Geoghegan that he had not teamed with his brother since 1969. 'You could be competing against your best mate and you'd carve each other up. It was a race. It wasn't a gentle tour.'

To the surprise of the factory followers, it was the privateer Falcon of Kevin Bartlett and John Goss on pole for a new-look Bathurst — over 1000 kilometres. They led the race but were caught up in a collision in the cutting, and the damage forced them out. 'Some of my Bathurst performances,' Bartlett recalls, 'might seem a bit ho-hum, but I can honestly say that every one of them was a true race. It was never just a drive. We were always on it.'

Goss had not long established himself on the mainland after starting his career in Tasmania but when he teamed with Hurstville Ford Dealer Max McLeod his career started to take off. Goss had bought the car in late 1972, and prepared for the 1973 season. It was the first racing version of the hard-top coupé. He had given it a shakedown at the Bathurst Easter meeting and was well ahead of the factory development. 'I'd proved to the team and myself that we could be competitive.'

They were not the only retirements. Nearly half the field would drop out, including Jane and Harvey, and Firth's skinny fuel strategy was looking like a winning ploy for Brock and 35-year-old co-driver Doug Chivas — until Chivas drove one lap too many on his stint. He ran out of fuel before he could reach the pits. He tried to clutch start the car as it rolled lifelessly down Conrod Straight. This was not only unsuccessful, but ensured that the car lost momentum. It stopped 100 metres short of the pits.

He leapt out, in front of a supportive crowd and a massive television audience, to push the car down the pit entry road. The rules stated that he could not be assisted. Brock and his crew were dancing around as if barefoot on hot sand as the painful scene unfolded. Officials allowed assistants to intervene just as the exhausted Chivas neared the entry line. It cost the team 3 minutes. Brock recalls the incident with great regret, but no blame. 'Poor old Chivo had to push his car into the pits. He was about 8 stone wringing wet. I was urging him on. He had a bit of a mild heart flutter actually, from the effort. I just flung him backwards and got into the car when he finally arrived. Honestly, I just flung him! The whole episode was caused, basically, by a miscalculation. Someone took their eyes off the ball. That's all it was.'

Moffat capitalised, with Howard Marsden throwing the Falcons through the pits in slick time, and at the end of the day Moffat stood on top of the podium with a deserving Pete Geoghegan. 'Compatibility with your co-driver was mandatory to win Bathurst. I had driven the previous two wins solo, but with the rule changes demanding two drivers for 1000 kilometres, I could not have had a better co-driver than Pete. He was actually a very funny fellow. The whole team worked hard. Howard and the Ford team would work all night on anything that we felt needed doing, and in those days the parts had to be maintained with great care so that we could drive them hard, faultlessly. No driver wins Bathurst on luck. The dedication that each team takes to the start line is what decides the outcome.'

Brock and Chivas finished nearly a minute and a half behind, with a similar margin to Bond and Leo Geoghegan. Leo had gone relatively close, without winning, yet again. Somehow that was appropriate in his final fling at Bathurst.

'Pete and I had won a long distance Sports Car race there in a Daimler, so I guess I had one big win at Bathurst! There are no regrets. The 1000 had come to be special and it was a worthy test for the driver, there's no doubt about that. A hundred miles around Warwick Farm in an open-wheeler kept you fit but at Bathurst it was also a mental drain because you were concerned about the car. The other problem was the traffic, a mixed field of cars with different speeds. Those different cars were populated by about 120 different drivers over the course of the race. Of those, about 40 were very good, another 40 good, and the rest varied from average to bad. You often didn't know when you were coming up behind one of them, about to overtake, which kind of driver you were up against. That took a lot of care.'

Harry Firth was starting to become frustrated with the HDT experience. 'We had everything sorted, but there were stupid mistakes all over the place.'

Jane and Harvey, amazingly, fought back to finish 4th. Harvey received a media award for the drive and regarded it as one of his most satisfying performances. 'After what had happened at Bathurst in the past, Bob had been a little edgy about taking a full stint. I drove the first and last stints and was very pleased with the effort.'

In typical sporting fashion, John Harvey never begrudged Pete his victory after all those years of trying. 'I reckon Pete Geoghegan was the best touring car driver, ever, in this country.'

Few people in 1973 paid attention to a young Queenslander who drove methodically into 5th place with Bob Forbes in a Torana. He was not a factory favourite, nor a wealthy entrepreneurial type. Money, cars and drives would never come to him from affluence or influence. He would have to earn every dollar, every trophy, every centimetre of bitumen between himself and the cars behind.

Dick Johnson was born in Brisbane on 26 April 1945, exactly 2 months later than Peter Brock. He was born to race and overcome obstacles. The first of those was family tradition. His father was a sales manager for a Holden dealership but wanted Dick to become a champion swimmer. Dick was good, setting a record for 50 metres freestyle that would last 25 years, but the only way his father could get him to a pool to train early in the morning was to let him drive the car — at the age of 8.

'From day one, that's all I ever wanted to do. I can't remember wanting anything else but to race cars.'

Like so many other children, Johnson would wait for his father to arrive home from work so that he could drive the car into the garage. He would rush to every race meeting he could possibly get to, often on a pushbike. His father sometimes went along, even his mother … just once. 'It was at Lowood. We had been camped for a while at the back end of the circuit, when Mum turned around and asked where my little brother David was. Next thing you know, there he was, walking across the circuit! My mother became terribly disenchanted with motor racing after that.'

Not Dick. He joined the MG Car Club at 14 and stared lovingly at yards full of sports cars, wishing one of them were his own. His parents only consented to signing his racing licence on the condition that he avoid open-wheel racing. That was fine by him.

Johnson would ride his pushbike from Coorparoo, more than 4 hours away, to Lakeside to watch his heroes.

'They had the Australian Touring Car Championship in Queensland in 1964. Pete Geoghegan won it in a Lotus Cortina. It seemed that everyone was there. Beechey, Muir, Bo Seton, Jim McKeown, Peter Manton, Brian Foley, Clem Smith. I watched Frenchy [John French] race there.'

Then there were the mug lairs, the part-timers, who brought a wry grin to Johnson's face with their lack of ability and abundance of backyard bravado. 'A lot of the local touring car drivers were posers. They'd drive around the suburbs of Brisbane in their race cars, with their helmet sitting conveniently in view at the rear windscreen. I remember one bloke just kept on going straight ahead at the kink one day and ended up in the lake. There's the arse of his car sticking out of the water and I could see him, still inside, just looking out the back window. They were real characters.' The whole spectrum of the experience captivated him.

He bought and prepared an FJ Holden for racing: the usual club expeditions, hill climbs, gymkhanas and circuits. He took up the obligatory job as a mechanic. It was fitting that he should compete for the first time at his beloved Lakeside, in November 1964. It was the final race of the day, open to all comers, and he won it. 'I think I was on the second row. I beat a Cortina driven by Kevin Johns. But then I retired. I had no money left!'

The next mission was to rebuild another FJ, an ex-taxi, in order to resume racing. 'It cost 80 quid, but the body was rusted out, so I bought another one from the wreckers for 15 quid.' The car in fact cost the Johnson family a lot more. Dick's second brother, Peter, was helping Dick and David panelbeat the car and copped a sledgehammer blow to the mouth. The dental bills ran to $1000. 'That left David and me. We had no money left to do anything. When it came to painting the car, we collected as many tins of paint as we could, but never enough of the same colour, so we mixed them all up and it came out as a kind of lilac, which we then applied with brushes. I borrowed parts from another bloke, so we shared the driving. That was good for a few races each. Then we ran out of money again.'

Racing, however, would not be a problem where Dick Johnson was heading. The price for being born just 2 months later than Peter Brock was that Johnson was also a target for national service. He even finished up at Brock's base, Kapooka, near Wagga Wagga. For months, Australia's legendary touring car opponents lived together without even knowing it. 'I had no idea at the time,' Johnson says with a laugh. 'I never knew Brocky, of course. I was fresh out of Queensland. He was from Victoria. I might have seen him, but I don't remember him. We later found out that his quarters were just three huts away from mine.'

Johnson was later posted to Bulimba, then Canungra in Queensland, where he was able to continue work as a mechanic, honing his skills and using the army's extensive workshop facilities. He came out of the military tunnel after 2 years — with $1086. Even the currency had changed while he was away. 'When I got out of the army in 1967, I bought an EH to focus more on racing, but the only way to raise the money to sustain that was to become a home-based mechanic, working under the house. I was thrown out of there, though, because I was working one morning with a block and tackle on a beam under the old man's bed at 2 am and he didn't appreciate it. I moved to a little workshop.' The EH was gradually honed into a decent race car, winning club and state events with lap times that were catching the eyes of the motoring journalists.

Johnson's first break came when he was signed up to drive for a state branch of Norm Beechey's famous racing team. The deal provided him with lubricants, fuel and a small amount of money. They also paid bonuses, in tens of dollars, for finishing 1st, 2nd or 3rd. Through parent sponsor Shell, Johnson was able to find work attached to one of their service stations, which he ended up running for 15 years. The business grew quickly. His passion did too.

'I never missed a Tasman series race at Lakeside. I'd lean on the fences and watch Jim Clark, Graham Hill, Chris Amon, Derek Bell, Leo Geoghegan, Jochen Rindt, Frank Gardner, Kevin Bartlett, Piers Courage, Pedro Rodriguez ... I was there when the big tall wings were introduced. I even remember when Hill's wing collapsed. He came into the pits, they pulled out a couple of hacksaws, cut it off and continued the race! My hero, though, was Jimmy Clark. They were all accessible in those days too. If you wanted to say g'day to any of them you just wandered around to the paddock and said g'day.'

Nothing seemed to weaken Johnson's commitment to emulating the drivers he saw at Lakeside, not even the ever-present danger. He saw a terrible crash which killed Cooper Maserati driver John Hough. He also saw Glynn Scott decapitated in a collision with Juan Tighe just prior to the dog-leg. Scott's car had dived under a metal railing. He saw Niel Allen firing like a bullet off the dog-leg, but somehow surviving.

Johnson raced wherever his budget would take him, progressing through the ranks to a Torana XU1, one of the first to be used in competition, and his first purpose-prepared race car. It scored him a point on 26 July 1970, in an Australian Touring Car Championship round at Lakeside. He then won the Stan Keen Trophy Race at Mallala, South Australia.

A new girlfriend also came in handy. Dick met Jill. It sounded like the opening line of a children's book, and it would indeed become one of Australian motor sport's most famous partnerships, but in the early days his motives were less than pure. 'I liked the fact that she had her own car,' he confesses, 'but it was only a Mini, and after I started taking her out I had to convince her to buy something bigger, because there was no way it was going to tow a trailer with my Torana on it. I talked her into buying a Holden.'

In the same year that Brock won his first Bathurst 1000, Johnson had pumped 16 championship points from 3 rounds — at Oran Park, Warwick Farm and Surfers Paradise. It was all he could afford, but the strike rate caught Harry Firth's attention.

1973 was a quiet year for Johnson, except for an offer from Bob Forbes to co-drive with him at Bathurst. He had experienced the thrill of Mt Panorama in an earlier meeting, and jumped at the opportunity. He prepared Forbes's GTR XU1 Torana 202 in Brisbane but ran out of time to complete it. That would have to be done at the other end. He towed it to Bathurst, taking turns with two mates to share the non-stop drive all the way south. The plan was for one man to drive for 150 miles (240 kilometres) while the other two slept. Johnson could not understand why he was so tired for his stints until he discovered that his mates had been waking him after they'd spent only about 5 minutes at the wheel. They camped at Orange, 60 kilometres west of Bathurst, and finished building the car at a Shell Service Station on the Saturday morning. He qualified the car on row 5 of the grid and was proud of his fifth placing, considering that Forbes was a few seconds a lap slower. The Queenslander's tireless, penniless campaign was light years from the factory-backed success enjoyed by his contemporaries, and there were no signs of bigger teams or wealthier supporters rushing to change that.

Ford withdrew from touring car racing again in 1974. They virtually abandoned the project overnight. Allan Moffat knew there would be repercussions from his 1973 win. Holden had been beaten by a V8 and were determined to come back fiercely with a V8 of their own, in the Torana.

Harry Firth, who knew how Moffat was feeling, was ready to capitalise. Two drivers inherited Falcons from the 1973 team. Fred Gibson, frustrated by lack of factory support, gave his to his mother-in-law. Allan Moffat put up a brave fight in a 1-year-old Falcon, but was never going to win the touring car championship, which Peter Brock did win after 6 of the 7 rounds. So consumed was Brock by the lure of the mountain that he barely acknowledged the title. 'I just concentrated on winning as many races as I could.' In the round that clinched the series, Surfers Paradise, Dick Johnson poked his head up again, driving a 6 cylinder Torana into 3rd place.

'I finally got that call from Harry Firth,' Johnson recalls. 'Harry was supporting Zupps Holden in Queensland and they offered me some drives but it didn't last long. The new SLR 5000 came out and the deal finished.' Johnson found a seat with John French in an Alfa Romeo — it turned out to be a dangerous fire-trap that strained their friendship.

It had been 5 years since John Goss had made his debut on the mountain. He had been disappointed enough after failing in 1973 after Kevin Bartlett put their Falcon on pole, but it seemed luck had really forsaken them in 1974 when Bartlett crashed his Lola at Pukekohe in the Tasman series. 'Even though we'd run pretty well the year before,' Bartlett recalls, 'I never went to Bathurst expecting to win. We got on well, had both driven Formula 5000. I was still getting over my crash, but I had hopped straight back into a Formula 5000 at Oran Park and got down to the lap record within 12 laps. Therefore I proved to myself that I still had it. Gossy would never hold back. He was an honest, straight-as-a-gun-barrel sort of guy. I drove for him for a pittance ... and was happy to do it.'

Goss had spent some time developing an XB Falcon for the race but ultimately settled on the older XA that he had used the year before. The car by then was nearly 2 years old, but Goss had tested it extensively, pounding around Amaroo Park and Oran Park. They received little or no attention, in spite of their previous efforts. 'I went to see KB while he was in traction at the Royal North Shore Hospital in Sydney,' Goss recalls, 'and he wasn't sure at first if he could drive but later in the evening, when his family had left his bedside, he called me back and said he'd do it.' Adding to this risky call was the set-up of the driving position and the handling of the car. Goss and Bartlett had very different styles and demands. They compromised, but neither driver was ever truly comfortable.

'I remember getting into the car,' Bartlett recalls, 'and I was still hurting a bit. I had just had a new hip put in and my leg was still not perfect. I was still using a walking stick. But John had so much faith in us doing the job; in fact he had more faith than me. He never hesitated, in spite of others urging him not to use me for the race. They were saying I couldn't drive because I was crippled. He waved them away and said, "He'll do the job." That, to me, was as important as winning the race.'

Frank Gardner had become the supreme being in British touring car racing. In 1973 he had taken his Chevrolet Camaro to seven wins and two other podium finishes out of 10 rounds, his third overall championship victory. In 1974 he competed in five European touring car endurance races, qualifying strongly and winning at Silverstone but failing to finish the others. He had been testing close to 200 Lola cars a year and enjoying that far more. One of them had been the Can-Am Lola, which he took to Silverstone — and at 44 years of age, he drove himself into the record books for the fastest unofficial lap of the old circuit. The time was approaching, however, when he would turn his eyes towards home on a more permanent basis than the Tasman series or Bathurst excursions.

He teamed with Bob Jane in one of 19 Toranas opposed to three Falcons, while John Harvey and Jim Hunter drove another. By this time Harvey had parted company with Jane and was missing the support of a large team. He had driven the Hunter entry in practice and was not happy. Like Norm Beechey a few years earlier, he hatched an escape plan. 'It was one of the situations,' he recalls, 'when I parked my car outside the track so that when the race car blew up I could get away.' He wasn't the only one who had thought of that plan. Not far from Harvey's car was Gardner's.

The Holden Dealer team took pole position, thanks to Brock, who was paired with Brian Sampson. Bond and Bob Skelton were on the other side of the front row. They started to dictate terms, and Moffat, driving with Dieter Glemser from 15th on the grid, was never going to be a factor following a series of problems peaking when the clutch gave out. At least they lasted longer than the Hunter/Harvey and Jane/Gardner entries, which were out before 7 laps had been completed. Gardner leapt into his car and headed for Sydney airport to catch a flight to Europe. Harvey was quickly on his way home to Melbourne.

Rain started to pound the mountain, but parts of the track were still dry. Goss crashed and was lucky to make it back to the pits with a broken wheel. Brock also wheeled back into the pits with smoke billowing from his car. He was 6 laps in front at the time. Mechanics scrambled, fans craned their necks from across the main straight to watch their hero's struggle. Lap after lap was bleeding from his lead, and shaking heads told the story. The car could not be started. Bond had also struggled with brake failure before spinning out of contention in the run-off area at the end of Conrod Straight. He later had an oil leak, which brought out the black flag a few times.

Kevin Bartlett, fighting the pain of injuries, the discomfort of a car that was not set up for him, the miserable mood of the mountain and a late challenge from Bob Forbes, finally produced a win at Bathurst. Allan Moffat described it as one of the greatest wet weather drives he had seen.

'It had been a tough old race,' Bartlett recalls. 'I mean those cars had no brakes at the end ... well, they never really had any brakes to start with. When it rained, typically, the windscreen fogged up. The wipers were blowing off the screen. I had to lean outside the window to see, and you'd get dirty and wet, sticking your head out while you're driving. It was no limousine ride. At the end of the day, the accomplishment of finishing, let alone winning, would have been enough for me.'

Goss would take his career to greater heights two years later, winning the Australian Grand Prix in a grand finish with Vern Schuppan, but there would be few more satisfying results, and none more famous than this one. 'We were a good team, not as quick as the works Holdens in practice but I'd done a lot of work to strengthen the chassis and solve the oil surge problem that we'd had before. It rained so hard so quickly that I aquaplaned off and only just made it down the mountain and back to the pits with very little left of the right front wheel. I had it hanging over the edge of the road, on the grass, wherever I could. Allan Moffat lent us the latest spec Goodyear wet tyres. KB drove the last stint in pain from his injuries. It was a great feeling because it had all the elements. It captured the philosophy of the era and the challenges of Bathurst.'

John Harvey, still grinning after his slick getaway, had been cruising down the highway in and out of rain storms, every white post that disappeared past his doors reinforcing his satisfaction at escaping an unpleasant experience. He pulled in at Albury-Wodonga for petrol, and as he walked into the service station to pay, glanced up at a television, just in time to see one of his best mates greet the chequered flag. With a shake of his head and an even wider grin he walked back into the early evening mist and those wet country fields suddenly smelled even better.

Firth and Brock clashed over driving tactics in that 1974 race and Firth felt that he no longer had control over the young man who had become a national celebrity, even marrying Miss Australia, Michelle Downs. Within a year, Brock was a privateer again. 'I sat back a few times and asked myself why,' Brock says, 'but I guess occasionally you just want new challenges in life. I suppose you could say I was busy with relationship issues and what have you, but really, I just wanted to go racing. I had no money. I had to just make it happen. We called up a few old favours, cobbled together some parts. We really had to win races to pay our way.'

Harry Firth's affection for Brock would not allow him to stay away, though. Like a divorced couple with an amicable agreement over custody of a child, Firth and Brock would stay in touch on technical issues in 1975. 'I was still mates with Harry,' Brock recalls. 'It's just that he was looking on me as this troubled young man with plenty of issues.'

John Harvey was also remaining unattached, keeping himself busy with the Holden Gemini series. Colin Bond, still driving for the Holden Dealer team, won the 1975 Australian Touring Car Championship and was Firth's only official competitor in the Hardie-Ferodo 1000, with John Walker his co-driver. Frank Gardner returned home to drive with Bob Morris.

Ford's best chances were the same as before: Goss and Bartlett were back. Moffat returned to his formerly successful combination with Pete Geoghegan. 'Peter Brock's split with Holden never affected me,' Moffat recalls. 'My duel was always with either the mountain or the financiers. There were never enough cheques from sponsors.'

After 163 laps of the 1975 Bathurst 1000 it was Brock 1st, Gardner 2nd. Bond, who had started on pole, finished 3rd after Walker was forced to pit with a broken axle. The win, with a limited budget, made Brock feel vindicated. 'I really drove with my head that year. It was hard to describe the team's elation. I was the only one who believed we could do it. The rest of the team were shocked. It was the challenge: another goal I set myself.'

Frank Gardner had achieved so much in a career that shone like neon above the rest of his rivals, from his engineering genius to his formative years with Brabham to Formula 1 to the Tasman series to British Formula 5000 to sports car seniority and touring car superiority. Winning Bathurst would have been a wonderful cap ... in his case a terry-towelling hat ... on one of Australian motor sport's most famous careers. His car had run out of brakes too far from the finish.

Tim Schenken had made a quick trip back to Australia to race an Alfa with Paul Bernasconi in class B. It was one of three cars run by Brian Foley. They lasted 140 laps. 'I realised that safety precautions in Europe had not been a big issue, although Jackie Stewart was by then starting to change that, but in Australia they were nonexistent. I had never been to Bathurst before. We drove the circuit before the meeting and thought how incredible it was. There was no guard rail on the inside of the track at the top of the circuit. I thought that if I came off there, I might roll all the way down until I finished up in the back of the pit area. With that in mind, I was chasing Marie-Claude Beaumont and John Leffler, who were leading the class in another Alfa, when I came up to McPhillamy Park, crested the hill, turned left, and the front wheel broke. I went across to the right, hit an embankment, launched into the air, somersaulted, and landed upside down across the track.

'I looked up the road, and cars were coming at me on either side. The yellow flag was out but they weren't slowing down. I panicked a bit, unclipped my belts and fell on my head, hurting my neck. I crawled out and up the bank to the spectator fence and sat with my back to the crowd, unaware of what kind of crowd it was on the mountain at Bathurst. Soon there was a tap on my shoulder. I turned around to see this massive bloke, tanned almost black, beer gut hanging over his jeans, can of beer in his hand. So I stood up and faced him. He shook my hand and said, "That's the best fuckin' accident we've seen all day." I then noticed the crowd, all drunk and out of control. So I figured it was safer on the edge of the track, where I spent the next few laps.' Schenken had seen enough. He never raced at Bathurst again.

Vern Schuppan had been invited back to Australia in 1976 to co-drive at Bathurst with Allan Moffat, who had won the Australian Touring Car Championship (ATCC) for the second time. 'It had actually been a very good year for me,' Schuppan recalls, 'having won the Rothmans Formula 5000 series earlier, been awarded Rookie of the Year at Indianapolis and raced strongly in the US Formula 5000 championship. I welcomed the chance to drive with Moffat. I found him not only professional, but very fair. He gave me enough time in the car to do a decent job. It was one of the more enjoyable experiences of my career.' They qualified on pole, but didn't finish.

'It was my first year as the Moffat Ford Dealer team,' Moffat explains, 'Ford's way of slowly coming back into motor racing. My Bathurst car was turned into a heap of twisted metal when my brand new transport truck went up in flames after an electrical fault in the Adelaide Hills in July. We built a brand new car, just in time, and it was extremely competitive, but the crankshaft balance pulley exploded while we were in the lead.'

It was a race packed with big names in various makes and models, but towering above them all were Jack Brabham and Stirling Moss in a privately entered Torana: 50-year-old Brabham and 47-year-old Moss attracted more fans to the circuit that year than anyone else, in spite of the unseemly fixation that

Australians had developed about their touring cars. Brabham had retired 5 years earlier and Moss 13 years earlier, but a willing band of sponsors had paid for the exercise. There had been a lot of fanfare, and the champions qualified a respectable 10th.

'We were supposed to have a new car,' says Brabham. 'They never had it ready, though, so we had to use the old, clapped-out car they had been using for a few seasons. In qualifying, I had one of the biggest scares of my life. I had come down Conrod Straight, put my foot on the brake to turn into the left-hander and my foot went straight to the floor. No brakes whatsoever. Frank Gardner was just ahead of me, about to turn left, but I had to go straight on, down the escape road. It was my only chance. I was catching him so fast with no brakes, I was sure I was going to hit him. I got so desperate, I jammed it down to second gear, revving the shit out of the engine, then dropped the clutch, and it locked the rear wheels up. That saved me. With my old speedway skills, I turned it sideways, missed the back of Frank's car by bloody inches, and slid down the escape road.'

Later, in pit lane, Brabham was watching the crew work on the car when he noticed Gardner walking towards him. 'Oh no, I thought, here we go. He won't let this go by without a bloody comment. He walked up to me, never said anything until he was almost past me, and then he just nudged me and said, "You're getting a bit untidy in your old age, aren't you?"'

'We needed a new gearbox, so we asked Holden if they'd lend us one. They said yes, but not until they had finished every bit of work that they had to do on their cars, which meant we got our gearbox at six o'clock on the morning of the race. There was no parade lap, so we hadn't really tested the gearbox. They were still working on it when we pushed it out for the start of the race. I tried to put it into gear, and it made a hell of a noise. Then it locked up on me. I bashed it to free the lever, and it came loose again, but when I dropped the clutch, it went backwards. It was stuck in reverse.'

It was one of Bathurst's most embarrassing moments. Brabham, starting the race, couldn't get the Torana off the line. The gearbox had jammed. 'I put my hand up, trying to signal people to drive around me. But it was too late.' He was slammed from behind by the Dolomite Sprint entered by John Dellaca and Terry Wade in class B.

Stirling Moss adds a little irony to the story. 'The point is, Jack was renowned to jump the start in races. You wouldn't normally get penalised.

Sometimes they'd dock you a minute or something if it was really obvious, but Jack was never that bad. So I said, "Look we're doing this together. You jump the start. It's your country. You'll get away with it and go quicker than I will." Then of course he got hit up the backside. I did get to drive, though. Fantastic circuit. We weren't in contention, but it turned out to be a great race. I always enjoy it when you have to try harder than you would normally have to, which we did.'

Their car blew an engine after 37 laps but all the fuss over them would be overshadowed hours later in a race that would become one of the most dramatic in Australian motor sport. Bond and Harvey seemingly had the race won, 3 laps in front with a third of the race to go, but they pitted to replace a fanbelt, following overheating. Privateers Bob Morris and John Fitzpatrick were left in front, and even won like battlers, Fitzpatrick coaxing their bright yellow Torana around its final lap hoping with every interminable metre that his blown gearbox seal and broken rear axle would hold on before a fast-finishing Bond/Harvey car could catch him. It was a highly emotional finish, with Morris and the crew in tears of disappointment at the breakdown, then tears from tension as the car crawled towards the crest before what they knew to be a winning descent, then tears of exultation at the finish ... all in the space of a lap.

The 28-year-old Morris had felt the politics of factory driving and didn't care for it much. This was the kind of win he wanted to have. He had enjoyed the privateer team of Ron Hodgson, confident in a more conservative set-up and 14 inch wheels while the factory cars opted for the latest 15 inch specification. The known quantities were crucial in a race of high attrition. It was the unknown, however, that really did it for them. 'We ran our car dry each stint, coasting to the pits to maximise fuel consumption and save a stop,' Morris recalls. 'We took our chances. We had a component failure at the end, oil leaking everywhere, but Johno's experience brought it home. Anybody who wins at Bathurst really deserved it. It's the best circuit in Australia.

'I had finished second with Frank the previous year, and believe me, coming second at Bathurst was a real downer. I really feel for blokes who have gone so close but never won because going close is such an achievement ... and yet it's nowhere.'

The ARDC had employed a new timing system for this 1976 race. Given the troubles experienced in the past, this was supposed to put to an end controversies such as the 1967 protest, which Firth and Gibson won, denying the Geoghegan brothers victory. However, even the best-laid plans ... Three people were stationed in a tower near the final corner, and during the race, while the Morris–Fitzpatrick entry made a lengthy pit stop, one of those people questioned whether the car had, in fact, passed the tower unnoticed. They decided that it must have, so they were credited with a lap. Amidst all the post-race euphoria, the ARDC reportedly discovered an error after checking their back-up system, and counts from other leading teams apparently confirmed it. Colin Bond and John Harvey had not finished 2nd. They had won.

Officials hastily called the Holden hierarchy to a meeting. 'What do you want to do?' they were asked. If such a mistake were discovered today, there would be no consultation. It would be an official matter dealt with by the independent controllers of the race. In 1976, things were different. Holden's Director of Sales at the time, John Bagshaw, was faced with an unnerving decision: award the race to their factory team, or let the minnows have their famous victory?

Whether it was generous or cowardly is a matter of opinion, but Holden's hierarchy knew that if they reversed the result, it would look like the big factory crushing the little privateer; hardly the image on which touring car racing had built its mass market appeal. And Ron Hodgson, who had sponsored the 'little privateer', also happened to be one of Holden's biggest dealers. They chose to do nothing. John Harvey and Colin Bond, according to a handful of ARDC officials, team members and Holden representatives, had won Bathurst, but could not claim the prize. Harvey, who had spent a couple of years out of striking distance, took it on the chin. 'They had a Holden 1st, 2nd and 3rd. Why would they want any aggro, something to go wrong? It pissed me off, sure, but I wasn't going to lose any sleep over it.'

'I wasn't allowed to do anything about it,' Harry Firth recalls. 'My drivers didn't get the credit they deserved, but I have to say, my relationship with Holden was fading before that.'

At a testimonial dinner for John Harvey 25 years later in Melbourne, Holden spokesman Ray Borrett, who had by then risen to the position of Director of Motor Sport, made a speech. In that speech, he admitted publicly for the first time that he and other company representatives had taken the win from Harvey in 1976. He apologised. 'I thought, "Jesus Christ, I didn't expect this",' Harvey says. 'When Ray got up at that testimonial, it just blew me away.'

Colin Bond was also informed officially of the Holden apology. 'Ray Borrett came and told me about the whole thing and I have to say, well, what's done is done. It's history. You can't change it now.'

Bob Morris, however, was deeply disappointed. 'I know we won that race. I'm amazed at what they said after all those years and it was absolutely incorrect. Their crew was the only crew in pit lane who had them winning. For them to come out and say that ... I was totally offended. In fact, I put a call in to Ray Borrett and he never returned it. I think that was a slur, when I had put in so many years of racing for Holden.'

Bond left Holden at the end of 1976. It had nothing to do with Bathurst, but politics was a factor. The news of his signing with Allan Moffat only deepened the fans' despair. For some, it was blatant treachery. 'Well, Moffat offered me the drive. It was worth a lot more money than I was being paid at the time. The car was a better car, looking ahead to 1977. I also felt that the budget was getting a little bit lean in the HDT operations. I don't know how to say this, but I could also feel that Harry wasn't comfortable anymore. In hindsight, if I had stayed on, it might have been better for me in the long run. Who knows?'

For all his success, it wasn't long before Holden's relationship with Harry Firth went the same way. 'They were getting beaten,' Firth recalls, 'and blaming me, but they would do no development whatsoever, and kept cutting the money back. I finished up telling them to get stuffed.'

Frank Gardner, having settled back in Australia, had launched a full-time comeback in August 1976, driving a purpose-built Chevrolet Corvair in the Australian Sports Sedan Championship. He designed and built the car using parts from a Formula 5000 Lola. With sponsorship from John Player, he started his late-season run at Oran Park in Sydney, finishing 3rd in heat 1, black-flagged in heat 2. 'There was some contention over scrutineering,' Gardner recalls, 'but I advised them that if they read the rule book they would find the car was all right. They were a bit keen on Moffat winning. They said I could race but couldn't win. As soon as I hit the front I got black-flagged. Later they pulled it all apart and it was 100 per cent squeaky clean.' From there on he was devastating, winning the next six heats at Calder, Mallala and Symmons Plains.

He drove a Torana with Allan Grice at Bathurst, where they lasted 140 laps before engine trouble intervened. Gardner and his awesome Chevy Corvair finished the 1976 season with 10 wins from 12 starts across Australia and New

Zealand. It was a debut that had dominant drivers like Bob Jane and Allan Moffat quivering. He vowed to return in 1977 for a full season.

Moffat confirmed his third Australian Touring Car Championship and second in a row in 1977. When he was not winning, his new team-mate Colin Bond was. They often finished 1st and 2nd. 'It was so dominant,' Bond recalls. 'We had a bit of fun with Harvey and the boys. If Moffat was up ahead, winning, and I was holding second comfortably, I'd often drop back and race them, sometimes even let them go past. They'd be working hard, but our cars were so good. Finally I'd say, "It's time I get going," and pass them again. I'd even drive alongside, looking at them, waiting for them to look back so I could wave to them. I had to have fun while it lasted. Of course I knew they'd catch up again the following year. That's the way it was in those days.'

'It was my first two-car team,' Moffat recalls. 'The problem we had in the previous Bathurst was a simple metallurgical failure. But in 1977, with an energised budget I was able to hire Carroll Smith to come out from the States for a year and help with the organisation, bearing in mind that when you move to two cars it's not twice the work, it's four times the work.'

Harry Firth had officially handed the reins of the Holden team to John Shephard, but would guide the cars through one final Bathurst preparation, part of arguably the strongest field ever assembled there: years of Australian motor sport heritage had somehow come together in a single, pivotal race. Legends from all categories and eras took part, some past their best, some in their prime, some on their way to greatness. Brock, Jane, Geoghegan, Bartlett and Harvey were there. Jack Brabham drove with his son Geoff, who had raced previously in 1975 with Bib Stillwell's son Mike. Larry Perkins and Vern Schuppan had returned from Europe.

Schuppan drove with Dick Johnson, who had been driving for wealthy Queensland businessman Bryan Byrt since 1976, and was struggling to put together a racing budget, as usual. 'Having driven Allan's car the previous year, I could make a comparison,' Schuppan recalls. 'I was told it was the same as Allan's. From my side, it was a handful. Dick could drive it, but I wondered how the hell he could. He was a tremendous driver and operator, and a totally great bloke. I didn't do a very good job for them because I just couldn't come to terms with the car, but he never got upset about it.' They would fare better the following year.

Allan Moffat and Colin Bond occupied two superbly turned out Falcons. The predominantly white Falcon coupés with their blue bonnets and boots and flashy red stripes were menacingly big and yet exquisitely sleek and powerful. They were great white sharks in a sea of struggle, a terrifying presence to those who did not love them. 'Don't forget,' Moffat cautions, 'there has never been a team that has ever gone to Bathurst that hasn't worried about its engine or anything else surviving for the six and a half hours.' Moffat imported the great Jacky Ickx to drive with him. Bond's co-driver was the experienced Alan Hamilton.

For all Moffat's success in the shorter races, there had been doubt he could sustain the form over the taxing circuit for 1000 kilometres. Even his co-driver was in doubt. 'Jacky came in after his first lap on the track,' Moffat recalls, 'and told me the car had no brakes. I jumped back in, did a lap, came back and told him the brakes were perfect. He said, "But the car doesn't stop ..." I said, "Jacky, I didn't say the car would stop. I just said the brakes are perfect. That's as good as they get." He then went on to tell me how every time he braked in his Porsche at Le Mans, he almost shot through the windscreen. I said, "You won't have that problem here!"'

There was conjecture over the performance of Ickx, who was blamed by some for going too hard mid-race when Moffat would have wanted the car nursed a little. After all, their rivals were floundering under waves of minor breakages. Bond recalls it as a highly strategic effort. 'Allan didn't want to at first, but we both drove the first 82 laps. It was a hard race, but it gave both our co-drivers a buffer. When Allan got out after doing his double stint, his hands were blistered from the effort. Then Jacky Ickx got in for his one-quarter race distance, and he did go too hard. He burnt the brakes out. Hammo was much kinder on ours.'

Moffat had the utmost faith in Ickx. 'He came to grips with the car very quickly, but I was concerned that he might use the brakes harder than I would like, because while the brake pads were thicker than standard, they were made to just last the thousand kilometres. Tiring as it was to drive 82 laps in one stint before giving Jacky one 41 lap stint, the order in which we drove the race was the best decision I made all weekend.'

In spite of that, Moffat's ailing Falcon started to show signs of a hard life over the final 20 laps, like a punch-drunk boxer. The good news was that he had Peter Janson's Torana safely held. The bad news was that his own team-mate was turning in lap times that added up to a storming victory. However, the overriding factor was that Moffat ran the team, and that entitled him to make whatever call would be necessary for the best team result.

'I remember in the final stint,' says Bond, 'picking up 10 seconds in one lap, more than 10 in the next, as Allan nursed the car. All of a sudden, I knew that I could win. I knew that I could catch him with about 5 laps to go. But I didn't want that. I didn't want to be sitting right behind him for 5 laps thinking about being able to win but not being allowed to.' The finish has been debated and feted, often at the same time, ever since.

Bond was following the orders of his pit crew when he ranged up beside his boss but refused to go past. The sign had said clearly, 'Form finish 1–2.' As the cars cruised down Conrod Straight for the final time, Holden fans slumped, searching for aspirin to go with their beer. It was especially painful to see one of 'their own' in his first Bathurst for Ford, figuring in this humiliation. 'At the time, it was a team effort, and I had no problem with that,' Bond recalls. 'Ickx came up to me later, shaking his head and saying, "If I were you, I would not have been obeying team orders … a win is a win." I had made a commitment. I've regretted it plenty of times since, but if I had my time all over again I'd probably do the same thing.'

Moffat said he would have had no problems with Bond winning if the team had not been so far in front. 'We ran exactly to the predetermined strategy. If we had a Torana on our tail, then I would have gladly let Colin take them on to make sure we won. I was in no shape to do that. We're not talking about a little bit of brake: I had zero brakes. I was breaking my ankle trying to push it through the floor, but there wasn't a Holden in sight and there was no need. Naturally, if Colin had been less than the absolute gentleman that he is, he might have tried to drive by me. Mind you, he would have found my car a lot wider than he remembered it, and I might have had to remind him who was signing his cheques! Seriously though, we were a team. That was it.'

The car in 3rd place was a lap and 24 seconds behind Ford's form finish. It was Peter Janson and Larry Perkins, in quite a debut for Perkins, who would soon be heading back overseas to pursue his Formula 1 dreams.

It was Moffat's fourth win in the great race and by far his most controversial. History, fate or whatever else you choose to believe in had also decreed that it would be his last. It would also complete the strangest trilogy in the history of the race — for Colin Bond. 'People often say to me that I really won three Bathursts: the one John Harvey and I lost in the lap-counting fiasco, this one, and the only one I actually got credit for, in 1969. There were plenty more that, on reflection, we should have won. But you know, it really doesn't bother me.'

'There were a few journalists,' Moffat recalls, 'who wanted to paint me as the big, bad cowboy who stole a race from Colin, but there was no stealing involved at all. The cards fell in our favour that day, which enabled us to run exactly to our plan.'

Bathurst in 1977 was also a defining moment in three famous careers. The first would be that of someone who had defined Australian race driving standards. Frank Gardner was 47. He had proved with his victory in the Australian Sports Sedan Championship that his skills and his quips were still worthy of each other. He left names like Jane and Moffat in his wake from February to October, a record of 26 wins from 30 starts, the last 12 in succession to bring the total victories in his extraordinary (now JPS) Corvair to 41 out of 49 starts — which became the title of a special publication recording his feat for posterity. While he'd delighted his fans and sponsors, Gardner also knew that he had ruffled some feathers. 'Bob had a few words for me once, after I beat him on his own track. If you leave out the four letter words there weren't many left. They were good scraps, but Bob was Bob.'

However, this time it was over. 'It's a split-second world, so you have to think in split-seconds. The only way you can do that is if your eyes are 100 per cent and they're relaying the information back to your brain and that co-ordination's working. If all these things aren't happening you're having yourself on; you're taking money under false pretences, you are miscast.'

Allan Grice took over the Corvair and, in Craven Mild colours, raced it successfully through the 1978 season, while Gardner took the opportunity to rest the ailing back that had troubled him for the past 5 years. Surgery was terribly risky, so physiotherapy was the only recourse. Fortunately, it was successful and Gardner felt 'human' again, but this most down-to-earth and pragmatic of drivers would officially retire, having nothing left to prove and plenty in the bank account. He wouldn't stay completely off the scene because motor racing officials, competitors and fans would for years make demands of a man who had just about the right measure of all the right ingredients: driver, engineer, personality, manager. His expertise in all fields would be a desired commodity because, above all, he had survived. 'There were plenty of people who were over the top, people who weren't going to die in bed. They were great to look at. Fantastic car control. But you can't push the boat out and out and out ... because there's no margin for error. Sooner or later, they're going to be Johnny on the spot. We drove in the days when cars were dangerous and sex was safe.'

Bob Jane, at 48, had also competed at Bathurst for the final time. He and Pete Geoghegan lasted 35 laps in their Torana A9X, which succumbed to oil filter problems. Curiously, the man who helped define the 'Great Race' at Bathurst actually competed in it only eight times for two wins and a second placing. His wins in the first two Armstrong 500s at Phillip Island, the precursors to Bathurst, must also be counted to appreciate his influence on the event.

Jane's final championship win as a driver had been the Marlboro Sports Sedan series in 1974, driving a Holden Monaro, but by 1977 he had become equally famous for his team management, winning the Australian Drivers Championship or 'Gold Star' with Spencer Martin in 1966 and 1967, along with the Australian Sports Car Championship with John Harvey in 1971 and 1972. He had brought exotic cars into Australian motor sport and fostered promising careers.

His vast influence, however, was far from waning.

Harry Firth was the third legend to depart the scene in 1977, this time as a manager. Like Jane and Gardner, Firth had made a good living from motor sport. He would take lovingly prepared MGs to many victories in historic racing over the next 8 years, but had effectively retired from the front line, factory-driven war that touring car racing had become.

Peter Brock may have left the team, but he would miss 'the Fox'. 'Perhaps the classic Harry story came from the early days of the XU1 Torana, when the fashion was to run wide tyres on the rear of the car, where the drive came from, and narrow steering tyres on the front. We had this on the Torana, but during one of its first meetings, Bondy came in and said the car was under-steering. We tried all sorts of changes which didn't work, and all the while Harry was sitting on his old camp stool, just thinking. Finally, he says to the guys, "Put the back tyres on the front, and the front tyres on the back." We just stood there. In those days, it wasn't done, but we did it and Bondy went one and a half seconds a lap faster. What effectively happened was, the rear of the car started to slide out, the fronts gripped more, and it turned in. It just wasn't conventional. The engineers might look at it and say, "Yes, but you'll also cause this, this and this problem." But at the time, it was the solution. I liked that.

'If you wanted the most effective car out there on the day, Harry would give it to you. They were ratty. They were grubby. They had finger marks all over them. But they were missiles.'

Firth would not miss anything, especially the politics, which he played deftly but with increasing distaste. Nor would he grow tired of the extra time he had gained to pursue his more relaxing hobbies, such as fishing, and collecting antiques and rare artworks. In the early days of retirement he would also take an administrative role that would have to be one of the most ironic twists in Australian motor racing: for 3 years, he was Chief Scrutineer.

CHAPTER TWELVE

Three Strikes

It's hard not to imagine a stick of straw protruding from Larry Perkins's mouth when you hear him speak. There's a straight-talking country kind of commonsense about him. He was born in March 1950 in Cowangie, Victoria. Like the Brocks, the Perkins were farmers, and their lives were as much about the manipulation of machines as they were about rough, dirt-stained hands and long sweaty hours in the dry, fresh air. Perkins loved the country, but he loved the machinery a little more. It started on his father's lap, in a short wheel-based Land Rover bouncing around the family property. 'I could only have been 4 years old, but my earliest recollection was driving ... and the urge to do that just got stronger and stronger.'

Perkins went through the same learning process as all mechanically minded future drivers, by experimenting with 'old bombs'. 'The whole exercise really was one of stupidity. How we didn't kill anyone was one of the great mysteries of the Earth.' Vehicles were traded like stamps among adventurous youngsters in rural Victoria who still didn't have their driving licences. A 1928 Dodge pick-up was swapped for a pushbike, which was swapped for a Renault 750. An FJ Holden gave Perkins his first experience of 'the limit' — he tried to swing the car between gate posts and collected one of them. His brother Terry rolled a

Standard Ten in a similar expedition; he finished up in hospital for a few days with concussion.

It was in the genes. Perkins's father, Eddie, had competed with success in Redex Trials and in limited touring car events. When he was 18, Larry decided that this would be possible for him too. He saved enough money to buy a Formula V in Bendigo and proceeded to 'test' it on the highway near Cowangie, with his mate Wally's garage as the makeshift pit area. He crashed, tearing the fibreglass chassis. 'Christ,' he muttered, 'this is harder than it looks.'

It wasn't long before he took the formal path, joining a car club and taking to the circuit. He spun like a ballroom dancer, and his first race was embarrassing, but within 3 months he was winning. He accepted an offer from Bib Stillwell to drive in Formula Ford professionally in mid-1970 and after starting at Warwick Farm he progressed quickly, to win the Australian Championship in 1971. He was awarded the Driver to Europe scholarship. Unfortunately for Perkins, it was just a ticket, so he chose to build up some funding and experience before cashing it in. The best place for experience was with Harry Firth. The best way to earn money was to work for him as a mechanic.

There were many would-be Firth disciples in those days, but if the old fox's characteristics rubbed off on anyone, it was on the worldly shoulders of the kid from Cowangie. He even picked up the Firth habit of calling his mates 'cock'. 'I had a good time there. I was a snotty-nosed young lad, keen as mustard. I remember when Harry first put the V8 engine into the Torana. I shouted louder than the others, begging him to let me take it for its first drive. I promised him everything: "Aw come on Harry, let me drive it home. I won't break the speed limit ..." Well I had it up to 180 kilometres per hour on the main street of Balwyn.'

While he worked in the Firth garage Perkins took an offer to drive for Gary Campbell in Formula 2 in 1972 in an Elfin 600B. He won eight of nine races and the Australian Championship. In late 1972, he planned his European assault. He arranged to borrow an Elfin 620 Formula Ford chassis from Garrie Cooper and paid for the car to be shipped to England. He needed an engine, but by then had run out of money. 'I went to Ford at first, to beg for an engine. They couldn't help me, but suggested I see Allan Moffat, who happened to be a hero of mine in those days. Allan asked me what I needed. I told him. He asked me how much. I said about $620. He just gave me a cheque, then and there, and said, "Go buy yourself an engine, and good luck."'

Moffat's faith was rewarded, but not before a sobering experience for Perkins. He met the world, and the world, it seemed, was full of Formula Ford drivers just as hungry as he was. 'I went out for first practice at the Formula Ford World Championships at Brands Hatch, then got back and looked at the time sheets. I turned over the first page, then the second page, then the third page. I had qualified 82nd or something. There were two other Australians there. Bob Skelton had qualified about 88th and John Leffler 104th. I couldn't believe it. I thought I was on the limit. I had to find another limit. The next session I qualified equal third, but ended up eighth on the grid because five of us did exactly the same time.' Perkins finished 5th in the race — already he was being compared with all the greats who had gone before him.

He stayed for another fortnight to race at the Formula Ford Festival at Snetterton, where he nudged, in frustration, a local driver off the track after being blocked for the lead. It was that, and his pace, which caught the eye of Australian Formula 1 driver Dave Walker, who was very helpful. 'He befriended me, and got me an introduction to GRD, a company set up by ex-employees of Lotus. They offered me a deal for the following season to run in Formula 3 in one of their cars, but the deal didn't include an engine, so once again I set about finding an engine. That's where another old family friend, David McKay, came in. He gathered up the finances, and he and Gary Campbell sponsored me. I bought a couple of Lotus engines and went racing.'

Perkins called for assistance from an old school mate, Charlie Coburn, and 'Team Cowangie' was ready to travel Europe. The 'transporter' was an ex-furniture truck. There was still no formal Formula 3 championship, but there were many races. The Aussies and their van went walkabout through some of the richest playing fields of the era, experiencing the lower end of the upper echelons of motor sport. Perkins was distinctive in another way. He had worn prescription glasses since he was a child and they had been a problem in his racing, but in the winter of Europe they were even worse. 'It was a constant worry. If it was a cold day or a wet race they would fog up.'

Still, the travelling was nice and the accolades nicer. 'I loved going to Monaco. I especially liked picking up the magazine L'Equipe and seeing that my headline was as big as Jackie Stewart's! Jackie was fastest in the Formula 1 session, but I was second-fastest in Formula 3, without having seen the track. That was considered an excellent debut, so they wrote about me. I tore the story out and sent it home. Pity I didn't finish the race.'

Perkins finished other events, though, winning in France and Sweden. In one of those races he was a lap down, but overcame his rivals when it rained. They weren't all successes. At Paul Ricard, in France, his car blew a tyre and he speared into some catch fencing. The crash cost him a finger, and left him in a daze in the medical centre. 'I also had various facial cuts, which the doctor at the track stitched up for me. I lost my glasses. There is probably some Frenchman still wearing my John Lennon glasses. But I went back to the car, which was sitting there in a mangled mess. Spectators had gathered in the paddock to look at it. One of them was Robin Herd, from the March Racing team, who offered me a drive in one of their cars for the weekend. While I was thinking about that, another bloke came up. It was Herbie Blash, who said Bernie Ecclestone would like to see me. Bernie offered me a free car. I had the engines and the truck. We did a simple deal. All he wanted was that at the end of the year I give him the car back, and that after every race I ring him and tell him how I went. Done.' Perkins became another Bernie Ecclestone protégé, and drove for him for the rest of the season.

Even in 1973, young Perkins was forging a reputation for fearless self-belief, straight talk and doing things his way. 'We still had our little van, which was rather unusual. We used to park it near John Surtees' garage when we were in England so we could access their equipment ... and stores ... whatever you like to call it. I also got on well with a lot of the mechanics in Formula 1. They also helped. But I didn't have an agent or anything like that. It wasn't until the end of 1973 that David McKay helped me get into Chris Amon's Formula 1 team for the 1974 season. In my second year in Europe, that was fantastic.'

Perkins would become a test driver for Amon's bid to make a successful Formula 1 car with a Ford Cosworth engine. The AF101 was to make its debut in the first European round, the 1974 Spanish Grand Prix at Jarama. Perkins was told he would get the chance to drive the car in a Formula 1 race at some stage that year. After only one season, he had almost reached the pinnacle of world motor sport.

Alan Jones, by 1974, had taken a more circuitous route to arrive on the doorstep of Formula 1. 'AJ', as he quickly became known, had been toiling away at what was looking like a futile 5 year campaign in a world where talent is only ever a small part of the equation. Jones, however, was of sterner stuff than many people realised. If they'd had the good fortune to see his father drive, they would have known that his success would only be a matter of time.

Stan Jones had been the archetypal daredevil racer, the kind a *Boys' Own Annual* might conjure for daydreamers. He raced fearlessly in an era that encouraged the fearless: there was little more to race for than thrills and pride. There were plenty of Stan Joneses who died on the world's finest circuits, but in spite of his reckless approach, he survived, winning the 1959 Australian Grand Prix in his Maserati 250F after many luckless attempts. By then he had earned the nickname 'Sorrowful'. It would remain one of the more popular victories in the race's long history and earned him the respect and friendship of his peers, Jack Brabham among them.

'I remember standing on a fuel drum watching the race,' Alan recalls. 'I was 12. Dad was dicing with Len Lukey in the Cooper. After the race, I hopped on the back of the Maserati and was waving to the crowd as we drove around. I also remember the day he clinched the Gold Star Championship at Phillip Island. I recall quite a lot of his races.'

There was always one thing missing, though, and it preyed on Stan long after his retirement: he had never competed seriously in Europe. Tony Gaze had invited him over with Lex Davison for the ill-fated 'Ecurie Australie' team, but that had been the extent of it.

Stan was running a Holden dealership when Alan started to turn, inevitably, towards cars. 'For me it was the simplest thing in the world. I was born into it. I often wonder how the butchers or the bakers get into motor sport; I can only assume they go along to a race meeting and get the bug. My earliest recollections in life were being on a race track. Dad would let me take time off school to go racing with him. I went to Perth, New Zealand. I travelled a bit, and really, going racing was a matter of when, not if.'

As a teenager he raced in karts before working in the family business and racing an 850 Mini. 'I was Victorian Junior Go-kart Champion, but then I was able to get my hands on Dad's cars. The Mini came into the yard with its engine in the boot. We gave it to Brian Sampson, and Dad asked him to make it as competitive as it could be. Well, he got a shock when he saw the bill! I raced it in the Geelong speed sprints, along the esplanade, then hill climbs, then circuit races at Calder, Hume Weir and Winton.'

Then he found an old Cooper chassis which he worked on in the home garage, but it was not an easy task. 'In my first race, I didn't have goggles, so I used a pair of sunglasses, and in retrospect that was pretty stupid, because if I picked up a stone it would have splintered them. Not good for the eyes.'

Trying his hand on the international scene seemed a formality: he had a genetic advantage, a culture of success, a willing tutor and a network of contacts. 'I had watched all the heroes coming out for the Tasman series. Dad had competed against them, so we'd go to barbecues and socialise with them. It just seemed natural that I go to England and try it out.' Alan had everything he needed to head for Europe except the thing he needed most: money. Running a car dealership might sound impressive, but for Stan Jones, it was not as profitable as driving. Times were tough, with dealers forced to hold a lot of stock, and the credit squeeze was choking him.

After an expedition to Europe in 1966 to meet and learn from a few contacts, Alan Jones left Australia for good in 1968. 'I got there the second time with 50 quid in my pocket.'

He and his mate Brian Maguire sold minivans to Australian and New Zealand tourists and Jones went through a succession of cars, starting with a Formula Ford which they lovingly maintained on the floor of their flat. The next project, a Lotus 41, almost killed him at Brands Hatch. He broke his leg, but was more concerned about losing his car, which had disintegrated. Next he hitched a ride with a motor sport promotional company which secured him a few Formula 3 races in Brazil.

Jones saved more money in 1971 and was able to buy a BT28, which he converted to the latest spec BT35 with a kit bought from Ron Tauranac. 'We formed this impressively named organisation called A.I.R.O., or Australian International Racing Organisation. We had a bright orange truck, with A.I.R.O. on the side of it, which was a mistake — while it looked really flash, we had the arse hanging out of our trousers. Everyone thought we had government backing or something.' He won some races in Formula 3, but not enough to make a statement. Those with helping hands still had them firmly in their pockets.

Jones's progress continued, with a trickle of support here and there, and deals so thin that he was unable to spare enough money to insure his equipment. He sold caravans to pay for food and rent, claiming that if it hadn't been for a close relationship with his bank manager, he would have gone the way of his father, but he kept winning races.

Then, in 1973, he was asked to become part of a three-car team backed by Scottish industrialist Dennis Dobby. 'I was paid £2000, plus expenses, to drive their Formula 3 car. Dave Walker drove the Formula 2 car and ex-Formula 1 driver John Miles drove the sports car.'

Jones became the star of the show when the Formula 2 and sports cars were not performing well. He was leading the British Formula 3 Championship going into the final round at Brands Hatch, where he needed to finish only 3rd to win the title. During the race, which he started on the front row, his engine misfired, and he drifted back through the field. He was trying to stay cool, but was worried by the time he fell to 3rd. A cursory glance in the mirrors revealed the driver he had to fend off to secure the championship. Right on his tail was Larry Perkins.

Perkins tried to pass. They touched wheels. Perkins was sent spinning off somewhere behind. No one else threatened, until, with 7 laps to go, a car again appeared in Jones's mirrors. Perkins was back. He had regathered his Brabham and resumed the chase. This time, Perkins gave himself plenty of room when he made his attack. He took 3rd place, and Jones lost the championship to Tony Brise by one point. Jones was shattered, and the two Australians clashed heatedly after the race.

The Dobby drive dried up. Networking, however, was reaping rewards. Jones had also picked up some work testing Formula 2 and sports cars for March at Goodwood. 'They never let me into a Formula 1 car, but it gave me great experience. I was working closely with Robin Herd and I learnt a hell of a lot about what the cars were doing. I had never been great at setting a car up, but I did learn to communicate to the engineer what I did and didn't want a car to do. That was invaluable for me. Let's face it, Patrick Head would later say to me, "Unless you've done a university course in mechanical engineering, just tell us what the car's doing or not doing, and we'll look after it."'

There was one opportunity with a Formula Atlantic team that did not look very promising, but it was Jones's only opening. He persuaded Robin Herd to lend him half a day of his time to help set up and improve the car, with which he won his first race at Silverstone. 'I figured I'd earned the right to make a few demands for the following race meeting,' Jones recalls. 'I told the owner exactly what I wanted done. But when he turned up the car had not been touched. So I not only refused to drive it, I also went up and down pit lane telling everyone why. I think that really raised a few eyebrows, convinced people that I was fair dinkum and wouldn't compromise.'

Another team boss, Harry Stiller, was impressed enough to offer Jones a test in his car — a March which had been giving them trouble. With Robin Herd's able assistance, Jones was not only able to solve their problems but slash a second and a half from the lap record. He was offered the drive.

Armed with his new March, Jones won races in Formula Atlantic, finishing 4th in the British Championship. The most important race, he recalls, was the curtain-raiser to the British Grand Prix. 'I did a time in that car that would have qualified me for the Formula 1 race. It's those things that get tongues wagging. I led from go to whoa, and everyone was getting a bit excited. Harry started talking about a Formula 5000 drive for the following year. It was only August — that was a record for me!'

The deal, however, fell through. Stiller had decided to head for the United States and run a Formula 5000 team there. Jones was back on the hustings, campaigning for a start. 'I would dedicate an hour a day just to working the phone,' he recalls. 'I'd get up, have coffee, then start networking.'

Vern Schuppan had enjoyed good results with the Mirage GR7 for John Wyer, including a 2nd in the World Championship 1000 kilometre race at Spa. His relationship with BRM, however, had fizzled by 1974. Options were few, friendships numerous. He had stayed in touch with businessman Teddy Yip since driving for him in Macau in 1972. Yip, who had also assisted Kevin Bartlett, took an interest in Schuppan's Formula 1 career, and introduced him to Mo Nunn's Ensign team. He would debut in Belgium on 12 May 1974.

Tim Schenken also returned to Formula 1 in 1974. He was still driving in Formula 2, waiting for the Rondel team to step up, but an opportunity came up with Ron Tauranac at Trojan Engineering (formed by Peter Agg and based at Croydon).

Schenken, Schuppan and Perkins, who was still driving for Amon, worked hard for their respective teams in a season packed with fledgling operations 'tinkering' at the top level. Some of them were run by intelligent and influential people who simply did not have deep enough pockets or the entrepreneurial flair to sustain their effort. Most of the time they struggled to even qualify their cars in events crowded by over-subscription.

Schuppan became the first driver in Formula 1 history to be disqualified at consecutive events, a distinction that would later be emulated by Michael Schumacher. 'The reason we were disqualified in the Swedish Grand Prix was some infringement the team had committed in the pits. In the Dutch Grand Prix I blew a tyre in the main straight, pulled over at the end of pit lane and the team pushed the car backwards into the pits, which was illegal. They were simple, but glaring, mistakes.

'It was a pig of a car. It never qualified well, even before I got into it. I wasn't getting on with Mo, who insisted the car was fine but the guys driving it were no good. He didn't rate his other driver, Brian Redman, and wasn't a very easy guy to please. It was one thing driving an uncompetitive car, but when you're driving for a guy that doesn't believe in you, it's an uphill battle.' Schuppan had no relief from the gloom when he made a diversion to Le Mans, where his Gulf Mirage lasted only 5 hours.

The 11th round, at the Nurburgring, was a rare moment in Australian motor sport history. Not since the 1965 South African Grand Prix had three Australians participated in a Formula 1 championship round. Brabham, Hawkins and Gardner had all finished in the top 12 in that race. This was not to be as momentous. Larry Perkins made his Formula 1 debut in the Amon car at the 1974 German Grand Prix, with Schenken in his Trojan and Schuppan in his Ensign. The Australians had stepped up to the plate, but it would be three strikes. Perkins had qualified faster than his team boss, who handed over the reins after falling ill, but neither time was good enough to make the field. 'It was under-funded. It was behind schedule. It was plagued with problems,' Perkins recalls. 'The car failed. I crashed, having discovered that wonderful feature of the circuit — it could be raining over the next hill without you knowing about it. It wasn't terminal, but it was withdrawn. I couldn't qualify it.' He would not get another chance. Schenken also failed to qualify. Schuppan did, but lasted only 4 laps before his gearbox failed.

It was in Austria that Schenken, by then building into a volcano of frustration, finished 10th, his most respectable result of the year. By this time, Schuppan, however, had had enough of Ensign. 'I got out of the car in Germany sick of the team and of Formula 1. I walked away from it.' His drive was taken by a British Formula Ford and Formula 3 driver Mike Wilds. He could not qualify the Ensign either.

Schenken lurched from frying pan to fire when he was recruited, following the collapse of Trojan's campaign, to drive the final round for Lotus in the ill-fated Lotus 76. 'That car was the car they had huge trouble with. Peterson and Ickx, who were the works drivers, had so many problems that they went back to the previous year's car, the 72E. I couldn't even qualify the 76.' Lotus started the car unofficially, and Schenken was disqualified after 6 laps.

He fared a little better in Formula 2, which was heading in the opposite direction to Formula 1. Fields for the various European championship rounds were strong and large, but they lacked the big names of the past: the pressures of the modern era were forcing leading drivers to concentrate more and more on the main game. Schenken drove for Rondel in a Surtees T515A with BMW power in six events, which included a 2nd to Patrick Tambay at Nogaro. Patrick Depailler won the European Formula 2 Championship.

In that time Schenken also picked up a drive in the German Porsche Championship and contested a variety of other events across Europe, recording consistent point-scoring finishes, but all of them just outside the top three. He drove a Carrera RSR to 3rd in a GT race at Hockenheim, and 5th at Monza. He finished the year in South Africa, where he and Rolf Stommelen drove a 911 Carrera to 6th in the Kyalami 6 hour race.

Teddy Yip had been quick to reorganise Vern Schuppan's season, by setting up a drive in a Lola 332 for Sid Taylor in the British Formula 5000 series. By the end of the year he would lead five races, win two, and impress Taylor enough to want to take him to the United States to finish the year there. He competed at Laguna Seca and Riverside just when the championship battle was heating up. He was little known, but qualified on the front row beside championship contender Brian Redman. 'The Goodyear representative for Brian came up to me and said, "You're not going to interfere with his winning this race, are you? There's a championship on the line, you know." I thought that was strange, but just before the start, Brian came up to me and said a similar thing. We lined up on the grid, I fired the car up, and, all of a sudden, it was spitting out water and making horrible sounds. I switched off. We later found out that someone had dropped an allen bolt into the air intake of the engine. It was deliberate, because we had a mesh screen over that air intake. To this day, I believe it was the Goodyear guy.'

Redman went on to win the title, the first of his three. At Riverside, Schuppan had some fierce dices in a heat with James Hunt, who finished up as his co-driver in the Gulf Mirage at the Nurburgring sports car race at the end of the year. They finished 4th. To top the year, Schuppan went back to Macau for Teddy Yip, and won the Grand Prix, following in the footsteps of Kevin Bartlett.

Kevin Bartlett was a Bathurst winner when he arrived at Sydney's Oran Park on 17 November 1974 for the Australian Grand Prix. He had a new Lola, but still limped from his early-season crash. 'A lot of us had "Lola limps",' he recalls, referring to the often experimental nature of the car. 'It seemed that whenever anyone got hurt, it was in a Lola. Terribly fragile cars. When you hit anything, there was nothing there to save you. You couldn't crash 'em and keep a straight bone. Mind you, one of the problems was that big lump of cast iron sitting right behind you. The momentum of that, with a tub that's not very strong … and you were sitting virtually inside a fuel tank. Most cars today feature a certain amount of protection built around you.'

Bartlett's attack on the Gold Star Championship was completely overshadowed by his friend, Max Stewart, in a Lola 330. The fifth round was the grand prix itself, by which time Stewart had sewn up the title.

The glorious days of the Tasman series were a distant memory as 11 cars qualified and 9 started. Bartlett had taken the lead and was roaring towards his first Australian Grand Prix victory. With 3 laps to go, his Lola started to cough, bark and shudder. It had, apparently, run out of fuel, but he knew that to be impossible. 'I was pissed off like you wouldn't believe. When I stopped, I just sat there in disbelief. It was a brand new car.'

A surprised Max Stewart flashed past to win his fifth race in a row and his first Australian Grand Prix.

Moments after Stewart won the race, Bartlett tried one more time to restart his car. It turned over. 'I drove back to the pits. We had plenty of fuel left, but it wasn't transferring from one tank to another. By the time I tried to restart it, some had seeped through. I got close, but there was no way I was going to win the Australian Grand Prix.'

There was one round remaining in the Gold Star series, at Phillip Island. Bartlett won it, but it mattered little. He was inconsolable.

By the end of 1974, Leo Geoghegan had emerged from two successful seasons in Formula 2 and Porsche racing, seasons that he never thought would happen. It was a bonus to be enjoyed, not lamented, especially as he watched the landscape change rapidly. Touring car racing was king. The Tasman series and the Australian Grand Prix were shrinking faster than his budget. It truly was time to go home … and this time, to not answer the phone.

The Geoghegan brothers had built their careers not on the gift of the gab, but on the simple promise of victory. They took their appearance money from promoters, but unlike other drivers, they didn't ask for money up front from their sponsors. Sadly, it never set them up for later life. They could not make a success of their father's car yard, and were not to enjoy a wealthy retirement, as many of their peers did.

Above all, the Geoghegans could count themselves among the lucky few Australian champions who tasted success and fame in all categories and enjoyed the privilege of racing the best in the world. 'I never raced against Stirling Moss,' says Leo, 'but I saw him race first-hand and he was as quick as anyone who ever got in a race car. The fastest driver I ever raced was Rindt. He drove like he was never going to die in a car. He was too quick. Too quick too often. You can go out to eleven-tenths every now and then, but he would drive at ten-tenths all the time. He was the fastest, but had a short future. The best? The best driver I ever raced was Clarky. He was in a class of his own. While I knew Rindt was going to get killed, I really didn't think Clarky would. Next was Jackie Stewart. His best attributes were cunning and determination — and he always seemed to be in the right car at the right time. The next three, on equal terms, were Sir Jack, Bruce McLaren and Graham Hill. They get their points for determination. But really, on any given day, any one of those blokes could win a race.' So could Leo Geoghegan.

In 1974, Vern Schuppan had been driving in the British Formula 5000 series for Sid Taylor in a Trojan, then in a Lola 332 that Frank Gardner had helped develop. 'Frank Gardner was a hero of mine. I had read all the stories about his exploits in Australia and Europe. Meeting him was a great experience and he was a real man, in terms of his racing and his outlook on life. He had that dry humour and he got on with the job.'

1975 would be another exciting year, with a few more drives in Europe before heading to a regular drive for Dan Gurney in the American Formula 5000 series. The Eagle cars tended to break — only because parts were not replaced regularly enough — but the series was popular, the crowds were big, and great drivers attended. His regular opponents were Al and Bobby Unser, Jackie Oliver, Brian Redman, David Hobbs, Mario Andretti and Warwick Brown. 'It was common to have 10 or 12 cars nose to tail, racing each other. It was one of the most competitive and enjoyable series I ever did.'

The early days of 1975 turned into weeks as Alan Jones worked the phone, probing for the slightest gap through which he might lever an opening into regular racing. It had been 7 years since he first established himself in Europe.

He had married his girlfriend Beverley. Their only income had come from turning their rented five-bedroom home into a makeshift boarding house for young Australian tourists. That alone was keeping his dream afloat. Nothing fazed him, though, as he dialled and delivered, chatting, challenging, cajoling.

Finally, a phone call came in. It was a bolt from the blue. It was Harry Stiller. He asked, 'What are you doing tomorrow?'

Jones gave the usual reply: 'Nothing.'

'You'd better jump in the car. Do you know where Lord Hesketh lives?'

'Of course I do. Just near Silverstone.'

'Well get over there. I've arranged a fitting for you.'

Jones was confused. A fitting ... for what? Perhaps they were running a Formula 5000 car. Perhaps a Formula 2. When he arrived and entered an immaculate workshop, he found a Hesketh 308 Formula 1 car, in Stiller's distinctive blue colours. 'I thought I'd died and gone to heaven. They placed a box on the ground for me to climb into the car. They asked if this and that were comfortable or if I wanted this shifted or that shifted ... '

Stiller was running his own single-car team, with support from Hesketh, who already had a Formula 1 entry driven by James Hunt. Jones's first race was a non-championship round, the esteemed British Racing Drivers Club (BRDC) International Trophy at Silverstone on 13 April. He finished 7th behind Niki Lauda, Emerson Fittipaldi, Mario Andretti, John Watson, Patrick Depailler and Mark Donohue. He beat Brabham Ford driver Carlos Reutemann, the man immediately behind him, by 28 seconds. It would be a fateful finish, certainly not the last time they would clash. Graham Hill, James Hunt and Ronnie Peterson were also in his mirrors. It was a grand opening. 'Harry got a bit excited.'

While the grand gates to Formula 1 had opened for Alan Jones, Tim Schenken had realised by 1975 that he had been locked out. He had waited for years for Ron Dennis to burst into the big-time, but Dennis just could not take the next step with Rondel Racing, for which Schenken had carved a reputation in Formula 2. The company collapsed. Like Frank Williams, Dennis had to keep reinventing himself to press on. By 1975 his effort had become known as Project Three; there would be more evolutions in later years.

'You seem to only get one decent shot at it. I had blown my chance, so I was forced to go to other categories. It's a hard thing to accept, though, because you always want to be up there, and to have been there, even for a little while … well, it had always been my objective, and I had lost. I tried at one stage to pick up a drive with Lotus. I had seen Ronnie Peterson testing, and while he was a great driver, he wasn't very good at finding the problems in testing, so I rang Colin Chapman and offered my services as a test driver. But Colin didn't like the idea. In those days there were no designated test drivers. It was always the works driver. I was ahead of my time!'

It was to be another Porsche season for Schenken. While it was not as high profile as his Ferrari sports car days, Schenken drove with great success in the 3 litre Carrera, scoring four podium finishes in the German Porsche Championship. He won at Misano and Jarama in the European GT Championship, won at Zandvoort in a GT 4 hour race, and drove a 917 to victories at the Nurburgring and Hockenheim. 'The 917 had a 5 litre turbocharged engine. At some circuits the turbo was tweaked to deliver 1100 horsepower. I was a little apprehensive at first, but the car was quite easy to drive. Lots of down force, huge tyres … it all worked well except when it rained and you were on slicks.' It was not Formula 1, but it was a living.

Larry Perkins had not yet suffered enough at the hands of optimists to be disillusioned. He took a part-time drive with a March-backed satellite team in a factory Formula 3 car, which he used to great effect at Monaco, shoving his team-mate, Giancarlo Cinzano, aside. 'He was holding me up, so I punted him off.' None of it was fruitful, but a piece of paper with a phone number on it was. Ron Tauranac had offered to help Perkins if he ever needed it. Perkins dismissed the cap-in-hand political routes and consulted Tauranac, who offered him a role in a Formula 3 team he wanted to start. Perkins's brother Terry flew over to join them, and Team Cowangie was born again. 'In our first race, at Thruxton, I put the car on pole position,' Perkins recalls, 'and I was in complete control of the race but got complacent and spun, which Ron was really at mad at.'

Perkins then dominated a race at Monaco so completely that a panic-stricken mentor David McKay actually rushed onto the circuit itself to warn him to slow down and conserve victory, with just 5 laps to go. 'I'll never forget it. He meant well, but it threw my concentration. The following lap my foot slipped off the brake pedal and I stuck it into the swimming pool complex. I was annoyed at him. He was annoyed at me. It took me a long time to get over that. It was one of the low points. There were 120 cars competing for spots in the final, and to win at Monaco is a massive boost to your career. I should have done it.' In spite of the setback, Perkins's plan was to win the first European Formula 3 Championship, and he did. Once again, Formula 1 would beckon.

Alan Jones, meantime, seemed to be going from strength to strength. Having made a stunning debut for Harry Stiller in a non-championship race, he drove in the Spanish Grand Prix, where he qualified 20th and retired after a lap 3 accident. It was unimportant, but events later in the afternoon were not.

Rolf Stommelen was driving for another new team, Embassy Hill, started by Graham Hill, who was sharing some of the driving duties in the formative rounds. Stommelen shot into the barriers after his rear wing broke, bounced back into the path of Carlos Pace, whose car launched into the crowd, killing five people. Stommelen was also badly hurt. The race was stopped at half distance and awarded to Jochen Mass.

Hill failed to qualify his only entry for the following round, at Monaco, then announced his retirement. He signed François Migault and Tony Brise, then sacked Migault and replaced him with Vern Schuppan for the Swedish Grand Prix. Schuppan broke a drive-shaft after 47 of the 80 laps. Alan Jones, by this time, was starting to acquire a feel for Stiller's Hesketh car, and finished 11th.

Before the next round, the Dutch Grand Prix, for all Harry Stiller's grand plans and improving results, the dream evaporated as quickly as it appeared. 'Harry,' Jones recalls, 'just suddenly decided to pull out and go racing Formula 5000 in America after all! This was the plan he'd teased me with at the end of the previous year!'

At the same time, Schuppan lost his drive with Embassy Hill just as suddenly, and in a seamless transition, the kind of good fortune that sustains the thirstiest of careers, Jones slipped into the Embassy Hill garage. With the more substantial backing of Hill's team he finished 13th, 16th and 10th for 3 rounds before climbing into the points with a 5th in Germany, from 21st on the grid.

'A lot of the focus,' he recalls, 'was on my team-mate Tony Brise, because he was British. It was a British team and he was very, very quick. But as luck would have it, I had scored their best result of the season.' The performance was even more impressive because of the difficulty Jones had working with Hill. He claims to this day, and other drivers have made similar comments, that to work for an ex-driver can be exhausting. Jones found Hill a little too set in his ways, and says he interfered too much with car set-up.

The season ended with some British Formula 5000 wins in a March run by RAM Racing, owned by British car dealers John Macdonald and Mick Ralph. 'You had to keep at it,' Jones says, 'working, driving something in their own backyard.' It was this persistence that kept his head above water, in view of team bosses.

It had been an ordinary 1975 for Kevin Bartlett in Formula 5000. He limped through the Tasman series, finishing on the podium twice. In August, on a slippery Surfers Paradise circuit, his was one of six cars that failed to finish as Max Stewart won his second Australian Grand Prix. Neither of them could take control of the Gold Star series, which was won by John McCormack. The struggle would continue into 1976.

Vern Schuppan shrugged off yet another disappointment in Formula 1 and resumed his Formula 5000 season with Dan Gurney's team. He finished 5th at Mid-Ohio and 2nd at Long Beach. Brian Redman won both events. However, it was frustrating at times, and he concurs with Jones's theory about former drivers running teams. 'Dan was notorious for changing things. You'd arrive at every race with different suspension settings. I think former drivers tend to be very tough team owners. They tend to believe that if they got in the car they'd be quicker than the guy driving for them.'

Schuppan also raced again for Gulf Mirage at Le Mans, with Jean-Pierre Jaussaud finishing 3rd. The other car in their team, driven by Jacky Ickx and Derek Bell, won the race. 'Le Mans is one of those places you really look forward to competing at, until about two o'clock in the morning, when you wonder what the hell you're doing there. Then if you're still rushing around on Sunday morning, you start to come good again.'

1976 marked the official end of the Tasman series. It was replaced by two 4-round series, one each in New Zealand and Australia. Some drivers, including Kevin Bartlett, contested both. Bartlett scored points in 3 of the 4 New Zealand rounds, but his total was nowhere near that of the series winner, Ken Smith. The Australian races were beefed up by the appearance of journeyman Vern Schuppan, on his way from the Macau Grand Prix, where he was unplaced. Schuppan, at 32, with 5 years of international competition behind him, was making his first appearance in an Australian series. 'It was unbelievable, actually,' he recalls. 'There was something missing in terms of my credibility with the Australian racing fraternity. No one had ever heard of me. There were times when I was written up as this "Austrian". To come home and contest the series was great.'

Schuppan's comeback to Australia in open-wheel racing was celebrated with victory at a wet Oran Park by 16.5 seconds. In the next round, also rain affected, he was unable to get from the team the full wet weather tyres he requested for the race start, and lost too much time changing them during the race. Ken Smith beat him. He was 2nd again, to John Cannon, at Sandown. The fourth race, at Surfers Paradise, was cancelled due to too much rain. Schuppan won the title.

For all his hard work, Alan Jones was not holding high cards for the 1976 Formula 1 season. He had hoped that Graham Hill would keep a place for him in the Embassy team, but before the season began, Hill and key members of his team had been killed in a light plane crash. He had been on approach to an airfield at Elstree, England. Five other team members were aboard. Tony Brise was one of them.

Jack Brabham was among those greatly affected by the loss of the legendary larrikin. 'He was a real character, like Frank Gardner. He used to always have an audience. I remember once in Casablanca, there was a floor show with these comedians and the like, and we're all sitting there watching it. Eventually, he got up there with them, and before long we realised that he was funnier than the rest of them. He took over.'

'I went through another of those depressing times when Graham was killed,' recalls Tim Schenken. 'I had flown a lot with him. I had raced with him. He was an incredible character. One of the funniest people you could ever hope to meet, as funny as any comedian. His funeral was the most heart-wrenching thing, his coffin being brought into this huge church, his helmet on the coffin. The atmosphere, you just can't explain it. People talk about cutting the air with a knife. It was like that. Then we went back to his place for drinks. I walked into the house and everyone was drinking and laughing and merry. I just couldn't cope with the two extremes. I looked at my wife Brigitte and she agreed with me. We just went home. Then you're racing the next week, and somehow it's all behind you again.'

It was back to the telephone for Alan Jones, talking, waiting. The next call was from John Surtees. In spite of his previous friction with Australians, he seemed keen to give another one a shot, although Jones was a little miffed at having to test for the drive: he thought he had shown enough in his stints with Hesketh and Hill. 'I can't abide these people who say they couldn't drive hard because it was their own car or they couldn't afford to crash the car ... I can't cop that. When your arse is in the car, you give it ten-tenths. Otherwise, don't get in it. I wanted to make sure that I left that test the quickest driver. I did.'

Jones was not impressed after some of the early races for Surtees in which he discovered the car had severe limitations, disguised only in wet conditions. 'The final straw was our sponsorship. It was Durex, the condom manufacturer! You'd get an MBE for driving with that on your car these days, but in those days the BBC wanted to pull out of the television coverage because of it.'

He struggled to qualify well but improved greatly in the races, without scoring points. There was more frustration in store. 'We'd arrive at a grand prix, bring the car out of the transporter, and the car would be set up exactly as it had been before the previous grand prix, instead of following up what we learnt from that race. You knew that every time we'd have to go through this stupid bloody ritual of re-setting the car to where we had it last time. You know, Surtees actually made the comment to me once, that our suspension was too good ... too good? He said that it was so easy on the tyres that we couldn't get enough heat into them and therefore, grip. I said to him, "Well, can we fuck it up a bit then?"'

Larry Perkins was also looking for a better platform to show his skills, signing up for the Formula 1 season with the Boro team, a Holland-based outfit run by two brothers who had made their money in the security business. They used a chassis from the Ensign team which had proved so frustrating for Vern Schuppan 2 years before and they were not scheduled to compete until the Spanish Grand Prix at Jarama. Perkins found, like Jones, that the racing was more satisfying than the qualifying. While Jones qualified 20th and finished 9th, Perkins started 24th, finished 13th. 'It was encouraging, because the car never felt good. We did some testing in Holland and my times were good, but the car was crook in the race. It had a sticking throttle which forced me to pit.'

Jones and Perkins were looking secure after the Belgian Grand Prix at Zolder, where Alan finished 5th from 16th on the grid, Larry 8th from 20th. 'I was starting to get my eye in,' Perkins recalls, 'passed a few blokes and thoroughly enjoyed it. I really felt I belonged there.'

He never had the chance to capitalise on this, however, because the Boro team folded before the French Grand Prix. 'I was not politically astute in those days. I was too naïve to think there might be a second option if I refused that one. I just thought, "It's a Formula 1 car. I'll drive it." Ron Tauranac saw the disaster about to happen at Boro and advised Perkins to keep going alone: to keep the Dutch team's equipment, some of the mechanics, and call on a few favours. Goodyear delivered tyres. The Italians who ran the Monza circuit also kindly let Perkins test there free of charge.

'At one point, during the Monza practice,' he recalls, 'I saw my Dutch apprentices pouring our waste oil into Lotus's fuel drums, by mistake of course. I have no idea what the outcome of that was. I didn't want to know.' He struggled on to the Dutch Grand Prix at Zandvoort, where he qualified 19th and crashed on lap 44. He knew then that his brave effort to continue alone could not last.

For Jones, another frustrating season was summed up by an incident one day in pit lane, when he turned around to find Peter Brock and a couple of mates standing there. Brock had won the Australian Touring Car Championship and two Bathurst 1000s by then. He was an idol in Australian motor sport. Jones was not so happy with his lot in what was supposed to be the biggest show. Brock too remembers this episode well. 'He seemed so impressed with what we were doing back in Australia with the Toranas and all that. I actually felt sorry for the guy,' Brock recalls. 'I thought here I am, doing really well for myself. Life's great. Then here's poor Jonesy, struggling away, the arse out of his pants, going nowhere. Of course, about 2 years later, that changed a fair bit!'

Vern Schuppan had continued racing for Dan Gurney's Eagle team in American Formula 5000. He too had been frustrated by lack of performance, fighting for midfield finishes. In one race, he saw Alan Jones streaking away to victory: Jones had commuted across the Atlantic for some morale-boosting races on behalf of Teddy Yip. If Schuppan needed any evidence that the Gurney failures were not his fault, it came from the most unlikely place. Gurney's disappointment was so acute that he replaced his own design with a Lola T332. Schuppan drove it to victory in the next round, at Elkhart Lake. 'Dan didn't even go to that race because he was so disgusted with his car. He went with his Indy Car team to Ontario. My win was announced over the PA system there, followed by a pause, and a second message: "Dan, you'd better stay away from more races!"'

Gurney gave Schuppan the chance to drive at the Indianapolis 500 in a spare car. It was exhilarating. 'It was one thing doing 200 miles an hour down

Mulsanne, but quite another doing it at the Brickyard.' Schuppan was forced to make an early pit stop for a puncture. He lost many positions, then resumed, and fought back to 12th by the time they declared the race finished because of rain. His performance was rewarded with a Rookie of the Year trophy.

All was not lost for Larry Perkins who, for the first time in his Formula 1 career, was given a serious car to drive at the end of the 1976 Formula 1 season. 'I recall Bernie Ecclestone asking me if I had any contract ties with the Boro team because he needed a substitute driver for the last three races. I said no ... but of course I did. I just couldn't refuse a plumb drive. We sorted that out later.'

Perkins believed that it was his final chance to impress; it was as if his future had come down to three races in which he simply had to do everything right, after all, agents would be hammering on Ecclestone's door with paying drivers on offer for the following year. Perkins qualified 19th and finished 17th at Mosport Park, then qualified 13th but retired at half distance with suspension trouble at Watkins Glen. He then withdrew after just 1 lap of a rain-soaked Japanese Grand Prix, believing that it was far too difficult to bring the car home in one piece in the conditions. His chance of driving for Bernie Ecclestone had washed down the gutters of the Mt Fuji circuit. 'I made my share of mistakes, didn't do a lot to help my chances. Would you believe it, I was still considered for a drive the following year — but when John Watson became available they snapped him up. Bernie said "Sorry, I've taken someone else." That's motor racing.' He had no idea that the sequence of Formula 1 frustration had barely begun.

Alan Jones was in an unusual position: he had performed well with Surtees, scoring 7 championship points by the end of the season, but did not want to drive for him again. All those years he had spent chasing a firm Formula 1 contract and there he was in his hotel room in Japan, for the last race of the championship, trying to avoid one. 'I knew that John had an option to re-sign me for 1977, but the deadline ran out on the night of the final race,' recalls Jones. 'So I was hiding from him in the Holiday Inn Hotel. He was looking everywhere for me. Finally, I realised how bloody ridiculous it all was, and went downstairs to grab a hamburger. Now, if there's one law stronger than Murphy's, it's Jones's. Of course I'm in the lift, the bloody doors open, and who should be standing right in front of me but John! "I've been looking for you," he says. "You're not answering your phone." He hands me the option! I had to be honest. I said, "If the only way I can do Formula 1 is with you, then I don't want to do it." Then I thought, shit, what am I going to do now?'

His first option was to drive at Macau, at the invitation of that great mentor of Australian drivers, Teddy Yip. The Macau Grand Prix in 1976 was still under Formula Atlantic specifications. Vern Schuppan had also returned, on Yip's invitation, hoping for his second victory. 'Jonesy was actually the quickest guy there,' Schuppan recalls. 'He had some trouble at Reservoir bend, while leading the race. He was driving the March that I had won with in 1974. I was driving a Ralt, which I didn't think was as good as the March, actually, but it was steady and reliable, and I came through to win the race again. I remember Teddy sitting on the back of the car as we did a lap of honour. It looked for all the world like he was sitting on my shoulders. People wrote in to the local newspaper saying it was disgusting that Teddy sat on my shoulders after I had driven all that way in the race.'

From Macau, Schuppan moved on to the Australian Grand Prix, on 12 September at Sandown, where he staged a brilliant finish in his Elfin MR8 with a determined John Goss in a Matich A53 with a Repco engine. It was another classical privateer story from the Goss archives. 'Frank Matich and I almost drove together years before when he was running the M10, but I couldn't raise the money; actually I probably didn't try hard enough to raise the money, from Ford. Colin Bond did a few races with him as it turned out. But I was more established when I finally bought a car from Frank in 1974, after he had retired. It was the last of the Matich cars. Laurie O'Neill loaned me the additional funds I needed for the purchase, and Frank also kindly gave me parts and spares to maintain the car, on a lend-lease basis, even the little van it all came in! He also hooked me up with his two mechanics, Grant O'Neill, no relation to Laurie, and Peter Hughes. They were fantastic and were a great part of my success in that car.'

Goss took the win by a length, after a desperate final corner pass from Schuppan just failed to come off. It was a wonderful drive from Goss, who proved that he deserved his place among the greats: he had achieved the rare distinction of being the only driver to win the Bathurst 1000 and the Australian Grand Prix. Goss could barely contain his emotions. He was in tears during the warm-down lap. 'I rolled around to the start–finish line, barely comprehending that I had not only won the Australian Grand Prix, but won it at a circuit in the city of my birth, in front of this massive crowd. The stands were full. I'll never forget the first person to congratulate me after the race: Diana Davison. That meant a lot to me.' It was a missed opportunity for Schuppan. 'I was running on 7 cylinders,' he recalls, 'but I believed I could get him on the last lap. I was very disappointed, but Gossy was totally over the moon, and I was happy for him. I also recall saying that I hoped the race was as exciting for the spectators as it was from where I was sitting.'

Kevin Bartlett's Lola T400 had qualified 15 seconds off the pace, thanks to a host of mechanical troubles in practice and qualifying. He charged through the field, only to fall out after 33 laps, his third consecutive retirement in the grand prix. 'My problem was always the same. I could never put together budgets and still drive competitively. I was always short of money. I was more suited to being a paid driver, but as it turned out, that was very rarely possible.'

Tim Schenken enjoyed more wins with Porsche in 1976, a turbocharged 934 taking him to victory at Hockenheim, Monza and the Nurburgring plus three podium finishes and a couple of 4th placings. He drove a 935 to 2nd place in the 1000 kilometre race at the Nurburgring, with Toine Hezemans as co-driver, and continued to campaign the 3 litre Carrera successfully. He was never able to finish the Le Mans 24 hour race, but it was not the fault of the intrepid German mechanics, whose maintenance tricks during endurance races knew no bounds. At one event, when Hezemans was stuck on the circuit, obliged by the rules to repair his own car before he could return to the pits, the mechanics smuggled a fuel pump belt to him in the middle of a French bread roll.

It was in 1976 that Schenken first tasted the bitter pill that many drivers have been forced to accept: team orders. Team boss Georg Loos had instructed him to let Hezemans win the final championship round of the season at Hockenheim, even though Schenken had clearly been faster. 'I thought, fuck this,' he recalls. 'I drove like a demon, as fast as I could. I must have had a 25 or 30 second lead. There were 60,000 or 70,000 people at the circuit, and on the final lap, I came into the view of the main grandstands, roared up to the finish line, and stopped. I waited for what seemed like hours. Of course it was only 25 or so seconds before Hezemans came into view. The moment he took the chequered flag, I put the car into first gear and moved across the line. The crowd went absolutely berserk. Then, when we went onto the podium for the prize, they all booed him. I was the hero. It was a riot. I got away with a reprimand from the stewards. They said it was unsportsmanlike ... but really, I thought it was very sportsmanlike.'

* * *

Australia was almost single-handedly sustaining the Formula 5000 category, but doing a very good job. The brave few who had battled through awkward and near-destitute years — Kevin Bartlett, John Goss, Max Stewart and others — were to be joined by a tasty dressing of international flavours, lifting the quality of what was still a relatively small grid of 15 for the 1977 Australian Grand Prix, run on 6 February at Oran Park.

Alan Jones in a Lola T332 and Vern Schuppan in an Elfin MR8 could not overawe the hardy Bartlett, who had seen them all come and go. 'I've had a lot to say about Jonesy over the years, because of the attitude that Australian Formula 1 drivers tended to have when they raced back home — although you never got that attitude from Jack Brabham. Brabham used to come back and he was exactly the same bloke. Other blokes, who weren't even champions at that stage ... well it's better left unsaid.'

Warwick Brown beat them all in the grand prix. Jones and Schuppan finished 4th and 5th. The luckless Bartlett finished 11th, but full of praise for the winner. 'Warwick was a very hard steerer, very good, but hard on the car, aggressive. He also acquitted himself very well in US Formula 5000. He was a brash character, but a great personality.' Max Stewart had entered his T400, but blew a piston in practice and withdrew. None of the fans at Oran Park that day had a clue that it would be his last Australian Grand Prix.

Just 6 weeks later, at Calder Park, Stewart was preparing for a $40,000 race with, as usual, his old mate Kevin Bartlett. 'It was a stupid, stupid accident,' Bartlett recalls. 'We were next to each other in the pits. We had been talking about changes to each other's car. We used to discuss things like that. He said to me, "I reckon I can knock a couple of tenths off this lap." I said, "All right. I'll go all out too." But I didn't. The next thing I knew, there had been this bloody big accident, and when he didn't come around, I knew.

'Ken Shirvington had broken something in his car and was going down the back straight. Max was doing two to Ken's one, catching him very quickly. Shirvington was in turn catching Vern Schuppan, who had dropped an engine and virtually stopped. He hadn't yet pulled off the track. Max must have come up on Shirvington, then ducked out from behind him, and there's Vern. He's gone straight into the back of him. The blade of Vern's rear wing hit him straight in the head, cutting through his helmet.'

The death of Max Stewart was the lowest point in Schuppan's career and has haunted him ever since. 'I had slowed right down. Next thing, I felt this tremendous impact. It felt like I had landed on my back after falling from a 20-foot wall. The car suddenly accelerated from this incredible force. Eventually I stopped again, without hitting anything, and got out of the car. Apart from a bit of whiplash, I was okay. I saw Max's car back up the road. The marshals were very quick to rush me off to hospital. I kept telling them that I was okay, but asking after Max. Later, I went to the hospital desk to ask. They told me he was critical and probably wouldn't live through the night. It was the most horrible night of my life.

'I had seen other guys killed. I certainly knew plenty of drivers who were killed. There was one young American driver whose throttle jammed open in Formula 5000, taking him into the wall. He was killed instantly. I often wondered why — why did it have to be that bloke on that day, when others have the same type of crash, and just walk away? Normally, like everyone else, I could shut it out of my mind in order to keep racing. Max was a bit different. It affected me quite deeply because I was the guy he ran into. If my engine hadn't blown, a great guy who was respected, enjoyed and loved by everybody would have stayed alive. It took me a long time to get over that.'

'Max was never going to survive,' recalls Bartlett. 'Rana, my wife, brought his wife down from Sydney. We stayed in the hospital that night until he died, at about two o'clock in the morning. Rana saw him. He was a mess. It was a terrible experience for her and the worst experience of my career. We were so close, and I have never been that close to a driver since. When he died, a lot of the fun went out of it for me. As a tribute, we raced the next day. He would have said, "Hey you silly bastards, why aren't you racing?"'

In Europe, Alan Jones was running out of options. The Formula 1 season would have to start without him while he maintained that eternal vigil by the telephone, but for Larry Perkins, the merry-go-round continued. Formula 1 just would not let him go. The Stanley-BRM team, which had promised so much to Vern Schuppan, was a shadow of its former self in 1977, but Perkins was no longer able to choose.

His second start for them, in South Africa, kept his name in the papers. 'I remember *Autosprint* magazine giving Lauda five stars for his winning performance and me five stars for persevering with a car running on 10 or 11 of its 12 cylinders! It was the last BRM to finish a grand prix, but clearly the worst ever.' Perkins had decided there that he would tell Louis Stanley what to do with his team. He had no idea, however, that the South African round would be yet another crossroads in his career. Tom Pryce, a 28-year-old British driver with the Shadow team, was killed in one of motor racing's most awfully ill-fated collisions. It happened on lap 22, and Larry Perkins saw the aftermath.

'I was racing along behind Jacques Lafitte, with Tom Pryce just ahead of us, when suddenly there's this flurry of debris that hits our windscreens going down the main straight. I wasn't sure what that was all about. Then Pryce, at the head of the queue, veers off the road. Next time around, I saw Pryce's helmet, just sitting on the side of the track, with his car stuck in the fence at the end of the straight. It didn't look good. I later realised that Pryce's team-mate, Renzo Zorzi, had parked his car in a slight hollow in the track. He had a split fuel pipe and it caught fire. Two track marshals had run across the track to extinguish it. They weren't looking, and Pryce's car came over the rise and hit one of them. The terrible thing was that not only was the marshal killed, but his extinguisher hit Pryce in the head, killing him instantly. The car just ploughed into a barrier.'

It was a tough call for Perkins to make. He was tied up in knots after witnessing the death but acutely aware that it had opened his only escape route from the ailing Stanley-BRM team. It was almost identical to Tim Schenken's dilemma in 1970, when Piers Courage was killed. 'I thought, what do I do? I got on well with the Shadow people and I was over the BRM thing. There was a big rule at the time which the Formula 1 Constructors' Association, FOCA, had agreed on. You weren't allowed to poach drivers from rival teams. It was a feared rule. I decided not to go and see them that weekend, but wait until I got back to England a couple of days later. By the time I made the phone call to Alan Rees and Jackie Oliver, they said, "Oh God. Sorry Larry, but we've just hired Alan Jones." I said, "What?" They said, "We thought about you, but you hadn't contacted us, so we assumed you were tied up." I'm convinced that if I had seen them on the day of the crash, I would have got the drive, and stayed in Formula 1 a lot longer.'

It certainly did not improve relations between the two Australians. 'I got a phone call from Jackie Oliver,' Jones recalls, 'asking me to join the team. I still had a contract with Surtees. I just wasn't exercising it. But it worried me a bit. Jackie said to get on the plane and he'd sort it out. We all met at Heathrow Airport. I had my solicitor there. We signed the contract. I then flew up to

Northampton to be fitted for the car. We were off to the US the next day to get ready for the Long Beach round. My team-mate was Renzo Zorzi.'

Another opportunity came up for Perkins when Brabham team driver Carlos Pace was killed in a light plane crash just 2 weeks after Pryce's death. Once again, Bernie Ecclestone was faced with a choice: give the young Australian another chance or take on the more experienced German Hans-Joachim Stuck, who had been successful in Formula 2 but scored only irregular rides in Formula 1. Stuck got the drive.

While Jones was settling into his new team, testing in the United States, failing to finish the first couple of races, then scoring a point at Monaco, Larry Perkins bounced back again like a pinball, following the sacking of Hans Binder. The only problem was that the man who did the sacking was John Surtees. Perkins was about to take up one of his last chances to cement a place in Formula 1, with the man who Tim Schenken and Alan Jones simply could not drive for. That wasn't the only twist.

Perkins had just returned from a meeting with Surtees, in which they settled the deal, when Alan Rees phoned back from Shadow to say that he had another vacancy. They had sacked Renzo Zorzi over a contract dispute. The prospect of an all-Australian team driving in Formula 1 had been literally only minutes away, but Perkins had to decline the invitation because he had just shaken hands with Surtees. 'I said, "Fuck ... I don't believe it!"' Perkins recalls, 'and Rees said, "Neither can we!" So I missed out.' Given their heated rivalry and the fact that no two Australians had ever been hired by a third party to drive for the same Formula 1 team, it would have been one of the most exciting combinations in the paddock. With Perkins unavailable, Shadow signed a 23-year-old Italian called Ricardo Patrese.

Driving for John Surtees would be just as demanding and excruciating for Larry Perkins as it had been for Jones and Schenken. He struggled to qualify in Belgium, working hard in an inferior car to finish midfield — helped by the attrition rate more than anything. He failed to qualify in Sweden. For Jones, however, there was more than a glimpse of light at Shadow, for whom he finished 5th at Zolder after running as high as 3rd.

By the time they both arrived at Dijon for the French Grand Prix, the pinball had bounced again. 'The Surtees team was a disaster,' Perkins laments. 'I remember Surtees had an eye for the Marlboro money, which Patrick Tambay had, so he replaced me.' The axe fell during practice. Tambay could not qualify the car. 'By that stage,' Perkins recalls, 'I was starting to become seriously disillusioned with all the bloody crap in Formula 1. I decided to just hang around for a while and do a few Formula 2 races which I had been asked to do.'

Patrick Tambay lasted one round with Surtees before moving on to Ensign. So much for the injection of money. But in yet another extraordinary development, his departure was Vern Schuppan's ticket back again.

Schuppan had been the typical driver-for-hire in 1977. He had raced for the fifth time at Le Mans, finishing 2nd with Jean-Piere Jaussaud to the Porsche of Jürgen Barth, Hurkley Haywood and Jacky Ickx. 'Jaussaud and I had agreed that whatever the cost, we would drive the car flat out. It was not the usual tactic for Le Mans, but our car was down on straight line speed, despite numerous attempts to tweak the turbocharger and make other adjustments. To complicate our strategy, it rained, as it so often does, but on only one section of the track, the Mulsanne Straight. We couldn't put wets on because there was too much of the circuit still dry. The rain spread. We stayed on slick tyres. I don't know how the car didn't break, but I knew that if we tried to look after it more, it certainly would have.'

He also had a deal to continue in open-wheel racing with Indy cars, driving the oval track series for legendary American driver and constructor Frank Kurtis, in a Wildcat with an Offenhauser engine. 'It had been a very good car for Gordon Johncock the previous year. It was still a good car, but Frank by then was a doddery old fool and the team was a disaster. We finished 5th at Phoenix, and were set for a second row qualifying position at the Indy 500 — but Frank forgot to put enough fuel in the car. I ran out on the fourth lap of qualifying. This would be the start of a 3-year period in which I drove in a variety of races for privateers in different cars ... and none of them was very good.

'I have no idea why I received that Formula 1 offer from John Surtees, out of the blue. I was in America when I got the call. I had been doing okay, I suppose, but I wasn't very happy. I had been following Formula 1. I'm sure most serious drivers do. I also knew what had been happening with the drivers in that team. I knew Larry, having met him a couple of times in the Formula 3 days when he was famous for driving what we called "The Araldite Special". His cars always looked like they'd been stuck together. He was never one for presentation in those days. So I knew it wasn't going to be easy, but I was so frustrated with Indy cars. I also thought that I might have been a little hasty in getting out of Formula 1 in the first place.

'I turned up full of enthusiasm, keen to re-establish myself, then found myself very much the second driver in the second car. All the good stuff — engines and anything else new that came into the team — went to Vittorio Brambilla, who crashed all the time, which usually meant me losing my race car and driving the "mule" car. Surtees would swear the two cars were exactly the same but we were not stupid. I took heart from the fact that Larry and Patrick had struggled to qualify and Jonesy had also had problems the year before.'

Schuppan wrestled with the car. His best finish was 7th at the Nurburgring. Jones, however, was starting to come to terms with his Shadow. At first he found it hard to get among the top-ten finishers. That changed in Austria.

Rain cleared on race day, leaving a partially wet surface at the Osterreichring, but most drivers chose slick tyres. Niki Lauda, James Hunt and Mario Andretti staged a three-way fight in the early laps. Jones carved through from 14th on the grid. 'She was a pretty heavy old girl in the dry, which wasn't bad for street circuits, but on race day the rain really helped.'

By lap 15 he had moved up behind race leader Hunt, who proved difficult to capture — ultimately, it was not necessary. Hunt's engine blew. For 10 laps, Jones had to hold off the 1975 World Champion, Lauda. 'I was shitting myself. All I could think of was, please don't break down … don't run out of fuel. The car might give a twitch that you wouldn't have given a shit about 20 laps earlier. Suddenly it was terrifying.' Alan Jones had become only the second Australian to win a Formula 1 race. Lauda was still 20 seconds behind when the flag fell. Hans-Joachim Stuck finished 3rd. Vern Schuppan crossed the line 16th.

'I'll tell you how unexpected that win was,' Jones recalls. 'They didn't have the Australian national anthem ready. A drunk played *Happy Birthday* on a trumpet. I couldn't care less. It was the best tune I ever heard. I remember saying to someone, "I don't care what happens. I've won a grand prix. I have won a grand prix." As it turned out, it would be the only grand prix that team would ever win. Shadow, of course, became Arrows.'

While Jones occupied the high ground, finishing on the podium at Monza behind Andretti and Lauda, filling up the season with consistent, if not brilliant, results, Schuppan suffered with Surtees' inflexibility on development issues and a pampered driver who not only crashed cars but commandeered his team-mate's when his own had run out. Schuppan claims that Brambilla crashed 23 times that year in testing, practice, qualifying and racing. Schuppan left the team in disgust and returned to the United States after failing to qualify for the Dutch Grand Prix; he vowed not to return to Formula 1. At the very next round, his replacement, Lamberto Leoni, failed to qualify. Brambilla? He crashed.

Schuppan arrived at Riverside for the final round of the Can-Am series. He drove an Elfin MR8 and finished 22nd. Alan Jones finished 33rd in the same race, the last of three unimpressive starts in a Shadow Dodge. The Can-Am series had taken over when Formula 5000 expired, and the conversion was not difficult for most teams. Can-Am was resuming after a 3 year hiatus, in the second phase of a life which started back in 1964. They were reshaped, single-seat Formula 5000 cars with the big V8 engines, attracting European-based drivers like Patrick Tambay, Peter Gethin and Gilles Villeneuve. Hollywood actor Paul Newman was planning to run a car in the 1978 series.

He was not the only famous entertainer that the Australians ran into in the American paddocks: Gene Hackman, William Holden, James Garner, Gene Kelly and Steve McQueen were all keen motor sport fans. George Harrison was also an acquaintance of Schuppan's from Formula 1 meetings.

Larry Perkins had by then returned to Australia and finished 3rd in the Bathurst 1000 with Peter Janson. He had contested 14 Formula 1 races without having to pay for his drives, but his performance had been limited by the resources of the teams and his choices would always be limited by lack of sponsorship. He felt comfortable with his ability, but it was time to make some decisions. He would return to England, and fight on for another year.

Alan Jones was stunned to learn that there would be no place for him in the Shadow team in 1978. 'There was a cloud over sponsorship for the following season. No one knew what was going on. For all my achievements, I was back to square one ... not Formula 1. But I had won a race. That must have impressed Luca di Montezemolo, head of the Ferrari team, who invited me to meet Enzo Ferrari for a chat. Then Frank Williams phoned me and told me he was building a car and wouldn't mind me driving it for him. My first reaction was, Ferrari or Frank Williams? Are you kidding? Frank's cars were always down the back. He had been running a March in 1977 for Patrick Neve, who we used to call Patrick "Naïve". But one thing I had learnt from my time in Formula 1 politics is that no matter how bad any new unknown offer sounded, you never told anyone to get fucked. You left the door open. With team owners, it's promise everything and deliver nothing, dog eat dog, so drivers had to play the same game. I told Frank that I was very interested and that it sounded like a great deal, all the while determined to drive for Ferrari.'

Ferrari's attitude was secretive, to say the least, in their dealings with Jones. Their warnings of confidentiality for the meeting with Enzo Ferrari were straight from a Le Carré novel. It made sense, because most drivers would turn down the Pope in favour of a meeting with Enzo. Jones broke into laughter when he arrived in Milan to find that his 'secret' escort was an Italian mechanic in dirty blue overalls with 'Ferrari' stamped on them, holding up a sign with 'Alan Jones' written on it. They walked outside and jumped into a brightly coloured Ferrari. 'If that was top secret I'd hate to see when they didn't give a shit.

'I nearly didn't make it to the meeting. My chauffeur proceeded to tell me, very angrily, during the drive to the factory, that he could have been a Formula 1 driver if it hadn't been for all these foreigners the team was signing, and the more he talked the faster he drove, until we were doing about 300 kilometres an hour, passing buses on the inside with a wheel on the grass. I tapped him on the shoulder and said, "Slow down, or pull up and let me out!"'

After a tour of the Ferrari factory, Jones was finally ushered in to meet the man with the most famous name in motoring. At this point, the mood changed from Le Carré to Mario Puzo. 'There he was, behind this big desk, as white as a ghost. I thought, this bloke's dead ... they're having me on. They've propped him up. He wasn't moving very much. Then he asks me, through an interpreter, why I want to drive a Ferrari. I thought, why would I want to drive a Ferrari?... what?... hello ...? I gave him all the routine about how great Ferrari were and how much I wanted to drive for them and how I wanted to become a world champion and they would make that possible. Then I actually went outside, talked to their accountants and signed a contract.'

There was one glaring proviso. Jones was told that he was not the preferred choice; the team really wanted to sign Mario Andretti, in order to improve their sales in America. Given that Andretti was likely to stay with Lotus, Jones remained upbeat. 'I went home to Bev waving a contract, saying, "If they don't get him, we're in."'

'Meanwhile, Frank Williams kept ringing me up. I'm saying, "Yeah, fantastic, mate. Can we meet next week?" I was stalling like buggery. Then I went down to Euston Station, bought *Autosport* magazine and read that

Andretti had signed with Lotus. I thought, you fucking beauty! I'm a Ferrari driver!'

Jones hurried back to that well-worn seat beside the telephone and waited for a couple of days for Ferrari to call, at the same time politely stalling a bemused Williams. Ferrari never called. So he called Ferrari, only to be met with an awkward silence. Finally, they explained that they had been so determined to sign a North American driver that they went for Gilles Villeneuve when Andretti was not available. 'I was stumped,' Jones recalls. 'I said, "What do you suggest I do with my contract?" I soon learnt a polite Italian expression for "Shove it up your arse."'

'Of course I was back on the phone minutes later. "Hello? Is that you, Frank?"'

By the end of 1977 Tim Schenken had added to an already impressive record in endurance races in exotic cars. He won the 1000 kilometre race at the Nurburgring for the second time in the turbocharged Porsche 935 and finished in the top four on five other occasions. He also competed in the European Touring Car Championship with John Fitzpatrick, in a factory Jaguar XJ12 which delivered enormous power but poor reliability and alarmingly weak brakes. He was enjoying not only the driving and development, but also the experience of competing with a co-driver to further improve performance, and at the same time, unlike in Formula 1, working in the same car towards the same goal.

At one disastrous round which ended before the race had started, Schenken, Fitzpatrick and crew were passing through the gates of the local airport terminal, on their way home, just as British Leyland officials were bringing corporate guests through in the opposite direction, on a special trip to watch the team race. The Jaguar publicity officer, when he finally transformed from a state of frozen horror to intelligible conversation, asked what was going on. 'We're going home,' Schenken said, with a shrug, and kept walking. He could only wonder what that episode did to Jaguar's client base.

There was no such nonchalance in his plan, hatched that year, to start a carbuilding company with his friend, former driver Howden Ganley. They called it TIGA Racing. The 'TI' was for Tim and the 'GA' for Ganley.

Larry Perkins was a little punch-drunk from his experiences in Formula 1. He maintained a home in England, and continued to work there for Ron

Tauranac, while assessing various offers to test and race cars from Europe to New Zealand. 'I wasn't paid much. In fact I suggested to Ron that he not pay me at all, because I didn't have a working visa anyway. It had been a 5 year drain on the finances, and I had profited nothing for the experience. All I ever got was enough to feed myself and rent a roof over my head. I enjoyed it, though. The mechanics liked me, because unlike a lot of drivers, I talked to them. In Formula 1 you're supposed to ignore your mechanics — or kick them in the head.'

For all his misgivings, Alan Jones was enormously impressed with Frank Williams's 1978 team and its new designer, Patrick Head. 'I liked the way Patrick was a straight-talker. The other thing that immediately impressed me was that the car had "Saudi" written all over it. I knew from living in London that the word "Saudi" meant "money".'

He soon learnt yet another Formula 1 lesson. The Saudi Airlines insignia was there to lure the sponsorship, not display it. There had been no money coming in at all. 'I think we went to the first round, in Argentina, on Frank's credit cards.'

Frank Gardner, the old genius who had seen every trick in Formula 1, was watching from afar. He found it unsurprising and vastly amusing. 'The one thing old "wanker" Williams was good at — and we used to call him that fondly — was languages. He was the best linguist. He could listen to people talk and work it out bit by bit. He got the Saudis involved by learning their language. He was a brilliant entrepreneur too, good on budgets. He could work out that if you sell this and keep that you could do this and that.'

Jones's 'insurance', which was vital for any driver, was to make a regular appearance for cigar-chomping millionaire Carl Haas — in a Lola T333CS with a Chevrolet engine — in the Can-Am series which he had appeared in for Shadow the previous year. Vern Schuppan, in his own Elfin MR8A, and Warwick Brown, in another Lola T333CS, were also scheduled for full seasons.

The average speed at most circuits in Can-Am was at least 180 kilometres an hour. Jones won the first race he started, at Road Atlanta, and went on to take four more victories, two other podium finishes, and the championship. 'I was doing one weekend in America, one weekend at a grand prix, and testing in between. There was one time I raced at Mid-Ohio, flew home Monday, tested for 2 days at Paul Ricard from Wednesday, and one of those was a 10 hour day with half an hour's break. It was a very busy season. But I got on extremely well with Carl Haas.' It was a relationship that would be rekindled on the track 7 years later.

Schuppan struggled through the Can-Am season, unable to contest all the meetings. His best result was 5th at Charlotte, but it was obvious that he needed a Lola if he were to compete for the championship. Brown had one and did that, winning at Watkins Glen, finishing runner-up in 5 other rounds, 3rd in another and 2nd to Jones in the series.

The focal point of the season for Jones, however, would be the continued development of the Williams Formula 1 car, which he was driving solo. There would be no team-mate in the early rounds to help push the envelope. Frank Williams, after years of hitting and missing — and frustrating top drivers like Tim Schenken — was on the brink of something special, pending massive financial support from Saudi Airlines. Patrick Head, controlling development of the car, was also on the threshold. He would soon be hailed as one of the great engineer–designers. Jones was about to discover that he was, unlike some of his predecessors, finally in the right place at the right time.

The 1978 season began poorly for Jones: he failed to finish in the first race, which was won by Mario Andretti at Buenos Aires. Then followed a series of top-10 results and the odd retirement with technical trouble before the French Grand Prix brought a marked improvement: 5th behind Andretti, who, with Ronnie Peterson, was making the most of a quick new Lotus. 'I'll always remember Bernie Ecclestone coming up to Frank after I had qualified the car 8th in the second round, at Rio, and saying, "You meet a nicer class of people up here." It meant, of course, welcome to the first four rows. By the time we got that result in France, Frank thought he'd died and gone to heaven. Then he invited all these Arab princes to the next round. I'm still not sure he had the money from them even then! But anyway, I qualified sixth for that race (at Brands Hatch) and was running strongly until I had an electrical fault which buggered us, and Reutemann ran away with the race. But I think we'd done enough to impress the princes.'

Hockenheim, Osterreichring and Zandvoort were ticked on Williams's list of failures to finish. By the time they all reached Monza, Lotus were in control of the championship and apparently light years ahead of their rivals. Jones had again qualified on the third row, and watched a horrifying pile-up on the first chicane. Ronnie Peterson was trapped in a flaming wreck, and was rescued by James Hunt and Clay Regazzoni. Peterson was considered very lucky to have survived — so many drivers before him had not lived through the kind of mass destruction that occurred that day. He was not badly burned and was expected to recover, albeit with severely injured legs. The operation, however, went wrong. A blood clot formed. By the following morning, Peterson was dead. Tim Schenken had lost another great friend.

'Sweden didn't have many Formula 1 heroes. There was Jo Bonnier, Gunnar Nilsson ... Ronnie. Brigitte and I were actually with him and his wife Barbara in Monaco celebrating our son Guido's birthday. Incidentally, Ronnie's daughter was Nina, named after Jochen Rindt's wife. That's how much he thought of Jochen. Ronnie drove off to Monza to race. We went home, saw the race on TV, saw the crash, but from all reports there was nothing to worry about. No one thought it was serious. Next thing you know we were flying to Sweden for the funeral. It was very, very hard. I hate funerals. I've been to too many. Many years later, Barbara took her own life. I don't think she ever got over Ronnie's death.'

Alan Jones and Williams produced their best result of the season in the penultimate round, at Watkins Glen: they qualified 3rd and finished 2nd. There would be hope, amidst the wreckage of another calamity.

Larry Perkins had been operating on the fringes in 1978, living in England, taking detours wherever opportunity led him. He drove in the Formula Atlantic series in New Zealand and was the best driver in the series except for one: a new talent from Finland called Keke Rosberg. 'It was a great series, a close series, with 10 races at five circuits — every photo I look at from that era was of Keke and me, side by side.' Perkins did some test driving for the Walter-Wolf team (which was formerly Walter-Williams) in Formula 1 and picked up a drive with Charles Ivey Racing at Le Mans. He finished 14th in a Porsche Carrera, 2nd in class, with Gordon Spice and John Rulon-Miller. Vern Schuppan's Mirage finished 10th. Then came the phone call that might have changed things forever. 'Bernie Ecclestone had another spot available,' Perkins recalls. 'This was before the end of the season. He gave me a call. I said, "Right. I'm back in Formula 1." I knew that Nelson Piquet was in the running for the same spot. He had driven for Ensign, then for McLaren in a couple of rounds. He had money from Brazil. I had none. Bernie rang me back and said he couldn't sign me. I understood that. I knew then that the writing was on the wall. It wasn't going to happen like it was supposed to.'

For all the disappointment he had suffered in his deals with Bernie

Ecclestone, Perkins still holds him in high regard. 'It was never Bernie's fault that I didn't get the drives. He was always a straight shooter. A deal was a deal. These days you hear people say things about Bernie, that he's a dictator and all that. But for every decision that he came out with for FOCA [Formula One Constructors Association], he would only have made up his mind after extensive consultation with the owners. He made sure he had support. There was no dictatorship.'

Perkins had not yet figured on cementing himself in Australia. Ron Tauranac wanted him to stay in England, to test drive and run his factory, so negotiations began. They haggled over Perkins's demands for a share of the business in place of wages, but the main sticking point was Perkins's lack of a work visa in England. That had been one of the reasons why he could not draw wages as a matter of record. When his application for a visa went through, he was told he had a week to get out of the country. Then he received the news that his father had been seriously hurt in a motorcycle accident back home. He had also met an Australian girl, Raelene, and decided to return home where they were married.

Kevin Bartlett was also puzzling over his future in the early days of 1979. Racing was no longer the satisfying adventure it had once been. The wearying grind of sustaining Formula 5000 on a threadbare budget in front of disappointing crowds was far removed from the glorious early days of driving successfully for Alec Mildren in competitive cars against the greatest drivers in the world. He had finished 5th in the 1978 Australian Grand Prix won by Graham McRae, but the prospects for the 1979 race were improving. 'I had a Brabham BT43, Formula 5000 spec, shipped out from the States. I was going to sell it, but had to get some results first, so I drove it in a couple of races and Colin Bond drove it for me in a couple of others. It turned out to be quite a good motor car and I sold it to a guy in Melbourne. Then he asked me to drive it!

'My first outing for him was at Sandown. It was running great. I was approaching the old causeway, just before the bridge — don't ask me where I was in the race — and it just snapped sideways on me. The rear wheel assembly collapsed. I went straight into the catch fencing, the wire-mesh fence put there for just that purpose, and slammed into the bridge so hard that it crushed the car in on me. It jammed my feet. The accelerator pedal went through my foot, and I broke my ankles ... again! I was trapped in the car for about 20 minutes while they were trying to free me. They had to cut the car in half, then get the jaws of life and spread the cockpit apart. But there was a lot of fuel aboard and we were all worried about fire, because I was stuck. There was one fire marshal who hopped onto the back of the car. He leaned over and said to me, "If this thing catches fire, I'm not leaving you. I'll drag you out by the epaulettes. It'll hurt, but I will get you out, no matter what." That's something, isn't it? Due to the circumstances, we were never really introduced, but I did meet him again years later. I told him that he was a bloody hero.

'I was in hospital in Melbourne, then Sydney. More operations. More pain. I said to Rana, "That's it for me. No more Formula 5000." She was pleased to hear that.' Bartlett had committed to drive in the Macau Grand Prix, but with arm in sling and hobble in gait he asked Vern Schuppan to take his place; he just helped to manage the team. 'Vern and I got on much better after we worked together. We've been mates ever since.' He would, however, find touring car racing much harder to resist. Bathurst had not seen the last of Kevin Bartlett.

Larry Perkins drove an Elfin for Ansett in the Formula 5000 series in those early months of 1979. He didn't win a race, but he did win a closely contested series. His team-mate was the promising Tasmanian John Bowe. The field for the Australian Grand Prix at Wanneroo Park, Western Australia in March was larger than in previous years. Perkins and Alfredo Costanzo shared the front row. The race was less than a lap old when Perkins dived under Costanzo in a move that was never going to come off, lost control in the dirt, turned back and shot over the top of Costanzo. Both drivers were unhurt, but they were also out of the contest. John Walker won. Perkins's next mission was another Formula Atlantic series in New Zealand, another 10 races at five circuits and, like the season before across the Tasman, when he diced with Keke Rosberg, it was another close defeat, this time to Teo Fabi. One of Formula 1's unluckiest drivers had been unable to leave the jinx in Europe.

The early rounds of the 1979 Championship Auto Racing Teams World series, which at that time included the Indianapolis 500, were historic for some. They were also the start of a glorious era featuring Gordon Johncock, Rick Mears, Johnny Rutherford and Bobby Unser. For Vern Schuppan, driving for yet another under-funded privateer team, they were just another frustrating sequence of midfield finishes.

Only Alan Jones was taking Australia's international recognition to new heights in 1979. The latest version of the Head-designed Williams Formula 1 car was launched in time for the season and it turned out to be a winning proposition. Development quickened with the arrival of Clay Regazzoni to drive a second FW07. Jones liked him immediately, though his affection was tempered by determination to keep Regazzoni in his mirrors at all times.

That was not easy in the early rounds, where both of them produced podium finishes, but at Silverstone came the result that all drivers dread: a win for their team-mate. Regazzoni gave Frank Williams his first grand prix victory. Not only had Jones done all the hard months of testing and toil beforehand, he had given the team its first pole position by a hefty 0.6 of a second and was leading the race until the 39th lap, before dropping out with an overheating engine. 'It really pissed me off. I had a 20 second lead. I was so pissed off that I hopped out, jumped in my road car and drove straight to London. I reckon I did the 150 or so kilometres in 45 minutes — with my wife shitting herself — only to hear on the radio that Regazzoni had won. I'd been with Frank for a while and I really wanted to be the driver who delivered his first win.'

It was typical of the hard-nosed, dogged way in which Jones had forged his career that he should turn up 2 weeks later for the following round, at Hockenheim, out-qualify his team-mate to claim a front-row start, and win. Regazzoni moved up to 2nd place, and the Williams team had achieved another first after 45 laps: a 1–2 finish. 'It was almost an anti-climax when I won that race. Frank couldn't believe it,' Jones recalls, 'He expected me to be jumping up and down too, but I wasn't ecstatic. I just went and had a cold Fosters. What I used to do was time it perfectly. I'd put the Fosters in the fridge of my motor home and — perhaps it was a bit presumptuous — but factor in the time it took to go up to the podium and then the press conference. I was always assured that it was just about frozen when I got back. It was an art, really.

'On race day, you know, I never used to eat. There were a few reasons for that. I didn't want food in my stomach in case of an accident. But it also made me feel leaner and meaner. I wanted to feel hungry. The problem with that was I'd lose 4 or 5 kilos during the race because I perspired a lot, and with nothing on my stomach, after a couple of cans of Fosters, I was anybody's!'

The next round in Austria proved easier still, and suddenly it was three wins in a row for Williams, two for Jones. 'Patrick just kept refining the car, little touches here and there. We knew the Renaults couldn't use all their turbo-power during the race because they'd either use too much fuel or blow up. But Patrick discovered a little aerodynamic thing that he put on the rear of the car — a little bit of aluminium. We checked it in a wind tunnel we hired. I wouldn't have thought it would make any difference, but the effect was just like a hand on the car, pushing it down. I could not believe the difference it made. That was when we scored our three wins.'

The complicated scoring system meant that it was impossible for Jones to win the world title, which was heading to Jody Scheckter, but he finished the season with a fourth win, at Montreal, and a third pole, at Watkins Glen. 'We had established ourselves as front runners.' The turn of the decade looked like producing a new world power, a new champion, but then, this was Formula 1. If a week was a long time in politics, in this game, a split-second could mean a lifetime.

CHAPTER THIRTEEN

The Next Champion

The necessary events had taken place, and as usual, there were casualties. The team owner, Frank Williams, had come through years of edge-cutting and occasional humiliation, harder and wiser for it, but he was unable to save some of the careers that had been left in his wake. There were two exceptions. Designer Patrick Head, who had made the Trojan — ineffective on the track but effective in wrecking Tim Schenken's Formula 1 career — had given up in despair before being lured back by Williams to work on the FW series. Then there was the unexpected, unheralded Aussie who, like most overnight successes, had in fact spent years grinding away with indefatigable commitment to work and self. It had been 13 years since he first ventured to Europe to make his name, 13 years in which the wheeling and dealing had also washed a few less fortunate souls, like Larry Perkins and Vern Schuppan, into the backwaters of Formula 1. That was the roulette wheel of motor sport. You had to keep breathing long enough to throw your marble onto the numbers and hope the right one came up.

Head refined his car again in 1980, to stay in front of his rivals. Everything in Formula 1 was a moving target. Clay Regazzoni moved to Ensign, so Williams hired another experienced driver: Argentine Carlos Reutemann. The chemistry in the garage would change from passive to volatile. Reutemann had bought Tim Schenken out of Brabham in 1972, then moved from Ferrari to Lotus, staying competitive, always hungry.

The season began in perfect harmony for Alan Jones: pole and victory in his team-mate's home grand prix. At the following round, in Brazil, Jones struggled for a good grid position for the first time in months, but such was his determination that he drove to 3rd behind René Arnoux in the Renault and Elio De Angelis in the Lotus. Reutemann, who had out-qualified Jones by three rows, failed again. There was concern in the camp after the South African Grand Prix at Kyalami, where Arnoux won again; Jones, qualifying 8th, failed to finish. Then at Long Beach in the United States, he collided with a lapped Bruno Giacomelli. Nelson Piquet took the win for Brabham. Clay Regazzoni crashed head-on into a concrete wall in that race. He survived, but was left paralysed from the waist down.

Williams seemed more at home in Europe, where Jones qualified on pole and finished 2nd in the Belgian Grand Prix. Reutemann won at Monaco. It was a rain-affected race, and Jones was out after 3 laps. After six races he was one of five drivers within 7 points of each other on the championship table. Nelson Piquet was leading.

At this stage, there was simmering heat between Bernie Ecclestone's FOCA and the Federation Internationale du Sport Automobile (FISA), a branch of the FIA headed by Frenchman Jean-Marie Balestre, had begun to affect Jones's title chances. There had been confrontations at Zolder and Monaco, where FOCA drivers had refused to attend compulsory briefings. The rumblings of revolution were still being heard. The following event, the Spanish Grand Prix, was to have been a championship round, but only FOCA teams competed. Jody Scheckter, Gilles Villeneuve, Jean-Pierre Jabouille, René Arnoux, Patrick Depailler, Bruno Giacomelli and Vittorio Brambilla were not there, so FISA ruled it a non-championship race. Jones won it, one of only six cars to finish. There were seven crashes and numerous retirements. 'I've always been credited with 12 grands prix wins but I say it was 13. I went there. They parked the transporter. I stayed at the hotel. I went to practice. I qualified. I raced. I won. I met King Juan Carlos, received the trophy. Now if Jean-Marie Balestre really had an axe to grind over the FOCA business, he should have called it off before we raced. I think the thing that really topped it off was that they didn't have a chair for his wife at the official box or something. He was a very volatile sort of frog.'

That only made Jones more determined to win the next race, in Balestre's France, especially when the home-grown Ligier team occupied the front row. FOCA and FISA had by then reached a truce to avoid further embarrassment for the sport, but Jones had suffered more than anyone. At Le Castellet he overhauled the Ligier cars and won, taking the series lead by 3 points. 'By that time they had the Australian anthem ready to play, but I couldn't find an Australian flag. So I really pissed off the French and drove my victory lap waving the Union Jack. Then I refused to get on the podium while Balestre was up there. They had to ask him to leave. The funniest thing, though, was that part of the prize was a Shetland pony, donated by the local amusement park down the road! This woman came up to the rostrum and even asked me to hop on it! So here was this Aussie, a million miles from home, with a Shetland pony. They told me his name was Dusko.'

The pony spent some weeks tied to the back of the Jones's motor home before being shipped back to Australia; this was no easy feat, given quarantine restrictions. Dusko, the French pony, had emigrated to the Jones's farm at Yea, Victoria, where he would live out his days in peace and contentment.

Jones had no shortage of horsepower in his workshop either, but the aerodynamically efficient Ligiers were a serious threat. They did, however, have the occasional breakdown, which was the only reason Jones was able to win at Brands Hatch. His championship lead extended to 6 points (over Piquet). Then it was pole and 3rd place in Germany, followed by 2nd in Austria, and an 11 point lead over Piquet.

The season turned again at Zandvoort, where Jones's problems with chassis damage from curb-hopping forced him to make an early pit stop and resulted in a pointless finish 3 laps down. Piquet won.

The paddock was solemn for the Italian Grand Prix following news that Patrick Depailler had died in a testing crash at Hockenheim. Piquet surged back into the battle by beating Jones into 2nd at the Imola circuit — it was the first time the grand prix had left Monza since 1949. The Brazilian had taken back the championship lead, by 1 point. There were 2 rounds remaining, but with drivers counting their best 11 of 15 rounds, under the 1980 points system a result would be possible after the following race, the Canadian Grand Prix.

Jones jumped Piquet in Montreal, where they shared the front row, much to the delight of the crowd. However, they came together when the Brazilian refused to give way going into the first corner. The crash caused so much chaos that the race had to be started again. Jones had suffered little damage but Piquet had to restart in a spare car. He was out 24 laps later with engine failure. The way was open for a fourth Australian victory in the Formula 1 championship. If Jones won, he could not be beaten in the final round: Piquet would need more than maximum points. Didier Pironi cared nothing for that, as he attacked Jones to spoil the occasion. It was a worrying time, until Jones was informed that Pironi was likely to be penalised for jumping the start. When that news was confirmed, he allowed Pironi to lead, and crossed the line 2nd. As predicted, Pironi was relegated to 3rd place. Alan Jones had won the championship by 13 points from Nelson Piquet.

'I had pole stitched up, but Bernie's Brabham team had made some pretty amazing adjustments to their qualifying set up, and in the last minutes of the session Piquet just blew everything else away. I was thinking, shit, I might lose this. Anyway, after that first rub, seeing him go into the fence, I thought I was away. Then they stopped the race. With Piquet's race car stuffed, they had to go back and use their spare car. It was just as quick, about 4 or 5 miles an hour faster than I was, but then it blew up. I won the championship.'

To confirm the title, Jones won the final race of the US Grand Prix, at Watkins Glen. Reutemann's 2nd placing also gave Williams their first constructors title. 'That last win was probably my best drive in Formula 1,' Jones recalls. 'I had a bit of a misunderstanding with Frank. He thought we had agreed on our deal for 1981 but I hadn't. It was a mix-up over pounds and US dollars. But the great thing about Frank was that he was one of the few owners who believed that if he was paying me all that money he should be listening to me. Otherwise I wouldn't be worth all that money. Other owners didn't subscribe to that. After I'd qualified fifth I told him the car was down on grunt. They changed the engine. I was quickest in the warm-up, made a blinding start from the third row, passed everyone then went off the circuit into the dust. I came back in 12th or 13th, but with nothing to lose, and the world title tucked away, I got stuck into it, and passed everybody. Carlos was the last one. He didn't want me to beat him but I went right around the outside of him. I won it by about 4 seconds. That and the French Grand Prix where I wore the Ligiers down were my best drives. Anyway, I quickly sorted out the deal with Frank after that.'

It was a relationship built on mutual belief and trust. Jones was not a conventional driver. He was not from the slim, sleek European mould. He was stocky, feisty and full of the best bullshit Australia could produce. 'Frank was a mad runner. Fanatical about jogging,' Jones recalls. 'When we were at a circuit he'd have a tracksuit on, ready to go for a run. A few people used to ask Frank what I did for fitness and he'd tell them, "I think he goes to the pub and has a few beers." That used to blow them away.

'I also used to act a bit naïve on occasions as well, telling people I didn't know things, that I was just lucky. There's a lot of "thought-planting" that goes on. Some drivers would admit to me, honestly, that they'd had a bad night's sleep or they felt nervous before a race. I couldn't understand why they'd tell me that. I'd never admit it. Half the races are run before you get in the cockpit, whether it's through psychology, physical fitness or mechanical preparation.

'Another advantage was that I was a fairly economical driver; that is, I wasn't white-knuckled all the time. When you're relaxed it doesn't sap your strength as much, mentally or physically. I used to race against blokes who could ride the Tour de France or run a marathon, but they'd still be fucked when they got out of the car. Rooted. What you do need is clarity of the mind.'

It is both wonderful and tragic that motor racing is so unpredictable. Just 3 years earlier, the odds that Alan Jones would be a world champion and Larry Perkins and Vern Schuppan would have given up on Formula 1 would have been massive. But that's what happened. By the end of 1980 Schuppan had established himself as a formidable Indy car and Can-Am driver in the United States. He started only 4 CART rounds, finishing 5th in 2 of them, but he still finished 10th in the championship — and every driver ahead of him had driven at least 9 rounds. It was tough but enjoyable. 'They were just all good blokes,' he recalls, 'the kind of guys who just wanted to drive something every weekend, sometimes during the week as well. That only changed when they grew a bit older and the series grew bigger. They just drove for fun. My problem was, I still could not get a look-in with one of the big teams, and if you weren't with them you couldn't compete.'

He prepared his own car, supplied by Tim Schenken's TIGA company, for the final 2 rounds of the Can-Am series, won by Geoff Brabham. Brabham was in a Lola T530, which was the car you had to have at that time. In most races, it filled the bulk of the top-10 placings. 'I remember when Geoff first started becoming interested in race driving,' Schuppan recalls. 'He and Michael Stillwell, Bib's son, were staying at our house in England in the 1970s when they decided to go to a race driving school at Brands Hatch. There he was, a decade later, beating me!'

While Geoff Brabham had landed, by 1980, in a strong team, Schuppan's car was well off the pace. 'I'd spent most of the year supervising the construction and development of that car at Tim and Howden Ganley's factory, which was quite funny, because for my entire career until then, I was barely on speaking terms with Tim. We of course became great friends. It was a pretty good car around corners, but for some reason it had terrible straight line speed. There was too much drag. So while I pursued this development for my own team, I kept on taking other drives to supplement the income.'

The scheduling of the Formula 1 season, the scheduling of the nomadic Australian Grand Prix and the evolutionary change of Australian open-wheel racing all seemed to favour Alan Jones in 1980. He was able to return home to a race that had long become inconsequential for the world's premier drivers but held enormous significance for this world champion. Australia had revised its racing rules in the 20 months since the previous year's event, and Jones was now allowed to use his Williams Formula 1 car against Formula 5000 and Formula Pacific, and the grand prix was part of an eight-race Gold Star series. It was none other than Bob Jane, with his enormous promotional power, who had driven this change, but the change was conditional on the race being staged at Jane's own circuit, Calder Park, which he had recently purchased.

'The Australian Grand Prix was in fact the second oldest in the world, after France, but by the end of 1979 it was almost dead, actually, it was probably dead,' Jane recalls. 'Alan Jones's father, Stan, had been one of my best friends for many years. So I had set about with a French friend of mine, Daniel Gerrard, to bring Alan with his Williams car and other F1 drivers to race here in 1980.'

Bob had lured national television coverage and a sprinkling of international names like Didier Pironi and Bruno Giacomelli. While the presentation of the event was not entirely smooth, the result was poetic. Jones won by a lap and history had come full circle.

As the motor sport world turned into 1981, there was a meeting that would change Formula 1 forever. The seeds of the famous Concorde Agreement were finally planted when FOCA agreed to fall into line with the FIA, of which FISA was the executive body. However, the teams assumed the lead role in financial and promotional arrangements and were involved in technical discussions.

Alan Jones had eyes only for a second world title, until it became clear that his own garage would be just as volatile.

Jones believes that had Williams raced as a team, they may have stopped Nelson Piquet winning the 1981 World Drivers Championship. Instead, the season became a self-destructive tangle of team-mates. Carlos Reutemann won the unofficial grand prix in South Africa, but Jones won the first race that counted for points: the United States Grand Prix at Long Beach. The duel flared quickly in the race at Rio, just 2 weeks later.

Reutemann had relegated Jones to row two in Rio, qualifying second behind home favourite, Piquet. The Brazilian, however, made a bad choice — to race on slick tyres when the track was still wet from earlier rain. Reutemann and Jones took control of the race. The problem came in the closing laps, when Jones expected Reutemann to allow him to pass. He refused. There were team orders in place. The World Champion was to be given every chance to defend his title. The crowd was aware of the situation when pit boards displayed by the Williams crew ordered Reutemann to move aside. The laps were ticked off, and on the final run, everyone expected the feisty Argentinian to make his point but pull over at the last minute. Instead, he rushed at the chequered flag.

From there to the end of the season the battle raged. Occasionally it descended into farce, such as in San Marino, where Reutemann drove into Jones shortly after the start, to prevent him from overtaking after a charge through the field. The champion responded brilliantly at Monaco, beating all but Villeneuve. It was a race he should have won. 'I was leading by 20 seconds, then had a fuel surge problem. Only the winner went to the podium at Monaco in those days, so I've never been there, and it's a race I dearly would have loved to win.'

The door remained open until the final couple of rounds, by which time technical problems had conspired with the sheer frustration of incompatibility within the team to deny Jones a second title. Before the season had even finished, he was teetering on a fateful decision. 'It's funny, really, but I had too much money. I was going home every Christmas where it's all sunny and there were barbecues going on. It was ironic, because all your mates are thinking, lucky bastard, he's going back to Europe in a few weeks, and I was thinking how much I wanted to stay home.'

The great event of the year was the final round. It was held in, of all places, a Las Vegas casino car park. Who would have bet that Alan Jones would have flown back to Australia to drive in the Bathurst 1000 then returned to not only win his last race before retirement, but use all his hard-won faculties to deny his obstreperous team-mate the title? 'My qualifying car was crook but my race car felt terrific. Carlos was on pole. He was a fairly emotional sort of person. I was beside him. I took him aside and said, "Carlos, the problem with where you are is that, heading into the first corner, there's a lot of shit on that side of the track. You know, being on pole, you're entitled to use whatever side of the track you want." I effectively talked him into heading for the outside and letting me have the inside line into the first corner! During the warm-up, I used that inside line as many times as I could to sweep the debris off it so that I could have the cleaner run. I not only led them all into the first corner, but he hit the shit and wound up 4th. From then I think he fell back. I lapped him.' Reutemann finished 8th. Piquet finished 5th and won the title by one point.

Jones, for all his troubles, was only 3 points behind Reutemann. 'Patrick Head reckons I drove better in 1981 than I did in 1980. It was just a couple of silly little mechanical problems that cost me the championship.'

Somehow, in the almost comical setting of that Caesars Palace concrete, it all made sense.

1981 was a better year for Vern Schuppan. If he were to risk his life at speeds approaching 400 kilometres an hour at Indianapolis, he might as well do it for himself. He acquired a McLaren M24 Band with a Ford Cosworth engine. 'I had this theory that the car would easily last the distance,' he recalls. 'I started 17th on the grid. I had a part-time pit crew; one was a doctor, another was a lawyer. I had the oldest car in the race and the only non-ground effect car in the race. It was so bad the mechanics didn't have the heart to tell me that we had a chronic fuel leakage which they couldn't fix in time; they just kept putting a blanket underneath it whenever it went in the pits, so the officials couldn't see it and disqualify us. I had no idea about that. All I knew was the car was too slow, but if we made good pit stops I could get close to their pace during the event, and that might be good enough.'

In Schuppan's home state of South Australia, West End brewers produced a commemorative beer can which they released at Indianapolis. It featured a picture of him and the car, including a biography. They may have overestimated his potential, but their optimism would be well placed. With Geoff Brabham also running a strong car in his rookie year, a Penske PC9,

Australia had its best chance of providing its first Indianapolis 500 winner. Not since Geoff's father raced there in the 1960s had they even gone close.

Schuppan's tortoise-like tactics almost paid off. He finished 3rd, behind the hares: Bobby Unser and Mario Andretti. Andretti, however, protested the result, claiming that Unser had passed under a yellow flag, and the top two positions were reversed. A later inquiry found that Andretti had done the same thing, so for a while there was a chance that both would be relegated and Schuppan awarded the victory. Stewards chose not to tamper with the result again. Andretti's win stood. 'For years later,' Schuppan recalls, 'every time I ran into John Cooper, who used to run the Indianapolis Moor Speedway, he would announce to everyone, "Well here's the man who actually won the 1981 Indy 500!" John reckoned that if I had been an American, they would have given me the race.' Schuppan's under-funded operation nevertheless banked a tidy $90,000, including bonuses.

Geoff Brabham finished 5th and won nearly $50,000; it was a brilliant debut and also made headlines in Australia. While Brabham continued in Can-Am for another successful season, Schuppan abandoned his plans to campaign the TIGA car. He had another more important mission: to win Le Mans, this time for the mighty Porsche team.

He had only been offered the drive for Porsche after Rick Mears, the Indy car champion, was burned during a pit stop in a race. Schuppan's team-mate was Jochen Mass. They qualified second, just behind the lead Porsche of Jacky Ickx and Derek Bell, and lost a couple of laps at the start, following some spark plug problems and a clutch failure. They fought back to second position and appeared to be travelling easily for much of the race. Then the car simply stopped, with Schuppan at the wheel, on the back of the circuit. It took him 35 minutes of radio instruction to work out the problem and bring the car back to the pits. He and Mass eventually finished 12th, an incredible performance given the stoppages they endured. Porsche were so impressed that they dubbed him 'the fastest mechanic in the world' and invited him back for another try in 1982, part of a full-time drive in the World Endurance Championship.

The year was far from over as Schuppan prepared to fly home for the Sandown Hang Ten 400 and the Bathurst 1000 with John Harvey. It would be a painful trip. Two weeks before, he crashed at 290 kilometres per hour in a CART race at Riverside, breaking some ribs. 'I suffered the second of two steering arm failures and the car went straight on at turn one, hitting a concrete barrier at an angle. It flipped the car, and I landed upside down on the infield. The roll bar saved my neck, but I was in a lot of pain, and stuck there. While I waited patiently for someone to get me out, I'll never forget hearing one of the track marshals warning everyone to keep away from the car because it was likely to blow up at any moment! They waited for a fire engine to arrive before they turned me over.'

Larry Perkins had made it to within metres of motor racing's Everest. He simply did not have the means to take those final few steps. It would haunt him for a while as he settled in back in Australia and pondered a new decade of adventure. 'I did go through withdrawal symptoms. For a couple of years there life was quite vague. I tried a lot of different things. I won the Australian Rallycross Championship in 1979, and raced with Pete Janson again at Bathurst, finishing 2nd. We were getting closer. Then we finished 2nd again in 1980 ... Brock and Jimmy Richards beat us both times. We had engine trouble in '81, the only time we weren't on the podium. I didn't really make any money. It still didn't bother me. We just lived in a flat in Melbourne.' He also became, with adventurer Hans Tholstrup, the first person to drive a solar-powered car across Australia. Perkins built the car with his brother Gary.

There was work on the engineering side repairing engines for Formula Pacific cars and some racing in that category's 4-round series. He won a round, but lost the title to Bruce Allison, who did not win a round. The enterprising Bob Jane had started to build Formula Pacific cars as the category grew to be the premier open-wheel feature. At the same time he continued his push to take the Australian Grand Prix back to the heights he believed it deserved as one of the world's oldest domestic grands prix. He was right on both counts. The 1981 Australian Grand Prix would be made up entirely of Formula Pacific cars. People would debate the right formula for the Gold Star series, however, for at least the next 20 years, as domestic open-wheel racing was crushed under the heavy herd of V8 touring cars.

Unlike the 1980 race, which fans had been sceptical of — they would give it a try on television but not fork out the price of admission — Bob Jane attracted 25,000 people to Calder Park. Alan Jones had decided to make a farewell appearance for the local fans, and was joined for the occasion by Nelson Piquet, the new Formula 1 champion Jacques Lafitte, who had been a title contender for much of the year and a 22-year-old Piquet protégé called Roberto Moreno, who ultimately upstaged them all. Can-Am Champion Geoff Brabham finished 3rd, just behind Piquet and just ahead of Perkins.

Alan Jones made his decision to retire at Donington, during testing for the 1982 season. 'It was so bloody cold you had to put the kettle on and pour boiling water on the door lock to open your car. I'm thinking, fuck this. I drove the new six-wheeled car. It didn't feel that much different. I hopped on a flight to Heathrow, then boarded a jumbo for Australia. It was dark and gloomy as we took off, but then we climbed, started to break through the cloud and soon it was just a white fluffy bed far below. With a can of Fosters in hand and all those familiar Qantas accents, it felt like I was home already. That seemed to confirm it for me. I got home and called Frank, told him I didn't want to go back.'

It was a feeling warmly welcomed by his wife and 3-year-old son, Christian, but that still did not make it easy. There would be dirty days spent on the seat of a tractor, grinding across those 2000 Yarra Valley acres. 'There were times,' Jones admits, 'when I'd shift my sore arse in the seat of that tractor, disturbed by a faint sound in the air, far above. I'd look up in the sky and wonder where that plane was going ...'

For a driver like Tim Schenken, who had seen plenty of talented drivers washed down the drains of world motor sport because they did not have the finances to climb from the gutter, making cars and managing teams with his TIGA Racing had been a strange experience. He gave drivers like Stefan Johansson, Jonathan Palmer, James Weaver, Andrea De Chesaris, Martin Brundle and Eddie Jordan their first serious entry into open-wheel racing. He even supplied cars for Vern Schuppan. And he may have despised the well heeled young men who tried to buy their way in when they were his rivals, but he had even come to feel sorry for the wealthy drivers who so often pushed more talented rivals out of a seat, but then lacked the skill to support their ambitions. 'You can teach them theoretically, but once they were in the car ...'

TIGA Racing would eventually fold, but Schenken left his hands-on role in the early '80s. He worked with John Fitzpatrick Racing in the United States, where he and Brigitte, by then with a son and twin daughters, lived happily for a few years. He had accumulated other business interests that would ensure a stable future for him and his family, and he eventually returned to Australia, where he took up the offer of a senior position with CAMS — he has been there ever since. He had been guilty of being in the wrong places at the right times, but had satisfied himself that the destination had been worth the journey.

Vern Schuppan in 1982 had proved conclusively that he would never be successful in the CART series, having taken another three-drive tour of the underworld with Kraco Racing. 'I was so sick of all those part-time drives in Indy cars that Jennifer and I decided to move back to Europe.'

By this time he had also witnessed the reality of the harsh concrete walls that lined America's oval tracks. He saw Gordon Smiley's car disintegrate in one of the most horrifying crashes ever seen at Indianapolis. Smiley's lifeless body, still strapped into the seat, which was still attached to the engine, was spinning awkwardly across the circuit. It was so bad that Rick Mears urged other drivers not to watch, saying that 'I couldn't go within 10 miles an hour of my previous pace after I saw it.' Schuppan also saw Danny Ongais slam into a wall; his car disintegrated, debris all over the track. 'It looked like a plane crash. I drove past and there was Ongais still sitting in what was left of the frame, his legs bent back towards his body at terrible angles. Lap after lap you watch while they clean it up. The weird thing is, you talk about ghoulish behaviour and people wanting to see crashes, but drivers are the worst. They can't help it.'

Porsche were a better bet, and there he finally found a home, though in some ways it would be a frustrating sequence of races. At Le Mans, he finished 2nd again with Jochen Mass to team-mates Ickx and Bell. At Spa, the pairings were switched, but even with Bell as a co-driver he finished 2nd to Ickx and Mass. In the Japanese round at Fuji, he and Bell failed to finish, while Ickx and Mass won again.

Alan Jones had been restless in retirement, winning the Australian GT championship with a Porsche 935 and dabbling in the Gold Star series in the Ralt RT4. Life on the farm was starting to tire him, especially after he fell off a horse and broke his femur. He was looking forward to having a crack at the Bathurst 1000 in a Mazda RX7 when a most surprising telephone call came from Europe. It came in mid-August 1982. Didier Pironi had crashed into Alain Prost in the Hockenheim Formula 1 race. Pironi's career was over. His team was looking for a replacement.

'Mr Jones ...' the voice began, 'could you please come and deputise for Mr Pironi?' The team was Ferrari.

Jones had a long memory. He had been sweating on a chance to pay back Ferrari for the rejection that had almost killed his career in late 1977. 'I couldn't believe my luck. "Yes, sure," I said. "Love to. No dramas." Well I fucked them around as much as I could for about a week. They'd ring up and I'd tell someone to put them off. I was always at the butchers, or the bakers or the hairdressers or something. It's funny. What goes around comes around, but then it goes around again. In hindsight, I should have just said yes, because I still had my eye on a possible comeback and it was foolish of me to close the door on that out of spite. On the other hand, my wife just about collapsed at the thought of my returning to Formula 1, so that influenced me a little bit too. But wait for this ... here's the best bit ... when they couldn't get me, guess who they did get? Mario Andretti. He then went and put the thing on pole at Monza. It could have been me sitting there. I really regret that.'

Jones put all that aside to shore up the field for the Australian Grand Prix 3 months later, but his engine failed in the warm-up and he didn't even make it to the start line. A deflated Calder Park crowd watched Alain Prost cruise to victory, followed by Jacques Lafitte, making it a 1–2 for Ligier. Bob Jane's ardent support of the event had borne fruit, with 26 cars ready to race before Jones's withdrawal. Jones's problem, however, was not just that the zest for racing had not quite been purged from his system. He had also inherited from his father the trait that he least wanted: an inability to consolidate his wealth.

The second phone call from Europe was the decisive one. 'Jackie Oliver was asking if I'd be interested in looking at a new car for the team that had evolved from my former employer, Shadow. It was Arrows, and they would be testing at Willow Springs. I said I'd have a look.'

CHAPTER FOURTEEN

Brock and Johnson

Australian touring car racing in the late '70s and early '80s had more than its own share of politics and power play. Only the scale of economies was different to the world in which Jones, Perkins, Schuppan and Schenken had immersed themselves.

Colin Bond did not believe that 1978 could be so different from the heady successes of the previous year. 'It was a bit of a disaster. The Holdens got their act together. We lost our team manager, Carroll Smith, had to return to the United States because he only had a one-year visa. The budget hadn't been increased. Really, the only good thing about moving from Holden to Ford turned out to be my rally involvement. I ran that team from 1977, using Escorts, which were fantastic rally cars. We won the Australian Rally Championship with Greg Carr driving.'

While Bond was able to shelter behind screens of dislodged dirt in the forests, Allan Moffat remained under increasingly intense scrutiny as the fans came to see touring car racing as defined by the fortunes of two manufacturers. 'To go from winning every race, to winning just one … you could say it was a horrible year.'

The only highlight for Moffat was off the track, and it was a very special one for an ex-Canadian. He was awarded an OBE in the Queen's Birthday honours.

'We had built enough credibility and prestige in 1977 to lay the foundations for another 10 years of factory dominance, had the appropriate financial commitment been made.'

John Harvey recalls the era with wonder, given the curious origins of touring car racing. 'Oh it was intense. It was more than just Brock–Moffat; it was Holden–Ford. That was the key to it. We had gone through periods when Ford had blown us away. Then Ford made the mistake of sitting on their hands after winning a couple of championships and Bathurst, when Moffat kept saying, "You can't just do nothing. Holden won't take this lying down." They did nothing. Holden built a better car, came on strong and got on the top of them. It even got a bit personal sometimes, when people wouldn't talk to each other.'

It was in the cyclical nature of Australian motor racing that Holden should be shovelling support back to their prodigal son, Peter Brock, just as Moffat's team was drowning. 'Holden rang me, out of the blue, and said they wanted me back,' Brock recalls. 'Moffat had that big win. They weren't getting much joy. John Shephard, the new boss, loved the idea of driving the opposition crazy. He would even make the guys park the cars in front of the pit area, just to polish them. It was about presentation. It drove the rival teams nuts and made everyone feel on top of their game. It's fairly common now, but in those days it was pretty new.'

Brock, driving for the first time with Jim Richards, won the 1978 Bathurst 1000 race by a lap. 'Richo and I were buddies. We just locked in. I would qualify the car and all that. He would just go up there, jump in, do his stint with no fuss. Off we went.'

Dick Johnson, teamed once more with Vern Schuppan, finished a powerful 5th. 'You know, I don't know why Dick had me back,' Schuppan says, 'after I had done such an ordinary job the year before. I was keen to redeem myself, actually.'

'Vern was so easy to get on with,' Johnson recalls, 'Not a prima donna. He drove within his limits — and those cars are not easy to drive after open-wheelers.'

Another startling result was Jack Brabham driving with Brian Muir to finish 6th. He had saved his best result in the great race for his final appearance. Within a year he would be knighted for his services to motor racing

* * *

Kevin Bartlett discovered in 1979 that in the cyclonic fury of commercial competition in motor sport there is sometimes a benevolent eye. He found it after an unexpected meeting with Kerry Packer. 'He called me to his office, but he didn't say much; still doesn't. He basically just offered me help when I needed it. We had known each other over the years and he knew how much I'd struggled. I said, "Well, I picked the sport. Nobody picked it for me." He's a very nice person and I respect him. A lot of the things that he does behind the scenes to help people, people who are less fortunate, are not widely known. He does charitable things that are never talked about and it's not my place to say any more than that.'

It had been a sequence of fruitless excursions to Bathurst since that famous win in 1974, but with sponsorship from Packer's Nine Network, Bartlett bought a Chevrolet Camaro; it was lighter than a Falcon, but had the same horsepower. The problem was that the teams which wanted to run Camaros were not allowed to use disc brakes, which were standard in the United States, where the car was built. There were more problems when, as late as the Sandown endurance event, CAMS had still refused to legalise them and they were left sitting on the dock. The irony of all this was that Bartlett would be unable to drive the car at Bathurst anyway. He still had not recovered from his latest horrific crash in Formula 5000. When he did find fitness, he found a new world of trouble with officialdom.

Brock, ever the restless spirit, took another detour in 1979 that tested Holden's allegiance to the limit. He insisted on taking their new Commodore on the Round Australia Trial, against the wishes of a Bathurst-obsessed management. In the footsteps of Brabham and Firth, he carved yet another special place for himself in the records. A mission that cynics had described as a publicity stunt became one of his greatest personal achievements as he fully tested his 'mechanical sympathy', teasing, urging, at times flogging the Commodore like a tired team of bullocks through the harshest of back country. He survived a near-somersault, when he hit a ditch at 180 kilometres an hour: the car skimmed the ground on its bullbar before deciding it wanted to rest on its wheels instead. It would not die.

Former team-mate Colin Bond led the event from east coast to west in a Ford Cortina rally car before crashing north of Perth. They repaired the car but it was never competitive after that. By that stage, only a couple of dozen competitors were still in contention. Then Brock took over. On one stage, estimated to take more than 4 hours, he covered the kilometres in just over 2. Two competitors were killed on a following stage. The trial continued. As the teams careered into the vast, wild territory across the top of Australia, drivers were starting to suffer from severe exhaustion. They were hallucinating. 'I remember asking my co-driver,' Brock recalls, 'is that sun going down or coming up? I remember seeing a black dog running along beside me. He was often there. The trouble was, I was doing about 170 kilometres an hour at the time. I had no idea what was going on.' By that stage Barry Ferguson, Wayne Bell and Dave Boddy, in another Holden team Commodore, had taken the lead. Brock was told to conserve 2nd place. He refused.

The trial ended for Colin Bond when his car hit a rock near Borroloola, pushing the sump guard through the steering rack, into the sump and breaking a rod. Adventurer Hans Tholstrup towed them behind his big Chevy for 100 kilometres to the end of the stage, at Borroloola. 'Most terrifying trip I've ever had,' Bond recalls. 'We were weaving back and forth on the end of a tow rope in dust so thick I could barely see his tail lights. I knew that I was never more than 8 feet off the road, though, because that's how long the rope was.'

Only 13 cars would finish the 20,000 kilometres. At the front, it was Holden, 1, 2 and 3. Brock's determination to take a historic victory that would sell thousands of Commodores was typified by one of the final desperate stages, in Victoria's snow country. 'I wasn't far in front, and had about 100 kilometres to go. I was in second gear, going up this logging track at about 60 to 80 kilometres an hour. When I got to the top, I couldn't change gear. The gearbox jammed in second. I called them on the two-way radio. We calculated that if I tried to finish the event stuck in second, I couldn't win it. They'd catch me. By that time, Barry, Wayne and Dave were trying to nail me. They were into it. We pulled out the WD40 and tried everything, but couldn't fix it. So one of us kicked it — just gave it a kick — and there it was. This humungous slab of mud just fell out of the gearbox. The gears were freed. Yeeeeeeeeees! I went from the lowest depths to the highest heights in a second. Off I went.'

The event almost destroyed him. An already thin Brock had been reduced to a disturbing state, several kilos lighter, eyes blackened from less than 30 hours' sleep in a fortnight. It took him weeks to recover, after living on determination and adrenaline for almost the entire trip. When he did recover, it was as if he had been reborn in some new impenetrable form. He had evolved into an even tougher, more confident competitor than before.

With John Harvey, who was still part of the Holden establishment, Brock inflicted some painful defeats on rivals over the next two seasons, but when it came to Bathurst, he and Jim Richards appeared to be invulnerable, completing a treble. 'In 1979 we still had basically the same sort of machinery as the year before, with a little bit of a tweak here and there,' Brock says. 'Some trick wheels. Bits and pieces. Bridgestone had also made a comeback and started making our tyres. They were terrific. But the Repco Round Australia Trial made us feel like we were on a roll. In that year, it was like we just couldn't lose a race if we tried. The funny thing was, I didn't win the championship, but it felt like I'd won everything.'

No one seemed to have the financial support or the skill to challenge them, but in 1980, one driver went very close. Dick Johnson, waiting with dirty shoes at the doorway to prosperity, had decided in 1980 to dig deep into his own pockets. 'I said to Jilly,' he recalls, 'that we really need to get back into this and have a serious shot at it. If it works out, fine. If it doesn't, tell me to call it quits and I'll walk away from motor racing altogether.'

With small purses from equally small but keen investors, Johnson bought a used XD Falcon shell into which he poured his best components. He mortgaged the house, recruited a makeshift team (which worked seven-day weeks) and gave up working at his service station to try full-time driving. By July he was on his way to Lakeside, hoping that he had not reached another dead-end. The car barely made practice, was hauled in for a wheel alignment, and went on to win both races. Brock beat him in the CRC 300, a dress rehearsal for Bathurst run at Amaroo Park, but there was hope and fire in those deep blue eyes. In Johnson's own words, fans had been 'bored witless' with Brock winning everything and it was time to strike.

He qualified second to Kevin Bartlett's Camaro at Bathurst. 'It was 10 grand for pole, zero for second. I missed out by a tenth,' Bartlett muses. Perhaps it was an omen.

When the race began, everything seemed to fall into place for Johnson. Bartlett had told officials time and time again that without disc brakes his car was not just ineffective, it was unsafe, and true to that prediction, he lost brakes and tripped over a Holden Gemini. Johnson had, for the first time, a powerful, light yet strongly built, well-prepared car that looked like upstaging them all. He was leading the race decisively after 16 laps. Moffat was in strife with mechanical trouble. Brock had made a long pit stop after crashing into a back marker and came out 1 lap behind him.

Johnson had predicted before the race that he could beat them all, but on lap 17, one of the most celebrated cases of misfortune in the history of Australian motor sport befell him. 'When I came through the cutting, the section just after mountain straight, I saw a flag marshal waving white, signalling that there was a pick-up truck on the circuit. What he didn't — or couldn't — signal was what the driver of the truck was about to do. The driver had noticed a rock and stopped to pick it up. I focused on the truck as I went past in second gear, at about 120 kilometres an hour. Then, as I moved over for what should have been an easy pass, I saw the rock. There was no room to go between the truck and the rock. I went further right, up the bank, to avoid it, but the left front hit it, and smashed. The tyre deflated, and I shot back across the road and almost cleared the fence before coming to rest. Brock will tell you that he had earlier driven past the rock and missed it, but anyone could have missed when it was on the track by itself. By the time I got there the truck had parked and left me with nowhere to go.' Johnson's race was over.

Bathurst had become the national focal point on the October long weekend, following years of dedicated and ever-improving television coverage. If the Melbourne Cup stopped the nation, Johnson's rock had stunned the nation. At 35, having seen chances go by like early trains, Dick Johnson now felt only one thing larger and heavier than that infamous object back down the road: the lump in his throat.

'Ivan Stibbard of the ARDC came up to me later in the pits. They had brought the rock back with the car. Ivan gave me the rock. He said, "Here's the culprit." The rock has stayed with Dick Johnson ever since, proudly displayed at his Queensland workshop. No one was ever able to determine just how it got there. No one owned up to throwing it or even innocently dislodging it. Claims of sabotage or conspiracy just did not make any sense, and were quickly washed away in the flood of moral and financial support that followed.

It had been Johnson's sixth attempt to win Bathurst, and clearly his best chance. He explained on television to a nation of sympathetic fans that he had staked everything on the race ... all his savings. The switchboard at the Seven Network was jammed with calls from people wanting to donate money. Edsel Ford himself made contact with them, guaranteeing that he would match every donation dollar for dollar. Ford and the fans raised $72,000. Letters, telegrams and calls came from all over the world. There was a downside, though. A couple of people whom Johnson thought were friends came up with schemes to offer money, get the matching half from Ford, and split the difference. Johnson was disgusted. One of the nicer gestures, however, was small-time sponsor Ross Palmer offering Johnson his entire marketing budget, $50,000, for the following season. When you weighed it all up, the incident occurred on lap 17 of 163. Anything could have happened in the next 146 precipitous laps of the mountain. There were so many ways Dick Johnson could have been mercilessly brought undone, ways that would not have generated such public sympathy. The rock, in its innocent, oblique way, had ensured that the crisis-ridden Dick Johnson Racing would be back.

By the time the 1981 Bathurst 1000 loomed, the term coined by television commentator Mike Raymond had sunk into the Australian psyche: Peter Perfect. Brock's achievements were acknowledged even by the Federal Government. He had won the Order of Australia Medal, at the age of 35. 'I remember sitting in the room with all these important people, and one guy there I spoke to was the head of ASIO. He's telling me all this stuff about international intrigue and spies and things and I thought, I've hit the big-time here. I did feel like a fish out of water. It seemed so strange, like I was watching all this happen to someone else.'

Allan Moffat spent the early years of the decade once again redefining his place in the tribal war. He was not idle, winning the 1980 Australian Sports Car Championship in a Porsche 934 produced by Alan Hamilton. He was given a shell by Ford, and in 30 days built a car for Bathurst. In the meantime he even took a one-off drive in Brock's second Commodore at Sandown. It was a promotional deal with the Sandown Light Car Club. They produced a 1–2 finish. Brock first, of course.

Moffat took up with Mazda in 1981, a relationship that would prove very satisfying. 'Mazda Australia approached me and asked me if I would race a rotary-engined RX7. It turned out to be a very pleasant chapter in my career that would last for 4 years.'

He would come back to Ford, but never again as the factory favourite: Ford had found a new hero, the lovable battler with the quick wit.

There had also been a curious, but significant comeback in the early '80s. Frank Gardner kept to his vow not to race seriously again, but there was still a treasure of knowledge in his head. BMW would make good use of it in 1980, employing him as an engineer and manager. Together, they established the

John Player Special (JPS) BMW team, based in Sydney, with Allan Grice driving a 318i turbo. There Gardner set new Australian standards in preparation and presentation of cars and teams and performance of pit crews.

Colin Bond, who had finished 2nd in his class in a Ford Capri in the 1980 Bathurst 1000, approached 1981 with a mind more intent on rallying. 'I had brought out the 1980 World Champions, Bjorn Waldegaard and Hans Thorszelius, to run in the Southern Cross Rally in a Ford Escort. It was a huge boost for rally fans in Australia. I also brought out 1981 World Champions Ari Vaatanen and David Richards for that event. I stayed friendly with Ari and Dave over the years. I remember Ari asking me one day "Colin, how many rollovers have you had this year?" I said, "None, Ari." He said, "I have had more than a dozen. How do you find your limit?" I admit that that was the difference driving overseas. We didn't have the budgets to wreck cars in order to push the envelope. Even in those days, overseas, drivers' wages were starting to go into the multi-millions. We were not on the same page as those people. As for Dave ... it's amazing to think that from there he went on to form Pro-Drive, running the Subaru World Rally team, take over the television rights to the World Rally Championship, and run the BAR Formula 1 team. He went a long way.' Bond's Capri finished 3rd in its class in 1981. In the following two years he would compete again for an outright win, first with Kevin Bartlett, then with Allan Grice, but regular employment was what was needed.

In the few months between that fateful 1980 Bathurst race and the 1981 championship season Dick Johnson made an amazing climb from despair to elation, thanks to generous support. But that support brought a new kind of pressure. He felt obliged to repay the debt. He had also risen to equal status, at least in the eyes of Ford fans, with his arch rival Peter Brock. Brock remained one of Australia's sporting icons, forever in the public glare. He was fascinated by the entire process of media, marketing, promotion and racing. From circuit to circuit in Australia and New Zealand he bounced, creating a tornado of activity that has barely ceased since. His special vehicles were selling, his race cars were winning, and his face was forever grinning. He made his third excursion to Europe in 1981, driving a Porsche with Jim Richards and Colin Bond at Le Mans. It was a rank failure, highly embarrassing for Porsche, which supplied the car and the crew but no one cared. He loved it all, not with the arrogance that some heroes succumb to. It was more of a boyish wonder.

Johnson, the blue-eyed battler, mustered everything he had to beat Brock in one of the great touring car titles. They traded race for race until it came down to the final round, which Johnson won by 0.2 of a second from Brock. Brock returned the favour in the Sandown 500, scoring his seventh consecutive win in that event. The impending Bathurst duel was making headlines long before they reached the mountain.

There were other chances. Kevin Bartlett's Camaro was back, with disc brakes at last, and he celebrated by taking pole position again, next to Johnson. He led the race for 23 laps before a clash with lapped driver Ron Wanless in a Commodore took him out of the race.

Brock, driving once again with Jim Richards, had broken a rear axle in what had seemed like an innocent rub with Bartlett early in the race. He spent a long time in the pits, leaving Johnson and co-driver John French in charge. It would turn out to be a very important lead. On lap 120, 2nd-placed Bob Morris and 6th-placed Christine Gibson, a few laps down, collided at McPhillamy Park, causing a massive pile-up, much like the one that stopped the 1969 race. This one, however, stopped it for good. Dick Johnson was declared the winner. Only three other drivers — Bob Jane, Allan Moffat and Peter Brock — had won the Touring Car Championship and the Bathurst 1000 in the same year.

'With all the support I had after 1980, I had never felt more pressure in my life. I didn't want to let anyone down,' Johnson recalls.

His victory also redefined the relationship between Ford and Holden. It was a true contest again. However, for the first time since the mid-1960s, when Alfa had been knocking on the door to outright victory, there were other significant players emerging. Allan Moffat and Derek Bell finished 3rd and won their class in the Mazda RX7, beginning a new period of touring car tension. In 1982 that would escalate dramatically.

'Moffat,' recalls Brock, 'was a pain in the butt with that little thing, especially on tracks that suited. He had dropped out for a bit, but he really started to come good again with the Mazda.'

'We could have won the race in 1981, had it not been for the crash,' Moffat recalls. 'With 20 odd laps to go we were sitting pretty, gassed up and ready to sprint to the finish, while the two fellas in front of us needed to make their final pit stops.'

*   *   *

Frank Gardner signed up Jim Richards to drive for his JPS BMW team in 1982 and was so impressed he believed Richards could have driven successfully in Formula 1 had he been given the chance. 'When I first rubbed shoulders with Jimmy I thought, shit, what a fantastic disposition. He had a good comprehension, understood his cars, wasn't afraid of work — the ideal composition for the professional driver. He was light years ahead of the others. He wasn't the commercial type. He didn't sell himself as well as others. But he was the best, and easy on the car. Other drivers might go through a few gearboxes in a meeting. Jimmy wouldn't. He had great mechanical sympathy.' They ran two black-liveried cars, the 635 in the ATCC and a slick little 318i turbo in the newly created Australian GT Championship. Success came several times in rounds of the latter, but not in the touring cars, where it really counted. Still, the sponsors were happy, for everyone could see they were always trying. For Bathurst, Richards was teamed with Englishman David Hobbs, with a second car for Gardner's old friend and 1967 World Champion, Denny Hulme, who paired with young Stephen Brook. Reliability got Richards and Hobbs's car to 6th place.

Replacing Richards at the Holden Dealer team in 1982 was Larry Perkins. Peter Brock had seen the potential that had been largely untapped since Perkins's return from Europe, and offered him work as an engineer and part-time driver. Perkins did not think it was a big deal at first, running the race team and workshop, as well as driving in the endurance rounds.

'I admit that when I went in there for the first time,' Perkins recalls, 'I made some very quick changes and Peter sacked some of his "good buddies" — who were fleecing him, in my view, on the payroll but not working.'

Perkins presided over another 3 consecutive years of Brock victories at Bathurst, although championship wins were harder to come by. In all those wins he co-drove with Brock; John Harvey joined them on top of the podium in 1983 following a mid-race change of cars. For Brock, it was a total of eight Bathurst wins. He truly was the King of the Mountain. 'I've got to tell you, '83 was good, but '84 was dynamite. I'd go home from a race and Bev would say, "How did you go?" and I'd say, "We finished third" and she'd say, "Oh? What went wrong?" It was just crazy.'

Allan Moffat raised the hackles of his rivals for 4 years with the RX7, which many believed was not a touring car at all. He finished 6th, 2nd and 3rd at Bathurst, driving with Japanese Yoshimi Katayama and former Australian motorcycle racer Gregg Hansford. He won the 1983 Touring Car Championship and competed for the Japanese factory at Daytona and Le Mans, where they won their class. 'I felt very humbled by the fact that the Japanese wanted to take a foreigner in their international team. They had very good drivers in Japan. They made me feel like I was part of the team and not just some ring-in from Australia.

'Le Mans was not everything I expected; it was more. This was the place that was world famous, in existence since the 1920s, at the heart of everything the FIA stood for. Terrific atmosphere. What I wasn't ready for was the speed of the car down Mulsanne Straight, and when the big ball in the sky went to sleep, corners that seemed fairly accessible became dark and difficult because of the ordinary lights on the car. The Japanese were not only so polite, but the preparation of the vehicle was excellent and the planning was so methodical: you're in, you're out, no flap in the pits. Never lifted the bonnet for the whole 24 hours, from what I recall.'

Dick Johnson found through the early 1980s that his misfortune at Bathurst had become a badge of courage which was worth almost as much as Brock's victories. He won his second Touring Car Championship in 1982; he regarded that as one of his most satisfying achievements.

The Hardie's Heroes run-off for the final 10 grid positions in the 1983 Bathurst 1000 will be remembered only because of Johnson's apparent attempt to make a tree house out of his Falcon. In one of the most horrifying crashes in the history of Bathurst, he was roaring through Forrest's Elbow, centimetres wider than planned, enough to lightly touch a tyre barrier placed on the exit into Conrod Straight. The steering arm broke and he sailed over the gully on the right side of the track and landed in a clump of gum trees. The car almost disintegrated around him.

'You really stick your neck out on those 1-lap dashes. If it hadn't been for that stack of tyres catching the front wheel, I would have been fine. I remember going into the trees and the car just stopping. I tried to get out of the driver's door. It wouldn't open. So I crawled over to the other side, and from the moment I opened that door till the time I walked up the back of the pits, I don't remember a thing. Brocky apparently picked me up when he saw the crash and gave me a lift.'

What happened next was just one of many miracles worked by the Bathurst TAFE College, whose students had again taken on their traditional role of repairing damaged cars in time for the great race. Johnson lined up in 10th, but lasted only 61 laps. It may have been because Kevin Bartlett was his co-driver — perhaps just too much bad luck for one car to handle!

One year later, Johnson charged back and won his third ATCC title championship, but Brock was still unstoppable at Bathurst.

Brock knew that whether he was winning or Johnson was winning, 'It was very much a rivalry that perpetuated what we both knew: there was an insatiable appetite for this Holden versus Ford stuff. I don't think it was ever more intense, not even today. It had been building to a crescendo. The fans were extremely vocal. It was fantastic for the sport. A lot of people involved with the sport think the other team should never be allowed to win, but I think that it's great. It makes us stronger. It makes the sport stronger.'

By this time, Brock had turned HSV into a thriving business, with Larry Perkins as his chief engineer and John Harvey running the team. It was a powerful operation and blending of personalities. 'I got on well with Peter and John,' Perkins recalls, 'and an important thing was that I wasn't a threat to anyone. A lot of drivers are headstrong in those situations and ego takes over. Now I was still only 34, and had every reason to be like that, having driven in Formula 1, but I had no trouble with the relationship at all.'

Then a bizarre chapter in the volatile Holden–Brock history changed all that. The change in the Brock philosophy started in 1984, when he and Bev had decided to embrace a new lifestyle. The smoking, eat-anything star of old had, on the cusp of his forties, turned to healthy food and alternative medicine. There was more. Brock's insatiable yen to broaden his boundaries led him to embrace radical scientific concepts, and one of those was the 'energy polariser'.

Perkins remains diplomatic, but firm. 'I was given the job of running the team. Brock sometimes would come in and put his engineering views forward, and I wouldn't always welcome them. I suppose I became less tolerant of that in the latter stages of the relationship. But it really came to a head when I heard that Brock had been into the factory and stuck all these crystal things on the engine while it was on the dynamometer.'

Brock was certainly one of many people who understood that crystals and magnets, operating together, had the power to change molecules. He also believed that if they were properly harnessed, it might be possible to improve the performance of a metallic instrument like an engine. He only ever applied the concept to the production vehicles, not the race cars, but that would prove an even greater problem when it came to manufacturer approval. 'My motives were always based on, "Well here's an idea. Let's give it a go." I was never hampered by fear of the unknown. Let's get it clear. The only other commercial application of a quartz crystal was in a quartz wristwatch and it worked in exactly the same way. The rest of the comments were based on ignorance and superstition and I'm not into either of those. You become a bit more circumspect as you get older, but I've always been just a curious human being. A lot of other people out there may be too ... but not necessarily in public. I explained it to some journalists, but they just stood there and asked me how were they supposed to write it. I replied, "Well, how do you explain how a light bulb works?" I think anyone trying to understand it should read a few books on quantum physics.

'Some time later, I was talking to Jackie Stewart about the whole thing and he said to me, "Oh, those things were everywhere in those days. Lots of people caught onto those. It became a hot topic in Europe too." Jackie told me that the mistake I made was in the application of the idea, not in the idea itself.'

Perkins called an urgent meeting. 'I never sought an explanation as to how the crystals worked. I treated it as nonsense, but I respected the fact that he owned the team. I just told him I didn't support what he was doing and that either he ran the team or I ran it. He told me that he wanted to keep using these things and I stood up, shook hands, and left. That was it.'

There were no hard feelings from Brock. 'I could sense that Larry deserved the opportunity to go and do his own thing. I really didn't want him to leave. I tried for a while to get him to come back, which I probably shouldn't have. I think it was just the catalyst for a change that was inevitable.'

The experimentation continued. Brock neither sought publicity, nor tried to hide from it. For once, he just did not anticipate what was around the corner. In the wake of Perkins's departure, the paddock was veritably simmering with whispers and sniggers. The fans seemed impartial, but the establishment was rapidly divided. Some were supportive, others contemptuous. Holden certainly could not see the point. Their marketing self-defence mechanisms switched on and barriers locked into place: after failing to persuade Brock to drop the polariser, they cut their ties with him.

'The general feeling of the employees was that they loved being there,' Brock recalls. 'We were turning out some pretty good cars. We became extraordinarily successful. Perhaps we'd become the target for a lot of people, too. I really couldn't believe it. What had I done wrong? I didn't realise for a long time that there was a concerted effort to minimise what we were trying to do.'

He never backed down. With Holden went an estimated $10 million of annual business to the Brock enterprise. 'I suppose I'm a pioneer,' he reflects, 'and they say pioneers get eaten by natives.'

Perkins, like Bond before him, went to the last place that Holden fans expected him to go: Dick Johnson. They would finish 7th after qualifying 3rd in the 1985 Bathurst, in a Mustang, before Perkins realised that he too was born to be a team owner. After all, he was as outspoken as Brock or Johnson had ever been!

The remaining years of the 1980s and the turn into the 1990s saw the character of touring car racing clouded by a new phase. In 1985, it went global. Group A was introduced to open up the category to all kinds of cars, provided they retained the shape of their production-line equivalents. Power-to-weight ratio and tyres were brought into parity by regulation. It gave Australian drivers the chance to compete in Europe, where there were plans for a world championship. That plan brought two old rivals together.

Brock and Moffat had previously driven for the same team once, in that curious Sandown start, but never together. It was a brilliant marketing move. Moffat had not even raced in 1985, floating for a year in the wilderness following 4 enjoyable years with Mazda. 'I got a phone call from John Harvey, who wanted me to have lunch with him and Peter to talk about driving for them. All I said was, "Do we have to wait for lunch? Can we make it morning tea?" The funny thing was, after all those years of competition, I didn't even know how to get there. I had to get a street directory out to find the address of Peter's headquarters! By that afternoon I was driving a Commodore home.'

They won the first event they contested together, the Wellington 500 in New Zealand, in January 1986. 'For so long I didn't know who he was other than this bloke I had to stay in front of. Then I was saying, "Why didn't we start this 15 years earlier?"' Moffat recalls, and Brock felt the same way.

Brock had mapped out a European campaign: he needed to learn the circuits, gather data and be ready for the first official World Championship, which was to start in 1987. Their best result was 5th at the Donington and Hockenheim endurance events. They also won the Kings Cup for highest-placed team in the Spa 24 hour. They returned to Australia and finished 5th at Bathurst, but by the time the 1987 season rolled around, Brock and Holden had parted over the polariser dispute. The entire Holden Dealer team operation had closed.

Moffat brought in his own sponsorship, bought a car and made an assault on the first round of the new championship at Monza. He and Harvey won. 'The car was brand new. It had never turned a wheel before we flew it to London, then to Italy. John and I then continued through to France, Spain and Germany. We also went to Spa again for the 24 hour race, finishing 4th, behind three Ford Sierras, but winning our class.' But neither funding nor inclination could carry them as far as Bathurst that year, especially after they'd seen how ineffective the Commodore had been against the Sierras in full flight.

'I have never heard anyone in the fraternity say a bad word about John Harvey in 30 years,' says Moffat. 'He was an unbelievably loyal, strong backdrop to Peter, exceptionally gifted with running the team, keeping it going while Peter was off doing other things. John is a credit to the sport.'

Solid success came to Frank Gardner's BMW team in 1985, with Jim Richards scoring 17 wins from 21 starts, including six straight in the ATCC and four out of five in the Endurance Championship. These results brought not only championships, but also international recognition, with the presentation of the BMW Achievement Award.

In 1986, Gardner and his wife, Gloria, keen on the warmer climates of Queensland, moved to the Gold Coast. There he revived the passion he'd always had for imparting the skills of driving to others. He'd written a book about it — an international bestseller — he'd run a school at Calder, given numerous lectures to car clubs and service organisations, and now, backed by three long-time friends — Dean Wills (Amatil/Coca-Cola), Ron Meatcham (BMW) and Rod Longhurst, brother of Tony — Gardner created his dream establishment. The Performance Driving Centre was a $3 million venture at Norwell, on the Gold Coast, comprising a 2 kilometre training circuit (with a shorter one for children), a 97 metre irrigated skid pan, buildings with lecture rooms, offices and restaurant, later an impressive car collection. The centre targeted 17–25 year olds and trained over 2000 in the first 18 months, including most of the entrants in the BMW Celebrity Challenge at the Australian Grand Prix, Adelaide.

Gardner not only managed and delivered the driver education courses, but also master-minded the racing team, along with the preparation of M3, M5 and M6 customer cars. The JPS team's endurance title was successfully defended, and repeated in 1987, with Tony Longhurst also backing Richards in his second Touring Car Championship. Even when the arrangement ended it was said that Dean Wills, on behalf of Amatil, was 'very pleased with the commercial success of the program'.

In 1988, Gardner built, prepared, even tested a Ford Sierra for Longhurst, who drove it competitively in the Australian Touring Car Championship. The crowning achievement was Longhurst's victory in the Bathurst 1000, with Tomas Mezera co-driving.

Frank Gardner had finally added a missing chapter in his already impressive résumé.

In 1989, he ran two Sierras. Longhurst, Alan Jones and Dennis Hulme taking one of them to 5th place.

Not even the Mt Panorama circuit could survive the tumultuous years of change unscathed. The race was touched with tragedy on lap 5 in 1986 with the death of Mike Burgmann. Burgmann was driving a Commodore, and duelling with Gary Willmington down Conrod Straight. The famous hump would claim another victim. It was the same problem that had killed Bevan Gibson in 1969. Burgmann's car became airborne, landed awkwardly, and fired at high speed into the bank in front of the bridge. He was killed on impact.

'They were almost touching,' says Dick Johnson, who had also been at Bathurst when Gibson was killed. 'Willmington's car was right at Burgmann's back door. The problem was when two cars came so close down there, it created a vacuum, and when both cars lifted off the ground, Willmington's car just touched the back of Burgmann's and he was off. They found him in the left rear corner of the car. He would have hit that wall at 150 miles an hour [240 km/h].'

After detailed inquiries, the straight would be changed. A kink was inserted where the infamous second hump used to be, slowing traffic before the bridge and the hard left-hand corner into the pit straight. The track length had increased slightly, so the race distance was reduced by 2 laps, to 161.

Motor sport insiders were relishing the multiculturalism of the times, while rank and file supporters tried to come to terms with BMW, Volvo, Nissan and Ford's turbocharged European Sierra streaking away in various events, depending on which direction the regulations were blowing at the time. If the average punter had cared to look through the history books, he or she would have noticed that foreign cars like Minis, Alfas, Toyotas, Chevrolet and others had in the past played powerful roles at Bathurst. However, the public perception was that it was meant to be all about Ford versus Holden, in whatever their respective family sedans happened to be at the time.

When Armin Hahne and John Goss won the Bathurst 1000 in a Jaguar in 1985 there was unease, and even in the next 5 years, when it was either a Commodore or a Ford winning, the ledger seemed unbalanced, because Ford were at first non-participants, and then involved via the Sierra, which was not only unavailable to the Australian buyer, but was also a turbocharged aberration — this brought howls of protest from those who sought on-track equality.

It just did not have the same feel as the previous years. Brock found the times tough, too, winning only in 1987, against the odds, in his second car, sharing with Peter McLeod and David Parsons. He was surprised at how well the Commodore ran when he drove it. 'Especially when it rained,' he recalls. 'The crowd cheering when I got it sideways ... the way it handled ... it was one of my greatest memories.'

Even then, the effects of the polariser controversy were lingering. 'I had been shunned. A lot of people still wouldn't talk to me. They'd turn the other way, didn't want to be seen near me because, somehow, I was, like, bad. Don't go near, you might get infected by it. There were threats! It was a very volatile time. The public didn't really buy into it and I never suffered from lack of support from them. The fans were the one thing that was constant. The problem was only within the system, when people starting talking, started convincing themselves that black was white.'

Brock's switch from Commodore to BMW to Sierra were desperate attempts to regain the dominance he'd once enjoyed. The next few years would be difficult.

Dick Johnson struggled too, at first. The Mustang phase lasted 2 years; it was an interim car, used until he could buy a Sierra, which he did in 1987. In that year, Shell came aboard as a major sponsor, starting one of Australia's best-known commercial partnerships in sport: it was still thriving 17 years later. Johnson admits that there were good races at times among the various makes and models in the late 1980s, but it was not what they hoped it would be.

He took all of 1987 to find his feet again, including a trip to England to learn the new turbo technology and the subtleties of the Sierra development. 'We blew about 37 turbos in 6 months.' Johnson won the championship in 1988. He and Gregg Hansford finished 2nd to the Sierra of Longhurst and Mezera at Bathurst.

Johnson made up for his loss the following year, 1989, winning the championship and Bathurst, and cementing what would become one of the greatest driver pairings ever seen on Mt Panorama. John Bowe joined the team as second driver in the championship and co-driver in the endurance races. 'It was a damn good combination and we complemented each other in many different ways.

'Bathurst in 1989 was spectacular, because we started from pole and led for every lap of the race. It was a great car, and we were cruising.'

The climax to this lawless era, however, was the double victory of the all-wheel-drive, turbocharged Nissan Skyline, dubbed 'Godzilla' — with a mixture of awe and affection. This amazing car, like the RX7, stretched the definition of 'touring car'. It would give Jim Richards another two titles, and, with the talented youngster Mark Skaife, two more Bathurst wins.

Skaife's career started in karting before taking a touring car detour that in so many cases ends in mediocrity, but for him it was quite the opposite. The Skaifes were friends with the Setons. Glenn was also in the early stages of his racing career. All those years spent watching the Bathurst 1000, and celebrating with his father Bo in 1965, had built an irrepressible urge within him. He and young Skaife were inseparable.

The Seton family helped Skaife prepare a Torana XU1 which he raced in the sports sedan series in 1984, before tackling the Ford Laser series in 1985 and 86. At end of that year he was offered a job with Fred Gibson's Nissan workshop in Melbourne, with the promise of a drive when it came up. Gibson was true to his word, and in 1987 Skaife drove a Gazelle in the 2 litre touring car championship. He progressed to the ATCC with the Nissan Skyline in 1988. Glenn Seton and George Fury were the other drivers in the team.

Seton, however, formed his own Ford Sierra team in 1989. 'Glenn and I have been mates since I was 5,' says Skaife. 'It's extraordinary that you could have such a competitive environment, especially when the two of us went to opposite camps from 1989 onwards — I mean we even had rival cigarette companies sponsoring us — and yet we've remained good mates.'

While Seton's departure may have been disappointing, Skaife had little idea at the time just how important it would be, for that is when Jim Richards was brought into the Nissan team.

'There's nothing in my career that I've learnt so much from than my time with Jim Richards. A lot of what you learn about how to approach motor sport comes from how you approach life. Jimmy's an incredibly honest and genuine person but the most mongrel competitive guy I've ever seen in my life. He would do anything to win a race, basically. What he also demonstrated to me was that to drive cars well you have to know what each car likes, but you've also got to drive them incredibly hard. All those blokes that used to say it's got to be smooth and lovely and don't hurt the car ... that is absolute crap. In the end you walk up to this modern piece of machinery with all the technology and the professional way it's prepared, and then you treat it like a matchbox. You smash it across whatever you have to, use every zac of power and grip to make it go fast. Jimmy taught me that.'

In 1990, the team was honed to two drivers: Skaife and Richards. It was a season that brought the modern-day Skaife, by then 22 years old, out of his cocoon. He out-qualified Richards for the first time at Lakeside. 'That was a big milestone,' he recalls. 'The next step would be to win a race. The step after that would be to win consistently. Then, your next step should be to win the championship. Each time you have to be able to apply yourself to making good, fast race laps within the limits of the tyres, brakes or whatever, but you're always seeking to optimise performance.'

While Skaife measured himself against one of the great drivers of his era, he was winning in open-wheel events. In 1991 he not only shared a Bathurst win with Richards but won the one-make Gold Star series in a Spa FB003 Formula Holden. By the spring of 1992, he had made all the necessary progressions. He not only beat Richards for the ATCC but repeated his Gold Star series win on the same day at Oran Park. 'It was just unbelievable. I had to win both races to win the titles. I remember getting up that morning, never felt so nervous. I figured that if I came out the other end of that day all right, it would be a fantastic thing.'

The second of their Bathurst wins however, would live in infamy. It was not only the catalyst for change, but another of the more controversial finishes in Bathurst's history.

Thick clouds unloaded some of the heaviest falls seen in the event. Cars started to slew everywhere.

The race was thrown into even deeper depression when Denny Hulme suffered a heart attack and died at the wheel. Witnesses saw his BMW slow, then move almost innocently to the side of the circuit. It would be one of the most poignant fatalities in the violent history of the sport. Frank Gardner felt it more than most. Not only had Hulme been an old friend, but Gardner had prepared the car. Since 1990, he had been involved for the second time in a works BMW team, with Tony Longhurst, Alan Jones, Paul Morris and Geoff Brabham taking drives at various stages. The team that day was shattered, but Longhurst and Johnny Cecotto would still drive to 4th place.

Jim Richards was leading the race, approaching Reid Park, when the wet road just stopped co-operating with his brakes. The GTR jammed into the wall, and a wheel ripped away. He tried to drive the car back to the pits, and after negotiating the winding road up and over the mountain, it seemed the pressure was off and he would achieve this. However, the 6.2 kilometre mountain circuit can seem infinite when such trials are thrust upon drivers. Richards skidded into a collection of crashed cars as he headed into Conrod Straight. The race was called off. The question on everyone's lips was, from which lap would the winner be declared?

Dick Johnson cruised down into the main straight, acknowledging the congratulations of the crowd. He was the first car to cross the finish line after the flag had been waved. It had been a mighty effort for him to even keep pace with the GTR, and he felt he had earned the victory.

The result, however, was taken from 2 laps before the accident occurred. Richards and Skaife had won after all. Johnson was in shock. 'I have had a lot of things happen to me in this sport, but that was without a doubt the hardest thing to get over. I knew that I had been robbed and that I deserved the win. It was a tortoise and hare sort of race and we drove it perfectly, tactically speaking. We drove well. The pit crew did a fantastic job. Had Jim not crashed for the second time, we would have won the race. He had his front wheel hanging off. I still feel bloody bad about it.

'It was nothing to do with Jim or Skaifey. It was the decision from race control that I thought was unfair.'

Boos flew like darts from the masses. Perhaps it was the way they won; perhaps it was the car they won in. Richards lost his cool, calling the crowd 'a pack of arseholes'. It would become, arguably, the most famous quote in Australian touring car history.

'It was the most dangerous day at Bathurst that I had ever seen. A good friend of Jimmy's, Denny Hulme, had died. Jimmy was driving the Nissan when it crashed, caught out on the wrong tyres. He wouldn't have made the mistake otherwise. He was emotional. For the crowd not to respect that we were out there doing our best, regardless of what brand we were driving, the reaction was extraordinary. I was also very disappointed. Those things tarnish you. They impact on your view of the game. Jimmy felt very strongly about it.'

Larry Perkins had made a couple of decisive career moves in 1986. Somehow, this gnarly character had become driftwood on the motor sport scene, and it was not right for him to be washing up in various garages when he had more than enough ability to take charge of his own. He had a few other issues. 'I had then become very knowledgeable about the touring car scene in Australia, and what was disappointing me was that these were cars that, to the public, were showroom cars, but there were some modifications that were apparently available only to the chosen few. I thought that was terrible. I decided to get my own car, even though I knew all the ins and outs. I reckoned CAMS had a bit of a nudge-nudge, wink-wink relationship with Holden, Ford and even Mazda, allowing them to use bits that in my opinion were illegal — because let's face it, no manufacturer wants everyone to see their cars breaking down at Bathurst — but if you were a poor Joe Blow down the back you got no help at all. I was determined to change it all.'

Perkins's other canny decision that year was to buy the exclusive rights to the title 'Australian Touring Car Championship'. That meant CAMS would be obliged to seek his permission to use the title. It would become very useful. He ran his own Commodore in the 1986 championship, finishing 10th. He also showed pace at Bathurst before falling back to 25th. From there, however, he continued to fight city hall, all the while building a team that would become so strong that no one could ignore him.

Colin Bond's affair with Bathurst was rarely dull. It had looked promising with Kevin Bartlett in 1982, however, but after starting from the second row, Bartlett flipped the car while running 3rd. In 1983 he finished 3rd with Alan Grice in a Commodore. Then followed 3 years of driving Alfas. In Bond's fourth try with an Alfa, in 1987, co-driver Lucio Cesario crashed in the esses after ringing a few warning bells with earlier mishaps. He was the first driver to bring out a safety car at Bathurst. 'He was a typical Italian,' recalls Bond. 'A nice bloke and really fast, but when the red mist descended ...'

Bond also hopped onto the Sierra bandwagon, dumping his Alfa 75. There were immediate rewards: he finished 3rd in the 1988 championship, and with team-mate Alan Jones, 3rd at Bathurst that year. He was feeling the breeze at his back for a change, and proving something to the knockers — at the age of 46. 'I think Alan was just about at his best that year. He had won the Formula 1 championship, retired, gone back, then settled in with us. Gee he was driving well. It was great to watch someone tie a car in knots and then get out of it. He could put down times that stunned me, and made me go faster too.' Bond and Jones would continue driving in touring car racing into the 1990s.

By 1987, Bob Jane had finally turned his back on competition, even as a manager and owner. His financial support of teams and drivers had run into millions over the years, including some bizarre excursions overseas, such as Peter Brock and Larry Perkins's uneventful and unsuccessful Le Mans campaign in a Porsche in 1984 and Allan Grice and Graeme Crosby's races in the US in 1987 in a couple of Australian-built NASCARs. He even claims to have put together Fosters' naming rights sponsorship of the Australian Grand Prix in Adelaide, a generous gesture given that the South Australian government trumped his own Calder Park to host the first Australian round of the Formula 1 championship.

Jane had turned his attention to a 35 million dollar development of Calder, the first Australian oval track, which he called the 'Thunderdome'. During its construction, he was quoted in a Melbourne newspaper as saying, 'The Pope's visit is looking less likely at the moment because the church doesn't think we will be ready in time.'

With the greatest respect for the Pope, Jane might well have side-stepped him to get into NASCAR, such was his love for the category. He was determined to establish a series in Australia. For the next decade, while he fought a continuous battle with CAMS over various issues relating to Calder and its development, Jane pressed his considerable wealth into making oval track racing work, and there were brief periods when the house was full. It would never quite catch on. For all his success in other endeavours, that circuit and the massive effort he put into it, remain perhaps the greatest testimony of Bob Jane's love for Australian motor racing.

Allan Moffat had decided at Spa, during his Commodore adventure with John Harvey, that Ford Sierras were the future. He acquired an Eggenberger Sierra and it was flown to Perth in May 1988. His best championship result was 3rd at Lakeside, and he won the Sandown 500 with Gregg Hansford. They suffered engine failure at Bathurst, where Klaus Niedzwiedz was the third driver. 'That Bathurst was the worst in my whole career,' recalls Moffat. 'We had a 3 lap lead with 30 laps to go. A 3 lap lead. Then a pace car came out for 12 laps. As soon as the pace car went in, Gregg radioed in to say the engine had blown. It turned out to be a cracked block. With all that slow running behind the pace car, the temperatures had fallen, and when the race went green again, the metal just couldn't handle the sudden rise in temperature.'

Moffat had been frustrated by being one of the nation's premier drivers and yet not able to win Bathurst since 1977. 'When you head up the mountain once a year for 20 years, you do become a little philosophical about it. You just have to treat every failure as it comes and work towards the following year. I remember the Managing Director of the ANZ Bank asking me after the 1988 race, "What are the chances of that ever happening again?" I replied, "About a million to one." He said, "In that case, we'd better have two cars in for next year," and ordered another one on the spot from Rudi Eggenberger. So, every cloud . . .

'I have to say, though, that the shock in 1988 was strong. Klaus and I were just waiting to wave Gregg home at the finish line. Bathurst is not the be-all and end-all of one's career. It's the be-all and end-all of one's life.'

Moffat's focus, in times of strict financial discipline, became Bathurst, almost to the exclusion of the touring car championship rounds. He would hold back resources for the Bathurst 1000, but even then, the pressures were extraordinary. 'Remember that $280 clutch that failed on my Falcon in 1974? Well to give you an idea of how things had changed, the clutch on the Sierra was worth $10,000. That wasn't the only thing different about those days. The public just couldn't relate to a car that wasn't for sale in Australia. The local manufacturers weren't supporting the sport. It took a few years for people to realise that the cost of running these sophisticated turbocharged cars was sending most teams to the wall.'

Moffat was not going to the wall, at least not in the short term; he was going to Japan. In April 1989 he took delivery of his second Ford Sierra from the Eggenberger factory, just as ANZ had promised. It became his second Bathurst car. Bathurst that year was another classic case of 'if only': he finished 2nd to Johnson and Bowe by 90 seconds after Niedzwiedz made an unscheduled stop to repair a loose wheel. They took the Sierra to the Fuji 500 in November and won the race. Moffat drove the car to the chequered flag. 'We were running 3rd most of the day, but really, we won by 25 seconds, and that was because we had a Bathurst pit crew that gave us 25 seconds with a fantastic final stop.'

It was enormously satisfying, but the win held much greater significance than anyone realised. 'When I went to Indianapolis in the 1960s I noticed a disturbing thing — there were many of these American drivers who were well into their fifties. When they weren't hobbling into their cars they were needing assistance to get into them. They had been through so many crashes. Half their bones were locked up. One particularly sickening sight was a guy called Jim Hurtubise, whose badly broken fingers had been reset in a perpetual curve so that he could still grip the wheel. That was not the way I wanted to end my career in motor racing. I made a deal with myself then that on my 50th birthday, I would quit. It's just that I had no idea that winning the Fuji 500 would fall on the same weekend.'

Moffat returned to the pit crew, passed his helmet to one of them, and uttered the immortal words, 'Thank you.' He was the only person there who knew precisely what they referred to.

The absence of Allan Moffat as a competitor at Bathurst in 1989 had almost slipped under the radar. That was partly because he had entered himself as a driver. He even drove a few laps of his team cars during practice. In effect, he was saying goodbye. 'I was more than happy with my participation. Was four Bathurst wins enough? One would have been enough.' Moffat would continue to run a team, but unlike so many legends, he stuck to his decision not to drive.

'No one is born with a steering wheel in their hands. I had the good fortune to become a race driver. I spent every spare second that I had in practice and qualifying ... not because I needed to learn how to drive, but to make sure I had the car at its very best to perform on the Sunday. I think we owed that to the supporters. I was happy to retire knowing that I had done my very best every time I went to the start line. My only disappointment is that 30 years went by like 30 seconds.'

After years of relative inactivity, Kevin Bartlett also said goodbye in 1990, when he teamed with Russell Ingall and Rohan Onslow in a Commodore VL at

Bathurst. They finished 17th. 'Russell wasn't quite the brash young fella he is today. He'd only just got back from Europe, where he had been racing open-wheelers. I didn't realise at the time that it would be my last race. I had suffered very, very badly from dehydration. My water bottle spilled. The tube fell out of it on the second stint. They'd changed the engine the night before and turned the heater on to bleed the system — and forgotten to turn the bloody thing off. The car was worse than an oven. Ingall got out. He was dehydrated. We had to put Rohan Onslow in and he didn't get past three-quarters of his stint before he was dehydrated. I hadn't recovered before they had to put me back in again. Shortly after that race I had a severe heart attack. I wonder why . . .' After a quadruple bypass operation, Bartlett decided he had had enough. In 24 of the Great Races, from the very first in 1963, he had started from pole position twice and won once. He was never on the podium in any other attempt. For such a highly respected, talented driver, that is a funny old statistic, except 'There's nothing really funny that ever happened to me at Bathurst. It was always a bloody tragedy.'

CHAPTER FIFTEEN

Like Father

After all the years of struggle, drifting from garage to garage, occasionally forming his own team, 40-year-old Vern Schuppan finally hit the jackpot in 1983. It would be a year that would define his career. He had signed to drive again with the Porsche team in endurance sports car races, including Le Mans, where he had already achieved more than any other Australian, finishing on the podium three times. By this time Schuppan had also gained enormous respect from international drivers and journalists. He had come to be regarded as extremely quick, but undone by his own quiet, unassuming nature in a world of brash egotists bent on self-promotion.

Le Mans was where more than a decade of hard work would pay off. 'We led the race for 21 hours; the only problem was a broken rear wing mount which cost us a couple of laps. But we were in charge, leading by 2 laps with 3 hours to go, when I came through the kink out of Mulsanne and felt what I thought was a terrific explosion. It was the door ripping off, at nearly 400 kilometres an hour. One of the hinges failed, and the air pressure was so great that it just ripped it out. Suddenly, the car had this huge gaping hole in it, with wiring flapping about. I was concerned about the rear body work peeling off as well. That's what had happened when Bruce McLaren was killed.

'I decided to keep driving. We still had a good lead, but the stewards black-flagged me. By then the team had a new door ready. They riveted on some aluminium strips, like band-aids to keep it in place. A rival team protested, because according to the rules I had to be able to open my door. The crew rushed back, punched a hole in the door and in the bodywork and fitted a leather strap, a crude hinge, which meant that technically the door could be opened. In the meantime, the engine had overheated because of the disturbance in the air flow.'

Al Holbert finished the race, with Schuppan and Haywood watching in horror as smoke billowed from their rapidly overheating car. It started to slow down. The second team car was catching them rapidly, but all Holbert had to do was get across the line. By the time he reached the finish, the car was barely moving; it was as if he were pushing it home. They had 53 seconds in hand, but the cooked Porsche could not have run another lap. Vern Schuppan had become the first Australian to win the Le Mans 24 hour race. '*Autosport* magazine claimed that after my nine consecutive finishes there I had driven more laps at Le Mans than any other driver in history.'

There were pins in his hips and weight on his frame. Alan Jones had raced only sparingly in the 12 months since he retired from Formula 1. His latest ride had been an unsuccessful one, on horseback, but there he was, standing in pit lane at Willow Springs, California, where the Arrows team was testing its car for the 1983 season. He was beating the cockpit with a hammer so that he could fit inside. 'I was always big for a Formula 1 driver, even when I was fit. I was 76 to 77 kilograms and they still called me the "big, burly" Alan Jones. But I hadn't been out of hospital for long, so I was definitely on the heavy side.'

The test was satisfactory, and Jones agreed to drive the car in the second championship round, at nearby Long Beach. The famous Californian coastal cruising lanes may have been shut down for the event, but Arrows' plan was still a two-way street. Part of the reason for their employing Jones was that he would help bring sponsors to the team. After all, it had been only 2 years since he won the World Championship. Jones qualified the car 12th in a field of 26, but his race ended after 58 of the 75 laps, due to the ill-fitting car. How often does the result sheet read 'driver discomfort' as the reason for a DNF? Jones finished 3rd in the non-championship Race of Champions at Brands Hatch but refused to go to the French Grand Prix. 'I wanted to see the colour of their money,' he recalls, 'and that didn't materialise, so I was out.'

Jones had always freely admitted that his future had been decided before he was born. The same could not be said for three brothers who were also sons of a race driver. Geoff was born in 1952, Gary 9 years later and David 4 years after that. Unlike Alan, they were not encouraged by their father to race, and yet together they were Australia's primary source of international motor sport success for almost two decades. In many ways they succeeded in spite of their surname, which was Brabham.

Geoff was born 3 years before his father won his first Australian Grand Prix. By the time he was 7, his father was a world champion. By the time he was 15, his father had won three world championships. They were different days, days when teams socialised and even co-operated in the sometimes bizarre off-track antics that characterised their celebrity. Geoff recalls the Brabham mechanical team stealing the Gurney team's hire car and lifting it onto a pedestal at an intersection where the Italian police stood to direct traffic. The car was confiscated, and the police refused to release it, so Gurney later stole it back from the police compound. Young Geoff and his father had to go to Gurney's room and pack his gear for him while he fled to the airport — Italian police officers were combing the city for the rogue racing driver. 'They raced hard and played hard,' says Geoff. 'Of course it was a lot easier to get away then, because most of the drivers had their own planes.'

The planes were often more frightening than the cars. 'Dad came in too hot one day at Oulton Park and had to throw his plane, a Piper Commanche, into a 90 degree turn, sliding it sideways to take some speed off, or we'd have crashed into this lake. It's a wonder more of them weren't killed in that era.'

'Young Geoffrey was at boarding school at the time,' Jack recalls. 'He came with me to watch me race. We were running a bit late, as usual. It was just on dark. There was no problem with that, but when I got on the ground I realised that the grass was all wet. They'd had a big shower of rain before we got there. It was as slippery as anything. I put the brakes on and nothing happened. So eventually I turned the plane and slid sideways right down to the lake, stopping about 10 feet from the edge. The wing tip was over the water. Geoff's never forgotten it.'

'When I was at an age to start racing, there weren't any second-generation drivers,' Geoff recalls. 'In some ways I think that prevented me from starting earlier. But also, Dad didn't want me to do it. He came from the era when people died, regularly.

'I think the other thing was, he didn't want me getting into racing just because I was a Brabham. I had to prove that I wanted to do it, and that I was prepared to work hard without expecting an easy ride. He took a little convincing of that, but once I showed him how determined I was, he was fine. I think that opened the gate a little for Gary and David.'

'It was dangerous,' says Jack. 'I just didn't want them to do it. But once they made their minds up and I knew they were going to be fair dinkum, I gave them every support I could.'

'By the time Dad retired and came back to Australia,' says Geoff, 'the dealership he was running got involved in Formula Ford racing. That was the chance for me to give it a go. I didn't really start until I was 18 or 19, which was pretty late.' Geoff finished 2nd in the Australian Formula Ford Championship in 1974, progressed to Formula 2 the following year, and won the title. He even drove in the Bathurst 1000 with Bib Stillwell's son Mike in a Ford Escort. They finished 12th.

That was when he chose to try his luck in Europe, almost exactly 20 years after his father had done the same. By 1977 he was winning in British Formula 3, but within 18 months had run out of money. He took up an offer from an American friend of his father's to drive in Super Vee, the US equivalent of Formula 3. 'My wife, Roseina, and I had spent our last dollars on the flight. Gary came over from Australia to join me and help out.' Geoff won the championship, and after a couple of impressive drives in the Can-Am series, he had bought his ticket to greater things.

'Team VDS called me and I finished up driving with them for 2 years in the SCCA Can-Am championship.' Geoff's first race for the team was in a Lola T530 Chevrolet at Golden State Raceway: he finished 4th behind Patrick Tambay, Elliot Forbes-Robinson and Bobby Rahal. He finished on the podium at two other events and won at Road Atlanta. Vern Schuppan contested some of the later races in that season.

In 1981, Geoff won the championship which Alan Jones had won in 1979. By the end of his 2 years with VDS he had also won two of three starts in a Ralt in Formula Atlantic, which further enhanced his reputation.

He even drove in the budding CART championship, which was in its infancy after the famous split with the Sprintcar Control Council of Australia (SCCA), for the same owners who had given him a start in Super Vee. One of those races was the famous Indianapolis 500, in which he finished a stunning 5th on debut. 'To give you an idea of how unimportant American racing was to Australians, the year I finished 5th, my rookie year, Vern Schuppan finished 3rd. Two Aussies in the top five, and I guarantee you very few people in Australia would have heard about it. Funny thing was, I remember passing Vern about 10 times during the race and I could not work out at the finish why he was two places ahead of me! His team was more switched on with their pit stops than mine was.'

Geoff found more work with his father's old friend Dan Gurney, but the team's lack of performance and Gurney's intrusion was frustrating. He signed up with George Bignotti's team, but would find full-time driving with a reputable owner just as difficult. 'It was a disaster. How I survived that year I'll never know. In one race, the steering wheel came off in my hand while I was doing about 400 kilometres an hour on the super speedway at Pocono. I banged the steering wheel, and luckily it fitted back on the splines. I straightened it up and missed the wall by millimetres. Back in the pits, I called everyone over, and when they had gathered around, I pulled the steering wheel off, left it there, and walked away. If I had stayed, I would have killed someone.'

In a year of breakages, he finished only 5 of 11 races, but accumulated 110 points, enough for 8th in the series. His best result was 3rd at Michigan behind Bobby Rahal and Mario Andretti. Team-mate, Tom Sneva, won a couple of races and finished 5th in the series; rumour had it that the best equipment and parts, including engines, were all going into Sneva's garage. This is a recurring theme in the world of motor racing.

Geoff was so incensed that he threatened to quit — several times. 'But it was one of those situations in which I was paid to drive, and couldn't really afford to quit. How was I going to live? On the other hand, if I kept going the way I was, I might not have lived at all. It was really dangerous racing in those early days of Indy cars. That year, Gordon Smiley was killed at Indy on qualifying day. It was the worst accident I've ever seen. He told me before the race that he was going to "run 200", that's 200 miles an hour [320 km/h], but he made the classic mistake of any road racer on oval tracks. The car got loose going into the corner and he counter-steered too far and shot the car into the wall. It exploded. They replayed it over and over again in the drivers' lounge. There was nothing left of the car, and Smiley's body was flying through the air like a rag doll.

'Then we went to Milwaukee the next weekend, and I was in the pits when a guy's throttle stuck open and he hit the wall. Two dead in 2 weeks. Other guys were smashing their legs up. Most of the accidents were head-first into the wall. There was a standard joke in that era: how did you know you were at an Indy car race? There were so many disabled parking spots for the drivers.'

One of the unusual aspects of Geoff Brabham's career was that he never had a sponsor. He was always a paid driver. In a way, it was a proud record, but it also made for some empty years in which he really needed to seek out sponsorship and, like so many others, boost his value by bringing money to a team. He never claimed to be much good at that. In 1983 Geoff contested only six races, and finished only two, but there was no regular drive. 'I drove for some good teams, but they were never good when I drove for them!'

He made a brief return to Team VDS, replacing an injured driver at Indianapolis. He ran in the top three after qualifying 26th and resumed a battle with his former team-mate, Tom Sneva. 'You know, that was one of my great regrets. I'd have given up just about anything to win Indy that year. I thought I would take the win. I was confident I could beat the only driver in front of me — Tom. The problem was, every time I made a pit stop, I had to hold my breath. The engine was not running smoothly, so I had to rev it hard to keep it from stalling during the stops and a strong wind was blowing the methanol fumes into the cockpit. It caught me out on the last stop, and I stalled it going out. It cost me a lap. I went from 2nd to 4th.' That was where he finished. Sneva won. The season closed with a few more drives for Kraco Racing, which had previously hired Vern Schuppan. Kraco signed Geoff to a full-time drive for 1984. Mario Andretti's son, Michael, was to make his series debut as his team-mate that year.

Geoff finished 8th for Kraco in the 1984 CART series, recording six top-five finishes, three of those on the podium, but the team focus was on the driver who brought money, and that was Andretti. 'It's always the problem for a paid driver as opposed to a paying driver,' Geoff recalls, 'and I had no problem with that. You just have to grin and bear it.'

Then Rick Galles signed Geoff to replace Al Unser Jr, and for 2 years there was more of the same: scattered podium finishes, hard luck stories and no victories. 'I was in position to win races and things would go wrong. It was really frustrating, stupid stuff.'

Gary Brabham started his career in motocross in 1978, but paddock-bashing on four wheels around the family farm soon became more interesting. To Jack's horror, he announced that he would also like to go racing. After helping Geoff with his American career as the 1970s turned into the 1980s, Gary returned to Australia to build his own racing résumé. He equipped himself for Formula Ford with a 9-year-old Birrana, and his breakthrough result was at Sandown, where he charged through from 11th on the grid to lead the race after 6 laps. He was so amazed at being in front that he lost concentration, and finished 3rd. He equalled the lap record, and captured the attention of local motor sport magazines. 'I remember when I was qualifying, Alan Jones came over to me and gave me a few tips on how to improve my speed on a couple of corners. I'll never forget that. I've still got the trophy. The logo was stuck on with sticky tape.'

The following season, Gary was off to Europe, where he drove a Reynard SF83 for Neil Trundle Racing and finished 11th in the British Formula Ford Championship, against drivers like Julian Bailey, Maurizio Sandro Sala and Mauricio Gugelmin. His best finish was 5th. He secured sponsorship from BP in 1984 and finished 6th in the championship. He'd been unable to break through for a win, but had finished 2nd a few times, led races, produced fastest laps and taken one pole position. He was forced to play second fiddle to his British team-mate, Bailey. In some cases, broken parts from Bailey's car were installed in Gary's. He assumed it was to save them money; he would usually be in front of Bailey until the parts broke.

In 1985 Gary won the Thundersports sports car race at Snetterton (in a TIGA TS84 Ford from the company Tim Schenken started), drove a Porsche 911 in British Rally Cross, finished 4th in the Grandstand Formula Ford series, took on Thundersports again, finishing 2nd in five races, and even drove in the British Truck Grand Prix. That is when his father decided he had had enough: he started a team for Gary to race in Formula 3. Gary ran the team himself.

In his eye-opening years with Jack Brabham Racing, Gary matched it consistently with drivers who were on the launching pad to greatness: Damon Hill, Johnny Herbert and Eddie Irvine. 'I'll never forget seeing Damon getting massages in his motor home while I was in the garage changing gear ratios.' Gary won not only races and awards, but also further sponsorship. He even drove a BMW M3 with Juan Manuel Fangio II at Bathurst, running 5th before Fangio hit a stationary car. They finished 16th. 'I always wanted to do Bathurst, because I saw Dad race there, and I used to watch the race with my mates when I was young. It was something I always tried to organise in my schedule.'

While older brother Geoff was carving out a career as a hired gun, never having to pay for a drive, Gary was on the hustle continuously, raising sponsorship to keep his team afloat. 'It wasn't planned. It just happened that way,' he recalls. 'In Europe you had all the South American drivers swarming in with plenty of backing. You had to compete with that, and on the track it was worse. Miss a gear change in qualifying and you'd be 6th on the grid.'

'It was definitely easier for me in America. Even as far back as 1977,' Geoff recalls, 'There were 80 Formula 3 cars entered for Monaco. I qualified last of the 20 who made the field. I passed only one car, but still ended up 5th, out of six finishers. The rest were hanging off the fences. That was the attitude back then. It was win or nothing.'

Some European officials favoured local drivers at events, bending or even changing the rules, to contrive a popular result and corporate liaisons would often ensure an imbalance in parts supplied that could mean up to 10 seconds a lap for the battlers. Stories of despair drifted back to Australia, as Geoff and Gary experienced the inequality of motor racing, but the third Brabham brother was only too keen to join them.

David was able to learn and benefit from the experiences of his older siblings, and by that time his father had come to terms with the fact that his sons were keen to continue the tradition. 'I don't remember any of Dad's Formula 1 career, but the house was full of trophies and all the visitors to the house would be interested. I didn't see much of Geoff either. He is 13 years older than me, and had left home when I was young. Gary and I spent more time together, but we were never in the same school because he was 4 years older. My passion was soccer.'

David was still uninterested in cars when he moved to an agricultural boarding school at Walla Walla, in the Riverina district of New South Wales. 'To me, a car is just a means of transportation from A to B. I'm not a car perv, not the slightest bit interested. I appreciate what a nice car is, its quality, but as a kid, when guys were talking to me about engine capacity, suspension settings and things like that I'd just go, "Yeah, sure." I didn't have a clue what they were on about. The main sports at boarding school were Australian Rules and castrating lambs.'

He left school to work on the family farm, which involved the usual paddock bashing, but that didn't motivate him either. His passion was fired when he went on a holiday to watch Geoff race in the United States. It was at

This was sophisticated for its day: the Geoghegan family transporter with touring car on the tray and open wheelers in the trailer.

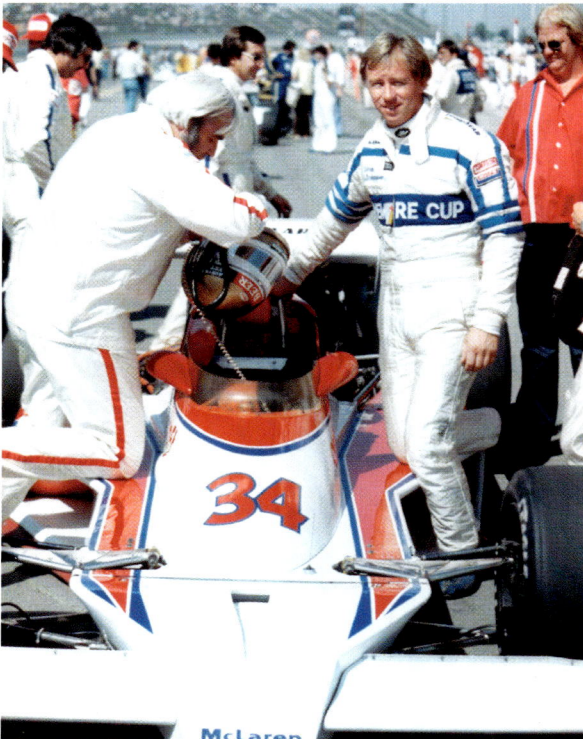

Vern Schuppan about to step into a recently acquired McLaren M24 at the 1980 California 500 Indycar round. He finished 10th, but developed this car into a podium finisher at the 1981 Indianapolis 500, the race many experts believe he actually won.

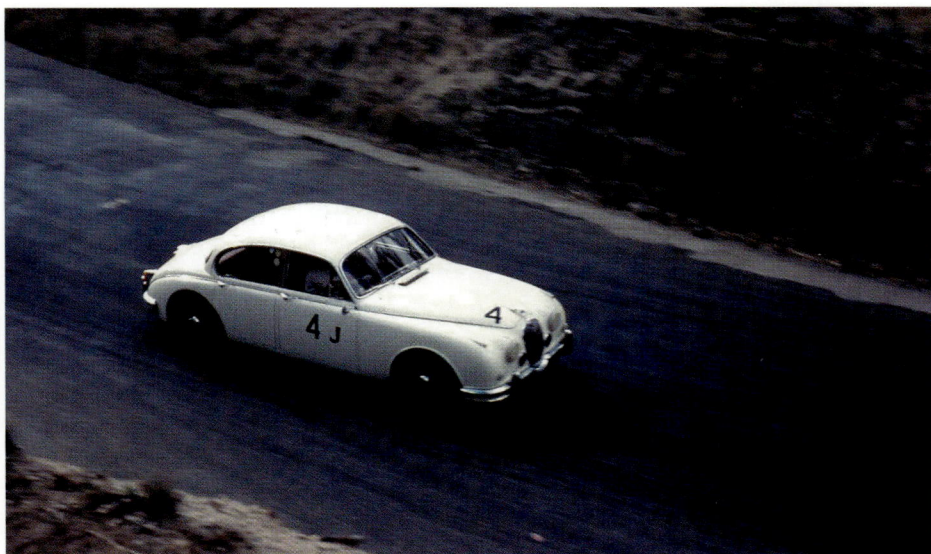

Bathurst, 1962. The Bob Jane Jaguar 3.8 Mk 11, unbeatable in its day.
(PHOTO: PAUL CROSS)

The Geoghegan brothers Falcon XR GT which finished second in the 1967 Bathurst 500. After a controversial finish Leo hoped he would never have to compete in the great race again. He did. (PHOTO: PAUL CROSS)

Allan Moffat, partnered by Jacky Ickx, on his way to victory in the 1977 Bathurst 1000, which turned out to be yet another controversial finish. (PHOTO: PAUL CROSS)

Alan Jones's amazing homecoming in 1980, winning the Australian Grand Prix in his Williams FW 07B, six weeks after winning the World Championship. (PHOTO: PAUL CROSS)

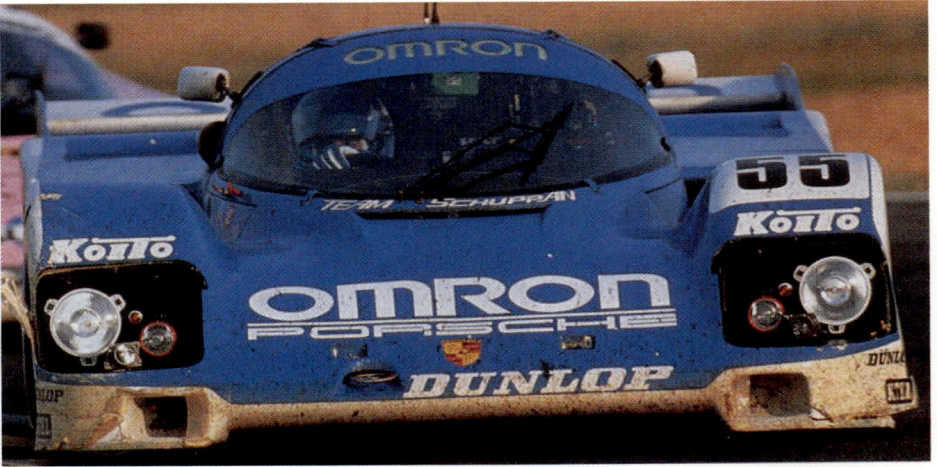

Gary Brabham, driving for Vern Schuppan in a Porsche 962C at Le Mans in 1989.
Eje Elgh was the third driver. They finished 13th outright.

A study in good ol' laconic Australian charm: Dick Johnson.

Bond versus Brock at Amaroo Park in the early 90s when the Blue Oval was too good for the Lion, thanks to a turbo-charged import called the Sierra, but both would be trumped by Nissan's 'Godzilla', the GTR.

In days when drivers were far more territorial, this was one to shock the purists. In 1985 Larry Perkins, having fallen out with Peter Brock, joined Dick Johnson in a Ford Mustang for the Bathurst 1000. There were only four Fords in the field, and if you thought all that was strange, John Goss and Armin Hahne won in a Jaguar.

Typical Brabham innovation: the BT26A, unleashed in the awkward era of early wing development in 1969. This model delivered four pole positions and two wins.

So near, and yet … Gary Brabham in 1990 in the Life Formula 1 car, which unfortunately never qualified for a grand prix.
Inset: But not for brother Geoff sitting proudly on his 1993 Le Mans-winning Peugeot 905.

Colin Bond on the edge, in more ways than one. The awestruck fans saw him somehow bring the Escort back on to four wheels moments later.
(PHOTO: DAVID R. MILLER)

Leo Geoghegan in the Repco-powered Lotus 39, Warwick Farm, 1969. He finished 5th behind Rindt, Bell, Gardner and Bartlett. 16,000 spectators defied the rain.
(PHOTO: PAUL CROSS)

Sir Jack Brabham gives the Midas touch to Mark Webber during his days as a test driver for Benetton. Webber would deliver, not only scoring Formula 1 drives for Minardi, then Jaguar, but signing with Williams for the 2005 season. Every move was a step closer to emulating his boyhood hero. (PHOTO: NEWSPIX)

Webber (right) celebrates 5th place with Minardi team boss Paul Stoddart in their Formula 1 debut at the Australian Grand Prix: a motor racing miracle. (PHOTO: NEWSPIX)

an Indy car meeting in 1981 that something stirred in David. 'It was quite amazing. I saw and appreciated racing for the first time. I still had no idea what it was all about. I went to a workshop with Geoff after he won the Can-Am series and watched him get fitted for the new season's car. I saw a go-kart sitting in the corner; a mechanic was working on it. I had a go-kart at home, which I built just for fun. I asked the mechanic, "Do you race these?" He was shocked that a Brabham could make such a stupid comment.'

David has never considered himself a technical person, but the concepts of aerodynamics and suspension interested him. He started discussing go-kart racing with the American mechanics and resolved to return to Australia to compete. 'Dad was gobsmacked when I told him, and wasn't particularly helpful at that point. I don't know if that was deliberate, to see how serious I was.

'I think the main reason Dad was never too enthusiastic about us racing was that he wanted to see just how serious we were. There's no point doing something if you're not going to be committed to it. He was never one of those dads who was always there, telling everyone what to do. Some of those can be a right pain in the arse. He was the opposite. He was there if we wanted advice, but he let us learn for ourselves.

'When I finally took the go-kart for a test, Dad decided to come along, just in case. He took a piece of yellow number plate, placed it on the track to mark the apex of the corner, and instructed me. When I did go around I found that I not only enjoyed it, but it felt like I'd been doing it all my life. It must have been in the genes.'

David had a tough initiation in his first races at a circuit in Griffith. His tactics were basic: see a gap, go through it. It worked well at first, but then a gap closed. 'Our wheels touched, and I flipped up in the air, end over end. All I had on was a pair of jeans and a jumper. All my back was stripped of flesh. It was hanging off everywhere, horrible. They changed the dressing a day or so later, and discovered that it was the wrong dressing. They had to tear it off. I still have the scars. It was a good test of how serious I was.'

David's mum was terrified. This was the fourth Brabham to put her through the rigours of racing. David never gave her cause for alarm again. The country racing progressed. The kart gave way to a better version, which in 1985 gave way to a Ford Laser sedan — in which he won three races during a one-make series. 'I wasn't technical. I just bought the car and raced. At the end of the year scrutineers checked out the car and discovered we had the wrong shocks on it. I had no idea. They also found out that Dad had tweaked the engine. I had no idea. After a tribunal, they gave me 4 months' suspension. When I called to ask them if I would be back in time to drive a Toyota Supra at Bathurst, they extended the sentence to 7 months. Mark Skaife got the drive.'

David made his comeback in 1986, in Formula Ford, and finished 4th in the Australian Championship. In 1987 he scored a drive in a Formula 2 race in Adelaide which carried the Gold Star Award that year, and was a curtain-raiser for the Australian Grand Prix. David had problems in qualifying, which meant starting from 27th on the grid. 'To make matters worse, Dad had found out that my girlfriend was pregnant. We had such a row that we were barely talking to each other. Dad's philosophy was that if you were a racing driver you just couldn't have women hanging around you, least of all a child, because it was a very selfish sport and if you wanted to succeed, you shouldn't make it harder for them or yourself. He said, "The chances of you ever getting to Formula 1 are finished." I just glared at him and said, "Fuck you!" and walked off.

'I remember sitting in the car, around the back of the field. I couldn't see the start line, and I was fuming about the fight with Dad. I was just really pissed off, which was probably good, because I drove the wheels off that car. It didn't matter who was in front of me, I was going to get past. One by one I steamed past them. The funny thing about it was, Dad noticed me carving my way through the field, so he grabbed Ken Tyrrell, dragged him over to the fence and said, "Have a look at this!" I won the race. I was standing on the podium, and there was Dad, nagging Ken Tyrrell and some Fosters people to put money behind me! All of a sudden I went from career finished, to Europe.'

1988 brought more fortune and less pressure for Gary, because he became an employed driver — at last — in Formula 3, under the umbrella of Bowman Racing. He drove a Ralt/VW RT32, finishing the championship 2nd to JJ Lehto, and winning four races as well as the Callnet and Scottish Super Prix. Damon Hill and Eddie Irvine were left in his wake. Gary remembers these drivers before they became world famous in Formula 1. 'Eddie was a wild man in his younger days, but a lot different from his character in Formula 1. Nowhere near as controversial or arrogant. Damon always kept to himself, never mixed much. I liked Lehto. He was a good bloke and a clean racer.

'That year I also gave my younger brother David a drive in class B, so I was still maintaining vehicles and running my own race team. At the Oulton Park

Gold Cup meeting, I won class A and David won class B. It was great, because Dad was there, and he'd won it a couple of times. Damon Hill finished 3rd in class A, and I remember Damon's chin being about an inch from the ground, because his dad had never won that race either.'

The Brabham tradition was not Gary's only asset. He raced at Macau, where he finished 5th, and won the Bruce McLaren Motor Racing Award. The next step was to test a Formula 1 car. Benetton gave him that chance, in Thierry Boutsen's car at Jerez in December. Benetton's team boss at the time was an Australian, Peter Collins.

David's ticket to Europe in 1988 was a funded drive in the Vauxhall Lotus Championship, which included three other sons of famous drivers: Damon Hill, Justin Bell and Guy Hobbs. Mika Hakkinen and Allan McNish were also competitors. He finished 10th, before he was offered the drive in Gary's Formula 3 team. David won five of the nine remaining races in class B and finished 3rd in the series.

That took him to class A, where he won six races — and the title. He then travelled to Macau to continue a strong Australian tradition, competing in the famous grand prix against the world's best Formula 3 drivers, champions from the various European nations. He also continued the tradition of learning the street circuit late at night in a cheap rented vehicle, just like Bartlett and Schuppan before him. He finished 2nd to Michael Schumacher in heat 1, but beat him in heat 2 to win the title on aggregate. 'I didn't really know Michael in those days. He was really quiet. He was doing Formula 3 in Germany. Hakkinen was also there, plus Irvine, McNish, Frentzen, Morbidelli, Zanardi — it's good pub talk, and I can tell my grandchildren that I beat all those guys at Macau.'

Schumacher would be back to win at Macau the following year, but David Brabham was ready to cash in on the vow he had made to his father back in Adelaide. 'It was a very significant year. Not only had I won the Formula 3 title but Gary had won Formula 3000 and Geoff had won International Motor Sports Association [IMSA]. It was a big deal.'

No one that year was more proud than Jack Brabham, who had only one word to describe his feelings: 'Unbelievable.'

By 1988, after six 2nd place finishes and no wins in his CART career, Geoff Brabham made a decisive move: to Nissan in the IMSA Sports Car series. 'It was probably the turning point of my career. Sometimes you can be lucky and land in the right place at the right time. That was my one lucky break.' After a few races to settle in, he and co-driver John Morton won at Road Atlanta, the first of an eight-race winning streak over distances from 150 to 500 kilometres (it was only in the 500 kilometre races that he shared the drive with Morton). Nissan was jubilant at beating the traditional GT juggernauts, Porsche and Jaguar, for the title. Geoff was not only a hero; he was also the winner of the US Driver of the Year award.

Geoff was earning a lot of money driving for Nissan, and more poured in as he won the IMSA or Grand Touring Prototypes Championship in both the next 2 years, counting the Sebring 12 hour race in 1989 among his many victories. He beat the best from Europe every time. 'It was really good racing up the front. The cars were really quick. Massive down force. The team was excellent, and after a while I had a lot of power within the team. I was calling the shots in terms of pit stop strategy and preparation, and that created its own set of responsibilities, which in turn made me drive even better. I didn't like using co-drivers, because I hated the thought of anything going wrong while I wasn't in the car. I ended up doing almost all the races on my own. Most lasted 2 hours.'

Geoff still did some Indy car races, driving once in 1989 for Team Penske in Portland, where he qualified 4th and was coming 2nd before engine trouble cost him a podium finish. 'It was when I finally landed that drive with such a big team — even though it was for only one race — that I knew I had been wasting my time driving for the smaller teams.'

The Nissan phenomenon peaked at the turn of the decade, and by 1992 it was over. The team and the series were fading into oblivion.

'One of my great disappointments,' Geoff recalls, 'was not winning with Nissan at Le Mans. The first year we went there we were joined with a European Nissan team, which didn't work. My co-driver, Arie Luyendyk, was one of the fastest guys around fast corners I've ever seen, and one of the most courageous drivers. He took the car out in practice, but after only 1 lap he came rushing back. He jumped out and grabbed a telephone. I asked him what he was doing. He said "I'm upping my insurance policy!"

'The next year Nissan ran a Japanese team, an American team and a European team, each running two cars. We had the best chance. We were nose to tail with the Walkinshaw Jaguar. Derek Daly was driving at the time, and the fuel tank split. He returned to the pits soaked in fuel. One spark, and he would have gone up in flames.'

Gary Brabham had tested with Benetton in 1988, and finished 2nd in Formula 3, but he did not get the break that he needed to drive in Formula 1. There was one chance before the 1989 season to join the team that bore his name. Herbie Blash phoned Jack and discussed signing Gary to Formula 1. 'Dad told him I wasn't ready!' Gary recalls. He did, however, win the British Formula 3000 Championship for Bromley Motorsport, taking four pole positions and winning four races. He also took up an offer from Vern Schuppan to drive with him and Eje Elgh in a Porsche 962C at the 1989 Le Mans, where he was running 4th before gearbox trouble knocked them back to 13th. It was the only Le Mans 24 hour race he ever contested. He was 5th at Macau again, and by the end of 1989 had conducted many hours of testing for a variety of teams and manufacturers, and from Formula 3000 to touring cars.

The original plan for David had been to follow Gary into Formula 3000 in 1990 — at Middlebridge, and with Damon Hill for a team-mate — but the team had higher aspirations, and bought the Brabham Formula 1 team, which was being run by Herbie Blash. Blash, discouraged at signing Gary, asked David to drive in the first round of the championship, at Phoenix. David refused, preferring to gain more experience and build himself up physically, but after some testing, he took up a second offer. 'I had no choice, really, because once they had bought into Formula 1, they ceased their Formula 3000 program. It was drive in Formula 1 or not at all.'

In 1990 Gary Brabham seized, as so many others before him had done — including Jones, Schenken, Schuppan and Perkins — the nearest rope dangled before him from the lofty heights of Formula 1. The Italian Life Racing Engines team was as strange as its title suggested. The car was a disaster. The engine blew after only 4 laps of the first session of the first round. In the following round, in Brazil, it lasted 400 metres; not the worst, but certainly one of the most embarrassing failures in Formula 1 history. During this time, Herbie Blash phoned Jack again. 'This time,' Gary said, 'Dad told him I was contracted to the Life team! I wasn't. That's why David ended up getting the drive.' Gary left the Life team in its death throes not long after that phone call, but the door to the Brabham team had closed.

It was back to Formula 3000, with the Middlebridge team, but this time without an engineer, due to budget constraints. His team-mate was Damon Hill. Gary fought to the podium a few times, against the odds, but was never in a truly competitive car.

His only race for a serious, fully funded team was when Nissan invited him to drive with Geoff and Derek Daly. They won the Sebring 12 hour race. 'It was one of the highlights of my career, winning a race with Geoff.' Gary later drove with Steve Millen in a Sierra at Bathurst, running as high as 5th but blowing a turbo after 128 laps.

'Most of my steady work was in testing. I not only enjoyed it, but started to get a real feel for it. I developed quite a reputation as a test driver.' One such test led to an extraordinary offer from Mazda in 1991. They signed Gary up to drive at Le Mans. 'The offer was £50,000,' he recalls. 'I didn't waste any time saying yes. I did all the testing. Then Bernie Ecclestone changed the calendar dates so that Formula 3000 and Le Mans clashed. Because I had a contract to race in Formula 3000, I had to say no to Mazda. Of course Bertrand Gachot, Johnny Herbert and Volker Weidler won the race!'

Gary gradually switched his racing to endurance events in sports cars, running mainly with Geoff for Nissan, but he also competed again at Bathurst, in a Sierra prepared by Allan Moffat, with Charlie O'Brien the co-driver. They were running 4th when the distributor broke. There were two drives in the Gold Coast Indy car races, in 1993 and 1994, one-off appearances for lowly teams, run mainly to boost local interest. 'A couple of opportunities came up to drive Peugeot in touring car events back in Europe. I tested, matched the main driver's times, but lost the drive because I wasn't English. My big problem, though, was with my middle ear. It had worsened over the years until it got so bad that it affected my last couple of drives on the Gold Coast. It wasn't just hearing loss, but loss of balance. A couple of times it would just hit me, and I'd end up on the floor. The house would be spinning, I'd be physically ill. It was as if I was paralytic drunk. I managed to get to the phone and ring a friend, and he took me to the doctor. They fixed it with surgery, but by then I'd made my decision to retire.'

His skills were in far more demand in the area of driver training, and that's where he focused his career after 1995. Gary Brabham has joined a list of great drivers to have come so close to — and yet so far from — success in Formula 1.

The Brabham Formula 1 team had a competitive car in 1989, when Gary Brabham had missed his chance to drive for them, so he watched his brother David in 1990 with mixed feelings: how would he handle his opportunity to drive for them? 'They started the year with the BT58, the previous year's car,'

David recalls, 'but by the time I came in to drive, they had the BT59, and it hadn't been shaken down. I hardly did any laps in practice. The car kept stopping. My team-mate, Stefano Modena, had a little more time in his car, enough to get the gremlins out. We also had to use last year's rear end, because the BT59 rear, including the gearbox, wouldn't be ready until halfway through the year. It was a fantastic experience to go through, but really, it was a shit year. Here I was on a roll through the Formula 3 ranks, then I came to Formula 1 and just stopped.'

It was a familiar scenario for drivers who have come in on the ground floor. 'The team ran out of money halfway through the year and we couldn't take delivery of engines until they got their money. Whenever parts wore out on Stefano's car they ended up on my car. The mechanics later told me this. Politically, too, there were problems. The old "Brabham network" was still there, even though Middlebridge had bought the team. These were people who didn't want me there because I had come from Formula 3 and they considered that, given the history of the team, they should have hired established drivers. I could understand that. I didn't have a hope.'

David failed to qualify for 6 of the 14 races he contested. He was forced to retire from seven others, with various technical problems. The only race he finished was the French Grand Prix, where he came 15th, 3 laps behind the winner, Alain Prost. Modena out-qualified and mostly beat him, but was also plagued by problems, particularly in the latter half of the season, when even he was feeling the squeeze on funds. He failed to finish six of the last seven races. 'Towards the end, I was qualifying within hundredths of a second of Stefano, but he was on the back of the grid and I was off the grid. It was hard for both of us, but Brabham was on the decline.' The ignominy was at its worst in the final round, in Australia, where he did qualify: the locals cheered as David struggled for 18 miserable laps at the back of the field before spinning out.

But David had at least learnt about timing. While Modena went to Tyrrell, David was back nosing the 'classifieds' to keep in work until he could find another opportunity. He raced four times in Formula 3000 before taking an offer to compete in a new series for Jaguar production cars. Drivers had been invited from all over the world for the 3 rounds. He was joined at the first race, in Monaco, by Jim Richards. 'Typical Jim,' David recalls, 'rocks up with no idea about the car, never seen it before, never seen the track, and he goes bang — third on the grid, and I'm fourth. I've got enormous respect for Jim. He's an awesome driver. I thought, there's no way you'll beat me in this race, mate. I took off at the start, got in front of him. I think he had a problem after that. Then I put on a good show with Derek Warwick, and that's when Tom Walkinshaw asked me to drive with Derek for him in the sports car.'

He won the sports car race at the Nurburgring with Warwick, for whom it was a very emotional race: he had just lost his brother Paul in a Formula 3000 crash at Oulton Park. David also won the All-Japan race at Sugo, with Teo Fabi. Then Jaguar pulled out of the championship. The highlight of the year was teaming with Anders Olofsson in a Nissan GTR to win the Spa 24 hour race. There were also some podium finishes for Toyota and some co-driving duties with Jaguar in the long-distance IMSA races, in which he finished 2nd at Daytona and 4th at Sebring — where he was only two positions behind Geoff in the Nissan team car.

Geoff's Nissan years may have seemed too good to be true, but the big drives were still coming his way. 'In 1993 I was still negotiating with Nissan, because they had pulled the plug on IMSA but I had 2 years left on my contract. Then I received an offer from Jean Todt, who was then running the Peugeot team, to compete at Le Mans. It took me 5 seconds to agree to the drive. Then I rang David. I said, "David, I've just got this drive with Peugeot at Le Mans. What can you tell me about the team?" There was deathly silence at the other end. He had been chasing that drive for months. I never found out why they chose me, except that the year Nissan went well at Le Mans, they must have noticed. I guess I must also have been one of the most successful sports car drivers around. David is convinced to this day that they got our names muddled up.'

Geoff was the only one of 200 team members who could not speak French. He tested for the team but was always a little confused as to why he was there. 'It was a special occasion, Peugeot's last race, Jean Todt's last race before departing to take over the Ferrari Formula 1 team. We were the number three car and my co-drivers, Eric Helary and Christophe Bouchut, were young guys who were also just there for the one race. One of the other cars was driven by Thierry Boutsen, Teo Fabi and Yannick Dalmas. Philippe Alliot, Mauro Baldi and Jean-Pierre Jabouille were in the other. So I expected that they would be the preferred entries.

'I have to say, it was unbelievable. The most fantastic car I've ever driven. You had to have neck braces on both sides because the G-forces were so great through corners — and that was with only 25 per cent of the available down force used! If they ever took it to a circuit like Magny Cours, where you'd be using maximum down force, I don't think you'd be able to drive it. It'd rip your head right off your shoulders. As for straight-line speed, well by 1993 they had introduced chicanes, but even with those the Peugeot was doing about 380 kilometres per hour, over a short distance. The physical demands on the body were so great that after the race I was shattered. I had to sit down for interviews to keep from throwing up. It took me a week to get over it.

'Eddie Irvine was in the Toyota entry and they were fractionally quicker than us, so every time we got in the car we had to drive it absolutely flat out, as if it was a sprint race. We just had no problems. The closest I came was when I was going flat out through the kink and a slower Porsche moved over. I thought he was letting me past, but then he veered back again. I locked up all four wheels and slid sideways right up underneath him. I don't know how we didn't touch, but I recovered and kept on going. My tyres were flat-spotted, and I was bumping along severely, afraid to come in for 5 laps lest we lose the advantage. I got on the radio, and of course I can't speak French. I tried to call out to them, "Tyres! I need tyres!" So I come flying into the pits, and they're all standing there with fire extinguishers! Eventually, they got the message.

'Apart from that, we were flawless. We took the lead after 12 hours and stayed there. With 3 hours to go, it was Peugeot 1st, 2nd and 3rd. I said to Roseina, "What's the betting they slow us up and let the other two cars past?" But they didn't. Not only that, but Jean Todt came over to me, having worked out the driver rotation, and asked me if I wanted to finish the race for them. I don't know why. For me, it was a great honour, in a team that was entirely French.

'Years later I ran into Jean at the Australian Grand Prix Ball and we talked about the race. I asked him again why he let me have the honour of finishing. He just smiled and shrugged his shoulders. So I still don't know!'

Le Mans turned 70 years old in 1993, and Geoff Brabham became only the second Australian to win it, exactly 10 years after Vern Schuppan broke through.

Remarkably, one of Geoff's favourite wins was not in sports cars or open-wheelers, but in a good old-fashioned American stock car. It came in the International Race Of Champions (IROC) series, which was a made-for-television spectacle pitting the best drivers of the major American championships against each other over four NASCAR events. The NASCAR specialists had a clear advantage, but that's what made it more satisfying for Geoff when he won two of those races, both at Michigan, in his 6 years in the series. 'My skills in NASCAR improved over the years. On one occasion I even beat the legendary Dale Earnhardt and Bill Elliot in a great finish, and Earnhardt was a hero of mine. That was my most satisfying win in a race car.'

David continued with Jaguar in 1993, finishing 15th at Le Mans. 'We won the race, but were then disqualified. It was the new prototype Jag XJ 220C. John Neilsen and David Coulthard were my co-drivers. DC was still a young driver at that point. He did a good job. He wasn't the quickest, but you rarely are in your first Le Mans. I drove that race with a sneaker on my right foot, because I had crushed my foot and couldn't fit a regular driving shoe on.' David also won a British Rallycross race, then flew to Australia for his first Bathurst 1000, in a Fred Gibson-prepared Commodore, sharing again with Anders Olofsson. 'It was so different from what I was used to. The lead car was Mark Skaife and Jim Richards. I just got into the top 10 in qualifying, ended up 8th after the shootout, but a long way from Mark, who had become a bit of a specialist around there. They finished 2nd. We finished 4th.' He had become a journeyman driver, apparently condemned to a life of paid drives for whoever made the offers. The next offer came from Formula 1 again, and David was forced to ponder the old 'bird in the hand' philosophy.

'I was desperate to get back into Formula 1. 1990 was not a year that I would have liked to be my last memory of it.' A new team, Simtek, invited David to drive for them, with Roland Ratzenberger as his team-mate. Formula 1 was exciting, with Ayrton Senna, Alain Prost, Damon Hill, Mika Hakkinen, Michael Schumacher, Gerhard Berger, Jean Alesi and Eddie Irvine among the superstars. David was arriving once again at the base of a very high mountain, looking up at the enormity of the task ahead. 'The team was again under-funded, financially worse off than the poorest teams today. We had Ford customer engines, and they supported us well, but we were down on horsepower compared with everyone else.'

Ratzenberger was qualifying at Imola when a front wing flap fell off his car. He was launched into a wall at 360 kilometres an hour. 'I was on the track at the time,' David recalls. 'I came round past the pits, saw bits of car on the track, and for some reason I knew it was Roland's car. Maybe it was the colours or something, but I just knew it was him. As I went past the gathering of marshals and medical people I could see the car, and see him, with his head forward, the visor up, blood on the visor. I knew he was gone. His neck had snapped with the impact. The whole team was crying. It was devastating.

'We decided to soldier on. I raced. But the whole weekend was really bizarre, I mean, so many accidents. Then there was Senna.'

After only 5 laps of an already tragic event, three-time world champion Ayrton Senna, hailed by many as the greatest-ever driver, was leading the race. As he entered his sixth lap, on Tamburello Corner, his car simply went straight on, in spite of his attempts to steer it. It hit the wall. The front suspension folded back from the impact, striking his head. He died that evening in hospital. 'I didn't think it was Senna at first. I thought it was a Tyrrell. Then, when we waited for the restart, everyone was saying it was Senna. Word also came through the pits that it was not good. No one could believe it. Roland on Saturday, Senna the next day? It was just impossible. I could not compute that at all.'

David was out with a puncture after 27 laps, but it all seemed insignificant under the cloud of that horrific day. 'That night, we were watching television, and learnt that Senna had died. Now, I don't care who you are, you're a human being. When you go through an experience like that it's going to affect you. It took me several races to find my confidence again, and I wasn't the only one. Especially the young Brazilian drivers ... they were deeply affected. Senna had such a presence, people were drawn to him. When he died, it was a bit like Princess Di. It was a global mourning.

'My strongest memory of Senna, strangely enough, was of him having a go at me back in 1991 in Adelaide. He had gone off on the first corner, in that infamous clash with Prost. We got in a courtesy van together later in the day. We knew each other and had spoken a few times, but you couldn't say we were friends or anything. But he started having a go at me. He said, "Someone told me that you said the accident was my fault ... " I was sitting there with the world champion, a bit of a hero of mine, and here he is, going off! I didn't know what he was on about. My wife was there. She said to him, "Are you sure you're not getting David mixed up with his Dad?" As it turned out, he had. When we got out, he was fine again. Of course, a year after that he admitted to taking Prost out anyway.'

David failed to finish 8 of the next 13 races. His best result was in Spain, where he finished 10th, 4 laps behind the winner, Damon Hill, who had come a long way since his struggles in Formula 3. For David it was the usual litany of problems caused by lack of money. In one race, a wheel fell off: unfortunately, after he had qualified higher than ever that season — 21st.

'My Formula 1 career doesn't represent what I could have done if I'd had a better shot at it, but that's the way it is. That's the way it's been for a lot of Australian drivers who've never had the money to keep going.'

Vern Schuppan had found a home at Le Mans, the very place in which his hero, Frank Gardner, had felt so uncomfortable. Almost every year had a story, an opportunity. He finished 6th in 1984 with Alan Jones in a privateer Porsche. In 1988, he was again presented with a 2 lap lead in the race, and believed he was set for victory — until the car's engine failed after 12 hours. In 1989, driving with Gary Brabham and Eje Elgh, he was in position to take 3rd, but again, mechanical trouble forced them into the pits. He would drive in 17 Le Mans 24 hour races before his retirement, finishing 11 times.

There were disturbing moments, though. In 1984, during a typical summer's night at the classic, Schuppan was alarmed to see a bright glow in the distance as he neared the Mulsanne kink. As he drew closer, he could see the scattered wreckage of a crash. Debris was everywhere, some of it on fire. The fuel cell from the car was up in nearby trees, still on fire. Before it landed there it had killed a marshal. Then, all of a sudden, he noticed a smouldering heap in the middle of the circuit, almost under his wheels. He swerved late, and just missed it. It was the driver of the car. 'I later discovered that it was a good friend of mine, John Sheldon. You know what? He survived. He had burns to about 60 per cent of his body, but continued to race. That whole mess, incidentally, was the result of a blown tyre.'

His staple diet in those years, from 1984 to 1990, was driving a Porsche for the Trust Racing team in the Japanese Sports Car Endurance series, where he became a prolific race winner and multiple champion. 'I really took to the racing there. I loved it, and I loved Japan. It was well-supported racing, with 70,000 to 80,000 people at the events. I decided to stay.'

This, in spite of the fact that it almost killed him. In 1985 he was driving his 956 at Mt Fuji in a downpour, leading the race, when a car spun in front of him on the ultra-fast straight. The impact, when he hit the other car, tore the brake master cylinders from the front bulkhead of his car and Schuppan was a passenger as it shot off the track. The massive crash seemed to last forever — until the car was stopped by a metal stanchion that almost split the chassis in half, ending at Schuppan's hip. If it had been a few centimetres the other way, it could have split him as well. 'I stumbled out of the car, heart pounding, and waited. Nobody came to get me. I had disappeared off the radar. I finished up walking back to the pits.'

Schuppan's achievements were finally acknowledged when he received the Order of Australia for services to motor sport. 'Jonesy had also received that award. We had a choice as to who we received it from. He chose Bob Hawke. I chose the Queen. I didn't want to miss the chance to go to Buckingham Palace. My kids were quite small, and they sat with Jennifer in the wings. As I received the award, and took a step back from the Queen, my daughter Paige, who was only 7, yelled out, "We're up here, Dad!" I remember that part more than anything. You know, I also got the keys to Whyalla, my home town in South Australia. That was a big thrill.'

Like most drivers on the verge of retirement, Schuppan started to feel less comfortable in the car. He also felt the weight of responsibility as Team Principal during the later years — especially at Le Mans, where the risks were great.

'My last serious drive was in a 1000 kilometre race at Suzuka in 1990. I was driving with Eje Elgh and Tomas Mezera in one of the 962s. I was halfway through the race, thinking, "I really am not enjoying this. Why the hell am I still doing it?" I went up to the guys and said, "I won't be doing another stint. You guys finish the race." That was my last recollection of racing. In 1992 I went to Daytona with the team. We were testing before the race and the boys had been having trouble with the car under brakes. I reckoned the wing we were running was too small. They didn't agree. I jumped into the car, did a few laps, came back and changed the wing. Then we all went out again for more laps. The car was much faster. When we finished, the crew chief, a big American by the name of Garry Cunningham, who'd been looking at the lap times, was laughing. "Look at this," he said, "This old bastard hasn't raced for a year and he's quicker than all of you!"'

Alan Jones had retreated to the farm again, then moved up to the Gold Coast, where he took on a succession of car dealerships. He was lured out of retirement for a second time in 1985: the Australian Grand Prix had finally become a round of the World Championship, coinciding with its 50th anniversary. The offer from the Beatrice team, run by Carl Haas, was rich: US$1.2 million for the first year and $1.5 million for the second.

The millions spent on the team were not unimpressive either. Jones threw himself into the gym, tuned up his body for the season and dived into a sequence of all-too-familiar problems. By the time the circus landed in Adelaide for the historic event, Alain Prost had sewn up the title, and Alan Jones's plans were unravelling. The Ford engines ordered by the team were never ready, and the Hart engine they used in the interim was suffering from palpitations.

Bob Jane had been propping up the Australian Grand Prix since 1980 and would have preferred to see the first Australian World Championship round run at Calder but it was never going to be that way. Bernie Ecclestone had told him that it had to be a street circuit event, preferably in Sydney or Melbourne. Jane unselfishly lobbied state governments, knowing their support would be essential, and surprisingly the most keen of all were not NSW or Victoria. The event was secured by a powerful state and local government-backed bid from Adelaide, which met the criteria that FOCA had demanded. It would become one of the favourites on the international circuit.

'Bernie Ecclestone had made a nice gesture,' Jones recalls, 'offering to let me be the first one to drive out and do a parade lap before the pit entrance was opened. Would you believe Ken Tyrrell blew up? He claimed I would be getting an unfair advantage, driving an extra lap!' Jones's primitive car was never going to win, but more than 100,000 spectators turned up to enjoy the world's richest international sport. Not since the days of the Tasman series in the 1960s had so much talent assembled at one Australian venue. But this was another level again: this was the sharp edge, honed by decades of dealing, desperation and destruction, fuelled by billions of corporate dollars. Jones qualified 19th, about 4.5 seconds slower than Ayrton Senna's pole time. His tactics were to wind up the Hart engine's turbo to the max and drive hard until it broke. It was going to break anyway.

It was the final event of the championship, and the final event in Niki Lauda's career — and at one stage he looked the winner. So did Senna, but both cars broke and Keke Rosberg took the win. Jones's car lasted 20 screaming laps.

A curious and lasting relationship had begun in that 1985 event. Frank Gardner, owing to his great stature in the sport and his friendship with the Formula 1 doctor, Professor Sidney Watkins, was asked by the professor to be his driver in the medical car. That role continues to this day.

In his book, *Life At The Limit*, Professor Watkins describes Gardner as 'a wizard in the car — in the wet or dry. He is also an astute judge of mankind, machinery and motivation, a delight to be with and his droll comments are unique. We were listening to the radio to the commentary during practice one Saturday afternoon, to the topic of discussion being the slippy condition of the circuit because nobody had gone faster than the qualifying times the day before. Then Senna came out and Frank chortled, "Watch — the circuit is suddenly going to get unslippy now Senna is on it." He was right. Ayrton was quicker than the day before. During the lull in practice Frank is always ready with a fund of funny stories, most of them hypothetical and told in a deadpan way — many of them unrepeatable in polite company.'

The following year was no more prosperous for Alan Jones, even when the Ford engines finally arrived for Beatrice. 'It was a beautiful little engine,' Jones recalls, 'compact, sat low in the car — but gutless.'

After a long sequence of failures, he returned to Australia to be running as high as 6th in one of the all-time great grands prix, the 1986 race in which Nigel Mansell, Alain Prost and Nelson Piquet were in contention to win the championship. Prost held on, winning a brilliant race from a fast-finishing Piquet to retain the title. Jones watched from the pits, having lasted only 16 laps. 'I thought, this is crazy. I'm not getting on very well with Teddy Mayer, who is running the team. I'm not enjoying this. I'm not going anywhere.' Except home. The Teddy Mayer he refers to was the same one who provoked the wrath of Frank Matich many years before. It seemed that the same heroes and villains just recycled in motor sport, spinning around like that roulette wheel.

There was one more chapter in the Jones career: he accepted a series of drives in sports car races for Toyota, in 1987. In the 2nd race of the All Japan Sports Prototype Championship, he teamed with Geoff Lees and Mansanori Sekiya to beat Vern Schuppan and Keiichi Suzuki in their Porsche 962c over 1000 kilometres at Mt Fuji, but it wasn't long before he found the Japanese far too conservative. Their serious-minded diligence and his knockabout sarcasm were like oil and water. He announced to the team at the end of the season that he would not be renewing his contract. They offered him more money. 'Then I made the worst mistake,' he recalls. 'I told them it didn't matter how much money they paid me because I would have to give half of it to a psychiatrist. They said, "You have a psychiatrist?" I said that I didn't, but I would need one if they kept driving me mad. They said, "We will get psychiatrist for you." I said, "See! This is exactly what I mean!"'

CHAPTER SIXTEEN

Eras

Motor racing, for all its back room deals and vast technological mazes, will always be defined by its drivers. Great races and championships are seen best from behind the wheel, no matter how many mountains of work lie behind those definitive moments from flag to flag. While Australian motor sport went through a relatively quiet period in the early to mid-1990s on the international scene, carried only by the Brabham brothers, three legends were helping reshape the future at home.

By the time the 1993 season rolled around, turning one era into another, Brock and Johnson (both 48 years of age) and Perkins (43) had written themselves into the psyche of every diehard fan. Their characters still defined touring car racing. Their names still sold it, even though they had all struggled, for different reasons, to maintain their strike rate on the circuit. None would win another title. They would, however, remain potent for another 7 years at the place that had most often sold their stories: Bathurst.

1993 saw the return to a style of racing that the fans seemed to demand. The Vikings were all but gone. New regulations were designed to reduce the number of manufacturers to just two, an almost unheard-of direction for a sport that usually encourages more manufacturers into the mix. The depth of the field was not great for the first race of the V8 Supercar era. Little more than a dozen cars fronted. Dick Johnson won the race. Within 10 years, however, it would be a worldwide success, pushing the boundaries of commercialism and mainstream popularity.

Allan Moffat had lived through a few cycles of change, and from the safe seat of retirement he thought this one was sensible, not only for the public. 'After chasing all that money to keep the cars running in the Group A days, the move back to purpose-built V8 Holdens and Fords, the formula we have today, has proved to be the smartest move — it has created the most popular form of touring car racing in our history.'

Frank Gardner, carried on at his Norwell driver training centre for several more years, even 'importing' renowned British engineer, Ralph Bellamy, to manage the program that converted the already high-performance BMW M3 into the almost lethal M3R for the burgeoning GT Production category. Come the new century he was, finally, fully retired, but firing one-liners to the end. He had employed several top drivers during his time with BMW and Ford on the domestic scene, including Alan Jones, but feared the reputation of none. He even told one very well known champion during a bout of impatience, 'Look, son, why don't you make up your own dais and stick it in your backyard ... because it's the only way you'll ever get to stand on one.' Actually, the driver had already had more than his share of success ... but he knew exactly what Gardner meant.

Honours have been plentiful in the life of Frank Gardner, but two hold special significance. In 1994, he received an OAM (Order of Australia Medal) for his services to motor racing and, 10 years later, a unique certificate, acknowledging his 20 year contribution to the Australian Grand Prix.

After driving for Gardner's BMW team, Alan Jones joined Glenn Seton's Peter Jackson Racing team in 1992, driving Falcons. 'I enjoyed driving for Glenn. It was very successful. We produced lots of 1–2 finishes, and that's how we finished in the 1993 championship. All I had to do was front up and drive the car — it behaved itself. I didn't have a problem with the arrangement; in fact, at a couple of events I slowed up and let him past.'

The Formula 1 World Champion found it hard to drag himself away from race driving, even after leaving Seton's team. 'Glenn had a bit of a falling out with the sponsor and I formed my own team, Pack Leader. I approached Ross and Jim Stone to work with me. I thought they were good operators. Turns out I was right. But at the time, I don't think the right people were in the right roles, and the team just didn't gel.'

Jones spent the rest of the decade picking up odd drives for various teams, including that of battling privateer Anthony Tratt. 'I drove with Tratty because, at the end of the day, I enjoy going to a race meeting, and I have to enjoy the people I'm with. It was fun. When I drove for Dick Johnson in 2002, it was not only a team that I enjoyed being with — they were also a top level team. They gave me plenty of testing and prepared well, but it just so happened that the team was having one of its worst-ever years. Jones's law kicked in again! I had no doubt that Johnson would be back. I just wish I could have driven for them when they were on top!'

By the end of 2002, Jones had still not announced an official retirement, but there was no desire to return. 'Half of me did, half didn't. I mean, I've still got an ego. You've got to have an ego to be a racing driver. You've got to honestly believe that if you're in a car that's the equal of anyone else's, you can beat them. But then there are certain sacrifices you have to make that I don't necessarily want to go through: going to the gym every day, watching what you eat, do this, don't do that ... well, fuck all that. It would have to be an awful big carrot for me to do it again. I don't know.'

Geoff Brabham had returned to Australia during the mid-1990s. He was 43 years old, tired of the international scene, keen to settle on the Gold Coast with his wife and baby son. He still won a host of races for BMW in the Super Touring Championship, including a Bathurst victory in 1997 with David. He enjoyed that occasion, but something was missing. 'I wanted to come home and just have fun,' he recalls, 'but what I found was that I couldn't race like that. I was so used to having to perform under enormous pressure that it was hard to find the motivation. Especially the Super Tourers, which were less inspiring to drive. After handling something with at least 700 horsepower for 15 years, coming back to less than 300 horsepower just wasn't doing it for me. I mean, we'd drive at places like Indy, where there were 500,000 people in the stands, and then I'd be heading out to Winton on a freezing winter's morning, with about 15 people attending, 14 of those being Brad Jones's relatives. I started to think, what the hell am I doing?'

He mixed those races with some V8 Supercar endurance drives, but not even the bigger crowds and budgets there could rekindle the fire. Geoff retired to a quiet life, and let his racing licence lapse. He had driven for 33 teams, winning more than 50 international races, including major endurance events with each of his two brothers. In 2004 he was inducted into the US Motorsport Hall of Fame. He was never injured in a career that spanned some of the most dangerous driving in recent history.

The cementing of the V8 category as the Australian Touring Car Championship created opportunities for some drivers, but dead-ends for others. It seemed for Colin Bond opportune to quit the rigours of competing full-time with his own team. The Ford Sierra had to be shelved, and he settled back in the freelance driver's seat and turned on the cruise control. 'It all got too hard. We simply never had enough funds to run the cars properly. You're driving, employing people, trying to keep your employees' wives happy, sponsors happy. I used to always run to my budgets, never ran over. A lot of people would run over theirs, then try to get more money from the sponsors. You were either asking too much, or spending next year's budget. I didn't want to risk that.'

His efforts would be restricted in 1993 and '94 to co-driving at Bathurst. Those drives, especially his final attempt in 1994, with Anders Olofsson, would remind everyone of his skills: 'I was a lap down, but got it back. It started to rain. I hit the lead. The track dried out. Safety cars came out. That shuffled the field. We ended up 6th. It was a satisfying drive, passing cars left right and centre. I was 52 then. I'd been doing it for about 30 years, and just noticed that I started to have to think about little things like what gear I was in. Things I never used to think about. Besides, how long do you want to go for anyway?'

Bond would retire for good to enjoy golf and his family. The three-time Australian Rally Champion and ATCC Champion would also expand his interests in sailing, in which he had already proven himself by contesting a Sydney to Hobart race. In 1997 he would become Driving Standards Observer for the V8 Supercar Championship. Like Kevin Bartlett, Bond's Bathurst strike rate didn't justify his status in the sport: one win and five other appearances on the podium in 28 starts. Peers regarded him as one of the most versatile of the great drivers and those who watched him race knew that in motor sport, success is not always measured in numbers.

*   *   *

Glenn Seton, Mark Skaife, John Bowe, Craig Lowndes, Seton again. From 1993 to 1997 the new guard took control of a touring car championship that was growing deeper and stronger and younger in appearance. It was commonly thought, in those years, that none of them could ever reach the same heights of popularity that their predecessors had, in spite of their much greater access to media and marketing.

When it came to Bathurst, however, it was still a case of the old bulls showing the young bulls just how fast they should charge down that hillside. There had been lean years for Larry Perkins in the late '80s and early '90s, but momentum was building. The peak was a podium finish at Bathurst with Tomas Mezera in 1990 until he teamed with Gregg Hansford to beat Skaife and Richards in 1993. It was the first Bathurst win for Perkins Engineering, with a 1-year-old sponsorship from Castrol that has lasted ever since. The team was shaping into a juggernaut of on-track performance and off-track sales.

'It was a turning point. I'd been in business about 6 years. Bathurst was so firmly entrenched in my mind as the event to win, that to come out of the box in a new category, still running the Holden engine when most of the opposing Commodores were running the Chevrolet NASCAR engine, was very satisfying. Holden allowed me to make modifications to the cylinder box and heads. They were homologated. We had pole and led all the way.'

They finished 3rd the following year, but early in 1995, a promising relationship was destroyed when Hansford crashed in practice for a 2 litre touring car race at Phillip Island. He was killed. 'It was very difficult,' Perkins recalls. 'He was a good driver and a no-fuss guy. He rang me in January wanting a release from his contract to go 2 litre racing and I wasn't happy about it. But he pestered me about it and I couldn't give him a full-time steer in the championship rounds, so I let him go. It's a bloody tragedy and a decision I'll regret for the rest of my life.

'It got a bit messy because the family asked me to have a look at the car because they weren't sure if there had been any structural cause of the crash and I did have a look. I made a report that there had been no failures, that it was caused unfortunately by an error of driving. That didn't go down very well with the family. I thought they deserved an honest answer.'

Perkins also played a key role in the formation in 1988 of the Touring Car Entrants Group (TEGA) which brought the team owners together in a united voice.

Dick Johnson was also a founding member. 'Frankly, CAMS didn't want to know about us. We were pushing shit uphill with a red hot needle. We had absolutely no control over our own destiny. Decisions were made by a bunch of bureaucrats who had a passing interest in motor racing while we had a real interest in what had become a business, our livelihoods.'

'I regard Larry as a close friend,' says Allan Moffat. 'And very few people are aware of what he has achieved in the sport. He was involved in the founding of TEGA. He told them that we had more things in common with each other than we had against each other. For my sins I was voted inaugural chairman, and for many years we worked effectively together on various issues — this was long before the series became what it is today. Larry was always trying to improve the formula, trying to make it a fraternity. That goes unacknowledged. I do so now.

'A lot of people don't respect his achievements in Formula 1 enough either, and if he didn't have to run on the backside of his breeches over there, he wouldn't have had to come back here to race. If you're going to do it tough, you may as well do it back home.'

Perkins's most famous Bathurst wins in the modern era were with his supercharged team-mate Russell Ingall. Ingall, back from Europe, where he had trodden the well-worn path through the formulas before running out of money, introduced energy and venom to the team when he replaced Hansford. Perkins and Ingall won Bathurst together in 1995. That year was probably typical of the way the mountain can give and take, often several times in the one day. Perkins started third on the grid, but found himself dicing with Craig Lowndes for the lead into turn one. They touched, he lost a tyre valve and had to pit before the first lap was over. 'We pulled into the pits at the end of lap 1 and it was heart breaking to watch every car flash past us. I couldn't believe it. But we calmed down a bit then because we had nothing to lose, and drove flat out for every lap of the race. Our pit stops were the best of the day. By the time we got to lap 80 I could see we were back in it. After that we passed car after car for whatever reason. Finally we came up to the top-three cars. I dismissed third and second fairly quickly so there was only one car left ahead of us. It was Glenn Seton. I couldn't make any headway on him. In fact he extended his lead from 4 to 6 seconds. Then, he blew up. One man's bad luck … you know … I thought I really must have done something right that weekend. I still don't feel for Glenn. We'd driven our car as hard as we could and it didn't blow up. It's just reality. It's a selfish game. It was a race I will never forget.'

For the next 7 years they would be a powerful two-car force in the championship, with Ingall going close to winning the title a number of times. They repeated their Bathurst success in 1997.

Everything went to plan … almost. 'I had a very big crash in the press day 4 or 5 weeks before the race. It was my mistake, and it was a big one, hitting the concrete wall at 160 kilometres an hour. It hurt, a lot. Didn't do the car any good. We had car speed, set the lap record in the first couple of laps, settled into a good pace. It was one of the most secure wins I've ever had. That record stood for about 5 years.'

Castrol Perkins Racing forged an intimidating record of consistency in the endurance races, thanks to careful preparation and no-frills strategies. Off the track, he continued to harass officials whom he believed to be misdirecting the sport. 'I had a lot of running battles with CAMS; not at grass roots level, they were dedicated people; but I felt the management over the years had lost the plot. It was no secret that I had a severe disagreement with John Keefe who used to run CAMS. It was old club type management when it should have been professional. It was all about mates and favours and goodness knows what else. At one stage, I sent a note to CAMS reminding them that I owned the ATCC title, and would have no hesitation withdrawing it again. I then said that while the CEO continues to exert the powers that he does I would not be interested in co-operating with CAMS, and if that ever changed I'd be happy to hand back the title on a long-term loan. I got a call a couple of months later asking if they could settle the matter of using the title, because the "deed was done". When I checked it up, the person in question was no longer with CAMS, so I gave them a long-term loan of the title. I guess you could say it was "mates and favours" that got rid of the mates and favours.'

The indomitable character of Larry Perkins would remain influential in the meeting rooms of CAMS, TEGA and AVESCO (which in 1997 became the commercial arm of V8 Supercar racing). These three organisations, by the turn of the millennium, had come to rule Australia's premier category, but he would never let them forget their roots.

'I made the first phone call to get TEGA up and running,' he recalls. 'I was the first man to put his hand up and vote for Tony Cochrane of SEL to market our sport. They're milestones. To find it has grown to this level is fantastic. However, the growth has to be managed and in the rule-making area that still leaves a lot to be desired. I'm not sure the board today is still acting in the best interests of the owners and the fans. I'm loathe to give it up and let them have a win ... but it's taxing.'

Perkins retired from full-time race driving before the start of the 2003 season, and fuelling that decision was an uncharacteristic error made in the 2002 Bathurst 1000, when he was again leading the race with Ingall. Scattered showers had left some parts of the circuit wet, including a small section of the pit lane entry road, which Perkins had not noticed. He slid off, losing valuable time, and damaging the car. 'I was undoing my seatbelts. I put the wheels on the wet curbing while on the throttle. That was unforgivable.'

The following year, with Ingall leaving the team to join Stone Brothers Racing, Perkins's lead driver was Jim Richards' talented son, Steve. Perkins chose to co-drive with Steve in the Sandown 500 and Bathurst 1000 but rued that decision when he hit the wall hard in practice at Mt Panorama, causing severe damage, and placing a lot of pressure on the team. 'I was still trying to run my business, employing nearly 40 people. I had been arguing with the stewards who were trying to make us all sign a document we objected to. It was designed to let them off the hook over safety. "Including negligence" were the words I didn't like. It had been with the lawyers in Melbourne. Those things were distracting me. I was not focused. The occasion sent alarm bells ringing in my mind. Was it time to hang up the hat? I've only ever gone to Bathurst when I was capable of winning and I felt I let Richo down there.'

In spite of commercial pressure to have another go, because his name was still one of the strongest marketing tools in Australian motor sport, Larry Perkins decided not to race in 2004. It was finally over.

Dick Johnson and John Bowe, together for 10 years from 1988, won three championships and two Bathurst 1000s, plus a host of podium finishes in both. They won Bathurst in 1994. 'I reckon that was probably one of the best drives I ever had; it was right up there with the 1992 drive in the rain. We knew that we couldn't have done any better. I had a great fight with Brad Jones, then Bowey got in the car and fought to the finish with Brad's co-driver, Craig Lowndes, who was driving in his first Bathurst. The kid showed us what he was made of.' Bowe won the championship the following year.

'If you look back over the records, we were in the top two or three at Bathurst for years during the 1990s. Of course there were a lot of bloody races we should have won, but didn't.'

Dick Johnson retired at the end of 1999. Unlike some of his contemporaries, he locked the door on driving. 'I could see the future of the sport was in youth, but I still have to run the team. Unlike most other guys, I have no other visible means of support. That team is my business. I have to make it successful or I'm buggered.'

Peter Brock had come full circle in 1994 — and there had been a few circles. He returned to the stable he knew so well after a 7-year cold war. The politics mattered little to his legion of fans, who never felt comfortable unless Brock was in the Holden Racing team. 'I thought well, okay. It had taken a number of years, since 1987 really, with a dedicated bunch of guys, and they deserved the factory support as much as I did.'

There was more than symbolism to the move. 'From 1988 to 1994, HRT had never won a single round of the Australian Touring Car Championship.' Brock utters the words as if he were talking about treason. 'That's what Group A did to us. Let's be honest. It may have been a period of Sierras and Godzillas, technical interest and sponsorship dollars, but it just didn't hit the mark with the fans. I broke the drought for the factory team at Eastern Creek.'

Brock retired at the end of the 1997 season, but with a nagging itch: he had not won that elusive 10th Bathurst title. It had been 14 years since his latest. 'I won the first nine so easily, I couldn't understand why the 10th just wasn't coming. I mean, dumb things just kept happening. There were mechanical failures which hadn't shown up until we got to Bathurst. Things that didn't used to happen.' He made one last attempt, in a celebrated comeback with the team that bore his name (in promotional terms only), for the 2002 race. The car simply was not good enough, but his presence alone generated a record crowd. Brock was smothered by fans for the entire weekend. Half the team strategy was freeing him long enough to get the necessary track time. 'I've always had a rapport with the mob at Bathurst,' Brock recalls. In this he is quite unlike other drivers, whose focus cannot allow them that awareness.

'The crowd on the top of the mountain. I'm always aware of them. I could pick faces out of the crowd, wave to them, no matter how hot the competition.'

The synergy of that race was extraordinary, with Bob Jane T-Mart becoming the naming rights sponsor, 50 years after Jane's Armstrong 500 win with Harry Firth at Mt Panorama.

Later in 2003, Brock won the Bathurst 24 hour race in a new association — with the return to racing of Holden's Monaro. There were mutterings about whether or not he could call it 'Number 10'; if anything, just to close the book, but for Brock, at 59, the Bathurst 1000 was still a habit he could not break. At the invitation of Mark Skaife, Brock agreed in 2004 to drive the second HRT Commodore with former British Touring Car Championship (BTCC) winner Jason Plato.

Could it ever be the same without them, these monumental figures who made Mt Panorama their Mt Rushmore? Of course it could. There would never be another Brock, Johnson, Perkins or Moffat, but there would be many incarnations. Mark Skaife is the only driver in history to win the Gold Star series, Touring Car Championship and the Bathurst 1000, and he did it in the same year. If Seton had come to deliver Ford from Holden, Skaife had come to deliver Holden from Ford, and that would redefine Australian motor sport.

Skaife had been hardened by the political realities of the times. Having fought through the controversial Nissan years, albeit sustained by rampant success, he then faced the letdown in 1993 of rule changes that effectively banned the BMWs and Nissans. Team boss Fred Gibson was wooed by both local manufacturers but chose Holden, and Skaife barely missed a beat as he found the dais in a Commodore. Seton, Skaife and Bowe filled the podium in the first round and set the tone for the season which Seton eventually won. 'We had some cracker races,' says Skaife, 'some really good races. Glenn's been one of the great drivers. I'll always remember shots of him in the rain at Bathurst, great car control and natural ability.'

In 1994 Skaife won the championship again, Holden's first title in 14 years. He failed narrowly to win it again in 1995, but by the end of that season, fortunes took an even steeper dive, as the government-regulated withdrawal of tobacco company sponsorship pulled the foundations from a number of teams. While his team-mate and mentor Jim Richards left to race 2 litre touring cars, Skaife and team boss Gibson soldiered on, with passive Holden support, in a white Commodore without livery that became an enduring symbol of the dramatic fluctuations that commercialism could muster.

'I probably learnt more in that period than I had in the previous 10 years. I had been, and I say this with reservations, lucky, because I had started with a fantastic team, learnt a lot from Fred and Jim. But this time I learnt more about the industry, how racing interacts with the car business, the marketing of the sport. If it's going well, then the teams go well. It was all right to have your head down and bum up, but you had to have the cheque book first.'

Skaife's carefully nurtured relationship with Holden paid off when they signed him for the 1997 endurance races as Brock's co-driver, ready for installation as full-time team driver for the following year. 'In our game you live for the "now". You don't think too much about where it's going to lead you. I did everything I had to do to be a better driver, without really knowing where I was going to finish up. Take all the crap away, and to be a race driver you have to be fast. When I figured out I was going to be fast enough, I also realised that you had to be more professional and global about it.'

His team-mate in 1998 would be Craig Lowndes.

The antithesis of the Skaife success was this fresh-faced young driver, nicknamed 'the kid', who had made one of the great Bathurst debuts in 1994, teaming with the talented Brad Jones to finish 2nd to Johnson and Bowe by less than 6 seconds. Lowndes was the first driver to unify the V8 Supercar titles for Holden in 1996, winning both the championship and the Bathurst 1000 — and doing it all more easily, it seemed, than anyone could remember (in years when playing fields were level). It was a command performance. He then tried his hand on the European scene, but lack of funds — and, perhaps, of readiness for the intensity of the competition — saw him return in 1998.

The pattern of behaviour resembled his Nissan experience. In 1998 Skaife often out-qualified Lowndes but lost the races. The following year he still out-qualified Lowndes but won more races. In 2000 Skaife won the title.

'It was like with Jimmy,' Skaife recalls. 'We were fiercely determined to beat each other but had never had a bad word. The crew used to say there was always an extra two-tenths in us because we were together because we wanted to beat each other so badly we would never have found the extra two-tenths any other way. That energy drove the team. It was expensive because you had to have two of the best cars, two of everything that made anything better.'

Lowndes agrees that his one weakness has always been that he is not a technical driver. 'I'm not as technically minded as say, Glenn Seton,' he told the 'RPM' television program. 'I'm a driver that relates to what the car is doing but then needs someone in the background to help me in the sense of what to do with the car to make it go faster.'

The other, less obvious component was being 'outmanoeuvred' when it came to management, even manipulation of the race team. 'If I was being really balanced about it,' says Skaife, 'I probably did teach him a bit about professionalism and application. To be really well rounded and be ultimately the most professional guy in the paddock and do the best job, you have to have the team with you.'

Any talk of a renewed intra-team rivalry was snuffed out when Lowndes made a stunning career change in 2001.

Lowndes was signed by Ford. It was not only symbolic of Ford's boss Geoff Polites' determination to balance the ledger, to restore Australian motor racing to the great factory struggle that gave birth to the Moffat and Brock careers in 1969. It was also a recognition of the two personalities who had stood out from the rest in the past decade. Skaife was the consummate professional: fiercely determined to the brink of arrogance, hardworking, politically astute. Lowndes was the laconic nice guy: always cheery, a man of the people, politically naïve. Ford simply could not give him what he needed to perform.

By 2002 Skaife had won his fifth Australian Touring Car Championship, known officially as the V8 Supercar Championship. He had also won his fourth Bathurst 1000, his third with the incredible Jim Richards.

This time, Richards was 55. 'The best thing that has ever happened to me was winning Bathurst again with Jim Richards in 2002. There has been nothing more gratifying in my career than doing it with my best mate, 10 years on from when we won it before.'

Lowndes three championships and one Bathurst 1000 seemed like ancient history, but ask the other drivers in the paddock who is the most talented among them, and his name would come up more often than any other.

'Craig Lowndes has more talent than any other driver in the country. He does it so easily.' says Dick Johnson. 'I had seen Mark Skaife in his early days of driving at Amaroo Park in a Laser and he was nothing special, but he was such a determined guy that he turned himself into a bloody good driver. They are totally different characters. Put Craig into the environment that Skaifey's in and he would get swallowed.'

It was a sign of the times in 2004 when Skaife took the ultimate step towards controlling his destiny: buying the Holden Racing Team following the bankruptcy of previous owner Tom Walkinshaw Racing. 'Having the guys behind you is important, you become mates. The guys that screw cars together are working on life or death stuff. We're out there risking our lives. When you have that relationship, that trust, you form a special bond. You don't want that to be disbanded.'

While the cadence of his former team-mate's career had barely changed in two decades, Lowndes had slowed to a near-stupefying crawl. Experts all over the industry lamented his inability to compete. He announced towards the end of the season that he would be moving in 2005 to Triple 8 Racing: his fourth different Ford team in 5 years. It had been an almost fruitless search for the right combination of talent to sustain him. In the end, the directional question may have been decisively answered by a contract rumoured to be in excess of a million dollars, but there was also a far simpler reason, oft-told in the history of motor sport, hard learnt in the HRT years: 'Triple 8 is based in Queensland where I've been living since I moved to Ford. Every other team that I've been with has been based in Victoria. It's hugely important to be able to go in there and interact with the guys and make sure that you know what's going on, you're up to date with the developmental changes instead of trying to do it over the phone or popping in from time to time.'

Skaife and Lowndes are still trading blows with Seton, Jones, Morris, Ingall and the evergreen Bowe. But there is also Jim Richards' son Steven, Dick Johnson's son Steven, Jason Bright, Greg Murphy, the Kelly brothers, Garth Tander, Paul Radisich and 2002 champion Marcus Ambrose ... the list goes on as V8 Supercar racing grows into one of the most watched sports in the nation, both on television and at venues. David Brabham saw it first-hand when he returned for a drive at Bathurst with Dick Johnson's team in 2003. It was the campaign for which, coincidentally, Ron Tauranac came out of retirement: he would consult with Johnson's team, which was performing far below the massive reputation it had set in the past two decades. 'The sport has grown so much everywhere,' says Brabham. 'You only have to look at the trucks, the garages with their telemetry and plasma screens ... all the bits are there. The cars are immaculate in their preparation. The crew are outfitted superbly. The level of competition —

everything — has been raised. There's really only one other championship like it, and that's NASCAR. They've managed to keep the costs down, which keeps more teams competitive. It's still not cheap, but it's cheap compared with sports cars, where some manufacturers spend 50 or 60 million quid to win Le Mans … now that's a lot of money.'

Brabham should know. Since shaking off the disappointment of a failed Formula 1 season in 1995, he has rebuilt his career to become one of the world's premier sports car drivers, winning the Japanese GT series in a McLaren sports car, finishing 5th at Le Mans, and finally taking an offer that led to a 6 year term driving for American sports car team and series owner Don Panoz. 'I remember seeing the car for the first time in *Autosport* magazine and thinking you're never going to see me in a piece of shit like that! It was quite ironic that this new front-engined car, which went against the trend for rear-engined cars started by my dad back in the 1960s, would become my meal ticket for so long!'

From his win at Laguna Seca in 1997 he built the Panoz name, winning the American Le Mans series championship at the end of that year. 'It was a great finish. I had won seven races that year while my team-mate Eric Bernard hadn't won any, and yet due to the weird points system I had to pass him to clinch it. He wasn't going to let me do it. We had a fantastic dice towards the end, through traffic. After that, Don Panoz took over the running of that championship and called it the American Le Mans series.'

By the end of the Panoz era, in late 2002, Brabham had won 7 of 24 Grand Touring starts, and offers were plentiful.

He switched to Bentley for 2003, the main aim being a victory at Le Mans. Bentley achieved it, but not with Brabham's car. 'We did three 24 hour tests. There was constant work. Compared with Panoz, where we rocked up, did a little bit of testing and never finished higher than 7th, there was far more testing and development. Bentley had more than 100 people on staff; Panoz had had about 16. They were great — and they're still good friends of mine — but this was huge. I'm not surprised we finished 1st and 2nd. It's just disappointing that my car finished 2nd! We were faster in qualifying and practice, but hit traffic, so they had pole and we were second fastest. Then our car seemed to have all the problems during the race — things like battery changes, a head rest that fell off — while their car had a smooth run, not one problem. It was a great race though, a sprint all the way.'

In 2004, driving for Zytek Engineering in their Le Mans prototype, he qualified 3rd for the 24-hour classic. They failed to finish.

David Brabham, still racing, is carrying on a tradition unmatched in Australian sport. Few families could claim to have reached such consistent performance at the top level of the same sport over 50 years.

'Remember that farm we bought after I retired?' Jack Brabham asks, shaking his head with all the world-weariness of a father in his late seventies. 'The boys wanted that farm. They pestered me to buy it. But slowly, one by one, they left to go motor racing. First there was Geoff, then Gary, then David. Suddenly, there was no one left to work the farm — just me, and I never wanted the bloody thing in the first place! I sold it.'

The problem for Australian drivers since the turn of the century has been finding the money to race when most of the major seats are bought with accompanying sponsorship or cash from wealthy parents. There is a long list of talented drivers who have run out of funds and returned home. Some, like Ingall, Lowndes and Ambrose, have bounced back to become successful in V8 Supercars. Others have managed to survive through various circumstances, finding just enough money to keep hammering away until winning factory support. It is a character-building adventure, and one character has stood out more than the rest, one young man who came along and played one of the most daring, persistent and clever tactical games and somehow rose above the political structure of European motor sport aristocracy.

Mark Webber, the son of a car dealer, as so many young drivers have been, rose from humble beginnings in Queanbeyan, New South Wales to plant himself on the Everest of his ambition.

He launched overseas after finishing 4th in the Australian Formula Ford Championship, and 3rd in Duckham's Formula Ford festival in 1995. He won it in 1996. The next steps were the usual mixture of performance and persistence, balancing the maintenance of physical and mental fitness which is so important in modern-day race driving with hunting through the enchanted forest in search of the right people to make things happen. He has had strong backing from Australian sponsors and powerbrokers, but nothing like the millions that many other European, South American and Asian drivers have at their disposal.

'The politics of meeting people and harassing them to death ... I mean I wasn't too worried about what other drivers had. There was nothing I could do about that. I just kept chipping away. It could so easily have gone wrong.'

He has had life-threatening setbacks, such as the spectacular end-over-end crashes in his factory Mercedes at Le Mans in 1999, destroying not only his car, but an entire support base carefully built by years of hard work.

With typically astute planning, Webber had reasoned that his signing with AMG Mercedes might propel him to their Formula 1 program. He had compiled thousands of kilometres in testing but during one Thursday practice session at Le Mans was unprepared for what happened next.

'I was following Frank Biela. He was co-operating with me, letting me through on the narrow straight, and I got light, and slowly, just slowly took off. Just like an aeroplane. There was no way I could get the car back down. Saw the sky, trees, grass, sky. I was just hoping it would stay inside the circuit and not fly into the trees but it landed back on the circuit, on its back, and stopped quickly. The roof was destroyed, the rear destroyed, but I somehow ended up on my wheels again. The marshal at the landing point hadn't seen anything, and thought I was just casually pulling up. He arrived at the scene very slowly and without any fuss told me to just pull off the circuit and I'd be fine.'

Webber escaped injury. The team built a new car for the Saturday race but as he embarked on his opening lap in the warm-up session, it happened again, and this time the television cameras were rolling. The spectacular pictures became worldwide news. Again, Webber was unhurt, at least, not physically.

'The first one, I thought, "this is it!" Then it happened again! Unbelievable. Shocking. I was very angry. All the drivers were angry. I was praying they wouldn't race and telling Bernd Schneider, who was like a big brother to me and the team leader, to say no. I knew the rest of the drivers' decisions would hinge on Bernd. We sat down and discussed it. He told me he had to race. I was worried about him. I was even worried about David Brabham. Dave wasn't in the team but I knew him and I couldn't help but worry if it somehow affected him.'

Brabham remembers the horror of the aftermath. 'Obviously, when Mark flipped it a couple of times it made everyone nervous: marshals, spectators and other drivers. You see that thing go up in the air, and it would not be very nice if it hit you.'

The team added down force to the two remaining cars and decided to continue. After 5 hours of racing, Webber's team-mate, Peter Dumbreck, was on board for the third somersault of the weekend. David Brabham was also in disbelief. 'When Peter came down, he landed on a stump, which stuck up through the wreckage just beside him. He was inches away from dying.'

'Peter Dumbreck was lucky,' Webber recalls. 'I was lucky. It was very interesting to see how the people at Mercedes reacted to that. The program just stopped from there. It wasn't so much me I was worried about, but what it would do to my career. As it turned out, it must have all happened for a reason.'

Webber did what an embarrassed Mercedes could not do with that ill-fated sports car. He rebuilt himself with more sponsorship, scholarship and inexhaustible effort. The knockers underestimated his ability to keep probing, to milk every moment he could get with the people who might help him progress, and somehow, through it all, maintain his integrity and dignity.

'It was quite a few months before I drove a racing car again and that was when my motivation stepped up. I trained ridiculously hard. So much that I was ready for whatever was going to happen. I was confident, knowing that those crashes in Le Mans were not about me not being good enough. I was so pumped to put it all back on the rails, I was offered a drive later that year in a Formula 3000 car in Pembray in Wales. I got up at five o'clock, went for a run. It was a 3-hour drive to Pembray and I knew that this was a big day for me, a step back in so many ways, but crucial to make the steps forward again. There was no way anyone was going to beat me that day.'

He worked his way back through Formula 3000 before landing a drive with the Minardi Formula 1 team, thanks in part to the patronage of Australian team owner Paul Stoddart, who accepted less money from Webber's backers than he could have taken from other drivers. It was one of the great moments of the modern era when Webber drove to a points-scoring 5th place in his debut race, the Australian Grand Prix at Albert Park in 2002.

'The longest the car had ever run before that meeting was 17 laps. I was just hoping it wouldn't be embarrassing, for me or for Paul. It meant so much to him. He said to me on the grid, "just bring it home". Then, later in the race when Mika Salo, whose Toyota was a lot quicker, was starting to catch me for 5th place Stoddy was on the radio saying "under no circumstances let him through!" I thought "bloody hell, that's all changed!" I then had to make sure when Salo caught me and made his first attack that he would be certain I was not going to just let him through. Then he crashed.'

Webber would go on to drive for Team Jaguar, with Stoddart's blessing, in 2003, and attract rave reviews for his astute handling of a car with only midfield potential. In 2004, as he tried to push the Team Jaguar project further ahead, he was snapped up by the prestigious Williams team, the same team that Alan Jones had won his World Championship with in 1980. Now, Webber too would be discussed as a future world champion because he had proven that he was the complete package for the new millennium: intelligent, articulate, charming, loyal, humble, fast, and — best of all — streetwise after those hard years in the jungle.

Alan Jones knows what that means, knows the painful reality behind the glamorous exterior. It is tougher now than it was when he was champion, relentless compared with the days of Brabham, almost horrifying when reflected against the golden years of gentleman drivers like Tony Gaze. Jones believes that Australia's 50 year history in international motor racing, formidable as it is, has always involved a fight for respect. 'I remember Lex Davison, Tony Gaze and my dad telling me about their adventure in the 1953 Monte Carlo Rally in an FX Holden. Can you imagine, a Holden in the Monte Carlo Rally? Ecurie Australie, they called themselves: "Team Australia". When they went to General Motors and asked for some backing, they were told, "Monte Carlo Rally? Australians? You're kidding." But they went there anyway. Not only that, they were running 8th outright at one stage. The next thing you know, they're getting all these telexes from GM saying, "Anything you want, boys, we're right behind you ... tally ho!" Typical of motor sport, isn't it? In 50 years, that has never changed.'

'Formula 1,' says Jack Brabham, 'couldn't be more different from what it was in my day. It's become a race to make money, a race for technology. It doesn't have the same interest for me that it used to have. Having said that, I think Michael Schumacher is the best driver of all time. He got Ferrari where it is today. He's done everything for that team that I did. He's done it all.'

It might be more than coincidental that Mark Webber has in recent years struck a friendship with Schumacher that few other drivers can boast. They first met in a gymnasium in Brazil in 2002, where the champion said to him, 'Well done in Melbourne.'

'Anyone who says he doesn't respect Michael is stupid,' says Webber. 'He commented on how busy I had been in Australia. That's what amazes me about Michael. He has so much going on, but he knows what everyone else is up to as well. If you asked him what position Felipe Massa was in after the first session in Barcelona, he'd probably tell you.

'One thing that drew us together is the level of motivation, getting the team to work as well as possible for you. He has a family. He's broken all the records. There are so many reasons why Michael could cool it. He's still out there, winning, enjoying it too. His drive is amazing.'

They've been talking to each other ever since and sit together as representatives of the Grand Prix Drivers Association (GPDA). 'What I get out of those conversations is how sharp he is, clever, a great driver and on top of the game.'

Then Webber smiles, with his typical Australian sarcasm, reserved only for mates. 'The sooner he leaves and lets us get on with the championship the better!'

In 2002, Webber walked onto the Spa-Francorchamps circuit for the first time in his Formula 1 career. It was relatively quiet, a few days before the event. Teams were unpacking. Officials and volunteers moved quietly and quickly about, methodically preparing. For Webber it was time, and there was very little of it available, to savour the experience of standing on one of the world's great motor racing circuits, just as Tony Gaze would have done almost exactly 50 years before. Decades of Formula 1 history enveloped the circuit like a fog.

Webber closed his eyes for just a moment, allowed himself to drift back in time, to feel that sense of history, to feel the rush of air from an HWM Alta as it roared from the distant past into his consciousness, sliding into Eau Rouge, its driver peering through bloodstained goggles and pelting rain, wondering in that frenzy of noise why he was there as he fought for control of a malevolent machine that could destroy him in an instant.

Suddenly, the vision was gone. Webber opened his eyes and smiled as a freshening breeze made him shiver in the warmth of the Belgian sun.

ACKNOWLEDGMENTS

It's well known that virtually no one bothers to read acknowledgments. So you're reading this because a) you expect to be acknowledged, b) you thought the book so terrible that you have to find out what the heck I was thinking or c) you're sitting on a plane or in a waiting room and you've run out of things to read.

Given that you're obviously still reading this, I should explain that *Legends of Speed* was never meant to be the definitive history of Australian racing drivers. It's just a story, connecting a group of famous men whose lives intrigued me for various reasons. The co-operation extended to me by the drivers interviewed for this book has been remarkable, in fact, touching. I cannot express enough my appreciation of their willingness to share their stories and opinions.

It's been a stressful, exhausting task trying to condense so much achievement and experience into one relatively small volume while still hitting the right notes. It's taken nearly 18 months of finding windows of time to write and research in the precious few hours left over from a full-time television career. Ever tried to squeeze an elephant into a phone booth? You get the idea . . .

The TV world is demanding not only in hours committed but the inconsistency of its timetables, which makes it impossible to plan efficiently. That brings me to my patient and supportive colleagues at HarperCollins, who were 'blooding' a rookie part-time writer and giving him miles of latitude in a world where deadlines are sacrosanct. Vanessa Radnidge, Alison Urquhart, Mel Cain, Karen Maree-Griffiths, Sarah Shrubb, Helen Beard, Sophie Hamley, Amanda Simons, Frances Paterson, Pam Dunne, Don Mace, Rod Stewart, Jim Sonter, Cheryl Rose, Graeme Jones and Judi Rowe . . . thank you so much.

This book could never have been written without the tolerance of my colleagues at Network TEN, who would have suspected at various times over the past 18 months that their grumpy host had been stretched a little thin. Not once did they complain. Thank you to Network Director of Sport David White, Network Director of News Kel Robards, Executive Producer of 'RPM', 'Formula 1', 'Lexmark Indy 300' and 'Motogp' Scott Young, Producer of 'RPM', 'Formula 1' and 'Lexmark Indy 300' Helen Collantonio. Executive Producer of the V8 telecasts Murray Lomax, Producer of the V8 telecasts Steve Wood. All the staff at the production HQ: Anthea, Melissa, Lynda, Gerard, Sam, Brooke, Tanya. What a team.

Of course the book had become the butt of many jokes among my closest workmates, the TEN commentary team, who were constantly bludgeoned with anecdotes as I tested the material, pummelled them with ideas and bled their knowledge. John Smailes was a willing motivator, supporter and bank of knowledge. Neil Crompton, Greg Rust, Mark Oastler, Daryl Beattie and Graham Brown have all been terrific. We 'have a laugh' as Barry Sheene used to say.

Nigel Greenway, who provides statistics for our V8 Supercar commentary provided the stats for this book.

The primary sources were the drivers themselves, who supplied personal records, memoirs, articles and photographs which they had collected over the years to support their various recollections of events. There is always, however, the need to confirm names, dates, places and results. There are literally stacks of magazines and journals with which to do this. Finding the right ones is not so easy, due to the sporadic press coverage of motor sport in years gone by. No blame on the hard-working journos, I might add. It's a bias that affects coverage today.

There are also many other books. Some of the drivers, like Jack Brabham, Alan Jones, Peter Brock and Dick Johnson have already had books written about them. The two reference books that I relied on most, for their impressive bank of research were: *Australia's Greatest Race*, a comprehensive history of the Bathurst 1000 published by Chevron, and *The 50 Year History of the Australian Grand Prix* also published by Chevron.

There are countless websites devoted to drivers, teams, cars and events. Two well-worn sites for cross checking Formula 1 results were grandprix.com and formulaoneworld.com. Le Mans and Formula 2 results can be found at lemansregister.com

In all the cross-referencing it's easy to find three or more conflicting reports of the same incident or information. I've covered a lot of major sport but motor racing is rife with disparate views of the same apparently straightforward incidents. For all the apparent camaraderie and respect there is a lot of disturbing underlying jealousy and resentment that sometimes taints opinion. It's difficult not to avoid such depth of feeling when participants stake their life savings on race teams. Walk up and down pit lane today and you'll quickly find out that what you think is black is actually white, blue and green according to various witnesses. One man's hero is another man's villain. One man's legend is another man's impostor. That's motor sport. We've done our best to please everyone, but we won't.

There has been a need for 'technical' support in the gathering of this research. My good mates at Subaru have helped me get around to various far flung places. CAMS may not be too popular with a lot of my subjects in this book, but then again, that's the lot of all referees and administrators and CAMS has been helpful in locating people and information.

A massive vote of thanks to the generous Paul Cross for allowing me to use photos from his private collection.

Each of the drivers of course had the opportunity to check what was written about them to prevent any inaccuracies, but a special thanks to Max Stahl, revered racing writer, who worked on Frank Gardner's memoirs to make sure they were in shape, and for persuading Frank to leave in a few 'Gardnerisms' that he had second thoughts about.

Finally, it needs to be said that there was one mighty motivation behind this book, and it's an unusual one. I had always wanted to write a book since I began journalism studies at university, but found neither the time nor inspiration while I was busy trying to earn some real money and feed a family. A few years ago, one of our promising young journalists at TEN told me that he was abandoning convention and turning freelance so that he could write books and pursue projects of passion. I was genuinely impressed by his courage and commitment. I'm pleased and proud to say that James Knight has gone on to make a great success of that bold change of direction, becoming a successful author, film-maker and reporter in his own right. But it also made me think: 'Hang on a minute, this bloke's so much younger than me and he's writing books ... I'd better pull my finger out!'

James not only motivated me to take on this challenge, but put me in contact with the great people at HarperCollins and gave me free advice on technical and tactical issues throughout the writing of this book. I'll be forever in his debt.

At 18, in my third year of university, when my course offered the option of writing a book as a final year assignment, I shook my head and smiled. That was for wankers ... I needed a job. I needed to earn and learn before I would be ready to write extensively about anything. I was an empty vessel waiting for a world of experience. Today, little more than 20 years on, there has been a lot of experience. Books are queuing up inside me, the inspiration overflows ... and I will find the time.

INDEX

Bill Woods is a journalist who has built his reputation as the face of motorsport on Network TEN while hosting the weekly motorsport program 'RPM' and as a commentator for their many motorsport events. He is a regular TEN newsreader and host of 'Sports Tonight'. *Legends of Speed* is his first book.